# THE RTI STORY

**Aruna Roy** resigned from the IAS in 1975 to work with peasants and workers in rural Rajasthan. In 1990 she helped co-found the Mazdoor Kisan Shakti Sangathan (MKSS). The MKSS struggles in the mid-90s for wages and other rights gave birth to the now celebrated Right to Information movement. Aruna continues to be a part of many democratic struggles and campaigns.

This book is a collective history that tells the story of how ordinary people can come together and prevail against great odds, to make democracy more meaningful.

**OTHER LOTUS TITLES**

| | |
|---|---|
| Ajit Bhattacharjea | *Sheikh Mohammad Abdullah: Tragic Hero of Kashmir* |
| Anil Dharker | *Icons: Men & Women Who Shaped Today's India* |
| Aitzaz Ahsan | *The Indus Saga: The Making of Pakistan* |
| Ajay Mansingh | *Firaq Gorakhpuri: The Poet of Pain & Ecstasy* |
| Alam Srinivas & T.R. Vivek | *IPL: The Inside Story* |
| Alam Srinivas | *Women of Vision: Nine Business Leaders in Conversation* |
| Amarinder Singh | *The Last Sunset: The Rise & Fall of the Lahore Durbar* |
| Ashis Ray | *Laid to Rest: The Controversy of Subhas Chandra Bose's Death* |
| Bertil Falk | *Feroze: The Forgotten Gandhi* |
| Hamish Mcdonald | *Ambani & Sons* |
| Ian H. Magedera | *Indian Videshinis: European Women in India* |
| Kunal Purandare | *Ramakant Achrekar: A Biography* |
| Lucy Peck | *Agra: The Architectural Heritage* |
| Lucy Peck | *Delhi a Thousand Years of Building: An INTACH-Roli Guide* |
| Madan Gopal | *My Life and Times: Munshi Premchand* |
| M.J. Akbar | *Byline* |
| M.J. Akbar | *Blood Brothers: A Family Saga* |
| Maj. Gen. Ian Cardozo | *Param Vir: Our Heroes in Battle* |
| Maj. Gen. Ian Cardozo | *The Sinking of INS Khukri: What Happened in 1971* |
| Madhu Trehan | *Tehelka as Metaphor* |
| Manish Pachouly | *The Sheena Bora Case* |
| Moin Mir | *Surat: Fall of A Port Rise of A Prince Defeat of the East India Company in the House Of Commons* |
| Monisha Rajesh | *Around India in 80 Trains* |
| Noorul Hasan | *Meena Kumari: The Poet* |
| Peter Church | *Added Value: The Life Stories of Indian Business Leaders* |
| Peter Church | *Profiles in Enterprise: Inspiring Stories of Indian Business Leaders* |
| Prateep K. Lahiri | *A Tide in the Affairs of Men: A Public Servant Remembers* |
| Rajika Bhandari | *The Raj on the Move: Story of the Dak Bungalow* |
| Ralph Russell | *The Famous Ghalib: The Sound of my Moving Pen* |
| R.V. Smith | *Delhi: Unknown Tales of a City* |
| Salman Akthar | *The Book of Emotions* |
| Sharmishta Gooptu | *Bengali Cinema: An Other Nation* |
| Shrabani Basu | *Spy Princess: The Life of Noor Inayat Khan* |
| Shahrayar Khan | *Bhopal Connections: Vignettes of Royal Rule* |
| S. Hussain Zaidi | *Dongri to Dubai* |
| Sunil Raman & Rohit Aggarwal | *Delhi Durbar: 1911 The Complete Story* |
| Thomas Weber | *Going Native: Gandhi's Relationship with Western Women* |
| Thomas Weber | *Gandhi at First Sight* |
| Vappala Balachandran | *A Life In Shadow: The Secret Story of ACN Nambiar – A Forgotten Anti-Colonial Warrior* |
| Vir Sanghvi | *Men of Steel: India's Business Leaders in Candid Conversation* |

FORTHCOMING TITLES

| | |
|---|---|
| Rahul Bedi | *The Last Word: Obituaries of 100 Indian who Led Unusual Lives* |

# THE RTI STORY

## POWER TO THE PEOPLE

Aruna Roy
with the MKSS Collective

Foreword
Gopalkrishna Gandhi

LOTUS COLLECTION
ROLI BOOKS

Lotus Collection



First published in 2018

The Lotus Collection
An imprint of
Roli Books Pvt. Ltd
M-75, Greater Kailash II Market, New Delhi 110 048
Phone: ++91 (011) 40682000
E-mail: info@rolibooks.com
Website: www.rolibooks.com

Also at Bengaluru, Chennai, & Mumbai

Cover Design: Vaasavi Kaushik
Layout Design: Bhagirath Kumar
Production: Yuvraj Singh

ISBN: 978-81-936260-4-7

Typeset in Arno Pro by Roli Books Pvt Ltd and
printed at Printways, New Delhi.

*Dedication*

This narrative is dedicated to the many who have paid with their lives, for combating corruption and the arbitrary use of power, by claiming the right to know.

*Tribute*

This book is a tribute to the large collective, from whose action, determination, memory and records a narrative has emerged. The stories, anecdotes and the common sense of its logic in the pages to come, including the many edited out – which remain anonymous for the time being, because of prosaic things like word limits and the number of pages – are its real authors. We are mere scribes.

# Contents

# Foreword

To know is to understand. To understand is to be at peace or – embattled.

To be in ignorance is to stay in the dark. To be in the dark is to stagnate, a condition which the human mind is not meant to be in. Knowledge is fuel, intelligence is energy. The two together, knowledge and intelligence, fuel and energy, race with time, keep step with every condition, every change, every challenge around it. In this talent, or skill, lies the human being's faculty for survival, for progress and happiness.

For an individual to be in ignorance is to let her or his intelligence run to seed. It is to let the human potential in herself or himself to atrophy. Worse, it is to imperil others dependent on the individual. If such be the dire result of an individual's ignorance, what of a collectivity of people, a whole peoplehood? For a citizenry to remain in the dark about its selfhood is to forfeit its collective destiny to slavery – the slavery of unknowing.

The struggle for our freedom came from a many-faceted struggle but, chiefly from a struggle against ignorance – of the slavery that British rule meant. Books like Dadabhai Naoroji's *Poverty and Un-British Rule* and Gandhi's *Hind Swaraj* and several journals like Gandhi's own *Harijan* and *Young India*, Tilak's *Kesari* (Marathi), Gokhale's *Mahratta* (English), Aurobindo's *Bande Mataram* (Bangla), Maulana Azad's *Al Hilal* (Urdu), Subramania Bharati's *Vijaya* and *Bala Bharati* (both Tamil) and Ganesh

Shankar Vidyarthi's *Pratap* (Hindi), among others, lifted the veil of India's unknowing of its political and social bondage. Our leaders were, thus, our teachers, leading us from ignorance to intelligence, from indolence to action, from apathy to energy. And, ultimately, from slavery to freedom.

India's independence moved us out of the valley of political thraldom and stood us, face to face, overnight, with the realities of our own multiple ills, our enervations and injustices, and the vice-like grip of several hegemonisms which two persons above all others recognized all too well – Mahatma Gandhi and Babasaheb Dr. B.R. Ambedkar.

Even in the few months that were given to him after 15 August 1947, Gandhi strove, tirelessly, sleeplessly, to make provincial governments and the new central government accountable for assuring human rights to riot victims, especially women, getting administrations to provide shelter and supply minimum rations and clothing to the dispossessed. Seeing men, women and children who had left or been driven out of their homes in Delhi unprotected from the rain and the winter's cold, Gandhi advised the administration on where and to whom blankets needed to be given and if raincoats were hard to find, to provide them stacks of newspapers to spread on the ground so that the women and children among them would not have to lie on the bare and wet earth. All this nudging of the administration he did as an 'ordinary citizen'.

Babasaheb's detailed and far-seeing crafting of fundamental rights guaranteeing our rights and privileges as citizens in the constitution and provisions in it for the accounting and audit of public funds were designed to open up our newly won freedom to public view, public experiencing. They were to save us from ourselves, help our lungs take in a new breath of our newly free air. The Constitution did not make these rights absolute or un-bridled but it did clothe them with what, speaking in the Constituent Assembly on 4 November 1948, Dr. Ambedkar called 'Constitutional morality'. This was a new and novel concept. The authorities of the state, he said, were empowered but their powers derived from the constitution and the laws and they were open to censure for all their public acts. He thus gave 'morality' a political dimension.

Ambedkar clearly had in mind the possibility that independent India would have and would exercise with verve its political rights, but the common man and woman would lag behind in the claiming of social and economic rights, which are the ethical dividend of citizenship.

In this claiming our experience – the experience of ordinary citizens without political clout or economic sinews – has been a glimmering but delusional mirage. 'One citizen, one vote' is an invaluable asset but is no substitute whatsoever to the retrieval of basic rights and entitlements – the privilege of a republican peoplehood. A vote is a vote; life is life. Hegemonies, oligarchies, cartels, caste and community cults from the past have crept out of the debris of the departing Raj and slid right into exposed cracks and joints in free India's body politic. And how they thrive there! Parasiting on its liberal masonry, they have enfeebled and all but destroyed it.

The governments that administer India through their multitude of beneficent laws have shown themselves to be – as they should be – creative and liberal in their ideals. They are in fact spectacularly so. But they are at the same time perversely rigid in their practices. They are progressive in concept, regressive in the actuality of execution. And despite the noble-mindedness of our administrations, several administrators – in high, middling and 'low' positions – have patented an ability to so distort entitlements, manipulate rights and hijack prerogatives as to make a mockery of all planning, a parody of Swaraj. Ignorance, illiteracy, the innate docility of our people before the high seats of office, render them open to exploitation, deceit and plain robbery. Our post-Independence laws and plans can be said to have been made by the learned honest for the unlettered innocent with sharp middlemen entrusted with their implementation. Result: dismay, disappointment, dejection.

And that is where – on the dust-laden street of revived spirits, gutsy agitations, arduous marches – for a new championing of rightful claims of rightful rights, this book takes its place, says what it says and does what it does. It gives us the story of how a lifeline came to be thrown to its claustrophobic polity, its suffocating republicanism and its malnutritioned democracy. In other words, to its 'constitutional morality'. How and why the uniquely inspirational Aruna Roy and her associates Nikhil Dey, Shankar Singh, his wife Anshi and others in their steadily growing team started the Mazdoor Kisan Shakti Sangathan in Rajasthan's rocky interior in 1990 is the start of the book's 'storyline'. It takes the reader through a series of defiant campaigns, stubborn resistances, touch-and-go negotiations, hard resolves, privation, persecution, and dangers beyond the ordinary, towards dispelling ignorance, sharpening understanding of the laws and entitlements, strengthening resolves and the plain guts that are needed to waken somnolent administrators from daytime slumbering. It is also the story of unexpected support, often from sagacious members of the very bureaucracy that was 'under attack', from intellectuals, writers, other NGOs, and from the hinterland of enlightened Indian opinion.

The stark simplicity of Aruna's life in Devdungri village, the severe yet spontaneous austerity with which she and her team lived and worked, not only affected the thinking and living of the village and its environs, it made their mission known to the world beyond in a way that recalled Gandhi's Phoenix, Kochrab, Sabarmati and Sevagram dwellings. The experience of very 'ordinary' persons, as real as they are unknown, described in this book, came to be known as little epics in heroism.

MKSS's campaign for an act that would confer and protect ordinary citizens' right to basic information on what is their legitimate due and in the public interest has been in the public's awareness. And yet a connected account of the stages of the campaign gathering momentum, catalysing other campaigns, and then culminating in 2005 in the RTI Act, eluded us. That is now with us, in this narrative. But the book is more, much more than a chronicle of successive events. It is a testament of the willpower, determination and resolve that comes from a people knowing that their cause is true and just, that it is not just about their 'claims' as individuals but about the veracity and indeed the necessity, in terms of social justice, of claiming that which is legitimate. It is a manifesto of truth-seeking, truth-telling and truth-living. Its author is no individual, no institution. Its author is the true word.

The RTI Act has been true to its mandate, faithful to its promise. From a ration shop in a hamlet to the president's residence in Delhi, it has done what it should be doing. Like any other law, it has had its saboteurs, abusers. A redemptive law should be judged by its successes, but be ready to be questioned for its failings. An Act that brings about accountability should not be coy when it is itself called to account. The Act has come, like all Acts come, from the wisdom of the Indian parliament. Curiously, it is in its birthplace, its own cradle, the Hon'ble Parliament, that the Act seems to have found some of its most vociferous detractors. They have their reasons. Sections of the political class and of the bureaucracy have also developed methods to tiptoe round provisions of the Act. They have their skills. This weakens the impact of the Act. There is another 'problem'. The Act's workforce, namely, the personnel in the information commissions, reflect all the diversity of our population. Our information commissions and their secretariats have had in their personnel from the many active to not-a-few slothful, from the many dedicated to the not-so-few sceptical. And they include, one might add, some fearful and some rather compromised. 'Compromise' does not need explaining. But all this does not dishearten the true harbingers of the Act who remain prepared to test its working against its experience. And there has been a great blessing: our first chief information commissioner, Wajahat Habibullah, has been the RTI establishment's pride. He has, through his principled and discerning rulings, established a great standard which has been, in the main, followed diligently.

Behind the RTI story lies one hugely dismaying fact: the lives of RTI activists and campaigners are at risk. As many as sixty of them have lost their lives. They are martyrs to the cause of the good state, of public accountability, constitutional morality. We honour them. But should such courage be met in our country by murder? It is a national scandal, shame and tragedy that they have been killed. Just as we mourn the loss of brave soldiers protecting our nation's territorial integrity, we mourn the loss of brave soldiers protecting our constitutional integrity. The tragedy is that one is killed by bullets from across the border, and the other by one of our own.

Yet, I believe that despite its many travails, the RTI Act's widening impact will grow, deepen and expand. Its detractors and saboteurs may win a few battles for ignorance and obfuscation in the short term; they cannot in the long term, for thanks to Aruna Roy and her pioneering team, and RTI catalysts like S.P. Gupta, the people of India know now, more than ever before, what it is to have and what it is to deploy the fuel of knowledge and the energy of intelligence.

– Gopalkrishna Gandhi

# Acknowledgements

In activism, documentation is often considered irrelevant, because the immediate absorbs all attention. The importance of keeping records for posterity, for learning, referencing or writing, is seldom a matter of priority. It is a task that is marginalized and seen at best as a mundane necessity. People who do so are often taken for granted and its relevance is seldom recognized.

This is to acknowledge those who have done so for the MKSS and the NCPRI. Were it not for a group of such people, the writing of this book – a collective labour of love – would have been much more difficult, even impossible. The writing of the chronicle has also been sourced from varied experiences and people who have been observers and participants for shorter periods of time in this long journey.

We would like to thank Kavita (Srivastava) and her office in her father's home in Jaipur, particularly for beginning the process of creating documentary support. The documentation office in Aruna's home in Tilonia has continually borne the burden of this extra work with grace. It played a significant role in providing the space and isolation required for sorting out miles of files and innumerable boxes of clippings, writings and collating them. A series of young people worked with dedication over the years and organized the documents, a vital support to all struggles and campaigns. Though they are too many to list, we must mention Sunita Vaishnav and Hansa Kanwar, who set it up, followed by Suraj

Kanwar, Samundara Chaudhary, Pushpa Kanwar, Nilofar Khan, Mukesh Chaudhari, Swathi Dhanesh, Laxman Singh and Ratan Lal, among the many who came and went. Shankar Singh, Sowmya Kidambi and Kheema Ram transferred and maintained records in the MKSS, before their transfer to the documentation office. The RTI Manch (Kamal Tak and Mukesh Goswami) also kept and transferred documents from Jaipur. A very important and special acknowledgement to Shekhar Singh and his home in Delhi, which became an institution in itself. It provided space, and Shekhar offered his huge storehouse of documents and information to help understand the legal formulations facilitating and recording the robust debates and discussions around each formulation. Through this entire process he taught us the immense value of keeping papers, documents and records in an organized fashion to support public action. This narrative owes him special appreciation and thanks.

The principal members of this writing collective were Laxman Singh and Ankita Anand. Laxman's knowledge of the RTI campaign and his quiet and persistent attention to detail were invaluable. He brought together a team responsible for collating material, sifting through all the written Hindi material, patiently assisting the process. He checked, referenced, footnoted and carefully looked at the annexures and the document, before it went to the publisher. He says he realized that he was threading together what he calls 'the marvellous anecdotes and stories from the MKSS experience into a book'. Ankita has been the persuasive force behind this effort and an ever-active link between the publisher and the authors. Her extraordinary and cheerful support was backed by her experience with the RTI, the NCPRI, of which she had been secretary, and her work with Penguin Books India. She read through chapters many times over, and accommodated the vagaries of time and place for important editorial sessions. She was our internal reviewer and timekeeper, pushing us to make time to write. She has also been a part of the writing, editing, and reviewing collective.

We would like to thank Mamta Jaitley and Renuka Pamecha of *Ujala Chadi* and Vividha Features, who have been fellow travellers in documentation and dissemination. The late Ajit Bhattacharjea said that this was a movement where the roles of the journalist and the activist overlapped. As the director of the Press Institute of India he facilitated the publication of the journal *Transparency*, edited by Preeti Sampat in

English, *Aar Paar*, edited by Bharat Dogra in Hindi, and provided space in the important journal *Vidhura*. We have drawn upon late Prabhash Joshi's editorials and op-eds in *Jansatta*, Kuldip Nayyar's regular syndicated columns, and late Nikhil Chakravarty's *Mainstream* for promoting the idea of a critique of the RTI movement. The prolific writings of Bharat Dogra are peppered with stories from the RTI struggles. These writings empowered us as they became the source material for a history of the movement. Rajni Bakshi describes the embryonic stage of this movement by making us a chapter of her book *Bapu Kuti*. Harsh Mander and his many publications, including *Unheard Voices*, and an account he wrote in the early days of the MKSS and the RTI movement, carried information about the people's journey towards achieving the right to information. Many mainstream dailies in English and Hindi and their special reports have served as source material in the book. We also referred to and wrote for *Raj Drishti*, a publication by the late Sri Prakash, a friend and contributor to the shaping of the campaign. Newspaper reports and comments formed an important part of the source material, and we would like to thank the late Prakash Kardelay for the campaign and support of the RTI in Pune. The rest of the innumerable sources used are part of the story and referenced for the reader.

We drew extensively from *Diamond India*, edited by Bhanwar Meghwanshi, a bi-monthly magazine published by the School for Democracy – a collection of comments and articles. It was almost like a diary of MKSS events. Bhanwar's persistence made authors of us all, and forced the literate activist to write. The flavour and details of many experiences would have been lost without this important publication. We have referred to and quoted from *Nirantar*, a daily edited and published by Ramprasad Kumawat from Beawar. This collection of editorials during April–May 1996 offer the best analysis of the beginnings of the RTI movement, and of the forty-day dharna that turned the local struggle into a national movement. All these have been important source materials for PhDs and books related to the RTI. This narrative has drawn substantially from the PhD thesis of Suchi Pande, who was very often a part of this narrative. Her research remained a constant point of reference to check the veracity of individual and collective narratives of this chronicle. Suchi also shared all her material with the team – including oral recordings of many prominent members of the struggle and campaign.

The photographs taken by Mohan, Ramlal, Bhurji, Ashok Sain and many others have been used in this book. We have also referred to films of Jan Madhyam – a forty-minute and shorter fifteen-minute version called *Hamara Paisa* (our money, our accounts). We would like to acknowledge Anurag Singh, who was always there at critical times, and Radhika Kaul Batra's film on Janawad, *Accounts and Accountability*. The rough footage, shot at different times by Mohan, Ramlal and our late friend and comrade Bhurji (SWRC) was extremely useful.

Amit Sharma readily translated the Hindi into English. Manini Shekher, Amrita Johri and Anjali Bhardwaj helped edit specific chapters. Shankar Singh, Nikhil Dey and Ramkaran of RMKM helped from time to time with locating important documents. Lal Singh, Narayan Singh, Kalu Ram, Sowmya Kidambi, Mohan Ram, and Chunni Singh delved into their memory and their papers to correct and enrich factual and other details.

The final edit team included Dr. S. Anandalakshmy, who went through the whole MS, and Siddharth, Nikhil Dey, Praavita Kashyap, Rakshita Swamy, Ira Anjali Anwar and Nachiket Udupa, who helped Ankita look at specific chapters. Bhanwar Meghwanshi helped with reading through pieces sent to him to make sure that they were correct. Vinay Jain helped with all graphic designing and a constant critique, so helpful in finalizing the document.

A special thanks to Sanskriti and its beautiful campus, and to Shri O.P. Jain, whose generosity of spirit and affectionate care facilitated the finalization of the manuscript.

# Introduction

The RTI has been a campaign blessed with the success of evolving into a genuine and vibrant people's movement. Many more arduously fought struggles have not been favoured with the fortuitous circumstances, such as those that enabled the passage of the RTI. It is a legislation that has arguably changed the contours of democratic governance in India. Even fewer legislations have been so popular as to help shape and strengthen a movement. The MKSS had the privilege to initiate and be part of the struggle that evolved into a powerful movement across India for the right to know.

As we write this introduction, we want to acknowledge some of the thinkers and writers who strengthened our resolve to put this chronicle together. Kosambi, the great Indian historian, understood history in 'terms of the dynamics of socio-economic formations rather than just a chronological narration of "episodes" or the feats of a few great men – kings, warriors or saints'. Howard Zinn's perspective, and a book called *Let Us Now praise Famous Men*, a volume dedicated to the ordinary people in the US who fought the great depression between the late 1920s and early '40s, reassured us that we were not alone in thinking that history was made by the unseen. Harsh Mander's book *Unheard Voices* reminded us that history is not only the construct of 'great' people. Vijaydan Detha's *Batanri Phulwari*, a magnificent collection and retelling of Rajasthani folk stories, chronicled the popular, collective commentary of people down the annals of history. It is a history of political understanding through fables that live with people though generations.

These are the recordings of events and narratives in that tradition, culled from the voices of people. Often such stories only feed into the research of scholars and become a footnote to documented history, largely unacknowledged and forgotten. The dominant narrative is always from the perspective of the ruler and single individuals. One had hoped that democracy would set it right. But the people who are the primary contributors to the discourse always remain on the fringes.

The RTI narrative is a celebration of ordinary people and their immense contribution to strengthening the pillars of democratic justice in modern India.

This collation attempts to capture the spirit, the humour, the hands-on feeling of action and the somewhat more methodical nature of reflection. It implicitly argues that action and reflection are categories that arise out of real life, where the two are often intertwined and inseparable. You can indeed think with your hands and feet, and act with your mind. These are people's stories which shaped ideas, and a legal tool to address corruption and the arbitrary use of power; two overpowering deterrents in accessing the people's right to live. The slogan: 'The right to know, the right to live' was crafted from their lives. Denial of justice often arises from the suppression of the truth and of information, keeping people away from access to food, work, health, justice, education, housing and the right to live with dignity. Corruption is the tangible manifestation of mis-governance and the arbitrary use of power.

Popular narratives are often set aside for the more scholarly efforts that follow a certain method in formulation and statement. In this narrative, people's experiences and theoretical understanding complement each other. Like all history, the story of the people who shaped the RTI in its initial years takes off from many points through multiple narratives. Some are oral and others are from written recollections. The causal sequence unravels how people come together for a single purpose, no matter how different the articulation and starting points. The players are from different 'sectors', who analysed and acted to change the nature of their immediate engagement with democratic institutions and governance. They all came to the conclusion separately that corruption and injustice could be controlled only if there was access to information as a right. This is the story of their coming together to shape that right.

The ordinary Indian citizen understands the Right to Information law. A 2016 report said that since 2005, a total of 1.75 crore RTI applications have been filed by users. Figures are often red herrings. But in this case it reflects continual vigilance and the citizen's responsibility to demand accountability from the state. In today's India, the RTI has made its niche as a law that has made it possible for every citizen to use it to access every other right. It has evolved as a tool universally applicable that is being used by a very wide spectrum of the Indian citizenry. Esoteric concepts like sovereignty have got defined in action. Being an enabling law to realize other constitutional and democratic rights, it has been aptly defined as a 'transformatory' legislation.

We offer this to our readers as both a story and an exercise in building theory through practice. It articulates the implicit argument that participatory democracy can be crafted to be constructive, inclusive and just. Its story celebrates pluralism and participation as important foundations of a democracy. It is a campaign that has been rooted in the complexities of Indian democratic processes while carrying the simple straightforward message of transparency to achieve its objective. This people's campaign has added to the lexicon of governance and its understanding by looking at ways in which people could engage with policy and implementation.

This collective history empowers young readers to understand their capabilities and possible roles in shaping governance. It offers some ways in which we can actually deal with conflicts in democratic processes between the citizen and the elected representative, between worker and scholar, between action and reflection, between individuals and collectives. Perhaps it will make us realize and recall the strength of the national movement that gave us Independence, and the constitution we then gave ourselves. The story offers hope that justice and equality need not remain in the tomes of legal guarantees but can – with judicious application – win some battles within the democratic and constitutional paradigm.

We have been extremely privileged to be members of the struggle, campaign and movement for the RTI. We hope that this chronicle has managed to bring together the diverse sets of voices, worries, concerns, songs, slogans, advocacy, struggle, reflection, campaigning, and the joy of collective action that helped build the movement.

The challenges of collective expression have been many. Activists move all the time and proof reading was very difficult. Notwithstanding these almost insurmountable hurdles, we hope we have been able to capture some of the energy and zest of the campaigns we were all part of.

Aruna Roy & the MKSS
Rajasthan
June 2017

CHAPTER ONE

# Devdungri: The Beginning

For many of us, it began on the dusty tracks by the bamboo shrubs, in a mud house in Devdungri in 1987, three years before MKSS was created. The hut was a shelter, an assertion, a symbol, a silent witness to the events and discussions that shaped the debate on the right to know. Ajit Bhattacharjea, former editor of the *Indian Express*, who joined the group of protestors in Beawar to demand the RTI in 1996, writes:

> Devdungri, a typical village in the heartland of Rajasthan, nestles on the slope of a spur of the bleak, rock-strewn Aravalli range, with a tiny Dev temple on its crest. The soil is dark and arid; water is precious and scarce, drawn from deep wells and preserved in ponds dug from the stony soil. The landscape is harsh but strangely evocative, relieved by patches of yellow grain fields, each surrounded by stone fencing making geometrical patterns in the dun landscape. They represent a long history of back-breaking toil to extract a livelihood from the stony earth.[1]

In a village, life is basic; boundaries between home and workplace are smudged. Important conversations and arguments happen while chopping wood, cooking, sweeping, and eating. They take place in half-broken sentences interrupted by a neighbour, loud thinking of tentative alternatives in the clutter of serving food, disagreements that need discussions and resolutions, in the middle of washing vessels. In these continuing discussions lie the seeds of critical insight.

Rajasthan is beautiful. In the middle of dry browns and dusty haze, there lies spectacular beauty. People who live in central Rajasthan are surrounded by the Aravallis – the oldest mountain range in India. Someone interested in discovering ancient relics can still find fossils and fascinating reminders of very old times. Now they are being quarried and entire hills are being broken down, for building and construction. This can be seen on the Jaipur–Delhi highway.

We – Nikhil Dey, Shankar Singh, his wife Anshi and I – began our work in Devdungri, when we moved into Haggu and Jait Singh's home in the hamlet of Chokkavadia in 1987.

The region still bears the scars of feudal rule. Life is hard, cultivable land scarce, and occasional drought makes it even harder. Most of those dependent on its produce go to bed hungry. Though the era of the feudal maharaja's rule is history, social inequity and administrative injustice still prevail. Amidst all this, the traditional culture of the region stays alive in the upright bearing of its people, their colourful clothes, engaging songs, fascinating myths, dialects and their laughter-interrupted conversations – evidence of a sustained vitality. The desire and potential for change persist.

> In 1987, forty years after India attained independence, three individuals from very different backgrounds chose to work and live in Devdungri. They were Aruna Roy, who had resigned from the Indian Administrative Service, Shankar Singh, a far-seeing local gifted with rare communication skills and Nikhil Dey, son of an Air Marshal of the Indian Air Force, recently returned from college in America, disgusted with its wasteful lifestyle. The stone and mud hut they rented, approached by a rough path from the main Ajmer–Bhim highway, still stands. They lived like their neighbours, sleeping on the ground, drawing water from a well, carrying buckets on their heads, cooking chapatti and dal on a choolah [stove], washing their clothes and utensils. They enlarged a goat pen adjoining the hut, into a kitchen and bathing area. The toilet was outside.[2]

They came from different backgrounds and experiences. Aruna was the eldest and Nikhil the youngest. Aruna had worked for seven years as a civil servant in the Indian Administrative Service (IAS), after teaching English literature in her alma mater, Indraprastha College for Women in Delhi. She had resigned from the Indian administrative services in 1975 to join a rural voluntary organization, Social Work and Research Centre (SWRC) to work with the rural poor in Ajmer district in Rajasthan. After nine years in SWRC, Aruna left in 1983 to live and work in a village, to enable the people there to access basic political and democratic rights.

When Aruna and Shankar met, they made friends as they shared a common concern about exploitation, poverty and inequality in villages. Shankar began his work with adult literacy. Like many concerned rural youth he had an innate understanding of rural politics. His maturity enabled him to place every personal problem in the larger political context. His inimitable communication skills helped him transform his perception into many modes of expression. Aruna and Shankar became friends. She was fascinated by his great gift as a communicator. There was never a dull moment when Shankar was around. The laughter and well-being he generated, even when he was being critical, increased his popularity. There was an ongoing debate between them on a number of issues. It included the huge divide between them on the way they saw gender, and also the subtle inequalities of caste and religion in the highly hierarchical society that is India. They quibbled on semantics, on theatre technology, on themes for plays – popularity alone could not be the judge of good theatre; applause can never compensate or justify debunking principles and values of equality or justice. Work became exciting for both of them.

Shankar and Aruna worked together when the first strike on minimum wages was organized by Aruna's friend Naurti in Harmara panchayat, Ajmer district, in 1981. He came armed with his puppets and his humour, to soften the antagonism of a strike. Their friendship ran an interesting course. Nikhil met them in Rajasthan in 1983. He was twenty. He had dropped out of an undergraduate programme at the last minute in the US after a brilliant scholastic career. His baffled parents could not understand why an intelligent, straightforward and 'good' student should drop out of college. His motivation was the growing disconnect he felt between his environment in the US and his obsessive concern with helping his own people. He wanted to become a part of people's politics and he chose to come back to India. Nikhil was attracted to Shankar's humour and his extraordinary gifts and wanted to learn more from him and Aruna, with whom he had made friends. All three of them discovered they had the same dreams of living and working.

They went to Jhabhua in Madhya Pradesh (MP) looking for an organization and a context to start work in rural India. It did not work out for a variety of reasons, and they continued their search. Their first requirement was in place: a compatible set of friends who shared political ideologies, principles, and lifestyle values. They agreed that people needed to understand the role of democratic institutions, and their rights as citizens. They were also clear that the organization and its structure should evolve with the people. In India this could be political work outside the party system, much in the tradition of Mahatma Gandhi, Jayaprakash Narayan and many others. Freedom was more than a change in the colour of the rulers. Freedom from hunger, untouchability, poverty and violence required sustained public action to change traditional social discriminatory practices. They believed that people's mobilization would help realize constitutional rights shaped by Dr. B.R. Ambedkar. They finally decided to work in Devdungri, which was close to Shankar's village, Lotiyana. Devdungri, though 35 kilometres away, was still dotted with his relations and his community; it suited Anshi, Shankar's wife, who wanted to live in her own area and be comfortable with the social milieu.

The poor needed work to earn a decent living, get equal wages, schooling, health facilities and all the rest that others take for granted. They were equals under the law. But everywhere they were treated unequally with disdain: by the government, the political system, and by a society divided by caste. They dreamt of a world with justice and equality. What began as a tentative journey still continues for Shankar, Anshi, Nikhil, and Aruna.

It is not very easy to find a place to rent, or even buy, in a village community. Shankar went looking for a place to stay. Haggu, Shankar's cousin, allowed them to move into her unoccupied hut, which used to be her home. The normally difficult entry into a tight-knit community was achieved with apparent ease because Shankar was a 'brother'. This also helped establish the early introductions of Aruna and Nikhil. The village was popularly known as Devdungri in Rajsamand district, and was 8 kilometres from Bhim, a small town on the NH-8 connecting Delhi with Mumbai.

The home, the hut, has a singular, personal and political value. It has been a reassuring place to come back to, and an effort to live the values of simplicity and collectivism. For this narrative, it is the special place where the lucid articulation Mohanji, a Dalit neighbour and small landholder, shaped the struggle for the RTI. Mohanji paraphrased the accusation of untruth faced by the poor in the hands of the authorities when they demanded their rightful wage. He said, 'If we do not get those records out we will always be liars.' This was a turning point in the struggle for the RTI. This simple statement traced the logical and critical role played by transparency as a tool against corruption and the arbitrary exercise of power.

The discussions and arguments in this house defined MKSS's struggle for the RTI.

Living with people was and is important for many reasons. It is the only way people's issues could be understood within the limitations of our lives. It is important to evaluate the work of any group through the eyes of its people. It was a good, practical way to share work and values. Aruna had learnt this in her nine years of work in rural Rajasthan, before coming to Devdungri. Shankar grew up with this understanding.

One of the earliest to visit Devdungri was Rajni Bakshi. A freelance journalist and a very good friend to the MKSS, she would often visit and live with the family. Her writing, which has become a chronicle of the early years, was an organic product of her many visits:

> **Devdoongri: Life along the black tarred road**
> At the northern end of the Aravalli range, on a low hill that stands apart, is a tiny temple made of rough stones and clay tiles. The gram deva, or village deity, who resides within, stands as a sentinel along a busy pathway that may be ancient….
>
> In the shadow of that low hill with its tiny temple, the devdoonger, lies the hamlet of Devdoongri. On its eastern edge, just below the slopes of a barren hill, lives an unusual family. Their mud-and-stone home welcomes a wide assortment of guests. Squatting on the packed mud floor of the kitchen a next-door neighbour could be sharing a meal with a senior bureaucrat from the state capital, a journalist from Mumbai or a marginal farmer from an adjoining district. Over the years I have often shared the strivings and laughter

> of this household. Sometimes, amid mundane domestic chores like sweeping the floor or feeding the goat, this home would remind me of the Bapu Kuti. But the likeness was difficult to voice. Any comparison with the Kuti or its history-making occupant would be embarrassing for my hosts. They were trying to live and work in simple ways that came naturally to them.[3]

As Bhattacharjea too elaborates:

> The house and its ambience began to draw people to Devdungri. Neighbouring villagers were soon attracted to discuss their problems with individuals who shared their spartan life-style but brought with them ideas of change from a wider world. Shankar Singh linked the dreams of his two partners from elitist urban India to rural reality. He was born nearby; his ability to weave new concepts into village idiom with songs, plays and puppets overcame limitations of language. Day by day, evening discussions focussed on how to resist inherited social injustice.[4]

Friends and sociopolitical activists were either curious or concerned about the apparent isolation of the Devdungri family. The continuing open-ended debates on poverty and inequality while living them kept the connections with the outside world alive. Reaching Devdungri was difficult. It was neither on any railway line nor near an airport and could be accessed only by road, as it was on the main highway between Udaipur and Ajmer. The NH-8 was like a giant TV screen of what the other India was about. Devdungri and its occupants watched the strange and puzzling technology in the form of fancy coaches, cars and cranes, lorries and trucks of various shapes and sizes pass by them.

Ajit Bhattacharjea and Prabhash Joshi, eminent journalists and former editors, were friends. Prabhash Joshi writes of his first visit in his inimitably frank manner:

> When I first came to Devdungri I had the same feelings I had when I went to Sewagram much earlier to visit Bapu's Kuti!
>
> Bhim and Devdungri were just names, as many places are when we don't get the opportunity to visit them. But I did one very hot summer afternoon on the 1st of May in a jeep. The sun shone ferociously on the Aravalli hills and the earth was ravaged by

> mining. The windows of the jeep reflected the sun and burnt one's eyes. Yet there were people working – building houses, digging in mines and removing mud and stone.
>
> We went back to Devdungri that night from Bhim. We ate roti and vegetable. Aruna made the rotis on a chulha. We all went to sleep on the mud platform outside. When we woke the next morning, we saw the sun rise from between the gulmohar and the bougainvillea.... Devdungri, dungri because of the hills and dev after Devnarainji, the god of the Gurjars. The temple, like the homes, was thatched with mud tiles and the floors and walls were plastered neatly with mud. The bathroom was a hut and the waste water fed the bamboos.... At the back there was a toilet. Also a mud hut...clean, neat and non-smelly...better than a 5 star hotel![5]

Friends were cynical; the whole exercise seemed romantic. Even the goat, which could be stall-fed and gave more milk than the native species, added to the image! Simple living, the goat – all appeared to be efforts to recapture the illusion of an idyllic village. The initial response was at best sceptical: 'We will not be surprised if you come back to civilization!'

Shankar recalls the early days, when no one knew whether anything would work at all:

> Devdungri is a small hamlet, with 15 to 20 houses, a small settlement where we got a place to stay, a small house with mud baked tiles with a kitchen.... Our initial days were spent in repairing and changing the house a bit. Aruna, Nikhil, Anshi and I started living there regularly from 1987. We were not quite sure how we would begin. But we knew what we would not do. We would not take projects or run an institution which would take funding.
>
> The minimum wages we needed for our survival came from studies of minimum wages which was monitored by the Institute of Development Studies, Jaipur. Along with the study we started to go to the nearby villages and started holding small meetings. We also met people individually.[6]

Living in the village with the community and participating in their daily lives was important. It gave the group an opportunity to consistently raise issues through simple, everyday action.

> It is through these sustained assertions that values were challenged and changed. They raised controversies and debates that began on gender roles [men fetching water on their heads, washing dishes in public]; untouchability [drinking water from the same pot, fetching water from the well]; issues of hygiene and health; norms of social interaction; difference between respect and ceremonial rituals; all become topics for argument and sometimes disagreement. The issue of sitting at the same level, or the same food served to all classes of people visiting provoked anger, criticism, astonishment. When the newcomers ignored these rules, in preference to equality and humanity, often potentially violent situations had to be faced and resolved.[7]

It is in dealing with conflicts in daily life that helps people reduce the gap between idea and action. It is important to have a daily critique of what one did or did not do.

**Getting to Know People**

Rural India could not imagine the apparently well-off Indian taking the risk of living in such adverse circumstances unless it was to exploit. Shifting from physical comforts of the city to difficult living conditions – no toilet, running water or electricity – was not an easy choice. Actually, a toilet was built more than a year after we moved in, with money donated by a friend, Anil Bordia. The questions people asked initially were based on what they saw: 'Are these people miners, or contractors in labour procurement? How does one account for people who did not come with the stamp of respectability?' Everyone's imagination went wild.

In a village there is not much you can hide. Indian villages live within an open frame. Doors are left open, except at night, and if anyone is denied entry it raises suspicions, also interpreted as a desire to hide. Then curiosity levels go up and change to inquisitiveness.

The moving of the few belongings in the hut was therefore watched carefully. There was much speculation. There was no standard furniture associated with the affluent; and the two iron beds had such small legs. Many came to see the odd beds, others to just have a look at the way the new residents lived. People came with varied assumptions. Most came out of curiosity; many came looking for opportunities for work. Some came to boast. Durg Singh came to announce he was a jawan (soldier) in the army and looked down on these poor, misled human beings.

The newcomers, Nikhil, Aruna, Shankar, and Anshi did everything: from fetching water from the well to cooking and sweeping the house. The goat came because milk was scarce, but it needed one person to be home to cater to its needs – animals, like children, need mothering! The water was fetched from the well of Nagodaji. Traditional hypocrisy prevailed when everyone drew water from the same well, but would not let Dalits touch their *mutki* or water pot. There was great opposition when Shankar's daughter asked Nagodaji for help to lift the pot. The entire village came to the doorstep and abused the inmates till they were threatened with legal action under the Scheduled Caste Atrocities Act.

But it was not all opposition. There were many others who came to visit. Many became good friends. Barring principles of equality and discrimination which were non-negotiable, differences were stated and debates began – on borrowing money from the money-lender, funeral ceremonies forcing the poor to overspend and get into huge debts, caste taboos, and of course gender prejudices, the hierarchy of seating, *ghungat* or women covering their faces, and on the social and political issues that needed to be taken up for debate. Gradually change began to be defined.

In the middle of all this speculation came Lal Singh. Nikhil and Aruna recall:

> Lal Singh lived in Sohangarh, about 12 kilometres away, and was visiting relations in Devdungri when he heard of this unusual set of people occupying Jait Singh's house. He came to find out more about them. As a police constable, he had joined a dharna by his colleagues protesting policemen being used for menial jobs for senior officers. The entire lot was dismissed. He came back home and while the others went to court, Lal Singh – for a variety of reasons, including having got fatigued by corruption in the police, decided that he had no desire to continue. The house needed a *mistri* [mason] to reconstruct the two goat sheds into a kitchen. He was recommended for his integrity. Aruna, Shankar and Nikhil were told somewhat cynically that they would get on with him, laughing at him and us for our "foolish" concern with honesty. Later it was apparent that, though a remarkable human being, Lal Singh's capacities as a mason were quite elementary. The first rain brought a flood of water into the kitchen. Anshi and Aruna spent

an afternoon bailing water out of a flooded kitchen. Considering how little rain Rajasthan gets, this was bad workmanship indeed. But this laid the foundation of a solid friendship and built the basis of the *sangathan* [collective].

Lal Singh was a reluctant leader, though the community reposed immense faith in his fairness and he became an arbitrator for disputes in his village. He was simple, intelligent, compassionate and fearless.[8]

Mot Singh, too, became a constant visitor to the hut. He was ill and unable to migrate and find work, and hence lived in Devdungri. Though he was the brother of Ram Singh, one of the few employed by the government as a mason, he was always on the verge of poverty. He was an intelligent and witty man. All villages boast of a few remarkable storytellers like Mot Singh who are not easy to forget. They seem to have walked out of fables and stories. Mot Singh was curious about the group, and was also looking for lively conversation. He knew his stories would appeal to the newcomers. The villagers were familiar with the tales anyway, but he chose his stories and his audience with the consummate skill of a communicator. He knew soon that this group had come not to mine. He was shrewd enough to draw his own conclusions from their concern for workers. It was also clear to him that theirs was not a business visit; looking at their open opposition to untouchability, which was creating unease in the village, he chose his story carefully. It is indelibly printed on the minds of the early supporters. It was the powerful, matter-of-fact allegory of famine, dignity, poverty, hunger and the tragedy when hope turns to despair:

**The pot on the rafters**

Once upon a time, when Rajasthan was affected by one of its worst famines, a family of seven – father, mother and five children who lived in a village – had a terrible time.

Their wells dried up. Nothing grew on their fields. Even the berries and leaves had all been eaten up. Cattle either died or were left to fend for themselves. There was no employment, and the father and mother decided to go looking for work. For if they worked and got money, food could always be bought.

When they left their home, they tied a little "hundi" to the rafters of their mud home. They told the children that the "hundi"

> contained grain, and that when they came home, they would cook it and eat it. The children waited, tired, and hungry for many months. They ate very little, only now and then. Their hopes were kept alive by the little "hundi".
>
> The parents came back, at last, with nothing. They were reduced to skin and bones, like the children. "Let's take the hundi down," cried the children. The mother brought the hundi down. It was empty. The shocked and horrified children died. When hope dies and despair grips us, life slips away.
>
> "The loss of hope is the ultimate end," Mot Singh said, "the government hangs the pot for us on the rafters of its edifice. But the wise know it's empty and those who have to exist believe that it may be full. Life carries on. Government's promises are like that, but what have you come to do about it?" A challenge that was a serious one indeed![9]

Mot Singh had tuberculosis brought on by poverty. Like millions of others all over India, he slipped through the invisible net and fell prey to a slow, early death.

Many people died, even the very young. Migration is a penance. Living conditions in cities are harsh, fraught with disease and alienation. There are no social backups, and people are indifferent, if not unkind. Even many of those young people who join the police and the army come back with diseases and medical debt-induced poverty finally kills them.

The initial phase of settling in to work in any community can be of any duration. Even when one has to first establish one's credibility by making friends with a sense of equality, the beginnings can be rough. Any and every thing can become a possible issue of contention. Listening patiently is the first step towards building an understanding. For the Devdungri group this happened more rapidly in a relative sense. This was partly because of kinship with Shankar and Anshi, and the comfort of dialect and culture. But for the many local people who visited, who had to drink water from a common water pot and sit at the same level, it was a challenge to their rules of social interaction laid down and rigidly maintained by tradition. There was constant friction, which sometimes became a loud exchange of arguments. The Devdungri family stood firm. The worst affected was Anshi, who was culturally closest to the women who got angry with her for breaking tradition.

It was not only the elderly who came to visit. Among the young, frequent visitors to the hut were Narayan and Devilal. They were an unusual pair. That was remarkable in a society where caste and discrimination drew dividing lines everywhere. They came to meet the newcomers who seemed different, a link to the culture hinted at by NH-8. The language these people sometimes spoke also opened up an academic possibility. These visitors could ask for help in the battle with the subject they feared, and failed consistently in – English!

A report done by Aruna, Nikhil and Shankar for the Institute of Development Studies (IDS), Jaipur in 1990, states:

> Kalu was home after he lost an arm in a machine because of bad factory management. He was sent home with nothing but a small compensation. Devilal was two years older than Kalu. They lived in a hut even smaller than ours. They were poor Dalits. They had mortgaged their land for a loan they could not repay. Hunger haunted their home. Devilal was a bright student and fought against all these odds to go to school and did very well. He won the scholarship of 2,000 rupees for the best student in the district in class eight, enabling him to study further. But in spite of this extraordinary achievement, he was working in a factory in Bhilwara, to earn a living. The facts were that he did go to the headmaster who said he knew nothing about the scholarship. When Devilal persisted he answered, much in the same manner as the factory owner had to Kalu: "Yes, I did get some money, but since you were not here I have returned it." Devilal continued to study and did his 10th privately. All the time he continued to work in factories and as farm labour.[10]

There were differences between father and son in Narayan's home. Ram Singh, though he appreciated the determined interest of Shankar and his friends, was not too keen that his son – in whom he had invested a lot – should wander into what we would call activism. Narayan persisted and became a friend and a comrade. Many who came to Devdungri in those early days were fascinated by the local youth who were frequent visitors to the hut. They saw hope in the determination of the young men and women working towards changing their condition. Rajni Bakshi was no exception. She was fascinated and writes in *Bapu Kuti*:

> Narayan was in tune with this perception. But he disagreed with his uncle's decision to distance himself from sangathan-like actions. Narayan found joy in being with his now well-known neighbours. Like his friend Devi Lal, Narayan found a reflection of his own dreams in the ideas and actions that flowed through the home with the gulmohar. So he decided not to go down the black tarred road like his cousin, Mot Singh's son. He completed school, with some tutoring from Nikhil….
>
> Soon, Devi Lal and he were working together on many errands and duties. Narayan found that this growing friendship bothered his parents. For them, all that was fine so long as it occupied its own limited place, but it just wasn't done to eat and drink with Devi Lal. Ram Singh, Narayan's father, enjoyed considerable power and influence within the hamlet of Devdoongri. It was unacceptable that his own son should be breaking basic rules. Thus, sometimes Narayan was forced to listen patiently as his father urged him to give up all this work. At other times, Narayan tried to explain to his father the needs of changing times. But, finally, Narayan did just what he thought was necessary.[11]

The National Highway is dotted with houses. As you come south-westwards down the highway from Bhim, the closest town to Devdungri, you cross Devilal's house. You could see a small cluster of houses from the hut. Traditionally, Dalit homes are on the fringes of villages. Homes are built according to caste, and in clusters; this practice continues for the most part, even today. Things have changed to the extent that Dalit children now go to school. However, even there, caste lines are clearly drawn. This too has not changed as rapidly as it should have. All over India, many schools in rural areas have separate water pots and separate sitting arrangements for Dalits.

Meanwhile, Rajasthan witnessed one of its worst droughts in living memory in 1987, the year this group began living in Devdungri.

An entry from the MKSS Diary states:

> Our work began in 1987 in the town of Devdungri, Rajasthan. The region was experiencing a severe drought that year, and local people were very concerned about getting work and finding a wage. We focused our work on these issues. Involvement with an immediate

> issue is important, both from the point of view of the poor peasant and worker's immediate concerns and the long term perspective of workers organizing for their share of development....[12]

The hunger was palpable. There were riots over getting names in the labour lists for drought relief work. Everyone wanted work, not a dole or even free rations. At times people are denied the right to land and work because they belong to a particular caste, forcing them to beg, like the Kanjars (a scheduled caste). To jump two decades into the future, it's people like them who have regained lost self-respect through the Mahatma Gandhi National Rural Employment Guarantee Act (MGNREGA). The Devdungri notes (later part of the MKSS Diary) state:

> In 1987 the Planning Commission sent a team to Rajasthan to examine the condition of people during the drought. We heard that such a team was visiting Udaipur and would travel past us to Ajmer. We requested that the team stop by. Dr. C.H. Hanumantha Rao, member, Planning Commission, was heading the team. Bunker [Sanjit] Roy, consultant to the Planning Commission was a member of the team. They agreed to stop and meet people. We walked to many surrounding villages and told people that they had a great opportunity and should come and meet the team. About 500 people gathered outside our hut that day. When the team arrived, the assembly of people demanded work, names to be entered in the muster rolls so that they could get "famine relief work". The most shocking information for the team and many of us present was when a woman, in answer to a query about food, took out a roti made from ground thorns. It was a dietary phenomenon seen only in extreme cases of drought, and recorded in the annals of folk history. Shock waves went across, enveloping the Planning Commission team as well. The Collector made many promises in front of the team. They also promised to make payments against famine relief work done at the earliest.
>
> Dr. Hanumantha Rao ate the simple rice and dal we offered and washed his plate. The village was both horrified and amazed. Everyone washed their own dirty plates in our home in Devdungri.[13]

The mud hut of Jait Singh and Haggu has become a part of the folk narrative of MKSS. In hindsight in one of the many reports, they say:

> It was such a blessing that Haggu and Jait Singh allowed us to use the house as our own. But when we lived as we did with equality, without caste discrimination, it excited people's anger. They took exception to the fact that people from all castes drank from the same pot. Narayan and Devilal were good friends and ate and drank with us. The villagers were appalled and very angry. Mohanji, Chunni Bai and Kheemu, all of them Dalits, entered our kitchen. The voices got more militant. After Devilal's land was released from mortgage to a Rawat, rage spilled over. They forced Jait Singh out of the caste [*jatbahar*] for allowing us to live in his house. We were criticized and came under pressure. But Jait Singh resisted this pressure and after a while he sold the house to us. Now these incidents are history and we live more amicably, our ways do not raise the kind of angst that they did earlier. Many social restrictions have changed.[14]

Whether it is a homestead or agricultural land, it establishes steady presence and inviolable claims. In fact, farming pays little dividends in an arid area like Devdungri. But possession of land remains one of the defining indicators of caste and class differences in rural India. Land is precious and an important security for the poor farmer. However miniscule that possession, it gives the person a right to be a legitimate member of that community, establish lineage rights and bear a host of other benefits which are culturally significant. In the case of Roop Singh, he had to migrate seasonally. He says, 'I was better off than those without land; they have it very bad. The small landholdings give a feeling of stability; it can be mortgaged to raise money. Also, the small harvest, in absolute terms, is an insurance against hunger for at least three months.'

For the slightly better-off, in no way comparable with big landholders elsewhere, investment is limited to mortgaging and extortion; it has a stranglehold on their imagination. It becomes a tool for exercising power and keeping their position secure. With moneylending as a side business, the better-off retain their positions of control.

The business of settling in was not so easy; it was fraught with daily dramas and the tension of being under surveillance for every act. As mentioned earlier, every act is under public scrutiny. One may ask why all this information is necessary for the entitlement of the right to know – it is relevant to understand the context of the people whose lives were open books, and the demand came from an understanding that access to basic information is essential. The common rural perception is that the urban and more endowed India often comes to 'exploit' and take away resources – material and human – leaving behind financial, physical and emotional debris that often takes years to address. They are contractors, miners and people who come to exploit cheap labour, acquire land and leave many ill, destitute, and in debt.

**The Struggle for Just Wages on Public Works**

As the acquaintance with people grew, the visits to surrounding villages began to become more focused. Discussions were often centred on the reason for the presence of this new group in Devdungri. Villagers began to understand their concerns. Bad monsoons and the persistent drought continued to be the broad preoccupation of these people. The main discussion and the articulated demand in these meetings was always work called 'famine' by the local people.

The word actually comes from the Famine Relief Code passed by the colonial rulers, to facilitate the opening of works in drought-affected India in 1878. This was subsequently revised in 1898 and 1901. Since Rajasthan is always affected by drought in part, the code was used every year by the Government of Rajasthan to implement works. Providing relief in the form of food was a tradition also among the erstwhile kings of Rajasthan. They used drought relief to build their forts and palaces, the rainwater conservation tanks, and lakes. The Pichola lake in Udaipur (circa 1362), Umaid Bhavan, Jodhpur (1929) are examples.

Independent India continues to implement the Famine Relief Code. It was therefore a part of both cultural and colonial history. People just abbreviated it to a cryptic 'famine', meaning drought relief work. 'When will famine open?' was a question that every newcomer to Rajasthan took time to understand. The Famine Act also did not pay minimum wage despite the passage of the Minimum Wages Act in 1948, which specifies that wages cannot be paid if less than the stipulated minimum prescribed by the state. This was overturned by the Supreme Court in a now landmark judgement in 1983. No public work anywhere could pay less than the minimum wage after this judgement, irrespective of who gives the work and who pays. The Act was and is, however, badly interpreted and implemented. The minimum wage is seen as a maximum rather than a minimum wage, as practice has shown in both government and private works.

## The First Mobilization and Protest: Dadi Rapat – The Beginning of the Work and Wage Issue

Dadi Rapat was the name given to a large 'famine' site near Chunnibai's village, Talai, just a kilometre or two away from Devdungri. Rajni Bakshi writes:

> In those days Chunnibai and Bhanwar and scores of others were digging sand at a work site of the irrigation department called Dadi Rapat. The sand was being carried some distance to bolster the "bunding" of a local tank. They should all have been earning Rs. 11 for a day's work, which was stipulated by the government as the minimum wage. Nikhil, Shankar and Aruna heard about this and started to investigate.[15]

The MKSS records of those days state:

> During the 1987–88 drought relief works, minimum wages were Rs. 11. For those who value every rupee they earn, as it means food, they were distraught over the denial of minimum wages. But the corrupt system denied them through a work system, never supervised. A penalty was levied on unfinished tasks. But if the task was never assigned properly in the first place, how was it ever to be completed? When there were false names on the muster rolls, people who worked on the site suffered. The so called penalty became a source of siphoning funds. People were almost resigned to the fact that they would never receive minimum wages on drought relief works.[16]

Lal Singh from Sohangarh is a thinker. He has contributed to every concept of MKSS, both ideologically and strategically. He says:

> For people, the Right to Information is really the right to live. The daily bread is concealed in the records of government offices. Dadi Rapat was the first place that this was actually realized by the workers. The junior engineer kept saying that people do not get the wage because they do not work. At that time the minimum wage was Rs. 11, but people got Rs. 4 and even 2! We talked to the workers and said, "If you do your full assigned task, you can get the full wage." The workers said, "We want the full wage and will work." Wheat was Rs. 2/kilo at that time. They said, "If we get 5 kilos of

> grain a day, we can stave off hunger. If the work is pre-measured and tasks are assigned we will deliver full work." Fifteen days' work was assigned to a large collective of people. Chunni Bai, Bhanwar from Kushalpura, and Mohanji – all part of the Devdungri group – were also workers. We went and talked to the junior engineer and he agreed to measure the task assigned before work began. After 20 days the results were amazing. The ones who had worked more got less, and the ones who worked less got more! The junior engineer said he had paid according to the measurement book. When we asked to see the book he said he would not show it. It became clear that work and quantum had nothing to do with payments. The Government did not want to honour its commitment to tasks and wages. What were they hiding? Actually, what is a measurement book? We too could not access it. The secrecy actually hid the fraud that was practised. They show 100 people on the muster roll and swallow 40 people's wages. How can work output ever come up to tasks assigned? People's rights were denied, they were denied food and life. Poor workers do not want to rule, they want the right to survive. The direct link between the paper and their lives became clear through this exercise.[17]

The news from the Dadi Rapat work site spread throughout the region. The work undertaken at the site came to be referred to as 'digging caves'. When the wages were disbursed, those who received higher wages (Rs. 7.40) were the workers from the previous weeks who had not worked at all. The workers who had actually dug the caves were paid less (Rs. 6). The mate who had assured workers that they would receive full wages for completed work vanished from the work site. Initially, all 140 workers refused to accept the truncated wage but it was only Chunni Bai and Bhanwar Singh who stuck it out to the very end. The others were duped into accepting their wages.

A very simple but effective way of denial of wages has been worked out by the government. Work is measured and assigned to every worker in principle. The junior engineer (JEn), who is responsible for the measurement seldom comes to the site. There is a 'mate' from the village who is appointed by the department. He (now there are women too) officiates for the government, gives rough measurements, and the work is allocated to an individual but measured group-wise for payment. The penalty, applied on everyone as the final quantum of shortfall in work (falsely claimed to have been measured), is divided equally among the number of workers on the 'muster roll'. The lazy or the ghost names of workers who are never there at the work site reduce the quantum of work. In reality the work is seldom measured – neither when it is given nor when it is over. The conflict between work given individually and measured collectively is that it uniformly penalizes the group for the shortfall. It inflicts an unfair penalty on the diligent worker who may have completed the work assigned. The workers understood that payment of wages had no direct link with how much they worked. Dadi Rapat was an exposé of the lies and cheating by the system. It illustrated that those who work more get paid less. What was the point in subjecting oneself to this exploitation and losing one's self-respect? People argued: why work at all if there is no justice? The government said, 'People are lazy; they do not work!' In this impasse the hard worker was left hungry, ill-paid and a victim of abuse.

Chunni Bai and her husband, Mohanji, were poor Dalits. But they were among the first to recognize the worth of a sangathan. Chunni Bai worked at the site and shared her story:

> The work in Dadi Rapat was strenuous. We had to dig and transport earth to the tank bund about half a kilometre away. We were 100 workers. We got anything between 4 and 7 rupees as wage. We tried an experiment and made 4 groups of 20 each and tried to bring some rationality into the work and wages. We decided we would work hard to finish our tasks and then demand full wage. Arunaji, Nikhilji and Shankar Bhai came to the work site to see the work. They talked to all the workers. This was the beginning.
>
> We worked more than required, one cubic foot more, not less! When the payments came, we went to the school to get our wages. We checked on the payments registered for the groups that had done more than the required work. I asked them to refuse to accept the wages if they were less than Rs. 11, that we would think we have built our own tank and bunded it. Bhanwar from Kushalpura was with us. I asked him to keep an eye on the proceedings. When payments were made they were Rs. 5 and Rs. 6 per day! We made applications to refuse payment and gave it to a "babu", a clerk sitting there. We gave one copy in Devdungri, one to the Tehsil and we kept

> one copy. When I went home I discovered that the wages denied by the workers were surreptitiously handed over to any member of their families that they could find. Bhanwar from Kushalpura and I did not take the money. On the advice of the Devdungri activists we went to the Jodhpur High Court and filed a case.[18]

Chunni Bai's recollection misses no detail!

Bhanwar from Kushalpura, who also worked and refused to take less than the minimum wage along with Chunni Bai at Dadi Rapat, has been a staunch supporter of rights. A poet and a writer, he hopes that by fighting defeat and pessimism in a free country, the poor will one day get justice. He expressed himself in verse which is paraphrased below:

> 16 December 1987 was a day with a difference. Workers, who completed their task, did not get full wages. Somebody other than the mate came to measure the work, and concluded we had worked less. The mate said, "You have cost me a lot of money for fuel, now watch me play my game. You also made complaints; I too am the one who can hold a grudge." The overseer needed to be convinced, but that was like trying to convince a politician. Less work more pay, more work less pay. This was done on purpose, we thought later. Everyone refused the wages; we knew officials were trying to fool us. Barring two, everyone got Rs. 6, according to their calculations. Two workers demanded justice. Officials are liars; this is what the workers say. But some day we will get justice; workers will also have a chance. Is the government fair, or is it occupied with feeding its officials? Says one thing and does another, like an elephant's teeth; one to eat with and the other for show. This is how the government treats us.[19]

The many months spent in organizing people to work and claim full wages followed its own logic. For Aruna it was a continuation of her preoccupation with work and wages for the poor since the late seventies. Soon after she resigned from the Indian administrative services, she started working in rural Rajasthan with the poor and their demand for work, including the struggle with Naurti Bai in Harmara, Ajmer district, which ended with a landmark judgement in the Supreme Court in a case on minimum wages.[20]

Shankar was the son of a patwari (revenue official). He knew the other side very well: the nature of petty thefts and the ways in which the system could be mismanaged. Nikhil was appearing for his final exams in law, and his innate gift for looking at the legality of issues helped a great deal. Aruna was 41, Shankar 33, and Nikhil 24. They had complementary skills and they worked well together.

Dadi Rapat established the intent of the group. It was clear to the workers in Bhim and Deogarh tehsils that now they could work with the Devdungri group to claim their rights.

CHAPTER TWO

# Sohangarh and the Struggle for Land

Events overtook us at Devdungri rapidly and the original plan – to wait and watch and proceed slowly – had to be set aside. The demand for work and employment, propelled by the continuing drought, introduced a kind of urgency to look for solutions, and Dadi Rapat called for immediate attention. If in Dadi Rapat the protagonist was the local corrupt and feudal administration, in Sohangarh it was the overwhelming subjugation of all rights by feudal and oppressive social structures, in collusion with a corrupt administration.

Lal Singh with Tej Singhji had started resisting Hari Singh, the Tal Thakur's oppression, even before Lal Singh had come to repair the roof of the Devdungri house. As he began to understand the ideology of the group, he saw potential in collaborating with them. He invited Nikhil, Shankar and Aruna to Sohangarh even while the Dadi Rapat mobilization was happening. The Devdungri activists began trekking about 12 kilometres to Sohangarh to hold regular meetings in the village.

## Hari Singh Tal – The Copy Book Oppressor

Hari Singh was the Sarpanch of Tal, which was the panchayat for Sohangarh. He was a former Jagirdar or traditional landlord, but becoming Sarpanch ensured his continuing authority. It was a merging of traditional feudal authority and newly acquired democratic power to conveniently circumvent every rule. If he could not get his way through foul means, he took to fouler ones by using the façade of the law. He used his fists, his mafia and his connections. All development works were either directly on his land or property, or sizeable portions were siphoned off. He retained illegal control over property that had become government land with the enactment of the Ceiling Laws. He levied cess or tax on the use of these lands by the people at will. He beat up women and molested them either through his family or his touts. Even mud taken from the government tank bed had to be shared in the proportion of 50:50 with him.[21]

### Tej Singhji and Lal Singh

In Sohangarh there were two steady opponents to the Thakur. Both of them were accepted leaders. Tej Singhji had studied only up to middle school and had been a part of the national movement for Independence. He spoke and wrote good English. A highly skilled mason, he was an ethical and fearless man. He had taken Hari Singh once, and had a broken finger to prove how violent and vicious the Thakur could be. People in the area also disliked the Tal Thakur because Hari Singh's father had burnt the Indian flag in anger, horrifying people when India got independence! Hari Singh compromised with independent India by insinuating himself into the electoral process. But the whole 'tikhana' (feudal leadership) saw the past as glorious and resented the equality that Independence and the constitution brought with it.

Aruna recollects:

Lal Singhji was a younger and important ally of Tej Singhji. Both of them were the leaders of the opposition to the Tal Thakur. They were courageous, principled and ethical. The women in Sohangarh were also exceptional. We met Kakiji and Bhuri Ya, both elders and leaders in the village community. Kakiji was strongly religious, and bound by her faith. Bhuri Ya, older and physically stronger, was more modern and a member of the panchayat. These two extraordinary women gave great strength to the battle against injustice. Their support opened doors of all homes in Sohangarh, and provided emotional comfort and security against physical violence that threatened the new comers at every step. Their presence was a strong inducement and invitation for other women

> to join the struggle. Kakiji was visited by "spirits" in her dreams who told her to support them! She saw a woman in a white sari and two men who came to help the village in its difficulties. They both gave me emotional and psychological support. I was empowered as a woman and as an activist. Their love has been a constant factor over the years.[22]

Frequent walks to Sohangarh became a routine thing for us. We were joined by Mohanji, Chunni Bai, Bhanwar from Kushalpura, and occasionally even Jait Singh. Chunni Singh came from Palona, miles away – he had become a friend because of shared values; Ramkaran and Naurti occasionally travelled from distant Harmara and Phaloda in Ajmer district, and were frequent companions.

**Sohangarh Village**

Lal Singh, who had invited the group to Sohangarh, took the responsibility of holding meetings and initiated the dialogue between the villagers and the Devdungri group about Hari Singh and feudal oppression.

Aruna's notes elaborate on their visit:

> The first trip to Sohangarh was a memorable one. Nikhil told me that Lal Singh was a very strict man and we had to be punctual at any cost. We had to walk half a kilometre to Chalis Meel, take a bus to Tal and then walk seven kilometres to Sohangarh. The walk was long and could have been fun, except that the tension of reaching at the right time made us jog! We arrived breathless in Sohangarh only to find no one assembled for the meeting. It started [as it normally does in villages] 4 hours late!
>
> In fact, later when I came to know Lal Singh, I was amused with our first impressions of him. Actually I have never met anyone more laid back than Lal Singh. Even a dharna and police action did not make him hurry or get tense!
>
> To top it all, when Lal Singh asked us if we were hungry, Shankar politely said, "No, we have eaten." I was baffled as Shankar knew I was famished. I knew that village custom permits comparative strangers to ask for food; I interrupted him to say that I was hungry. They were very happy to feed me. Eventually Shankar and Nikhil ate more than I did![23]

When the meeting began, the issue needed no introduction. The village faced oppression from Hari Singh and his family every day, and this was hardly surprising because he terrorized the whole area. He and his family levied tax on government land, charged for grazing cattle, and demanded that a percentage of clay or mud dug from the tank bed from what was now government land be brought to their 'rawla' or feudal home! He brought all the traditional horror stories to life. It was unbelievable that such acts were possible at the end of the twentieth century. The extortion was appalling, and if it were not so serious it would have been absurd.

For almost a year, these meetings in Sohangarh helped establish a relationship of trust and understanding with the people. The staging of a play provoked the wrath of Hari Singh. He openly confronted the group and threatened all of them personally, and as a group, with violence. Larger meetings continued, undaunted by these threats. It soon became clear that the primary source of Hari Singh's strength came from his excessive control over illegal land holdings. It was also apparent that small battles against his actions as sarpanch would not succeed in undermining his power base. On the contrary, it only singled out, exposed and threatened those who were courageous enough to take him on.

## Prashasan Gaon ki Ore

> The Government of Rajasthan had planned to take the administrative machinery to the villages in a programme which was appropriately called "Prashasan Gaon Ki Ore" [PGKO]. It was a method of redressal of grievance related to allotment of unoccupied government waste land to the poor, and other revenue related matters.
>
> The intervention by the Devdungri group was seen as a method of forcing the government to publicly recognize its own stated laws and regulations and implement them. It was decided that the villagers would apply for collective allotment of unoccupied government land for Sohangarh villagers in the camp to be held in Tal. It so happened that almost 1000 bighas of this land was under the illegal control of Hari Singh and his family.[24]

When they started holding meetings in Sohangarh, it came as no surprise to the Devdungri group that detailed and verified information about land was not accessible. Rumours intended to instil fear coloured discussions, and most of them were started by Hari Singh and his family. Illegal control was sought to claim ownership in the names of the Thakur's family members. It was clear to those who knew the Land Ceiling Act that it was impossible for this family to have legal control over the quantum of land it claimed as theirs. But there was apparently no public information to prove that the claim was wrong and the control illegal. The patwari, or revenue official, was frightened of, and controlled by, Hari Singh. It was impossible for ordinary people to enter the office, let alone look at land records. Questions from the Devdungri group to the patwari were evaded and no answers seemed forthcoming. Revenue information is public information, but it was a jealously guarded secret for obvious reasons. Because disclosure would break the controls of the corrupt and the power mafia, only a select few were allowed to access it.

The extent of the former jagirdar's control over the revenue administration soon became clear. Land can only be allotted if the 'khasra' number (property identification number issued by the revenue department) of the specific land is notified for allotment. Hari Singh made sure that the number of that land was not in the allotment notice. Allotments could not be made at the camp because it was procedurally wrong to do so. What the Thakur managed to do with his access to information and control over the local administration was diabolical.

The Devdungri and Sohangarh groups had managed a huge mobilization. A number of people who could take up the matter further came forward, such as Mahesh Bora, advocate and friend, who had come from Jodhpur especially for this purpose. The frightened villagers gathered enough courage to stand up and apply for allotment in spite of fears of facing dire consequences from the jagirdar. But the Thakur won the first round by manipulating the notification. No allotments were made that day.

The Devdungri group accessed this information informally from the subdivisional magistrate (SDM) and the forest department. This was perhaps one of the first public lessons of how vital transparency of official information was to every struggle. It was the beginning of understanding the importance of records, the transparency of public procedures and notifications, proactive disclosure and the interplay between official and unofficial information systems. All this dramatically proved that information *is* power.

Fortunately, the SDM was determined to render justice and his sympathies were with the socially underprivileged. He made sure that the notification was reissued and that the numbers deliberately left out earlier were included. A fresh camp was held.

Once the information as well as the intent was in the public domain, battle lines were clearly drawn. It was not unexpected that threats of violence and hostility would follow. For several months Hari Singh retaliated in multiple ways to protect his illegal control, all mobilized through his caste identity. He was very smart and though barely literate, was well versed with the rules of the game. He was inseparable from his black briefcase. It contained a number of papers related to land and the various cases he was involved in, which were whipped out periodically to prove a point.

The solution for Sohangarh lay in sidestepping the logic of Hari Singh and his power games. The village held secret deliberations and decided to form a 'mahila' or women's sangathan. This was a master stroke, and significant for several reasons. The government was allotting land for social forestry and women's groups were at the top of the list and seen as priority, while the men could not claim membership. Women were at the forefront of the land struggle, led by Bhuri Ya and Kakiji. Though upper-class Rajput women are supposed to be in strict purdah, working-class women are not restrained from working outside home. The process of forming and registering the samiti was an extraordinary experience. Signatures were obtained secretly and papers were taken to the district headquarters in Udaipur overnight. After much effort the samiti was registered and was allotted 25 hectares of land by the collector at Udaipur. The land continues to be collectively owned and managed even today.

The local administration was petrified of making the actual allotment, while Hari Singh continued to be in the dark. The SDM had to be cajoled into actually measuring the land. The whole process was fraught with anxiety. The tension was palpable when the SDM finally came to oversee the measurement of the land for allotment. Those who were asked to hold the measurement chains looked over their shoulder for fear that the Thakur would emerge with his men to attack them. The administration was tense. Under the SDM's orders the villagers held the measuring chain.

Aruna, Shankar and Nikhil, Chunni Singh, Mohanji, Chunni Bai, Bhanwar from Kushalpura, and friends from nearby Jawaja had reached Sohangarh well in time. When a motorcycle was heard approaching, the terrified villagers dropped the chain. The administration stood rigid in its anxiety. The chief inspector from Deogarh, Ayub, stood ready to act. The SDM said, 'Pick up the chains,' as the Thakur got off and made his way to the spot shouting revenge. Bhanwar, Tej Singhji's son and Lal Singhji held the chain to measure the land. Hari Singh realized that the administration was in charge and he could not brazen his way through, so he abused and threatened everyone as he left: 'This is not the end. I am coming back.' There was temporary relief from immediate violence, but the pall of tension was conspicuous as the land was hurriedly measured.

The Devdungri activists wanted to spend the night in Sohangarh, but the administration persuaded them to go back to Devdungri, which they did, reluctantly. Aruna went with the authorities in the first jeep that left Sohangarh. Nikhil and Shankar had decided to walk back with Chunni Singh, Madhusudan Jhala and others. However, they were surprised to see the police jeep return. Ayub had come back worried, as his police jeep had overtaken a tractor with Hari Singh and his subordinates, armed with guns and swords. The tractor was ordered to turn back by the police. Ayub ordered Nikhil and others to climb in, which they did after protesting that it was unnecessary. Anshi and Aruna were relieved to see them come back unhurt. But the tension continued, with fears for those in Sohangarh. Hari Singh's threats were real and his interests had been seriously threatened. There was anxiety, and it was another sleepless and anxious night for them.

It was later proved that their anxiety was more than justified. That evening, after they had left, the Thakur's men returned to Sohangarh. The armed team entered 'Sujaba ka Pol', Sujaba's home, where Lal Singh and Bhanwar had sat down to finish the paperwork and accounts. They terrorized Lal Singh and Bhanwar with a sword, and imitating a scene from the Hindi film *Sholay*, a fellow Rajput stood guard on the terrace with a gun! A neighbour, Koom Singh, and his wife saw the man. An enraged Koom Singh went in to bring out his gun, but his wife, frightened that there would be bloodshed, shut the door on him and bolted it from outside. She ran with her scythe (*dantli*) screaming, 'Help, danger from the Thakur,' around the village, gathering people from every home.

Hordes of people emerged in the evening dusk armed with every kind of agricultural tool. As they ran in one direction, Hari Singh's men fled from the other. Had they come face to face that day there would have been violence and death.

Chunni Singh, courageous and irreverent of feudal authority and threats, came to stay in Devdungri and was a regular visitor to Sohangarh. Chunni Singh was feared by the exploiter and respected by the poor. He was a rare champion for justice. His father had died when he was four, and had left the family unprovided for. An uncle fed them for a week. Soon enough, the irritated uncle began airing his worries publicly about the economic strain on his slender budget. He said to Chunni Singh, 'How long will I have to look after you?' Chagrined and his dignity hurt, though he was only four, he persuaded his mother to migrate and take him along. He spent his childhood washing cups and plates in dhabas. He grew up to be a modern-day Robin Hood in Baroda, Gujarat, taking on any oppressor of the poor and helpless workers. His face was marked with numerous mementos of encounters with the local mafia. Chunni Singh returned to his village, Palona, thirty years after his father's death, determined to reclaim the land which had been mortgaged, and settle down to make it work. He joined the group and gave it his courage and oratory, both highly valued. He became a constant companion in the months of terror that gripped the villagers of Sohangarh.

The village of Sohangarh decided to deal with this issue creatively and politically. The activists in Devdungri realized that Hari Singh and his caste network had to be countered by a group committed to protect the marginalized. The Van Utsav, on 'hariyali amavasya', was an annual event that celebrated the taking over of land; it was traditionally understood and lent itself to peaceful mobilization and a show of strength. On this occasion, hundreds of people assembled to celebrate the formation of the Shramik Mahila Vikas Evam Anusandhan Samiti, Sohangarh. This body was made responsible for nurturing and ensuring the collective use of the land which had been released from Hari Singh's control. Some of the more enlightened and sympathetic bureaucrats of the state, such as Anil Bordia and M.L. Mehta, came to the occasion. The ex-raoraja (some sort of a senior thakur) of Deogarh, Nahar Singh, who had taught at Mayo College, also came. He managed to help break the local stereotype associated with his class and caste. Eminent persons like Mahesh Bora, advocate from Jodhpur, Bunker Roy, Kishore Saint, Ajay Mehta, political leaders, and traditional jati panchayat leaders, all assembled to plant trees and welcome the collective 'social forestry' venture.

The samiti applied for and got a grant from the Wasteland Development Board (WDB) to build a boundary wall. It distributed work equally to all the households and was a transparent and wonderful collective effort. The money for wages was disbursed in Sohangarh once a fortnight by Shankar, Nikhil and Lal Singh, along with a representative of the WDB. Shankar and Nikhil were always picked up by the representative on a motor bike. One evening, as they were returning from Sohangarh, a drunk Hari Singh waylaid them at a crossroad in Tal and tried to beat them up. Because he was drunk, the three of them managed a get away, though they were manhandled – Shankar lost his spectacles and his slippers. They drove immediately to the police station in Deogarh and registered a complaint. Anshi and Aruna were worried when they did not return at the usual time. They came back late to relate their story, and everyone who had gathered in Devdungri was reassured that the injuries were not serious, and life continued.

Two nights later, when all of them were sleeping in the courtyard, they heard the thumping of sticks and sounds of footsteps. The children were hastily bundled inside and Nikhil, Aruna, Shankar and Anshi stood up to accost the strangers. In the darkness, a series of heads appeared, one wearing a miner's helmet. It looked as if they were ready to attack. When Shankar called out, 'Who's there?', Vijay from Sohangarh replied, 'Friends, we have come to see how badly Shankar and Nikhil were beaten by Hari Singh. We will go to Tal later for justice.' Hari Singh, boasting of his exploits in an attempt to instil fear among the villagers, had made a grand pronouncement. He had claimed, 'I have broken all the thirty-two teeth of those…'; he alleged that he had beaten up the two men who worked with Aruna so badly that 'they will now forget their way back to the village.' That night as the news about the so-called thrashing spread, thirty-five to forty people from Sohangarh and Dhapda, close to Sohangarh, decided to come to Devdungri, armed with sticks, iron rods, some even wearing helmets. They examined Shankar and Nikhil to reassure themselves that they were not seriously hurt.

Later, a discussion carried on late into the night. This was the first strategy meeting, in one sense. The villagers wanted to go and beat up the

Thakur and his family, and they had come prepared. The first discussion on peaceful protest and use of public space began with a reluctant acceptance of a rally and a public meeting in Bhim. The Devdungri group was able to persuade the villagers that physical retaliation is a spiral that would eventually affect the real demand for justice.

At a meeting in Dhapda the next day, it was collectively decided that the villagers would march in protest to Bhim and submit a memorandum to the SDM there.

**The Rally to Bhim**

The rally which began in Dhapda grew in numbers as people joined it from many villages en route, from Thana, Goma ka Badiya, and other hamlets in the 12-kilometre walk to Bhim. The first slogan at the rally had begun with full feudal propriety: 'Kunwar Hari Singh, your tyranny will not be tolerated.' Later the respectful prefix was dropped and it became Hari Singh and finally Hariya. This was a significant turning point, as abbreviations and derivatives are generally reserved for the lower castes and those who are socially oppressed. The idiom often reflects the power equation, and is more of a yardstick than stated ideologies. Articulation is the first step in the process of empowerment.

Bhim looked on with curiosity and apprehension at the first public meeting MKSS organized in this small town. Standing next to a cobbler, on a slightly raised platform, at a crossroad, Chunni Singh delivered his maiden speech, and established himself as an orator. He said:

> It's years since we got independence. But the poor and rich remain unequal before the government and the police. If a rich man's rat is beaten up, the police will drag the culprit to jail and beat him. But if someone kills a poor man, the police will do nothing![25]

He spoke his truth, and did not care who heard him. His maiden speech as an ordinary worker made him a rock star, and people flocked to hear him. They still do.

Much later, the police brought Hari Singh before the SDM. It was the first time that anybody had the courage to file a police complaint against the tyrant. The rally and public meeting managed to dramatically break the stranglehold of fear that Hari Singh had exercised over the area. This victory heralded a steady decline in the power of Hari Singh. The

Sohangarh story became folklore and gave many people in the area the strength to oppose the many forms of oppression.

Shankar, recalling this episode in an article in *Diamond India*, says:

> This struggle helped lay the foundation of the MKSS. There was a genuine recognition that coming together pays great dividends. No one had dreamt that the Thakur could be humbled. But a collective managed just that. It gave us great strength and taught us a lot. It underscored the power of collective strength. It led to the formation of the sangathan.[26]

Dadi Rapat and Sohangarh were processes that led to public understanding of the power of information, concealed in public records and offices. The continuation of colonial control over information in independent India became clear. This also amply demonstrated the nexus between oppressive social hierarchical domination and bureaucratic controls.

This process educated the people about collective strength and its ability to dismantle illegal power centres. It organically led to the formation of the sangathan. The heady feeling of solidarity and power that collective action promotes had to continue and locate itself in a systemic structure, which could channelize the energy over a period of time. The seeds of MKSS were sown.

People began to understand the need for a transparent administrative system, and information was no longer an abstraction, it was a means to land that they could or could not access, and to the minimum wage that continuously eluded them.

### A Footnote

> It was much later, when the mahila samiti was in control and the land was a healthy forest. Kakiji and I sat on a rock one Hariyali amavashya, the annual event to celebrate the taking over of the land. I heard Kakiji humming Gandhiji's famous bhajan, "Raghupati raghav..." I asked her how she knew the song. She said casually, "I learnt it from Bapu." I thought she meant her father. She corrected me to say, it was from the bigger Bapu, Gandhiji at Sabarmati! Her father looked after the cows there and she lived with him as a child.

Diminutive as she was, she was a unique woman, wise and fearless, literate till the 5th. Her support for the struggle was an organic part of her upbringing. Rural women never cease to astonish me with their strength.[27]

CHAPTER THREE

# The Concept and Birth of the MKSS

The extraordinary and unexpected success of the land struggle in Sohangarh demonstrated the potential power of collective action. It inspired people to hope and to move toward forming an organization. It turned around the helpless self-fulfilling prophecies like 'nothing will change!', to a positive assertion of strength, '*hum apna adhikar jante, nahin kisi se bheekh mangte*' – we know our rights, we have not come begging.

The struggle for land allocation set people thinking along the lines of possibilities. The time had come to form an organization. Devdungri became the hub of many meetings that took place to discuss the nature of the organization, its scope and objectives. Every issue was discussed; even the name that the sangathan gave itself went through many deliberations. Finally, it was Mazdoor Kisan Shakti Sangathan that pleased everybody. The *mazdoor* (worker) was also a marginal *kisan* (peasant) and this was an organization that would work for their empowerment or *shakti*. The logo, worked over by many and collectively designed, put the gender balance straight: a man's fist in black to show struggle, a woman's in red to show change and revolution – a woman leads the demand for change! And the sangathan thus took shape.

Poor people understood that there was no alternative to collective struggle to change their predicament. The Kushalpura wage struggle and the Sohangarh land struggle were indeed mass awareness programmes – 'learning by doing'. Sayings like 'You can break a finger but not a fist' were part of their cultural expression. Traditional understanding of collective strength was transformed into a working reality.

The Devdungri group understood that people need to discuss issues in their own idiom. The sangathan was not formed on ideological or theoretical discussions but on mutually agreed principles, and a code of democratic ethics. For poor people, their condition of deprivation and injustice formed the basis for sharp political analysis. The formation of the sangathan was their articulation of this understanding. Rural communities are practical; they have an information system, knowledge and understanding rooted in their daily lives. The sangathan allowed the coming together of individual experiences to create a powerful voice of reason, difficult to ignore or dismiss. A people's organization has to grow from people's thought processes and give them time to assimilate newer ideas and systems. The sangathan grew naturally, reflecting on every action and reaction. It became the vehicle for deliberative and analytical change. In the middle of the process of formation of the sangathan, Hari Singh was arrested, increasing the hope for justice and organized change.

**The Use of Street Theatre**

Shankar brought his enormous gift of a master communicator to all political action before and after the formation of the sangathan. His energy, strength and power of innovation brought politics into theatre, in the idiom and language of the people. He was equally at home on the stage in its formal mode and in acting and creating street plays. The political messages of the sangathan were transformed into street theatre, songs and slogans. It had a direct and powerful impact on changing people's understanding of theatre as mere entertainment. His performances made it much easier for the sangathan to communicate quickly and effectively. The oral scripts were based on people's experiences and crafted collectively. They were written down much later, more as a record than as a literary piece. There was a different play for every issue. It was a part of every *pad yatra* or *jatha* (foot march), travelling from one village to the other to raise issues of greater common interest. There was no professional actor or local troupe; those who acted were researchers and local people. All of them gave time voluntarily and easily slipped into the discussions and arguments that followed the performances.

The friends and people of the sangathan were happy to be a part of this process. The first testing ground was Sohangarh, at the height of tensions with Hari Singh. Apart from being a powerful tool of communication, a play cannot easily be stopped, particularly if it is popular. The street theatre scripts mixed humour and satire, and were hugely popular. The first drama workshop was with Uma Shankar, who came from Bangalore in early 1990. He helped establish the tradition of evolving a new play in a workshop, followed by a jatha/pad yatra in April every year, preceding the May Day celebrations. The tradition continues to this day. The play sets a broad agenda for the next year and invites people to come.

A political street play has to have topical relevance. It has to be in the local idiom, and include contemporary and popular references, which place it in the context of local experiential history. The implicit political message became clear. It set people thinking of the relationship between their own experiences and the political debates they heard so often. Subsequent MKSS plays followed this tradition every year. The workshop was therefore as much an exercise in political and economic analysis as it was in dramatizing a dilemma people faced.

The participants brought their own rations for the workshop and took almost a month off from their work to formulate the play and take it from village to village. Twenty-seven villages were mapped out in the adjoining districts of Pali, Bhilwara, Ajmer and Udaipur (Rajsamand was carved out of old Udaipur district). It was an experience that was new for everyone.

Apart from Uma Shankar, the MKSS has had the support and guidance of Tripurari Sharma from the National School of Drama (NSD) and comrades and fellow actors of Shankar, Shiv Singh Nihal, Ramnivas, Ramlal, Hameed, and Bodhu. Tripurari, with her manifold gifts, was Shankar's drama guru. Along with Lakshmi Krishnamurthy, she initiated Shankar into the art of formal theatre. Shankar's commitment to fighting injustice and poverty was closely linked to his gifts of communication, acting, puppetry, and his natural wit and repartee. His presence contributed to recognizing the talent and gifts of many others. His enthusiasm and energy were infectious.

The call of the mazdoors and kisans was to come together to make a declaration through the formation of the sangathan. It was one answer to the series of questions that were persistently being asked.

## Communicating through *Parchas*, Pamphlets and Wall paintings

Campaigns use pamphlets or *parchas* (handbills) for communicating with people. In the years leading up to its formation, the MKSS used parchas to disseminate information. The first handbill that was distributed announcing the sangathan served its purpose. In rural India people read handbills – they do not suffer the fate they do in urban India, where they are immediately used by vendors to sell eatables or added to the pile of rubbish.

The traditional painting on walls was a participatory exercise; many groups of young people, armed with a pail of brick dust mixed with water as paint and a twig with some old cloth as a brush, volunteered to paint walls and enjoyed doing it. In fact, many of these wall paintings can be seen even today. It has been as useful for rural communication as social media is in urban areas today. '*Bhim chalo bhai, Bhim chalo, 1 May ko Bhim chalo*' written on many walls in the villages around still exist as a testimony to the popularity of the May Day Mela.

A collation of statements and questions brought together the burning issues of survival and a series of pledges to address them in the pamphlet distributed before May Day 1990:

> This land is ours, the remedy lies in our hands, our number is our strength, and we must unite to ask these questions. How do we get our rights? What prevents us from getting work here? How do we improve our plight? How can we get our rightful wage? How do we protect our sources of water? How can we make the brown earth turn green?
>
> The final resolution summed up the determination that all questions need to be addressed and answered collectively. The two fists – "muthis" – bring us together. To find answers to all these questions all mazdoors and kisans are invited on the 1st of May to announce the formation of the Mazdoor Kisan Shakti Sangathan [MKSS] at the Patia ka Chowda, Bhim![28]

## Slogans

The MKSS slogan was very compelling and echoed the desire for equality, justice and dignity:

*Nyay samanta ho aadhaar*
*Aisa rachenge hum sansar*
[We will create a universe with justice and equality].

Slogans are powerful. The advertisement jingles prove it. But the slogan, unlike the jingle, has a different intent. It encapsulates a huge idea in a few simple words. It is chanted and travels quickly, working on the minds of people, persuading them to think. *Mazdoor Kisan Shakti Sangathan – Zindabad, Zindabad* (Long live the Mazdoor Kisan Shakti Sangathan); *Jab tak bhookha insan rahega, dharti par toofan rahega* (As long as people are hungry, struggles will continue to storm the earth); *Bhrashtachar – Hai, Hai!* (Down with Corruption!); and the MKSS slogan, *Nyay samanta ho aadhaar, aisa rachenge hum sansar.*

All effective campaign songs have appealed across sectors. The Right to Information campaign too, later, owed its popularity to the appeal, the lilt and the lyric of many a song. The songs were often created spontaneously and sometimes deliberately to carry messages. With every play there was at least one song that carried the message much further than the play could. The year the sangathan was born, it was the pathos of the migrant worker's song. He leaves home with great expectations but returns with his hopes crushed, to face questions he cannot answer. Workers face expectant families, drought and hunger, all over again. The sangathan provided a possible answer, which took them on a long trajectory towards a legal guarantee of employment through the MGNREGA in 2005.

Struggles and people's movements have expressed themselves in powerful collectives and interactive songs. MKSS was no exception. Since 1987, the community of workers and peasants continued to sing songs and chant slogans. In 1990, the song most remembered was: '*Paredesasu aayo bhaya*':

*Paredesasu aayo bhaya rama shama leejiyo re*
*Ghana dniaon aaya thanka haal sunao re, Marno hadhario*

It talks of migration and the futility of it all. It asks the worker and peasant why he does not stay back to address the real problems. Set to lively and familiar folk tunes, these songs and slogans are popular even today.

*Jao jao desh, pardesaon desh*

> How long will we suffer the oppression of migration, the result of continued drought and poverty? We neither have enough land nor do we have work to stave off hunger. The workers go to the mines in "Bijolia" [a dreaded place where we are bonded under inhuman conditions], into the wells of Kathiawad, in brick kilns, in factories of Pali and Ahmedabad, and our children get their life blood sucked out in dhabas and hotels. They bring back ill health and disease, but little money. The last line is a firm resolve, we will eat half a roti, but we will stay to find solutions.[29]

The second song invites everyone to resolve to make their surroundings green and bring well-being to their villages. It asks them to take control of their lives and become a part of the process of local government. *Bol Sathida Re* is set to a very catchy folk tune and the lyrics outline the agenda of MKSS:

> You netas and babus listen carefully; this predicament is perpetuated by you for the rich. But listen carefully, we will not migrate and we will bring work here. We will plant trees and make this land green….

## The Street Theatre Workshop

When Uma Shankar came from Bangalore, the group looked for a quiet and secluded space to create and practise for the play. They chose Rawli guest house, a government building in a very quiet spot, away from the village at the edge of a forest, with panthers and hyenas sighted from time to time. In spite of the pressure to earn and feed the family, a group of fifteen young people got together to shape and design the play, and perform in scores of villages over twenty-two days. This powerful intervention encouraged people to think of the issues of common concern and motivated them to join the group to form the sangathan.

The yatra before the formation of the sangathan set up a tradition which has carried on for twenty-five years. Forming groups of ten to twelve people, in the month of April, the actors travelled on foot to over sixty villages inviting people to Bhim for May Day 1990. The play also explained why the sangathan was being formed. They performed wherever there were groups of people in the course of the day. They culminated their daily trek with a play in the village centre where people gathered to discuss the issues well into the night. The actors – activists – ate and slept in the village in people's homes.

Titled *Duvidha* (the dilemma), the play focused on the predicament of a worker who migrates, juxtaposed with the life of a peasant left behind in the village to struggle with a hostile environment. The worker resolves the dilemma by deciding to not to migrate again, and battles with issues at home. The final question still remains: 'Why can't we find our own solution?' The MKSS Diary reminds us:

> This process continued for three weeks and culminated in the formation of the Mazdoor Kisan Shakti Sangathan on 1 May 1990. Almost 1000 people came for the formation day meeting and after almost twenty-five men and women had spoken, the pledge was taken and the sangathan was formed. The colourful procession with placards was captured in photographs, with the young and old walking together with hope.
>
> The sangathan passed its first resolutions which were to have an immediate impact in the next three months. The resolutions passed unanimously stated that minimum wages was a basic right of every worker, and that every attempt would be made to see that no worker in the area received less than the minimum wage. The second resolution stated that members of the sangathan would fight corruption and dishonesty and would personally not pay bribes to anyone anymore.
>
> At the end of the meeting on the 1 May 1990 a rally went walking through the streets of Bhim, which culminated in a public meeting in the Bhim Bazaar. Bhim had never seen a gathering of non-party workers and peasants get together. It was the first rally of the poor, stating fearlessly to the comparative elite in Bhim that they were going to organize to fight for justice and equality. It was an appeal to the people of Bhim to support such an effort, and a public proclamation of intent.[30]

Amidst a group of over 1,000 people on 1 May 1990, the creation of MKSS was announced with cheers and raised fists. The May Mela has been taking place every year at the Patia ka Chowda since 1990.

All our friends who supported the Dadi Rapat and Sohangarh battles came to Bhim to express solidarity with the sangathan. The first May Day Mela in Bhim in 1990 ended with a resolve to struggle for minimum wages and a determination to fight inequality, double-speak and lies. The role of the 'sarkar', the government, was to serve people and it had to obey the law as much as anyone else. People went home with a determination to fight, but this time with the strength, solidarity and support of MKSS. In a report on poverty alleviation, MKSS writes of the memorable speech by R.N. Misra, a respected senior English teacher at the senior secondary school in Bhim. Originally from Madhubani in Bihar, he brought his innate understanding of politics of inequality and exploitation to support MKSS:

> As Mishraji rose to address the rally, most of his acquaintances expected a revolutionary "communist" message. But Mishraji spoke simply of a struggle by ordinary people, against the structure that makes good men corrupt. "Let us rise," he urged, in his usual fiery manner, "against the everyday corruption all around us."[31]

Rajni Bakshi recalls in *Bapu Kuti*:

> "This work we have taken up is not some individual work, it is common to people all over the world," Devaram of Dhapda village was telling the inaugural gathering of the sangathan. A sangathan like this was necessary, others added, because none of the existing institutions – jati panchayats, political parties, religious organizations, government agencies, village panchayats – could help them fight for justice. The 1000-odd people who had come together to form the sangathan, were defying the pervasive feeling within their communities that ordinary villagers couldn't change anything.
>
> Tej Singh, an elderly friend and mentor of Lal Singh, had once single-handedly fought Hari Singh years ago. Now he leaned heavily on his stick and spoke with fervour, "I am with you even if I can't walk." As though smiling at his own missing teeth and grey, frail countenance, he said: "Never fight for yourselves but for your neighbour. He is not human who can sleep while his neighbour remains hungry."
>
> Surinder said: "We don't want to leave this area and go out; we must get work here, so that we don't have to work ourselves to death in the mines of Bijolia."
>
> "Once dacoits lived in jungles, now they live in bungalows," said someone else. Another person recalled history and drew inspiration from Gandhiji's call for a united struggle against British rule.

> Chunni Bai went behind the mike and delivered her life's maiden speech, with her ghungat falling almost to her waist, clenched fist confidently raised in the air. A stranger observing the gathering could have mistaken her for a seasoned "pro". R.K. Mishra was a school teacher who taught English in a local school. He was a feared and respected teacher, because he went to school and taught his curriculum fully and well. He was sceptical of this new bunch of "revolutionaries". He was not sure that this group of people living like the poor, who were also pacifists, could make any difference. Yet, he was drawn to them and they became good friends, who liked to argue and discuss. From the days of Sohangarh, Mishraji acted as a support and a sounding board for the Devdungri activists.[32]

The scraggy town of Bhim, witness to the formation of the sangathan, had mixed feelings. The market was worried with the workers' mobilization. The townspeople were curious. But the workers and small peasants went home with hope and the determination to make the sangathan work.

CHAPTER FOUR

# The First Hunger Strike, 1990

The first day of May 1990 saw the sangathan announce its intent of empowering workers to get minimum wages for their work in government public works. The relevance of work, employment and wages for ordinary people has to be seen in the context of a drought-prone state, which has, for centuries, pushed its workers to migrate. Rajasthan is categorized as both drought-prone and semi-arid. Management of drought has been a concern since the days of the 'Rajwada',[33] i.e., the kings who continued to rule Rajasthan till Independence. The Rajasthan government established public works under the 'Famine Relief Code' to counter drought.

In 1990, poor peasants in the villages of central Rajasthan were living in deplorable condition. They had practically no land. If they were allotted any land, it was still under feudal control. If by chance they were allowed to occupy it, to cultivate it was still a struggle. There was a cycle of daily wage employment, daily payments, and buying food every day depending upon their ability to get work and wages. Because there were no savings, poor families could not use the ration shop to buy their monthly quota of rations. This condition bound them to seek work that paid every day. Even employment in government programmes that delayed payment, if only by a week, presented a dilemma. On bad days they bought food on credit, at shocking rates of interest, at times as high as 20 per cent on a rupee, and compounded on a monthly basis. The land or belongings mortgaged to the moneylender were lost irrevocably, and families were bonded for many generations. This was the stark reality of the people at the bottom of the pile, and also for those who were slightly better off than them. Work, employment, wages and hunger formed a chain of reality that demanded daily and immediate redress. Logically they were the central foci of all concerns. Shankar recalls:

> It was evening and the village was busy cooking food. The MKSS team had gone to meet people and tell them that there will be a meeting after dinner. Shankar went to a Bhil [tribal] home to ask the elderly woman inside to come for the meeting. She invited Shankar to sit down and said to him, "I cannot really do hard work. I am dependent on my son and daughter-in-law for food. They will send it to me. I will come after I have eaten." Shankar looked at the empty containers and the very few belongings she had. He was very upset and he sat and waited for the food to arrive. After half an hour, no rotis came. She then said, "They probably did not get work today. If they had, I would have got some of the leftovers at least."[34]

Aruna and Shankar had known the importance of employment for survival and a decent life for the people at the margins. Being in the Indian administrative services from 1968 to 1975, Aruna had seen that the neediest fall out of the net. Working in the rural areas of Ajmer and Jaipur districts, from 1975 to 1983, with hundreds of women and men, Aruna tried to understand the reasons for their continuing poverty, which made her empathize with their priorities – the persistent, constant need for immediate work. 'When will the famine relief work begin?' was a question around which their lives revolved.

Shankar was born in a village. His father, a patwari, died when he was young and his widowed mother worked on daily wages to bring him up. He had worked in seventeen places while still a student, till his graduation. Shankar's stories of battling with unemployment are powerful and humorous. This particular anecdote of his brings together the multiple predicaments of poverty – he recalled with his typical wry sense of the absurd:

> I had finished my higher secondary in the seventies and had done many jobs. But I was out of work often as they were all short term. I felt I should relieve my mother of some of her financial burden,

> and I set out for Ajmer. Apart from being the district headquarters, the town offered many jobs. I went and stayed with a relative, and he told me that the poultry industry was asking for workers. I set off to a poultry farm, and asked for a job. The owner asked me how literate I was. When I told him I had passed my higher secondary, he dismissed me and said, "Sorry, no work." As I was standing outside wondering what to do next, a man came out. I asked him what his fate had been. He said he had got the job! When I asked him how literate he was, he showed me his thumb and said, "*Anghuta chhap* [literally thumb print, meaning illiterate]!" I was surprised, but thought I would try again.
>
> When I went to the next potential employer, I was ready with my answer. He asked me how much I had studied; I replied I hadn't been to school. He promptly gave me the job – to pick eggs, put them on a tray and number them. I had a bad memory and had to keep count. I marked the wall with a piece of coal, to pretend that I was an illiterate worker. When he came he was most appreciative and sympathetic. He gave me a notebook and a pencil to make the marks to record the trays. I was actually doing my B.A. privately. When I passed the final exam, I went to the owner with some sweets. He took one and asked what the occasion was. I told him I had passed my B.A. He almost collapsed with shock.[35]

Illiterate workers were cheaper to hire and also perhaps less prone to question the exploitative nature of employers. Shankar knew how critical daily employment was, even to those who were not starving every day but could find no work in the week that followed. His mother still worked as a daily wage worker in her village in Lotiyana.

The priorities of the MKSS were decided by workers and peasants. For them, employment was critical, a passport to life without hunger and want. Work with government public works was a key which could open the door to a better life – changing the pernicious cycle of unemployment, debt, poverty, hunger and bondage. Naurti's poster made in 1985 in the Mahila Mela held in Tilonia, Rajasthan, is a graphic description of their reality. It shows women going to the collector to ask for work. Naurti[36] was Aruna's guru, who had taught her Dalit women's and workers' politics. Naurti's history is the rare story of a successful Dalit woman in independent India. She faced threats with great courage and made use of legal entitlements. She opposed the infamous burning of Roop Kanwar on her husband's pyre as sati in 1987, was an important part of the protests against the gang rape of Bhanwari Devi in Rajasthan, and spearheaded the minimum wage struggle in 1981. It was on the basis of her work that a landmark minimum wage writ, filed in the Supreme Court of India, established the right to equal wages on government works, leading to striking down the differential wage structure in the Famine Relief Code in 1983.[37]

The relevance of development programmes for meeting minimum needs was well established. Even where primary sustenance comes from agricultural occupations, seasonal employment in times of drought was crucial and its non-availability a constant nightmare. The only 'safety net' was government work programmes.

The marginal farmer was a worker who migrated for six months every year. The migratory worker believed he could leave the family behind in the safer environment of the village, persuaded to believe the flimsy promises of a corrupt system. The Pradhan Mantri Gram Sadak Yojana (PMGSY) and later the Jawahar Rozgar Yojana gave on an average 15 days of work in a year, and covered about 10 per cent of the workers who needed work. The extremely small number of days became a major preoccupation for the poor, making them fight for the few opportunities and also driving them to organize roadblocks en masse on the national highways. Even those few days were not accessible to the really needy and powerless, because of bureaucratic corruption and inefficiency. Shankar recollects:

> In 1990 when the MKSS was formed, the sangathan made a resolve to tackle both the demand for work and legal wage rights. The workers in Sohangarh had tasted the fruits of solidarity. They needed no persuasion to mobilize when they went to work on a PWD [Public Works Department] site. They remembered the apparent failure of December 1987 when in Dadi Rapat of Bhim Tehsil 140 workers mobilized and demanded minimum wages on a work site of the irrigation department. They failed to get their demand or alter the corrupt system.[38]

On May Day 1990, the MKSS passed a resolution that workers would not accept anything less than the minimum wage. On 15 May, works started in several parts of the region under the Jawahar Rozgar Yojana and Famine Relief. Workers asked the supervisors to tell them if there had been any shortfall in their work, and they categorically stated that they won't accept anything less than the statutory Rs. 14 per day (the minimum wage rate those days). In spite of all this groundwork, on 28 June 1990, there was great anger when the first payments were made. After working sincerely for eight hours in the heat of Rajasthan summer, 300 workers refused to accept the six–eight rupees per day that the government public works and the irrigation departments offered to pay them.

The first representation of a group of 20 workers went to meet the subdivisional magistrate (SDM) in Bhim on 14 July 1990 and gave him a notice that they would not accept less than the minimum wage. He asked for three days' time. When they went again on 17 July 1990, he rejected their application. On 18 July, 300 persons (with 175 women) went to Bhim and sat on a day-long dharna to demand minimum wage for full attendance and work completed at their respective work sites. The MKSS Diary entry says:

> We were assembled in Bhim Tehsil, inside the quadrangle [chowk] waiting for the SDM. We came to ask for minimum wages due to us, and we had been promised that we would get an answer. The SDM had fled to Deogarh and did not return all day. We sat there, determined that we would not get up till he met us. The day dragged on. The anxious babus made many calls, worried that we would not leave. At the end of the day, they wanted to close the doors. But we would not let them, demanding the SDM come to meet us. They panicked and called the thana [police station] and about eight to ten constables came running with their lathis. They began beating people indiscriminately. They hit a young boy and cut his forehead. Blood ran down his cheek and hell broke loose. Teelu from Sohangarh was furious and all the other young men began using their fists to fight the constables. Nikhil and Shankar shouted to quieten the crowd, "We are here for wages, not to fight with cops." But to no avail. Chunni Singh shouted "Mazdoor Kisan Shakti Sangathan", and everyone responded with, "Zindabad, zindabad" and in the few seconds' silence, Shankar's request for non-violence got heard.[39]

The workers settled down and the SDM came after frantic calls were made asking him to return to Bhim. He came under duress but once again postponed the decision and promised an answer in a week's time. His plea was that he had to consult the district collector to find a solution to the problem.

On 25 July, 150 persons returned to Bhim because the collector had assured them that both the executive engineers would be present to hear their grievances and demands, to settle the matter. But the administration was absent; neither the SDM nor the tehsildar was in their office. After waiting for them the whole day, twelve persons (including three women) sat on an indefinite hunger strike. By 27 July the number of people on hunger strike had increased to seventeen.

The MKSS Diary notes:

> The seventeen workers and sympathizers on hunger strike included Devilal, Nikhil, Chunni Bai, and several others. One of them was Trilok Singh from Dhapda, who was a sympathizer from the time of the Sohangarh struggle and was now an MKSS member. He was also a member of the panchayat. His anxious mother used to come every day, with a roti hidden in her odhni [veil]. She pleaded with Aruna, "Please let me give him a bite, my poor boy will waste away." And every day Aruna said the same consoling words, "No, of course not. It is a hunger strike and we cannot go against it, can we? The powers you believe in will protect him and in any case he drinks water, and he will not waste away. There are sixteen others with him, and there is the sangathan. We will not let him die, do not worry."[40]

The obdurate and insensitive administration kept repeating that they could not do anything. The local MLA, Mandata Singh, publicly restrained the administration from resolving the crisis. He maintained that nothing could be better than the population being reduced by the death of these seventeen people! The residents of Bhim started supporting the struggle and their numbers steadily increased. Important, though unexpected, support came from the prominent citizens of Bhim, who decided in a meeting on 30 July to support the workers on strike. The merchants committee, Vyapar Mandal, declared after the meeting that if the demands were not met by that evening, they would organize a *bandh* (closure of the market) in Bhim.

Bhim became tense, and this forced the collector, who was headquartered in Udaipur city, to start negotiations. Anil Bordia (additional secretary in the Ministry of Education), who happened to be in Udaipur that day, came along with the team to meet the collector. The collector, sensing the urgency, drove to Bhim on the evening of 30 July 1990, the sixth day of the hunger strike. After talking to those on hunger strike and the MKSS, he agreed that the wages of the workers would be increased as per their demands, and that payments would be made in the next three to four days. A public declaration of this agreement was made and the hunger strike ended.

The MKSS wanted to pursue the matter with the state government and some of them went to meet the chief minister. As noted in the MKSS Diary:

> Two persons met the chief minister of Rajasthan, Bhairon Singh Shekhawat, on 8 August. He gave his word that the assurance made by the collector would be fulfilled. He also assured them that a meeting would be organized and the policy regarding the wage-rate on Famine Relief Programmes reviewed. Almost a week after the hunger strike was lifted, on 10 August the irrigation department repaid the wages. The wage rate was again lower than the assured rate. The public works department returned with the same muster roll in which there was no change in the wages to be paid to the workers. With a protest registered in writing, the workers accepted the payments from the irrigation department. The PWD muster rolls were returned without taking any payments.[41]

The demand was so basic and minimal. The poorest staked their legal claim to get the minimum wage, so critical to give them freedom from hunger and access to basic services. The government gave a fortnight or less of employment on public works, under the government drought relief and work programmes. Their demands were that the government should set up systems that enable workers to actually get the minimum wage, and they could work on a time or a task basis, i.e., either be made to stay eight hours or finish a task of allocated measurement. Legally speaking, a worker cannot be subjected to both norms, it is unjust. In conclusion the demand was that the worker should not bear the fallout of systemic failure, and if measurements cannot be made with logic and justice, workers who had been on the site for eight hours should be paid full minimum wage. This is called 'time wage', determined only on the basis of eight hours attendance. Rajni, the chronicler of early years of the struggle, says:

> **Hunger Strike: A Singing Dharna**
> There was clearly no danger of the tehsil headquarters being stormed. But the SDM was taking no chances. The heavy iron-bar gates of the tehsil office were shut tight at night. But the two harmless-looking police constables on an all-night vigil were more often than not to be found under the tent protecting the MKSS dharna, where merry singing continued late into the night. This was no ordinary late-night bhajan-mandali. The tent beside a grand old tree sheltered fourteen men and three women of the MKSS who had been on a hunger strike for five days by then. The strikers ranged in age from young Devi Lal to the wrinkled Bhuriya. All the strikers [except Nikhil] had worked on somc famine relief site and had been denied the full minimum wage. They were determined not to eat or leave that spot till their full wage was paid.
>
> During the day there were speeches and revolutionary songs to keep the public's attention focused on the dharna. This was no sleepy dharna like the ones people were used to seeing, where the agitators idled away time playing cards or dozed in defiance of buzzing flies. The MKSS volunteers kept the dharna site alive by using their collective talents to inform, communicate, and attract others to the cause. In the process, some of the most powerful communication and experiences were being forged. Some of the most enduring and effective songs and skits evolved during such dharnas.
>
> "Why this struggle?", a hand-bill of the sangathan asked in bold letters. The wafer-thin hand-bills, printed on cheap pink paper, were circulating all over Bhim. The question was answered by a brief and succinct statement of how workers were made to toil all day without any assurance of how much they would earn. The dharna had three demands: payment of full minimum wage; the wage criteria must be either time rate or piece rate; the work must be measured on individual and not group basis.
>
> With each passing day, Shanker became more frantic. He began to wish that he was the one on hunger strike. Watching Nikhil, Bhuriya and others starve was much harder than running

> around managing the logistics. Jait Singh, the Devdoongri family's landlord, was otherwise never very involved in the sangathan. But he couldn't bear to see these people starving. From the third day he just sat at the dharna-site all day and stopped eating.
>
> Many residents of Bhim watched the event closely, quite sure of finding that the strikers were sneakily eating on the side. Some doctors, apparently impressed by the cause, offered to file false reports and urged the strikers to take some nourishment. As it became clear that these strikers were truly hungry and simply would not cheat, emotions began mounting among the townsfolk.
>
> Slowly, and first imperceptibly, the hunger strike was changing the sangathan's relationship with the town of Bhim. The stoic perseverance of the starving protesters gave the sangathan more prestige in the eyes of people who might not have been very impressed by the May Day rally, a few months earlier. The sangathan succeeded in also widening the issue by emphasizing that poor wages also mean poor purchasing power.
>
> On the sixth day of the hunger strike, the shopkeepers and traders of Bhim held a meeting and declared their support for the dharna or bandh of the MKSS. Their threat to observe a bandh the next day had the desired effect. The SDM immediately met a delegation of the strikers and agreed to pay the full wage to all workers within two days. Amid much jubilation the strike was then called off and all the strikers were lovingly fed fruit juice by their anxious *sathis* [comrades]. This promise was not, however, fulfilled and the sangathan learnt an important lesson.[42]

This conclusion left the MKSS uneasy. The ending of the dharna was based on an assurance by the collector when he came and ceremoniously broke the strikers' fast with a glass of juice. But the collector did not keep his word. And when the muster rolls came back with hardly any change, the MKSS resolved to take the battle further and geared for the next phase of the struggle.

The MKSS was now prepared to build a discourse on the workers' predicament and the betrayal by the state government in not keeping to its side of the bargain, in either improving supervisory systems or paying the statutory wage. The first step was to build solidarity with other such organizations struggling to establish the sanctity of the minimum wage for the survival of the worker at the bottom of the pile. Bhim was the venue for the first set of collective deliberations.

The matter would then have to be examined in the context of policy and statute. The academic, economic and legal frameworks also had to be discussed in an appropriate forum. Many concerned people expressed a willingness to look at the academic side of the problem, and come to Bhim for a convention. The Institute of Development Studies (IDS) in Jaipur and its director, V.S. Vyas, agreed to host a workshop with eminent people drawn from varied disciplines to discuss the matter with senior government officials after the convention. With policymakers and economists, the scene shifted from action to reflection. It took the MKSS from Bhim to Jaipur.

**The Arbitrariness of the Wage System and its Opaqueness**

The hunger strike contributed to the emerging discourse on transparency of government systems by a systematic analysis of the continuing predicament of workers being denied the minimum wage. It also broke down the problem into parts and looked at the whole process, step by step. At one level there were flaws in policy which ended up contradicting the entitlement, and at another level an examination of the process made it clear that the corruption and cheating in the implementation of the entitlement was made possible because of a non-transparent administrative system. The arbitrary use of power and corruption are two sides of a syndrome of administrative denial of access to services. The abuse of power leads to privileges meant for the poor reaching the village elite. The family and the community of powerful people always seem to have undue advantage in accessing benefits. This predicament once again underscored the importance of voluntary disclosure of records maintained by the government. Constant contradictions between government records and reality re-emphasized the need for transparency. The logic for demanding transparency was, therefore, being strengthened by every struggle of the MKSS.

CHAPTER FIVE

# The Bhim Minimum Wages Sammelan

The first hunger strike on minimum wages in Bhim ended inconclusively. The collector's promises were just part of a strategy to end the strike. It became clear that there was need to reflect on the details of legal entitlements and policy.

This deliberation and reflection was important to understand why repeated efforts at justice for workers were getting stonewalled. The MKSS organized a state-level convention of peasants and workers on 24 and 25 October 1990.

On the 24th, despite a nationwide bandh and a bus strike, workers started gathering since morning. Many came travelling long distances, using different modes of transport. Workers struggling for minimum wages and their representatives came from all over Rajasthan and gathered in Bhim. They were affiliated to trade unions and workers' organizations across several districts of Rajasthan – Ajmer, Udaipur (including Rajsamand), Bhilwara, Pali, Chittorgarh, Kota, Bikaner, Jaipur, Dungarpur, Banswara, and Sawai Madhopur. Workers even from Jhabua in Madhya Pradesh and Delhi participated in this convention.

The MKSS slogans, street theatre and songs were shared and sung in chorus, as an expression of solidarity with the issues and the importance of collective deliberation. Strategies for communication were also discussed during the course of the convention. The use of creative cultural forms for understanding issues is a part of the tradition of the MKSS and Shankar had become the face of that effort.

On 24 October, the first day of the convention, the 2,000 peasants and workers from Bhim and other places marched down the streets and bazaar of the town, shouting slogans. In the middle of the bazaar, the rally turned into a meeting. The podium was a cobbler's platform, and the audience sat on the road under the shops' awnings. The small effort at modernization, the 'chhatri', like a gazebo, in the middle of the crossroads in the centre of Bhim, became a raised place for the elderly to sit. The issues covered that day included the lack of uniformity in wage payments in different parts of the state and the country. The speakers were heard with great seriousness. Ashok Mathur, who ran a newspaper in Bikaner, Mahesh Bora, lawyer and comrade, Moti, a supporter and fellow traveller from Sankalp, Chandra Bhandari from Sewa Mandir, Naurti from Harmara, and Chunni Singh spoke, among many others.

On the 25th, the convention was held in Bhim, and B.D. Sharma, IAS, commissioner, SC and ST, Government of India, and K.B. Saxena, IAS, joint secretary, Ministry of Rural Development, addressed the gathering.

Lal Singh of the MKSS initiated the discussion and elaborated on the hunger strike, the dismal conditions and the workers' determination to take the issue further. A powerful and persuasive speaker, he drew their attention to huge differences in wages between the privileged government employees on the one hand, and the workers on the other. His question was related to the quantum of work and output. He argued that since there were no norms for 'babus' they could get away with no work; and yet they grudged the payment of this small amount to the workers. If the output is low, ensure that the conditions of work and tools of measurement are such that work allocated can be completed. He admonished the government and said, 'Do not do what you did at Dadi Rapat – paying the ones who worked and delivered full work less than those who scratched the ground. This wage is just enough not to die from hunger.' Responding to Lal Singh, some of the workers said, 'What do we really want? *Mazdoori, roti, kapda, shikhsha, swasthya aur makan* (work, food, clothing, schooling, health and housing or shelter) are the basic minimum.' This was universally endorsed by the gathering. The unanimous demand was that the government has to pay the minimum wage. Under no circumstances can it pay less than that, as it sets the norm and is obliged to stand by it.

Addressing the gathering B.D. Sharma said, 'I am with you, but in my opinion, these demands are not enough, you should demand more.' He said that the poor should have full rights over all natural resources and they won't get this right without struggle. In the end, he emphasized that the peasants and the workers will have to unite to achieve success in this struggle.

Ashok Mathur from Bikaner, Mahesh Bora from Jodhpur and many others made fiery speeches and demanded that government's promises must be kept in a democracy. The poor, no less than anyone else, have a right to survive with dignity and without hunger. The minimum wage is a basic guarantee. The obligations have to be met. The MKSS notes recall that:

> We were determined to make the government see reason. The 1000 highly committed workers and sympathizers met in Bhim, in October 1990, at the same Patia ka Chowda where we had declared the sangathan formed 5 months ago. B.D. Sharma, commissioner, scheduled caste and scheduled tribes, an eminent civil servant, and K.B. Saxena, a joint secretary in the ministry of rural development, heard our case and agreed with us in principle. It was an important day for us. But for the CID it was a day of utter confusion. B.D. Sharma was in a dhoti and kurta; K.B. Saxena, with longish hair, unkempt and in a pair of rubber slippers did not look like the suited and booted collector sahib. The police came and asked, "Who are these men?" Our reply did not satisfy them and they continued to be skeptical. Unable to contain their curiosity they asked again, "Tell us the truth, are they revolutionaries?" We laughed and that got them really worried. But what finally convinced them was when a reluctant SDM came to greet B.D. Sharma and K.B. Saxena; protocol helped win the argument![43]

The convention also concluded that even to solve the problems of implementation of the Famine Relief Programme, the government needed to consult and seek the participation of the local people. Only then will the community be able to perceive the need, not merely for employment and wages, but also for creation of village assets.

An IDS report documented:

> The convention ended with resolutions, endorsed by the workers and their representatives and by B.D. Sharma and K.B. Saxena. The consensus was that the government should ensure that all the workers are paid the minimum wages, that workers should be employed either on time-basis or the task-basis, not on both. If the task-based measurement is adopted, then the payments should be made on the basis of the task performed by every individual and not by a group.[44]

The minimum wage debate in India today is ill-informed. It is dominated by the prejudice and illogic of the privileged. India cannot afford doing away with the guarantee of the minimum wage (Rs. 201 per day as on 1 March 2017 – just over 3 US$ at current exchange rates). Haunted as it is by poverty and increasing differences in income and access to services, the richest 1 per cent in India owns 58 per cent of the country's wealth, according to the latest edition of not-for-profit Oxfam International's global inequality report, released on 16 January 2017 by *Live Mint*. Those on salaried incomes do not understand the precarious existence of those who live on the edge of unemployment and hunger. A salaried worker seldom looks at the wage worker as a competitor for the spoils of government resources. The 93 per cent of the workforce of this country that is unorganized needs to make itself heard as citizens and voters in independent India.

An MKSS Diary entry asked:

> Now, why is it important that there should be a minimum wage? And why do the rich dislike it as do industrialists and big farmers? And why does the government and even the court sometimes take a negative position? A minimum wage defines the lowest amount that can be paid to a worker. There was a law passed in 1948, soon after Independence that this minimum wage should be a guarantee for the worker. The worker is a free citizen in a free country, but due to circumstances beyond her or his control, is born in deprived circumstances. To taste the fruits of a better life they cannot anymore be exploited in an independent nation without minimum guarantees. The minimum fixed according to nutritional needs in fact covers just the need for staple, which is wheat, rice and so on. In 1975 it was Rs. 3 and by 1987 it had risen to Rs. 11. Even so, no worker gets

> work every day. What we are really looking at is a survival wage, not a minimum wage. Even if you do not look at equal rights and access in the manner in which the MKSS does, it is inhuman. Most of the opposition comes from God-fearing people! Every dharma of every religion begins with charity and compassion. The children of these people do not beg, they work in dhabas and as domestic help in affluent homes. They work 12 hours a day for a pittance.[45]

The Bhim convention had prepared the ground for a meeting with policymakers, economists and lawyers in Jaipur.

Some months earlier, S.R. Sankaran, secretary, Ministry of Rural Development, Government of India, headed a team that came to Devdungri to learn more about the delivery of government programmes. The MKSS handed over a memorandum that began with a demand for transparency in all records on public works and ended with a demand for an Employment Guarantee Act. There was a positive response to both demands. He said that there is no reason to hide information from people. The government should function in full visibility and scrutiny should always be possible. Offices should be 'like a room made of glass'. He suggested that a meeting be held in Jaipur to look at these issues in greater detail.

### The Institute of Development Studies (IDS), Jaipur Convention and Workshop

Minimum wage is generally considered a straightforward issue and a basic entitlement. The debate is centred on setting the wage level, periodic increases and affordability for the employer. Arbitrariness and lack of transparency in minimum wage payments has much to do with the MKSS's demand for the right to information. Every single demand for minimum wages will be resisted by the employers on unethical grounds, and fair payment will be dependent on complete transparency, which was seen by the workers as non-negotiable for accessing this entitlement. The minimum wage is a minimum guarantee of protection from hunger, illness, and want.

Shankar often explains this through a local allegory that when the teeth are clenched the only cure is to block the nostrils. It forces the mouth open. The transparency of the muster roll is the nose; it sends the authorities scuttling to make payments.

Even in its early years, the MKSS had disciplined itself to reflect and write. It helped engage in dialogue with specialized groups outside the geographic area of Devdungri, and sometimes even outside Rajasthan. These reflections were written in Hindi and in English. This excerpt is from a report that was submitted and discussed in the Institute of Development Studies (IDS) in Jaipur.

> **The Convention on Minimum Wages at the IDS, Jaipur**
> Our experience in rural Rajasthan had already underscored the importance of the minimum wage. The sammelan in Bhim confirmed this assumption, when people from all over the state came despite curfews and a nationwide bandh. Workers and peasants came from most districts and from different kinds of organizations. There was consensus about issues and agreement that workers should come together to demand full implementation of the legal right to the minimum wage.
>
> The Bhim convention also emphasized the need to garner more broad based support. At the local level workers have to struggle with the contractor, the mate, the junior engineer and the sarpanch. The poor know that their oppressors have powerful links to Jaipur and Delhi. Local battles may be won or lost, but wars are lost far away where the workers have no representatives, and no one to speak for them.[46]

The MKSS knew that this was not only a local issue or a matter for the SDM or the collector. Even at their levels they could do a lot, but policy was beyond their power. In November 1990, IDS Jaipur invited policymakers, top officials of the government, educationists, economists, legal experts, and representatives of NGOs for a two-day convention/workshop so that open and extensive discussions could take place on the issue of 'minimum wages' in the government rural employment programmes. Professor Vijay Shankar Vyas, economist and director of IIM, Ahmedabad at one time; Upendra Baxi, eminent jurist and later vice chancellor of Delhi University; Professor Narula, director, IDS; S.R. Sankaran, secretary, Ministry of Rural Development; Anil Bordia, secretary, Ministry of Human Resource Development; M.L. Mehta, secretary, Government of Rajasthan; Dr. Kanta Ahuja, economist and later vice chancellor, MD University, Ajmer; Dr. Indira Hirvey from the

Gandhi Labour Institute; Dr. Sharada Jain, other civil servants and many other senior activists from Rajasthan and other states sat to deliberate on the conclusions of the Bhim sammelan.

Here are some excerpts from the report on the delivery systems of poverty alleviation programmes for the rural poor:

> The Convention's final session, chaired by Prof. V.S. Vyas, ended with a consensus and important resolutions were passed stating that: i) Minimum wages must be paid on all government sponsored employment works including Famine Relief Works; ii) Payment of wages be made within a week of the completion of the muster-roll; iii) In general, either time or wage rate should be the basis for payment of minimum wages on all government works. Only rarely should exceptions be made and that too in cases where the workers themselves make specific decision to this effective; iv) Voluntary agencies, trade unions and other field-level agencies should also concern themselves with ensuring productivity of such works; v) Resource-allocation at the macro-level be reviewed from the point of view of the needy and allocation for employment works be increased substantially. Care should be taken to discourage development of the type which favours only the rich and the entrenched interests; vi) Information is of critical importance to enforcement. Special attention was drawn to the following:
>
> - Information about the work, including the name of executing agency, duration of the work and employment to be provided and wages to be paid should be displayed prominently at all work sites;
> - The National Commission on Rural Labour be requested to invite a group of concerned people from the state before finalizing its recommendations on minimum wages;
> - In selection of works and their execution, special attention may be paid that these add to community assets.
>
> This meeting not only gave inter-disciplinary public sanction to the demands of the workers but facilitated prompt support when the next struggle took place.[47]

The convention endorsed the conclusions of the Bhim sammelan and that the minimum wage rate must be paid in all government construction works, including the Famine Relief Programme. There was a consensus that wages should be paid on time basis, and that exceptions to this could only be made when the workers themselves decided otherwise. The report on poverty alleviation continued to say:

> In January 1991, the Rajasthan government issued some guidelines for the implementation of the Jawahar Rozgar Yojana and included the views of the representatives of the NGOs and other participants of the convention/workshop.[48]

A review of these events shows a construct taking shape. In a democracy, engagement with the government becomes an important part of the struggle for equality and justice. This recognition of continual engagement as advocacy, and the alternate use of action and reflection eventually defined the inclusion of governance as a critical issue of concern for alternative peoples' politics. This engagement with government did not end with the passing of the law in 2005. It is part of a fundamental continuing discourse on governance and citizenship. The government, by obligation, has to engage with its citizens. Representatives to assembly and parliament borrow their sovereignty to govern for five years; they cannot betray that social contract.

But this process, initiated long before the RTI was specifically articulated, was already looking at dialogue across sectors and engagement with institutions. The MKSS was looking for platforms to promote discussion and dialogue to unravel the issue and contextualize its significance. Street struggle was seen in the true Gandhian spirit of satyagraha, non-violent civil disobedience, but the state was seen as Ambedkar visualized it – an institution that must deliver constitutional promises. The notion of engagement with the state, opinion-makers and policy began to take shape.

There was seminal learning from this very important dialogue. For the marginalized to have just and equal access to development, administration and governance, different sectors of society need to deliberate together. Democratic discussion can be creative and impactful and also deliver justice, if there is mutual respect and adherence to democratic and constitutional promises.

The demands from the worker's assembly in Bhim dealt with both the right to information and the right to work. These rights were consciously tabled together for the first time. The demands of the workers resonated with the views of eminent jurists like Upendra Baxi, as is evident from his article published in the *Indian Express,* titled 'The Making of the Right to Work' (15 September 1990).

CHAPTER SIX

# The Second Hunger Strike, 1991 – A Watershed

The first hunger strike in 1990 had left the workers and the MKSS frustrated.

The second hunger strike was a tough but popular dharna in 1991, etched in the collective memory of Bhim. It is now a part of the area's folk legend. It had drama, haunting songs, and political correctness. It was dotted with stories of courage and determination and, above all, great humour. This was the turning point of MKSS's political role in Rajasthan.

Just before the hunger strike, and soon after the conventions in Bhim and Jaipur, Udaipur district was bifurcated. The new district of Rajsamand was constituted on 10 April 1991. It was a long geographic entity stretching from north to south, and Bhim was at its northernmost tip. The town of Rajsamand, south-west of Bhim, became the headquarters of the district. Though closer than Udaipur, it was still a long way from Bhim and Devdungri.

There were the usual meetings on the mud platform outside the Devdungri house (and now office) as well. In 1999 the small hut could not provide space for the increasing tribe of the MKSS. Nikhil, Aruna, Shankar and Anshi (having lived frugally and saved money from their minimum wage honoraria) managed to buy Jamna Bai and Roop Singh's adjoining mud hut and the space outside it. It also had the great distinction of cradling the largest neem tree in Devdungri. At the behest of the villagers, the tree was left outside the boundary of the 'office' to show it was still common property.

Protests were organized and petitions continued to be given. People from Sohangarh, Talai, and many more villages gathered together to think and plan. The far-flung districts of Kota and Jaipur, the closer ones like Ajmer, Bhilwara, and Pali, agreed to come together to make a demand for minimum wages in Rajasthan. Mamta Jaitley, writer, woman activist, and journalist wrote and supported the earlier struggles and later the MKSS minimum wage struggles. The Rajasthan Mazdoor Kisan Morcha, with its headquarters in Kishengarh, was also active. Naurti, Aruna's guru and comrade, and Ramkaran, a young colleague of Aruna from her SWRC days and now a strong supporter, also came to the meetings. Moti from Sankalp came too. Mahesh Bora and Ramesh Nandwana, lawyer friends from Jodhpur and Udaipur, were part of the advisory group. Bharat Dogra, Rajni Bakshi and Jeremy Seabrook, writers and commentators, encouraged the fledgling MKSS in their visits and writings. Late Deepak Gyanchandani, research fellow in the IDS assisted in many ways, and supporters from Rajasthani NGOs – Sankalp, SWRC, Sewa Mandir, and many others from a huge fraternity of supporters – came forward to help.

The MKSS worked on a strategy. Narayan and Devilal, then postgraduate students on vacation, and who continued to be friends, offered to work on a Jawahar Rozgar Yojna (JRY) work site in Barar panchayat, Rajsamand district. They would try and work the system, insist on rules being followed, and also ensure the implementation of work norms. Narayan says:

> In 1991, a JRY road from Devdungri to Tejaji ka Than was started. My friend Devilal and I worked on this site. There were twenty workers on this work site. We had regular meetings in the MKSS and we decided to give everything in writing to the sarpanch, the pradhan and the BDO.
>
> The sarpanch decided to show off his power. He passed a formal resolution in the panchayat, that all workers would be paid an even wage of Rs. 11 per day. This was an illegal and unconstitutional resolution. Actually this provided sufficient grounds for disbanding the panchayat and the resolution should have been declared null and void.

> The entire episode gave us proof that there was in fact no real connect between the work output and the wage. These so called processes were a farce. Nevertheless, the establishment carried on responding to the worker's demands when it used the norms of work measurements to be completed by every individual worker, on the basis of which the government claimed it would decide dues. They measured the work on the work site innumerable times, when however the decision to pay a flat rate was pre-decided. The MKSS understood the importance of transparency. The muster roll and measurement book of this work came into the public domain. It dawned on all interested that justice was linked with access to these documents.
>
> In actual fact the dereliction of duty is of the supervisor if there is a shortfall in output, and he should be penalized.[49]

Narayan and Devilal had made reasonable demands in writing. The demands were that work should be properly measured when tasks were assigned and measured again after work was completed, on a daily basis by the supervisor. If there was any shortfall, workers should be informed so that they could work extra to fulfil the norms, to ensure the payment of full minimum wages. Narayan continues:

> We submitted a letter to this effect to the BDO and the sarpanch. Going against the request, the sarpanch passed a resolution in the gram panchayat with a full quorum that in all the works – whether JRY, Famine Relief or SGRY [Sampoorna Grameen Rozgar Yojna] – all workers should be paid a wage rate of Rs. 11 per day. This went against all work norms that insisted on task and could levy penalties only if there was shortfall in payment. Penalty was money deducted from minimum wages due if the task was not completed. It was strange that whatever the quantum of work, whether we worked worth Rs. 22 or Rs. 17, we should be paid a flat rate of Rs. 11.
>
> When they started making the payments, Devilal and I protested. We said that we wrote so many times to you and requested that you give us full wages and still you have entered those very 11 rupees in the muster-rolls. We refused to accept that payment and returned the money.[50]
>
> Narayan and Devilal were friends and studying for their MA

> with great financial strain. They used their vacation to work on JRY work sites to earn their fees for the next year. Since they had grown up with the MKSS they decided in 1991, that they would exercise their right to see that all records were strictly and correctly maintained at the work site and demand minimum wages. In the course of that fortnight, their vigilance paid off great dividends. Their persistent demands to see the records frightened the corrupt sarpanch and the panchayat. They hastily convened a meeting and passed a resolution to uniformly pay 11 rupees as against the statutory minimum wage of 22 rupees per day.[51]

The MKSS decided to take it up with the panchayat in Barar, but there was no response. A memorandum was submitted to the BDO and the pradhan, and nothing happened. The small dharna in Barar forced the SDO to come and he made promises. The BDO and the pradhan did not keep that promise. May Day was fast approaching, and the MKSS decided to call for protest on the same day. The May Day celebration shifted from its usual place in Patia ka Chowda to the front of the Tehsil and the SDM's office in the chowk (courtyard) in Bhim, and turned into a dharna. Initially the protest was about the twenty workers who had worked on the road under JRY from Devdungri. Soon there were supporters from all over. There was popular support for the demand that workers should get full wages. When the SDO failed to meet the demands once again, the MKSS decided to go on hunger strike.

In this indefinite hunger strike the strikers came from five different districts and many organizations. They demanded the payment of wages in Barar, and also asked for normative policy changes and strict adherence to implementation of rules all over Rajasthan. The resolutions passed by the Bhim and IDS conventions on minimum wages were reiterated.

**The Dharna**

The tent was pitched and Bhim, now more familiar with the MKSS, was prepared for some action-packed days. Every day more than 600 workers, sometimes even a thousand, would come from the hinterland of Bhim – from the districts of Rajsamand, Pali, Bhilwara, and Ajmer. The negotiations were punctuated with speeches and songs.

The demand was for minimum wages on a JRY work site. It was a central government scheme that promised a few days of work for every worker every year at minimum wages. The MKSS approached the state government but also wrote to the Government of India. There was an obligation for the government to meet its promise of work and wages. A central government team came to Bhim to negotiate and went to the 'dak bungalow', the government guest house, to discuss issues. The news that came from there was that there was no consensus between the central and state governments regarding payments to workers.

In the hot summer month of May, when the days are long, people on dharna slept out in the open. The evenings saw songs and skits. 'Saaki', a traditional interplay between voice and drum, verse and dance, was very popular. It was impromptu and contemporary issues got woven into the verse. The question and answer, and the frenzied drum and dance, drew crowds. The drunken jailer of the Bhim sub-jail was the star performer. He even donated money and grain to the dharna fund but requested that his name should not be disclosed. One of the abiding popular lyrics of this dharna, which was to become important for the RTI as well, was Mohan Ba's song: '*Haan re zamano choran ko*' (Oh! The times of the thieves!). The lyrics of the song were composed and sung by Mohan Ram (also called Mohanji, or Mohanba, a term of respect and affection). Mohanji, a Dalit Kabir singer, was famous in the region. He had the largest repertoire of Kabir songs. An illiterate poet, his political lyrics spread the message effortlessly and sustained MKSS protests. His energy was boundless and his commitment could not be faulted. '*Ude che bhai ude che, Dharna di-do re, Aa choran ko mundo balo* (Burn the faces of these thieves!) *Haalat Sari bigad gayi, Ladai votan ki, Duniya ulti reet batave re, Prashasan ko budhi do bhagvan*.'[52]

Bhim was tense. Bhairon Singh Shekhawat, the then chief minister of Rajasthan, was due to visit the district, and the whole official machinery was nervous. The hunger strike had begun; the strikers were on lemon and water, wasting away. Ganga Singhji was the representative of Rajsamand district, Keli Bai from Pali, Moti from Kota, Kishore from Ajmer, and Rukma Ma from Jaipur district. Barring Moti, they were all frail and delicate people. The others grew less hungry, just looking at their fasting comrades. Meanwhile, negotiations were going ahead in the new district headquarters. Mahesh Bindal from Sankalp and Deepak Gyanchandani from the IDS continued to meet and discuss issues with the state government. Local officials kept scurrying around all day in Bhim.

Rajasthan's famous *dhol* (a big drum) is used in many ways – an accompaniment for dance; a signal of danger; the beats can be a warning sign to alert people. Rajasthanis love to dance, and many feet lift as soon as the drums roll. The days began with songs, slogans and the roll of drums, followed by speeches and stories of non-payment and hunger, and the evenings were celebrations of the working people of Rajasthan. As the MKSS Diary notes:

> The SDMs and the deputy superintendent of police had their office and home next to each other. The SDM and the Dy SP were acquainted with the MKSS, and had often met in more pleasant circumstances. But this was a protest on socio-political issues and the sentiments were respected. The administration was anxious for the matter to be resolved. The hunger strike had taken over Bhim. The SDM had failed to act when he could have. The police was only anxious that no untoward incident occurred. The Dy SP's father was an honest and devout man and would not eat from the earnings of his son. He is alleged to have said that with a policeman one never knows where the money may have come from. His grain came from his home for his frugal diet. The Dy SP had often come to the dharna to appeal that the noise be muted as it prevented his father's meditation. The volume was toned down for a while. The SDM had two children aged 2 and 4. The children drove him mad with the slogans and the songs they heard every day. One slogan drove him mad particularly. The slogan went, "*Gyarah rupiah lelo bhai, nahin lenge, nahin lenge, nahin lenge*," going up rupee by rupee, from 11 to 22, till the crescendo ended with, "*Bayees rupiah lelo bhai*" and the response was "*Pura lenge, pura lenge*". The dharna chanted in response. This was repeated many times a day. The children found the lilt exciting and chanted and lisped their way through it. His irate wife demanded why there was no solution.[53]

When the dharna had continued for five days, Chief Minister Bhairon Singh Shekhawat visited Bhim. A delegation went to meet him and he also visited the venue of the dharna and assured the gathering that full wages would be paid. He asked the SDM and Tehsildar to come with him to Nathdwara so that they could discuss how to resolve the matter. In Nathdwara, the CM expressed his decision that there should be police action to disperse the strikers and supporters from the dharna. Friends who were negotiating in Jaipur called to say that in all probability the strikers would be lifted that night or the next day.

The night began quite normally. People had their frugal meal and went to sleep after carefully dispersing the hunger strikers to various locations. At midnight there was sudden activity. Two police jail vans full of cops arrived, and in their typical style they got off the vans with a thud of their shoes and silently stood in formation. The SDM came and asked the hunger strikers to step into his court for medical examination. The *dharnarthis* (participants in the dharna) asked the SDM to get the doctors to the tent, as the MKSS was not willing to send the hunger strikers to an office at midnight. After haggling for a while, the SDM must have ordered the cops to surround the dharna.

The MKSS was prepared for the attack. The hunger strikers had removed their black armbands to prevent identification. It was decided that when the police attacked, the women would form the outer ring. The dhol would play the SOS beat called 'varu dhol', signifying danger. The women would immediately switch on the microphone and wail like they do when someone dies. This was again a powerful traditional alert. No one would use violence and men would prevent women from being hit by the police. It happened with military precision. The police went into retaliatory action. They broke the microphone; they smashed the bulb, making it very dark. Finally they pierced the drum, making a big hole in it. About 100 to 150 policemen came and started thrashing the people sleeping at the dharna site. They picked up some of them, assuming that they were the people on hunger strike, but many were not. They picked up Shankar, Naurti, and Ram Lal, who were not on strike, and left behind Keli Bai and Kishore, who *were* the strikers.

But the town of Bhim was rudely woken up by the dhol and the wail of the women. Its citizens gathered at the Tehsil office – the politicians, the shopkeepers and many more. It was not a silent, swift midnight pick-up. On the contrary, the SDM and Dy SP were made to answer questions raised by the citizens and the politicians of Bhim. There was a general and strong comment on police action, which would leave a residue for the local administration to deal with.

Meanwhile, the ride in the jail vans was full of dark humour. Moti was made to lie on the floor and a cop put his booted foot on his stomach, till he was 'persuaded' to take it off with a threat of public action. His question, '*Arre yaar*, are you smugglers? Why the hell did government pull us out of our beds if you are not dangerous?' made conversation possible, and Shankar convinced them that they were not dangerous. In fact all they wanted was minimum wages. Those cops who listened were confused. Naurti, who was not on hunger strike, shouted at them and resisted being lifted. She recalls,

> When they started lifting the hunger strikers, they pushed us around and cuffed us. They could not find out who the hunger strikers were. One of the policemen pushed me and propelled me towards the police van and picked me up and dropped me in. The cops sitting in the van pulled me in. There was a lot of scuffling and roughing up. Shankarji was also lifted and dumped with me in a similar manner. Neither of us was a hunger striker. The police got fifteen of us in this manner and took us first to Nathdwara. On the way they asked me if I was a hunger striker, and I said "Yes", though I was not. Because if I had said I was not, they would have abandoned me midway, in the dark on a highway.
>
> As we got off at Nathdwara we started shouting our slogans: MKSS zindabad! Not a paisa less than 22 rupees, we demand our rights, we have not come to beg! The police took us shouting slogans into the hospital. The doctors and patients could not understand what the hell was happening. The police tried to push needles into my arm and I resisted, I even bit the fingers of the person who was twisting my arm. Some of us were hurt in the cuffing that followed. From there, for some reason, they took us to the bigger hospital in Udaipur. They brought juice, milk and fruits for us to break our fast. Shankar said he needed to go to the toilet. As I was protesting, a desperate cop came and gave me his baton and said, "Beat me as much as you want"! Ajay Mehta [Sewa Mandir] was contacted by Shankar, I don't know how. He came and helped us. We went to his home, ate there and then left for Bhim. We entered Bhim that night, when all was silent, with our slogans.[54]

Ramlal was offloaded about 30 kilometres from Bhim. He came back to a tense situation in Bhim, shouting 'MKSS zindabad', alone and fearless.

The following day saw thousands of supporters. Mothers, grandmothers, and children of workers, came pouring in. Shankar's mother Noji, called Ya or 'grandmother', made a memorable, fiery speech. The gist of it was not fear and intimidation but the gutsy cry of people who only wanted their share of food, housing, and other minimum needs. The meeting also recalled how they had stripped a Dy SP to his underwear and made him run around for sexual misconduct. There was a big hooray for people's power. Late in the afternoon the dharnarthis returned and found Aruna and Mamta Jaitley[55] on a hunger strike.

The government had meanwhile held up a 100-crore instalment due to the Rajasthan government for payments under JRY, based on the report of their committee that had visited Bhim. The 0.95 paisa paid on a site near Bhim and the 11-rupee wage (half the minimum wage rate) for the work site where Narayan and Devilal worked had set off a series of basic questions. The minimum wage issue was again in focus. This made the state government spring into action and they hurriedly made the payments on the dharna spot itself. For the first time the muster rolls were brought in, and those twenty people were paid 22 rupees per day rather than 11 rupees. The extraordinary victory was one of principle. The amount demanded was less than Rs. 2,000. The Government of Rajasthan had spent a colossal amount of money to protect corruption, misgovernance, and mismanagement. What a travesty of governance, rights, and a commitment to people!

It was learnt later that the hut in Devdungri was surrounded by policemen and all the roads leading out of Bhim were blocked that night. The myth of the MKSS being a 'Naxalite organization' was being constructed. In fact, Bhairon Singh was to ask Aruna pointedly (at one of the negotiations) why he should not send her to Andhra Pradesh to learn to become a Naxalite. Later, a letter came to them from the collector's office in Rajsamand, with a CPI-ML suffix. When the cops came to lift the dharna, they posted constables outside all exits from Bhim. There was also police outside the home in Devdungri! Some young performers who had come to support the dharna in Bhim were distraught. They panicked and ran to R.N. Mishra's home, a friend and supporter who lived in Bhim and taught English in the senior secondary school, only to find cops outside his home as well.

## A Conclusion and a Beginning

What did the minimum wage struggle have to do with RTI? How did a group of so-called 'illiterate' villagers, often deliberately defined as 'uneducated, illiterate', incapable of 'thinking or thought', or even 'understanding', arrive at this very intelligent, politically smart definition of information rights? Minimum wages was a need linked to survival. Blocking of wages with a series of lies made it necessary to stop the lies. The simple and sharp reasoning of how it could be carried out was effectively done with common sense and understanding by the best of the people – the ordinary toiling Indian who works to survive.

Aruna was granted the *Times of India* fellowship, which facilitated the detailed study of local conditions called 'Living with Dignity and Social Justice'. As per the MKSS report:

> The issue of minimum wages on government works had been repeatedly raised and there had been numerous failures of organized attempts to get the minimum wage paid. Sustained efforts continued, and a year-long campaign culminated in a dharna.... The MKSS converted a dispute into a major policy issue. At this time, a committed core group with a strong ethical base demonstrated that it had the capacity to take on forces much greater than itself. The struggle was enough incentive to project this method of work as viable and attractive. When a small sangathan from small town Bhim [with no municipality and only a panchayat] managed to get policy changed, despite the state government's very clearly pronounced intention to oppose payment of wages, the credibility of such efforts increased manifold.[56]

The efficacy of collective struggle was established, as was the need for a dialogue between those who struggle and the government. The importance of engaging with governance no longer needed persuasion and argument to convince activists. Political arguments and debates continued, and some crystallized into modes of public action. The continuing dialogue and support of the print media began to be recognized and understood. Usha Rai, with her piece in the front page of the *Times of India*, forced the Government of Rajasthan to acknowledge the embarrassment of a cut of a 100 crore in its JRY budget – a clipping of which remains in the MKSS archives. It is cherished as an honest journalist's report that immensely contributed to the livelihood of millions of poor Rajasthanis. It set the tone and standard for support from the media.

**Learning for the RTI Movement**

This dharna taught the MKSS how critical it was to access official documents for justice in wage payments, and consequently the right to food and life. The hunger strike demonstrated that policy needs to change and one case in point can demonstrate how and why. If the policy changes, it will enable and empower millions of workers to access justice on a large number of work sites. A step-by-step documentation of arbitrariness and injustice shared with people leads to an understanding of the need for transparency in governance. The unfolding of the illogic of misgovernance strengthened arguments and exemplified the bias of a corrupt and arbitrary system. It was obvious that it was intended against the worker ever being able to get the minimum wage. It became clearer that the documents were at the power centre of the issue, and specifically the visibility of the muster roll was the key to unravelling corruption.

CHAPTER SEVEN

# Exposing the Myth of the Free and Open Market

It comes as a surprise to most people that the MKSS runs grocery shops – the Mazdoor Kisan Kirana Stores (MKKS). It is a strong local identity nevertheless.

If the poor worker has more problems beyond the lack of access to wages and the shortage of money to purchase essential goods: it is the exploitative market. The traditional role of the 'seth' or the shopkeeper is well known in India – he denies credit to a hungry family to buy food but extends credit to meet the expenses of marriage and death, mandatory traditional social obligations. In a poor household, loans are taken against collateral, land and jewellery. The debt can never be repaid as the compound interest is prohibitive. Families get ruined and lose small pieces of land and whatever meagre savings they may have, including all their silver jewellery. None of it could ever be reclaimed from the shopkeeper. The repayment of interest is all that they can cope with.

The migrant Rajasthani shopkeeper can be found everywhere in India. Synonymous in some places with pawn brokers and extortive sellers, they engage workers from their 'native' villages on a pittance. Many of these workers come back with bad health and some end up being bonded because of debts. But they learn how to run shops.

This chapter is about the market and the worker, the new face of the market and the controls within it, explaining how no market is really free and, like all other systems, has its share of corrupt practices and oppressive structures. How can this system, built on individual profit, replace the structures made for distributive justice in a society riddled with inequality and injustice?

The first acquaintance with the issue of market liberalization, the 'free market', came with the 'Dunkel draft', essentially a copy of the provisions of the European Patent Convention, which became the foundation of the WTO in December 1991. It was a widely discussed policy document spelling out the vision of new economics with the market as the centre of the paradigm. But this did not make any sense to rural India. In the early 1990s India decided to liberalize the market and allow imports and foreign investment in India.

Any critique of the market is labelled 'anti-market'. But we know that investment and capital are for those who have privileges. The myth of the market as a solution to all problems should be examined and opened up for debate.

The market is necessary for the poor and the aspiring middle class as much as it is for others. The question is: what kind of market would meet the demands of an ordinary citizen?

Two issues bothered the MKSS in the early 1990s. One was that of intellectual property rights, which allows the idea of patenting traditional and collective knowledge by individuals, who are smart enough to package it and apply for a patent. The other was funding governments by multilateral financial institutions – based on the same logic as the local shopkeeper lending to poor farmers, but in the context of international borrowings. The country is often only able to pay the high interest rates. The capital remains mostly unpaid. Chunni Singh, self-taught and barely literate, understood this immediately, and spoke about it fluently in his speeches at the Bhim marketplace.

The nature of a free market and monopolies (both contradictory principles), the question of who determines the price, the relationship of the market with democratic rights, were all sources of immense interest to workers and small farmers. The MKSS took time off and met at the Chapli Dak Bungalow in Rajsamand district for three days. Accommodation in government dak bungalows was made available partly because local MKSS members had relatives who were class-IV employees and worked in these bungalows. Rules were adhered to and payments made. Sometimes the collector also gave the premises free.

Recalling the history of the kirana (grocery) stores, the MKSS reminisces:

> Those were the early days of the sangathan. There were discussions on various topics including the Dunkel Proposal. While discussing this proposal, MKSS, village-based members came to know about the World Trade Organization, IMF, World Bank, etc. The policies of the WTO had to be understood, but how could a small insignificant sangathan intervene at a national or international level? Nevertheless, the problem remained and it had to be addressed. Concerns were shared about the big companies in the WTO which wanted to expand their business all over the world and wanted to control the entire world commercially. The East India Company had also come for trade once and then they started ruling the country.
>
> The MKSS was thinking of strategies by which the issue could be addressed through public action. This question of intervention was answered by the decision to establish the grocery store. Just like the WTO, there are trade organizations in every town and these trade organizations connived to loot the buyer. How could we save ourselves from this looting? At least the MKSS could begin to address this small, but significant, problem. The worker was impacted by work and wages, and when paltry amounts were indeed paid, the market cheated them of what they had, and often left them bonded. "We'll remove the middlemen, we'll end the exploitation of the market," was the conclusion of these deliberations. It was decided that the MKSS will start a grocery store in Bhim.[57]

In 1992, when there was talk of setting up the Mazdoor Kisan Kirana Store, the local members welcomed it, but many supporters saw it as a dangerous and foolish step. Most of the people believed that a sangathan involved in struggle is actually incapable of doing business, and if it did, its very existence would be threatened. The rules of trade and those of struggle run along different paradigms. The best of the market system is based on money, profit and inequality. The worst is entrenched in acts of hoarding, dealing in black money and cheating. It was feared that this effort could become counterproductive. Either the MKSS values would be traded off into commercial principles or the stores would go bankrupt. These warnings came from long-term friends and well-wishers.

The MKSS Diary notes:

> Aruna's arguments against coupling struggle and commerce were based on her experience of working with crafts. Her education in the business of collective economics had begun in 1974–75 when she created and developed the crafts centre at SWRC. She had worked with Dalit and poor weavers and leather crafts persons. The odds against the poor craftsmen were immense. Banks treated them on par with business but they were burdened by bondage and indebtedness and a predatory market. This led her to question the inherent contradictions between commerce and development of the crafts persons. They laboured with a constant sense of loss and underpayment. The resultant dilemma was between the needs of production and the compulsions of marketing.[58]

To quote Rajni Bakshi from *Bapu Kuti*:

> Why do we talk of the poor forming cooperatives to fight a capitalist market? The bigger the market, the greater the emphasis on individual profit and gain? As soon as the leather workers cooperative got some benefits, its inner strength began cracking.... I learnt that no rural traditional income generation activity could be scaled up, without addressing this dilemma. The artisans had to look for an outside market if they produced re-designed goods. The outside market demanded investment in a pattern of marketing and credit in which the per capita amount required was too high. Poor crafts persons never had enough collateral. Above all, income generation activities of this sort emphasized either individual profit or the income of the organization. Where income is individualized the craftsperson would put personal gain over the collective. The really vulnerable are always workers supplying the market, through the NGO. Profit is channelled back, but not shared.
>
> The Harmara leather workers have prospered, but their social conscience for collective action and their co-operative has, if anything, come down. They are now ready to make charitable gestures, but cannot think of using their economic clout for real change in the village.[59]

Aruna's fears were discussed and addressed. Though she understood the difference between a grocery store and a craft shop, she still had reservations, due to the difference in clientele and the proximity between the seller and the buyer. Her reservations of the impossibility of the same organization being a part of both struggle and commerce were accepted. It was decided that a new entity would be created to deal with the grocery store. Since the majority supported the idea of the store and the MKSS intervention in the market, the Mazdoor Kisan Kirana Store came into existence.

On the other side, the market in Bhim and competitors in the grocery business also dismissed this effort for another reason: they questioned the ability of workers as managers. The MKSS was sure that there was only one way to give them a befitting reply, and that would be to run a shop managed by workers in the open market. The challenge had to be faced, through practical demonstration rather than a logical or theoretical argument; in the end, answers had to come through action. The MKSS discussed markets in detail, Ladu Singh and Tulsa Singh understood the elements of the local market and the relationship between traders and persons who managed the shops. The control over the 'till', the cash point and the exploitation of workers were recurrent themes. Ladu Singh and Tulsa Singh began to discuss the possibility of a shop for groceries run by the MKSS that would impact the market. They were hopeful that it would also control, to some extent, the pattern of indebtedness and bondage fostered by exaggerated prices. With this as background, the MKSS began to plan the setting up of a grocery shop in Bhim. The money came from 'crowd funding', 10 rupees from workers and 100 rupees from salaried workers; pad yatras were organized and many people contributed Rs. 10 against receipts. They were loans without interest returnable in two years. About 65,000 rupees was mostly collected from the area. A few friends who believed in the venture made small contributions. Questions were asked: why were institutional donations not accepted by the MKKS? The reasons for not accepting donations were argued out. Basically the shop had to be sustained economically by the people, and owned by them if it had to survive. The shop, owned by Shanti Lal, in the middle of the market in Bhim, was taken on rent quite easily – because it was believed to be cursed. Since it had no prospects it was given on a lease for three years. In normal cases shops were rented only for eleven months.

The grocery shop opened on 16 November 1992 in the Bhim market. The entire market was furious when the Mazdoor Kisan Kirana Store decided to announce prices of groceries over the mike. They were cheaper than the other shops, as the MKKS had collectively decided that the sale price would be marked up to 1 to 2 per cent of the net profit. The usual mark up is up to 25 per cent. The net profit to the shops is 1 per cent after deducting various expenses, like rent, electricity, transportation, salaries of workers and small incidentals. The shop tested the argument that markets cannot be transparent because it cuts at the root of profit-making, and proved it wrong. The secret of pricing and selling low-quality goods is another method of earning higher profits. All these arguments fundamentally separate ethics from business. Later, the RTI Act exempted 'trade secrets' and placed all commercial activity under Section 8 of the Act. But that is jumping chronology.

The first day was both a day of caution and excitement. The shop was stocked but not fully, as no one could predict the quantum of sales. The Kirana Store was inaugurated in the Sadar Bazaar of Bhim. R.N. Misra, the school teacher who was feared and respected, and a good friend of the MKSS, inaugurated it with a short prayer. It was a very simple event. Some MKSS songs of different struggles were sung. Slogans were raised and *gud* (jaggery) was distributed to everyone who came. The microphone used for the struggles was used for announcing the day's rates for various items at the store.

The response to the announcements was astounding. Buyers abandoned purchase from other shops and flocked to the Kirana Store, so much so that the shop ran out of its three days' stock by the afternoon of the first day. There was a huge difference between the rates of the other shops and the Kirana Store. When people heard the rates of jaggery, oil, sugar, etc. and thronged towards the sangathan's Kirana Store, other traders were forced to bring in competitive rates. The shopkeepers were in a dilemma, torn between seeing another shop do better and their reluctance to lower profits.

The MKSS gathered important principles for transparency. The mazdoor store demonstrated how one store could blow the myth of the free market by merely using transparency and exposing the mark-up rate and the market's dismissal of ethics in favour of exploitative profit, echoed by the popular Rajasthani song:

*Seth minnakuru lohu chatte*
*Bhari dhupahri jeban katte*
*Do numberri lachmi wallah*
*Bole mitha man hai kala*
*Dagahbaaj aur desh lutera*
*Khave deshra pran re*
*La pooncharo pran re*

Merchants taste the blood (of profit)
They cut pockets in broad daylight
They store black money
Speak sweet but have black hearts
Cheats and looters
They swallow the life of the country

In a typical marketplace, looting, high prices, cheating on weights, adulteration and lies is daily business, as the refrain carries on with, 'everything is fair in business'. Soon, the traders united and came to the Kirana Store to request that the microphone be switched off. This was an issue on which there could be no compromise by the MKSS; rates continued to be announced several times in a day. A delegation of traders from Bhim went to the district collector and complained that a new entrant in the market was spoiling the atmosphere by using a microphone. The collector asked, 'What do they say on the mike?' The traders said they announce the rates. The collector answered that he found no reason why they could not; even the official radio Akashvani announced prices. He could not stop a fair activity. He suggested that the merchants should also do likewise.

The traders started diversionary tactics. They started playing songs loudly and showing films in the shop just opposite the Kirana Store, to drown the volume of the mike. Though people came in hordes to that shop to watch the movies they bought groceries from the MKKS store next door. When the traders realized that their tactics were actually harming them, they stopped showing the movies.

The next attempt was to force a ban on supply by wholesalers to the Kirana Store. The wholesalers in Bhim were threatened that those who supplied goods to the Kirana Store would be fined. The Kirana

Store started buying stock from Beawar. Some Bhim traders started supplying stealthily to the Kirana Store. The tension continued for a few days but soon everything returned to normal.

At that time, in 1992, Lalu Prasad Yadav stopped L.K. Advani's Rath Yatra from advancing into Bihar. There was a call for a Bharat Bandh protesting this move. Politics entered the town of Bhim and its market when this bandh was enforced. The traders attempted to forcibly close the MKKS store, but failed. The Kirana Store did not pull its shutters down, as the sangathan did not agree with the demands for a bandh. A team of hooligans came and threatened the store. The workers in the Kirana Store stepped aside and said, 'Do as you wish, but remember that there are 2,000 financiers of this shop who will come tomorrow and call you to account.' The insulting and belligerent group backed out. Shopkeepers hate to lose business; and the brisk trade of the Kirana Store could not be resisted by them. Slowly the shutters went up and within an hour, by 11.00 a.m., all shops were open.

The Mazdoor Kisan Kirana Store does not merely sell groceries it states a point of view in the sociopolitical milieu in which it is located. Following the Babri Masjid demolition, the sangathan joined the Kirana Store to take a public pledge to the preamble of the Indian Constitution, outside the shop in the middle of Bhim on Republic Day in 1993. They were joined by many people despite hostility.

Slowly, the number of shops also increased. The turnover in the first year of the shop in Bhim, in 1992–93, was 36 lakh with an investment of 65,000 rupees.

In 2015, five such stores were being run by MKKS in Bhim, Jawaja, Surajpura, Todgarh, and Vijaypura. In 2013–14 the turnover of the five shops was approximately 4 crore 93 lakh rupees. The shops pay for all their expenses and in addition support a few MKSS workers.

What makes the Mazdoor Kisan Kirana Store special? It works for and within the reality of workers' basic needs and the local market. Two things that preoccupy workers in the market: the right price and the correct weight. By having workers manage the shop, accountability and transparency could be maintained. A worker at the Kirana Store was one of them, who drew the same minimum wage as the MKSS workers. It was easy to converse with as an equal. By looking at workers' needs, the Kirana Store went beyond prices to question customs in the marketplace. Local markets shut down on the only day of the month that workers get off – *amavasya* or new moon. The Kirana Store, on the other hand, remains open on that day, as traditionally it was the only guaranteed holiday for the workers and they were free to go to the market. The 'vyapar mandal', or the traders' organization, tried its best to force the closure but it failed.

When the workers went to Beawar to buy spices for masala-grinding, they were shown the crushed remnants that traditionally go into ground spices. They were informed that the good quality spices are sold whole. The MKKS decided to buy the best quality of spices and grind them to prevent adulteration of any kind. This is one item that costs more at the Kirana Store than the rest of the market.

There is complete transparency in the accounts of the store. Anyone can see the bills/vouchers, etc., of any purchase or sale from the shop. On the last day of every month, a stock-taking exercise takes place and every single item is counted or weighed laboriously, so there can be a check on the stores. In the journey of twenty-five years, many experiments have challenged market rules. In fact, the story of MKKS is not only a distinctive effort in itself but also a big source of learning and understanding.

> The Mazdoor Kisan Kirana Stores are not mere shops but could become a movement. The whole world talks of nothing but the market and big business. They are being run for the profit of big companies. The influence of businessmen and companies has now taken over the running of entire countries. They have assumed an important role in the policy-making of governments. From the "vyapar mandal", the trade organization in a town, to the World Trade Organization, it is a chain supporting small and huge empires. Even countries like the USA have become mere puppets in the hands of big corporations. The politics of the world are now heavily influenced by capital. Poor people are mere customers/consumers, while the actual control is in the hands of the owners of corporations and their top management. The middlemen [who merely buy something from a place and sell it at some other place] in small local markets, are guided by the same motives; they also earn much more than those who actually produce the various commodities. The MKKS cannot take on corporations, but it can and does control a small amount of the trade in small towns. Many such attempts will probably make a great impact. Perhaps we all

> know that the big is made up of small efforts. In all our languages there is a saying that, "small drops of water make the mighty ocean". Mere intervention in vote-politics will not be enough. We'll have to intervene in the economic paradigm as well.[60]

Bharat Dogra, well-known journalist and friend, has visited the MKSS every year for the last twenty-five years. He came in May 1993 and wrote:

> **Fighting inflation at the grass roots**
> Recently, a peasant and workers' organization based in Rajasthan demonstrated an important but neglected aspect of the fight against inflation – that citizen's initiatives are as important as macro-economic policies.... The effort concentrated on reduced retail margins and quality control to provide goods at lower prices. It was decided that since those who ran the shop were dedicated MKSS activists, they would take no more than the legal minimum wage of Rs. 22/day... the MKSS also helped to ensure that high quality was maintained by personal supervision of the grinding and cleaning work.
>
> Predictably, the response of the consumers has been very favourable. The news of good quality and low prices spread rapidly, first among MKSS sympathizers, and then among other people as well. A high turnover within a short time enabled the new venture to meet its target of being able to function at a margin of just one per cent.... The MKSS venture succeeded in bringing down the market rates to some extent as other retailers were forced to cut their high margins to compete with them. This had a favourable impact on inflationary trends far beyond the items sold directly by the new shop.
>
> Lakshman Singh, who buys spices worth Rs. 20 daily for his dhaba, says that he not only saves Rs. 5 a day now by going to the new shop but the quality of these spices are much better too.... Lal Singh, a peasant, says that even people from villages nearly 10 km away prefer to buy their groceries from the new shop. Nikhil Dey, a leading MKSS activist, says that prices have come down by about 15 per cent since this experiment began about five months ago.
>
> The Mazdoor Kisan Kirana Store at Bhim is a pioneering effort at proving how careful planning backed by honest, dedicated work

> can defeat inflation at the grassroots and also improve quality. Hopefully, the local administration will do their utmost to protect this effort [and similar ventures in other areas] from the local vested interests.[61]

The purpose was not to take over the market but to control market prices through the shop and to demonstrate the possibility of doing business fair and square. The money the first shop received as a loan was publicly returned after two years. The workers claimed that in two visits to the shop they recovered the ten rupees in savings, because of correct pricing. The shop has helped demystify the working of markets; to that effect it has been a great educational success.

As the MKSS Diary points out:

> The very same people who were the strongest defenders of the "free" market did not want an even playing field. We have seen how every market is manipulated, and the string of middlemen who exist between the farmer and the retailer. The small and marginal farmer once again gets the worst of both worlds. The farmer has to sell cheap and buy expensive. The local market is most familiar and an area of strength for the MKSS. It has therefore been easier to see through, overcome, and outmanoeuvre the local traders with comparative ease. In fact, the kirana store has been able to control the market through its retail price on some items, so that prices in Bhim are sometimes as low as wholesale price levels in Beawar.
>
> However, in the larger wholesale market the MKSS was out of its depth. Larger markets are even more manipulative than the ones in Bhim. But exposing the internal contradictions of a so-called free market is a very effective path to a greater share for its exploited consumers.[62]

The MKKS is worker-managed and has proved beyond doubt that management is not an invention of business schools. It is a systematic method known to people for centuries. The workers have managed the shop with efficiency and integrity.

The success of the shops has been dependent on the strength of the sangathan, in terms of both, the numbers that support the sangathan and the expertise available. One important learning was that people can be motivated by considerations other than profit. The ethical commitment of those working in the shops has ensured their continued success. All those who work with the sangathan and the Kirana Store earn minimum wages. Temptations of higher wages and better conditions have failed to lure the workers away.

It is not possible to question the powerful international business networks in practice. Local efforts provide the best space for questioning assumptions and defining counter-ideology. Practice and success provide conclusive arguments for theory. Very often creative action, which fundamentally questions the values of the establishment, is the most effective way to expose it. The principles underlying the MKSS's role as a protest and pressure group had to be transferred to its new function as an economic collective intervening in a conventional market, subject to all the forces that exist in a free-market economy.

The Kirana Store is not a philanthropic organization, nor does it see itself as doing *tyag* (sacrifice) or *sewa* (charity). It needs to break even economically. The store presents an alternative value base to operate and control economic relationships, using the market for not merely profit but also providing a service that is effective and ethical. The Kirana Store established new principles of market mechanism. It was built – contrary to popular understanding – on the principles of transparency and collectivism, considered inimical for the market, shrouded as it is in secrecy of various sorts. The whole exercise contributed to a holistic understanding of use of information for ethics, which shaped the RTI movement. Chunnibai said:

> You told me that I should not pawn my jewellery and mortgage my land. I know and you know too that it leads to complete slavery, bondage and economic servitude. How come the "intelligent" leaders have done the same to the country? How do you [or can you] explain such conduct? Is this short-sightedness or opportunism?

Chunni Singh, another sangathan member, addressing the May Day rally in Bhim in 1992, managed to communicate the importance of the shop, in relation to not only its control on prices locally but also inflation. He called upon the local traders not to see this shop run by the mazdoors as a threat. He cautioned them that they were victims of a system that would soon finish off the small traders so that 'bigger seths' would prosper. He went on to refer to the Bharat Bandh, to say that communalism was always a threat to the sanity of living. The horrifying fallout of religious strife is an extreme example. Inter-caste oppression and then intra-caste divisions are all manifestations of the same limiting, exploitative, and oppressive nature of humankind.

The myths that were broken (as recorded in the MKSS Diary):

**The market argument**: A worker will remain a worker and cannot run a shop, a trader will do the trade.
**Our experience**: When the shop in Bhim started, the neighbourhood traders and the people in the market saw that those who were shouting slogans and working as servants to merchants were in fact running the shop and taking all the decisions. Handling a shop/ business is not hereditary. The workers of the MKKS have not only successfully run these stores but some of those who left have also set up their own shops later on. With some training anyone can learn to run a shop. This has been our learning from experience.
**The market argument**: There should be only one owner of a shop, partnerships do not prosper.
**Our experience**: The store not only ran in partnership, it did wonderfully well. When the traders opposed us, banned the supply of goods to us, tried to force us to close our shops, they had to face not one owner, but all the workers and peasants of the area. Workers gave time to challenge threat and opposition. They helped with physical chores like lifting the loads, faced the threats with counters based on numbers, collected the capital, kept a vigil, faced communal and political attacks. Whenever the sangathan called upon them, they came and showed their solidarity and partnership. Today, there are five such stores and there are demands from many places to open stores there. The people value them because these stores have benefited the common person.

The question that bothers the person involved in dealings with the market is, "How open is this market? The market argument keeps repeating that profit is the key to the market. This shop will lose because of its ideological disbelief in profits, it cannot do well."
**Our experience**: On the first day when the store opened, a trader came and said, "Today, we have decided that *gud* [jaggery] will sell at this rate, asking for compliance." The MKKS declined to sell at that rate. This made us realize how much arbitrary control is exercised

in the market system. Their basic mantra is control and through that profit, the open market ends up being nothing but a sham.

How did we have a turnover of 36 lakh in the first year [1992–93]? Because we managed to break into monopolies and call their bluff, and brave it out when they threatened. We sell at cost on all festivals and major festivities, yet we did not incur losses. The normal tradesmen cheat with wrong weights and adulteration, and market-thievery profits are manifold and huge. We understood that the market is a mere medium which can be converted by anybody to perform, it is not an independent mechanism with a will of its own. The mantra of profit belongs to the traders; what is the mantra of the people in this market-system? It is honesty and service.[63]

## The Right to Information? Even Here?

The market was shocked that the RTI assumptions could also be applied to them. The business world has thrived on opaqueness. Could indeed a shop do business and break even, based on what were apparently absurd premises?

**The market argument**: Transparency in business is impossible.
**Our experience**: Initially, the stores and their accounts were run on the basis of trust. But the MKSS pledged to be transparent and accountable towards the people and the use of their money. Even in these stores, some discrepancies emerged and the answer to resolving even petty corruption comes from the Right to Information: Keep the accounts clean. Inform and be transparent about the rates of buying and selling. Keep every penny accounted for and if there is any irregularity then seek accountability. On this basis, not one, not five, but thousands of shops can be operated.[64]

## Postscript

The Sangathan Kirana Store exercise has been a great success in many respects. The right to information campaign took up a lot of time and attention of other sangathan workers, and supervisory responsibilities were neglected. As a result there was a loss, some misappropriation, and the sangathan had to take some decisions which stalled the expansion process. The second shop in Bhim

> and the shop in Barar were closed down. The monitoring and accounting systems were strengthened. A decision was taken not to open any more shops till the management, monitoring and accounting systems were made stable and effective. An important decision was taken to make the shop transactions transparent and educate the citizens of the area to use the Right to Information in the shops, so that they could monitor its functioning, and prevent any misappropriation and mismanagement themselves. The decision to apply the learning from the information campaign to the functioning of the shops has not only helped integrate two apparently disparate kinds of processes and activities but also holds a lot of potential for opening up new fronts and widen the scope of the Right to Information campaign. In any case, through this whole unstable phase, the consumer has not yet directly suffered. Loans have been returned on time. Prices have been kept low. Quality continues to be maintained.[65]

The MKSS play that toured the area with the yatra in 1994 looked at the advance of market forces through the lens of these shops. The appropriate name of the play was: *Aur Raj Karein Vyapari* – And the Trader Rules.

> This journey has taught us a lot. The market is a part of every person's life. If we have to challenge the profiteers we will have to understand their rules and their games. Mazdoor Kisan Kirana Store is a successful initiative and also an initial step. It is not a business but a movement, and if the businessmen are proficient in business, then we are also experts in movements. Not every movement can run merely through sloganeering. A movement is run by people's participation. In this movement, many people have come together. Its future depends upon the efforts of a community and the MKKS.[66]

CHAPTER EIGHT

# Articulating the Demand for Transparency

Most struggle-based organizations working with people locate themselves in the midst of their community to work with them. The MKSS continued to live in Devdungri. But like all villages Devdungri too has a daily interaction with the nearest town, where all the services and the local government are housed, not to mention the market or bazaar.

The relationship of Bhim, the subdivisional headquarters for Devdungri, and the MKSS is an interesting story. It began in 1987 with great hostility. Any critique of the establishment by the MKSS was perceived with disfavour by the town's privileged inhabitants. Shankar's presence was a powerful support and it diluted the antagonism for the rest of the Devdungri family. Traditional prejudicial and irrational categories were used but failed to brand the MKSS. Shankar's family – his aunt, cousins and other relations in Bhim – gave the MKSS a local respectability.

Though the local shopkeepers called him in for chats, Shankar was invariably asked why he played the role of Vibhishana. This was a reference to the Ramayana, where Vibhishana switched sides, betrayed his brother Ravana, and joined Rama in the war to retrieve Sita. The reference in this case was to Shankar's bringing in Aruna and Nikhil, outsiders from a different part of India, to threaten the cosy arrangements of local oppression. References to myths and folk stories are used as political commentaries in Bhim, as they are in other parts of India and the world.

The town itself could have derived its name 'Bhim' from the character in the Mahabharata, or from an important local luminary!

The hunger strikes and the opening of the Kirana Stores established a working, everyday relationship between the MKSS and the town of Bhim. It was not smooth then, and perhaps never could be, because there was always an undercurrent of apprehension. But in the long run, it was seen as inevitable. The MKSS was accepted as a continuing presence.

The minimum wage issue was an ongoing struggle of the MKSS. The worker's life and well-being depended on access to the daily wage. The structure of delivery, i.e., governance and the enabling requirements, rules, office orders and even legislation, were a link to their very existence. It was inevitable that there were frequent engagements with government offices at the subdivisional level in Bhim. Whether it was to ask for work or wages, the workers and the MKSS began to frequent Bhim's government offices. The offices were very hostile to start with, but were eventually forced to recognize that they were not merely power centres for self-aggrandizement, but institutions created to function for the people.

An entry from the MKSS Diary tells us:

> In the MKSS's early years, in 1991, Aruna had gone to the BDO in Bhim, to get a copy of the BPL [Below Poverty Line] list. The BDO was a woman, and her being a woman helped. [The BDO] claimed she was sympathetic to Aruna's request, because she was a woman. The published copy of the BPL list was brought out with great stealth and shown to Aruna. The BDO was nervous and drew the curtains of her office, and for reasons beyond anyone's understanding, behaved as if she was going to be court-martialled for sharing a public document. Ultimately, her good sense overcame her fears and she allowed Aruna to take the copy overnight for her to read and give back. But Aruna was told that she must take it from the BDO's home in the evening!
>
> This was an important lesson for Aruna and the MKSS. They had not understood the extent of misuse of the Official Secrets Act [OSA], and the fears of the junior officers. The Act was passed by British India to prevent information leaking out of their offices, through the Indian babus. The terror of being transparent was inherent in the bureaucracy and even innocent officials feared the act of disclosure. The irony was that the BPL list was published for dissemination!

> Government, said, "Let them die. There will be seventeen less in an over-populated country!" The pressure after the first few days began to show in the deteriorating health of those on strike. The collective itself found it difficult to watch fellow members wasting away, and lost its appetite for the struggle. We recognized a dilemma: if the hunger strike continued indefinitely, the MKSS would have had to appeal to the same administrative machinery we were protesting against if we wanted to save the lives of the strikers.[69]

It was at this point, in 1994, that Mota Ba, a village elder, came to the MKSS from Amner village, not far from Devdungri. He came with a complaint of non-payment of full minimum wage. But unlike most others, he had additional information. He had seen the muster roll, which had an entry for Rs. 22 per day, but all the workers were being paid only Rs. 11 per day. He had asked the overseer why he was being paid less than what was entered. The answer was that he alone would be paid Rs. 22, but that he should refrain from telling other workers what he had seen, or even mention that he had been paid more than them.

This information was converted into a complaint to the local administration. When the enquiry took place, the MKSS members informally managed to see records of buildings listed as complete but were found to be unfinished when inspected. In one instance of misappropriation of funds, Rs. 36 lakh was paid to a fraudulent company called Bhairon Nath and Sons.

After the enquiry it was clear to the MKSS once again that access to the records was a means to challenge the misuse of power by the powerful and influential in the administration. Asking for information was an effective method to establish the right to question, the right to equality and accountability. Until that moment, people had been battling a system in which they were discriminated against on the basis of poverty, caste, religion, and gender. Here was a tool which the poor person could use to realize a fundamental right to demand transparency from a system known for its refusal to share information. When the poor ask for rights, they become victims of the system, sometimes with false cases against them. The system knew that information was power, and that sharing it would reduce their controls. People were now beginning to understand that as well, and the administrative system felt hugely threatened.

The discussion on modes was another turning point in the history of the MKSS struggle for the RTI. The MKSS was invited to Delhi to attend a public hearing of an environmental group. This invitation was discussed in Devdungri and interestingly it turned into a debate on the mode of public hearing and how it could lend itself to the demands for placing information in the public domain. Suppose the public hearing on corruption and its manifestations, non-payment of minimum wages, unspent balances returned to the government, fraud, incomplete works, etc., is held in an open public space, how would it work? Could there be a public hearing without information – at least some documents are required? How could the MKSS gain access to these records?

Writing on the years of initial struggle, Neelabh Misra says:

> When workers on government employment works in villages of central Rajasthan found that they were not being paid the standard minimum wage and that despite increased spending, rural infrastructure was nonexistent or sub-standard, they decided to demand copies of the accounts of money spent in their name, either as payment of wages or on infrastructure. This was the beginning of what is generally known as the MKSS movement for the people's Right to Information in the mid-1990s. Under the slogan "Hamara Paisa, Hamara Hisab" the MKSS launched with the peasants and rural workers of central Rajasthan a movement that has had a direct impact on the lethargic and corrupt functioning that plagues the development machinery of our country.[70]

Many voices and perceptions gave substance to this understanding:

> It is obvious that seeking justice from an establishment which is responsible for the fraud in the first place, will not produce results. As the list of complaints grows with no real action taken, frustration levels and cynicism also rise.[71]
>
> It was this dilemma of seeking justice from the same system that malfunctioned and misappropriated, that led us to explore the mode of public hearings, where the strength of the platform emanated from the people. In other words, the journey of participatory governance might begin with seeking information, but there is a parallel need to develop institutionalized mechanisms

long journey of struggle and defining the right to know. It began with a demand to access public records, for claiming access to basic rights of food, livelihood, and shelter. Denial by an obdurate administration shaped the consequent hunger strikes. Government efforts to liberalize economic policy and privatize everything made the MKSS intervene in the market, weaving information into the unconventional area of business. The discourse spread further into the four districts of Ajmer, Bhilwara, Rajsamand, and Pali. It slowly became the topic of discussion in Rajasthan. Friends, activists, journalists, NGOs and others across the spectrum were drawn into the debate, either by discussion or through participation.

Kavita Srivastava, a friend and colleague from earlier days, fresh from the Institute of Development Studies (IDS), Sussex, and familiar with women's struggles, became a part of the process. Kavita had met Aruna when she was an undergraduate student at Kanoria College. The friendship grew when she assisted Aruna and Mamta, who published the Rajasthani tabloid *Ujala Chadi*, to record the process in a training of 'Prachetas' or block supervisors under the Women's Development Programme (WDP) in Jobner in 1984. It was an ambitious programme initiated by Anil Bordia as development commissioner in the Rajasthan government. Kavita, after an initial period of work with the IDS, Jaipur, went to the IDS, Sussex. She returned to work in Rajasthan and was drawn into the issues as a friend, participant, and sympathizer. Other empathizers, friends and fellow strugglers included Renuka Pamecha, a political science professor from Kanoria College; Moti and Mahesh from Sankalp in Mamoni; Ramkaran and Bunker Roy from SWRC; Sawai Singh, the well-known Sarvodaya worker; Deepak Gyanchandani and Ramanathan from IDS, Jaipur; Sanjoy Ghosh from Urmul; Ajay Mehta from Sewa Mandir; Sharada Jain from IDS Jaipur; Anil Bordia, then secretary of education GoI; and Professor V.S. Vyas, director, IDS, Jaipur. Many others joined as part of the larger circle of support concerned with issues of equality and justice. After *Ujala Chadi*, Mamta later set up Vividha Features as an alternative media centre, and she was a part of the group from the days of the Sohangarh struggle. Ramesh Nandwana from Udaipur and Mahesh Bohra from Jodhpur, both lawyers, lent invaluable support.

## Continuing Battle for Wages: The Records and the Fraud

In an inquiry conducted by the SDM on a complaint for non-payment of minimum wages in Amner, Bhim panchayat, Bhim Block, Rajsamand, Shankar and Nikhil peered over the shoulder of the SDM and saw a bill from Bhairon Nath and Sons. The enquiry confirmed that payments had indeed been made to the company, which apparently had its office at the bus stand in Bhim. It was purported to have supplied the Panchayat Samiti cement worth Rs. 36 lakh, and other raw materials for construction. The MKSS demanded an investigation, and the SDO was compelled to hold it. The testimonies revealed that no material had in fact been supplied. The administration had to admit that even though accounts had been audited, a major fraud had gone undetected. A company had been formed with the active connivance of three persons working in the BDO's office and an official's wife. Cheques were issued and cashed while material was supplied only on paper. The company had no office, no income tax or sales tax number, and was not registered anywhere. The government enquiry resulted in suspension and consequent action. The audacity of such scams could only be stopped by transparency and public/ social audit. This public space for enquiry and testimony would allow a collective quest for the truth of statements made by the government and the contradictions observed by people. Who was right and what was wrong could not be left to internal assessment in the government; the system could not be the accused and the arbitrator. In any case, the administration has a reputation of covering up theft and fraud. The argument of the people kept coming back to the basic guarantee that in a democracy, public servants and people's representatives are honour-bound to respect the constitution. They are obliged to meet the demands of veracity within its paradigm of laws, rules, and regulations.

## Public Hearings: In Search of an Appropriate Platform

The process of public verification needed a public platform. Public hearings offered the space and the architecture for such a process. Though public hearings, under the Environmental Protection Act, were recommended; they were not mandatory and thus seldom organized. The MKSS decided to use this mode to verify the documents related to public works. The contribution of the MKSS was to use this mode persistently and effectively.

The happenings in Kot Kirana were shocking. The facts exposed the arrogant corrupt practices of a blatant, cheeky and brazen power structure. The ghost names, the incomplete buildings billed claiming completion, the falsified bills for building material recalled local tales of duplicity.

The MKSS campaigns have been enriched by the familiar and rich folk traditions of fables and legends. Vijaydan Detha, famous writer and folklorist, collected and reinterpreted the folk stories of Rajasthan to share with the people. Written in beautiful Marwari (i.e., the language of Marwar – Jodhpur, Bikaner, Nagaur and Jaisalmer), a dialect of Rajasthani, he captured the beauty, wit and straightforward power of the art of storytelling. The story below is from *Batan Ri Phulwari*, a collection of such stories. Shankar, always the communicator, recalled the stories of Vijaydan Detha; this time the story provoked by the incident in Kot Kirana was of the naiveté of the innocent and the audacity of the cheat.

> There was a Thakur, who was in failing health. He was an alcoholic and the end seemed near. He was worried about the state of affairs and engaged a servant to make sure he drank a glass of milk every night before he slept. The servant obeyed the instructions dutifully for a while. The Thakur relaxed his vigilance and over a period of time, the servant helped himself to one-fourth of the milk, and added water to compensate for it. The Thakur got suspicious and engaged another servant to make sure that he got his nightcap. The milk got drunk according to plan for a few weeks. Slowly but gradually, the second servant was persuaded by the first to dip into the can. The Thakur again started showing signs of weakness. He engaged a third servant to keep a check on the first two. Again, for a few days he got milk properly but then all three servants in cahoots started drinking two-third of the milk and served only one-fourth to the Thakur. His health started getting worse. He then kept a fourth servant to keep a check on the other three. This time all four colluded and drank the milk and served the Thakur plain water. When he complained he was hungry and questioned all the four servants, they told him that there must be some other reason for his hunger as they had given him his milk the night before. The following night they drank up all the milk again, and smeared some cream on the inebriated, drunk Thakur's moustache. When he woke

> up and complained again, they showed a mirror to the Thakur and said, "We gave you the milk, see, there is cream on your moustache even now." The Thakur, though suspicious, had to be content with their answer. He knew he was being conned, but what could he do?

The context of the story and its allegory did not need explanations to the residents of the area. The story highlighted the siphoning of money from development programmes at every stage. A series of agencies: the vigilance department, the anti-corruption department, and so on take their cut. Like the servants in the fable, they collude and misappropriate. The people, like the foolish Thakur, are duped by the cream on the moustache. They have misplaced their trust and fooled by knaves are warned to act before it is too late. What they will have to do is go beyond the obvious and ask in this case for accounts or 'hisaab' (details) of the milk. The mere raising of the question gets the government into a state of apprehension.

Late Prime Minister Rajiv Gandhi had once said that only 15 paise out of the 100 paise in a rupee reach the people, and the rest are swallowed by the intermediaries. The jan sunwais sought to get to the truth of the missing 85 paise with people's information and participation.

It was not surprising that the call for the jan sunwai raised the alarm and the system responded with typical bureaucratic reactions. The reaction of fear was a compliment to the efficacy of the process. An excerpt from the B.V. Narayana Reddy memorial lecture bears witness to the effects of these public hearings:

> It is difficult to recapture the excitement and the energy that the series of public hearings generated in December 1994 and in January and April 1995. The radical nature and the potential impact of the demands dawned soonest on the lowest level functionary: the panchayat secretary or the gram sewak. The union went on strike to warn the state government that any attempt to disclose information would lead to resistance from them....[76]

**Jan Sunwai and its Demands**

The modalities of the jan sunwai were thought out carefully. The presentation of the information and the method of testifying were discussed with different groups. Help came from many quarters including

> from the local people who had been cheated, many of whom were powerful local citizens.
>
> We normally sleep in the school building. But the villagers insisted we sleep in people's homes the previous night. Hira Singh, ex-deputy speaker [BJP], had mobilized the local mafia to beat us up. He had in fact forcibly taken people who had given testimonies in front of the acting BDO Nirmal Wadhwani – IAS probationer – to Raipur and made them sign counter affidavits. The atmosphere was very tense.[78]

The panel of citizens – an academician (Renuka Pamecha), an activist (Sawai Singh), and consultant to the Planning Commission (Sanjit/Bunker Roy) – travelled a long way to make it to the public hearing. The press was contacted and several requests were made for them to attend. Eventually, a lone reporter, Pradeep Lodha from *Navbharat Times*, Ajmer, came with some reluctance. In the public hearing, ordinary people without any clout or status spoke out against their more powerful neighbours, naming people and reconstructing crimes. It was not surprising that the government officials invited to the public hearing, represented by the BDO and the official from the CID, sat 500 yards away, watching the proceedings with hostility and misgiving.

The issues raised in a jan sunwai have to be clearly articulated and asserted. Waffling, and raising issues that are irrelevant, would be shouted down. If people get up and leave the jan sunwai, it would be a final judgement on the irrelevance of the disclosure. If people stay to listen and participate, and the issue sustains their interest, the proceedings are of importance to them. The jan sunwai makes the organizers publicly accountable to the people by placing authentic documents in the public domain, and the discipline with which the proceedings are conducted ensures that equal space is given to all for expression of dissent and difference.

In the words of Renuka Pamecha, one of the panellists:

> So, that's how people understand as to how verification is done. By putting the bills, vouchers, etc., in front of the people. So this was the first process in which we said that we'll read out [the details], people will speak [to vet or reject the details presented].[79]

As another formal study notes:

> When names of a hundred people on the muster roll [the official document that records the names of those employed on a particular site] were read out in the hearing in Kot Kirana, outraged people came and testified that they had never gone to those work sites, that false signatures had been used, and that on the muster rolls there were names of people dead and gone and others unheard of. The responsibility for these discrepancies lay with the retired teacher Mot Singh who had entered the names, the Gram Sewak who made the payments and the Junior Engineer who had certified that work was done and payments made in his presence. They fearlessly spoke against the former Deputy Speaker of the Rajasthan Vidhan Sabha, who had camped in the village prior to the hearings, intimidating the villagers to change their statements against the alleged miscreants and corrupt officials. The vouchers for the unfinished Patwar Ghar were read out and the people learnt that they had a "complete" Patwar Ghar, on paper – as they sat facing the same [unfinished] building.... When bills and vouchers for the unfinished Patwar Ghar in the village were read out there was uproarious laughter. The papers showed payments for roofing material, doors and windows, while the structure stood close by, devoid of a roof and with gaping holes where doors and windows were shown on paper. As the laughter died down, anger took over. Soon after the public hearing, the acting BDO, an IAS officer under training, filed a First Information Report [FIR] against the Junior Engineer and the Gram Sevak.[80]

Sawai Singh, one of the members of the jury and the panel, had this to say:

> Before this, such an open hearing had never taken place in the state.
>
> We were among the panellists for this hearing. Some people reported to us that there is some fear of the Sarpanch in the village and in the area. If someone raises the issues of corruption in the panchayat, then they might be in danger. We also came to know that the day before the hearing the Sarpanch had openly warned the villagers against participating in the hearing and to be ready to face consequences if they raised their voice. But when a person is free from fear then there is nothing which can stop him/her. During

> the Independence struggle of the country, even Gandhiji did the same, he freed people from fear and a non-violent people stood up against the mighty British empire. The same was done in the RTI movement by the MKSS.
>
> The first public hearing in Kot Kirana was like the foundation stone of the RTI movement. In this public hearing, karyakartas [activists] and villagers exposed grave corruption in the development of the village. After this hearing, the RTI movement picked up pace across the state. Slowly, not only from villages, but even from cities, the voices against corruption started getting raised. Along with the MKSS, social activists from across the state started getting agitated. Dharnas and agitations started everywhere and demands for the Right to Information came from several places. People of the state were feeling that they would be able to wipe out corruption with the help of the RTI. A spontaneous tide of people's power emerged which resulted in getting us the mighty tool to fight corruption – the Right to Information. It can be said that the voices raised in Kot Kirana spread across the country and empowered the people.[81]

There was consternation, anger, and eventually an official FIR against the junior engineer and Gram Sewak. The exposure of the fraud committed by the son of the retired master resulted in his losing the sarpanch election a month later. He had been seen as the popular candidate expected to win.

**Bhim (District Rajsamand) Jan Sunwai, 7 December 1994**

The Bhim Jan Sunwai followed a very dramatic exposé of the defrauding of money by the system without any work on the ground. Nikhil, Shankar, Narayan, Lal Singh and several others were present in Amner village when an enquiry was instituted on the complaint of Mot Singh on non-payment of minimum wages. The SDM came under pressure after many small but significant protests, and was persuaded to conduct it in the village. As he was examining the papers, the MKSS sathis happened to look over his shoulder at a series of bills issued by Bhairon Nath and Co. – Bus Stand, Bhim. They were intrigued and continued to investigate. The bus stand in Bhim had a chai shop and a ticket counter, which was no more than a tin roof protruding from the wall. After scanning the entire town and verifying that there was no physical existence of the company mentioned in the bills, the MKSS demanded an enquiry. The enquiry was conducted and lakhs of rupees were confirmed to have been defrauded. The public presentation of this scam by a fraudulent company was the focus of the public hearing in Bhim. In one financial year, the company had cheated the government and the people by defrauding the block office of Rs. 36 lakh through the collection of illegal payments. It was not surprising to find that the company was owned by family members and wives of the block officials. The fearless and detailed testimonies of people in front of the block office, where the jan sunwai was held, was further proof of the truth of their testimonies. The government officials, though invited, did not attend. But an FIR was lodged with the anti-corruption department.

The MKSS Diary narrates how...

> ...poet Harish Bhadani, a great people's poet, recited a popular poem, which is a favourite with workers and those who fight inequality: *Roti naam satt hai* [the ultimate truth of hunger]. The recitation left us moved and electrified for days.[82]

The panel in Bhim included Justice V.S. Dave, former chief justice, Gujarat High Court, and formerly chair, Rajasthan Law Commission, who continued to be a strong and powerful supporter of the demand for the RTI; Harish Bhadani, poet and vice president of the Janvadi Lekhak Sangh and other eminent citizens. Evidence of corruption worth lakhs of rupees in Bhim Panchayat Samiti was unearthed. This was a review of just six months. Dharnas were staged, enquiries were set up, officials were suspended; but some important questions were still left unanswered – when would the money which had been siphoned off be recovered?

**Vijaypura (District Rajsamand) Jan Sunwai, 17 December 1994**

The Vijaypura Jan Sunwai was focused on the issue of illegal distribution of prime land on the highway by the panchayat. The hearing saw the unravelling of a fraudulent public auction where the panchayat's grazing land worth over Rs. 70 lakh had been auctioned off at throwaway prices. It became clear that not a single one of the 800 people had been to the so-called public auction, although many of their signatures had been falsely affixed. Once again, the government officials did not attend, but an FIR was lodged in the land case.

Anganwadi (ICDS) workers testified in detail about complaints regarding two supervisors, and suspicion about the scam in payment. People listened in rapt attention as they were told how the supervisor had taken bribes, stolen rations, and pilfered cotton, buckets, chairs and tables, durries, and even the paracetamol tablets provided for the community. A quick public calculation estimated that the graft was not less than Rs. 14 lakh for a four-year period.

**Jawaja (District Ajmer) Jan Sunwai, 7 January 1995**

Jawaja followed the excitement and interest of the three preceding jan sunwais. There was the escalating fear among corrupt government officers and public representatives who were implicated, as well as those alleged to have misappropriated money from government works. Despite unseasonal rain on a cold January day, which could have stopped the jan sunwai and prevented participation, the Jawaja Jan Sunwai was attended by a large number of people. The panellists here were Marudhar Mridul, an eminent lawyer from Jodhpur; Tripurari Sharma, a professor at NSD, Delhi, who had been writing and directing plays for many years; Mahesh Bora, a lawyer from Jodhpur; and Ramesh Nandwana, an advocate from Udaipur. This public hearing took place on the same day when the chief minister made an announcement in the state assembly stating that all citizens and elected representatives would have access to all records of development works. This was reported in *Dainik Navjyoti* on 6 April 1993.

In Jawaja, unlike the three previous public hearings, there was no access to government records. The Jawaja public hearing's source of information was the people themselves. The experiences of Kesar Singh from Baghmal were the focal point for discussion in the absence of authenticated public records, As the MKSS Diary elaborates:

> Ex-serviceman Kesar Singh supplied all the material [through his tractor] for all the works that were done in his Panchayat – Aasan, in Jawaja Panchayat Samiti, Ajmer district. Kesar Singh was asking for his dues [from the Panchayat] on the basis of entries in his diary. The sarpanch paid him only half the amount and the outstanding was about 16,000 rupees. Kesar Singh kept asking for his money from the husband of the sarpanch [Meethu Singh]. For three

> years he [Meethu Singh] did not deny that Kesar Singh was owed money. But he did not pay him. Finally Kesar Singh gave a written application to the MKSS. MKSS applied to see and get copies of all the records [bills and muster rolls] containing the accounts of those construction works [for which Kesar Singh had supplied material], from the panchayat samiti [Jawaja]. The filing of this application electrified the Jawaja panchayat samiti. The officials got so worried that the upa-pradhan, the cashier, and the secretary went to Kesar Singh's house that same evening. The government vehicle with six or seven other people and these officials arrived at Kesar Singh's house. They promised to make payments the next day. They were even ready to pay interest for those 16,000 rupees. It was astonishing that they were ready to give 20,000 rupees illegally rather than correctly pay the 16,000 they owed Kesar Singh according to the books. All they asked for was that the MKSS be kept out of this process, and that he withdraw his application. They assured him that the payment will be done and begged him not to ask for the papers/records. Kesar Singh said, "I only want my 16,000 rupees and the hisaab will be done with the MKSS and only after looking at the records."[83]

Kesar Singh was subjected to immense pressure. People from his entire caste (Jati Samiti), 500 of them, gathered to chastise and punish him. They (and the sarpanch) pressured Kesar Singh to take 50,000 rupees rather than 16,000, on the condition that he withdraw the application. But he refused and said that without MKSS and without the records no compromise would happen.

The Jati Samiti disintegrated with an interesting exchange. Kesar Singh was threatened with social boycott because his actions would jail a member of his community – euphemistically called 'bhai' or brother. His retort settled the day. He said, 'Wasn't he my brother when he swindled me? Why didn't the same feeling of community protect me then? This is not a question of community but ethics.' His courage kept the demand for the records open.

Ultimately the Beawar SDM – though he didn't give photocopies of the original records – gave the permission to make handwritten duplicates of the records. The MKSS did that and read out the muster rolls, bills, vouchers, etc., in the village and saw that there were contradictions between the records and the reality on the ground – there were names of dead people, those who didn't live in the village and those who had never worked on any sites. Eighteen names were such that they had been shown to work at two different places on the same day. The bills in the name of Kesar Singh were missing. There were bills of a person who had never worked.

When all this came to light, an enquiry was set up to investigate the complaint. On the day of the enquiry, the Beawar SDM, Shri Nehra, came to Aasan village. All the fake names in the muster rolls were called out to depose. Some 20–25 of the MKSS workers were waiting for the SDM when, to their astonishment, some people came on motorcycles, jeeps and cars and gathered at a distance. Among these, there was the pradhan of Jawaja panchayat samiti and many sarpanches of nearby villages. All of these people had come to help the Aasan sarpanch, Narbada Devi, and her husband Meethu Singh.

The SDM came and everybody gathered there. All the sarpanches, under the leadership of the Jawaja Pradhan, advanced menacingly towards the MKSS workers. There were at least thirty of them. They almost gheraoed the MKSS workers. The SDM asked questions and Chunni Singh started speaking. He hadn't even completed a sentence when voices rose in volume: 'Thrash them, kill them'. Narbada Devi, the sarpanch grabbed Chunni Singh's collar and tore his shirt.

The MKSS protested loudly. The SDM halted the enquiry. The sarpanches had assembled to disrupt the enquiry at any cost. The MKSS insisted that the enquiry be completed that very day. The SDM recorded statements inside a room in the school. One person at a time from both sides was asked to record their statements. Shankar was sent from MKSS and Bhikhamchand (Barakhan panchayat) came from the other side. The other sarpanches tried to dissuade those who were going to record their statements. 'Why are you courting trouble for yourself? You'll have to do rounds in the court. These people [MKSS] will leave in a while but you and we have to continue to live here. We are caste brothers and you should save your caste brothers.'

Meanwhile the enquiry continued, and the SDM kept recording statements. Fake attendance was exposed in the statements. Bhikhamchand (from the sarpanches' side) became impatient and said, 'We spend so much in the elections. We'll have to indulge in some [corruption] to make up for it. Otherwise where will we raise it [the money] from?' The enquiry was conducted on the basis of the FIR that was filed, but the police were bribed and they closed it with a final report (FR). Kesar Singh's payment got stuck again, but his determination was extraordinary: 'I only want the money owed to me, the money for which I worked, and nothing more.' He fought till the end and eventually got his 16,000 rupees, legitimately.

K.R. Venugopal, who had just resigned as secretary at the prime minister's office, attended the enquiry simply dressed in a dhoti and bush shirt and was a silent witness to the proceedings.

The authenticity of their information was proved when two days after the hearing the pilfered money began to be returned to individuals and the community. For example, five scheduled caste families had testified that their gram sewak had taken Rs. 1,500 from each of them as a cut from their Indira Awaas Yojana (IAY) housing grant. The gram sewak came to their houses and returned the money within forty-eight hours.

The issue of access to development information crystallized during the course of the hearing. The collector of Ajmer district sent the matter to the state government for a decision as both the Gram Sewak Sangh and the sangathan began to step up pressure on the district administration to make records transparent.

### Stiff Opposition from Gram Sewaks

Fearing that their misdeeds would be unearthed, all the gram sewaks – secretaries to the panchayat – got together and submitted a memorandum on 22 December 1994. Apart from other demands, they also demanded that information be denied to anyone other than government officials. Later, on 2 January 1995, they staged a dharna at the district collectorate in which they repeated their earlier demands. The gram sewaks said that the sangathan (MKSS) wants copies of all documents including the muster rolls, and this, they feared, would result in their being charge-sheeted and cases filed against them. Despite the boycott and opposition by the gram sewaks, the public hearing in Jawaja exposed the fraud of governmental development programmes which only existed on paper, like the incomplete Saksharta Bhawan of Rawatmal, which was shown as complete in records. Years had gone by, but the workers had not been paid. An older checkdam was refurbished to pass off as new. The school building was complete only on record, but in reality the children had to study under the open sky. The hundreds of people present in this hearing decided to start a movement to disclose information about every development work in every village. As always there was black humour, such as when the gram sewak said that the muster roll had been eaten up by goats, when he was accused of not paying wages.

In an effort to understand the sociopolitical situation of the area they were working in, the MKSS conducted many studies. According to one of them, the study on modes of learning for youth conducted in 1995 by MKSS and presented in IDS, Jaipur:

> The block offices are overwhelmed by a sense of fear. There has been a clamour for transfers out of the area. The rural middle class living in the nearby mofussil towns had gone out of the way to emphasize the need for citizens' control over resources and expenditure. The gram sewaks [panchayat secretaries] of the entire district decided to go on strike on 4 January [1995], three days before the day of hearing in Jawaja [Ajmer], rather than give access to bills and muster rolls.[84]

Afraid of public audit of their works, which included physical verification called social audit, the gram sewaks submitted a plea that their work could only be subjected to a government audit. The people, however, had a derisive and critical response to this – they said that this reluctance implied that the gram sewaks were actually pleading guilty by proposing to hide facts from the people. Although the hearing was to cover only seven panchayats of one block, it threatened the community of gram sewaks all over the state of Rajasthan, so much so that the State Gram Sewak Sangh took a delegation to the state development commissioner to protest against being asked to provide such information in the first place. This converted a local protest for information into a state-wide campaign in its projection and reaction.

As soon as the administration realized the impact that this tactic would have on their functioning, there was resentment and reaction. The first organized protest was in January 1995, when the gram sewaks decided that they would release information about their records only to their seniors in the government or to auditors.

In the words of an MKSS worker:

> We always sought as much information as possible before organizing a public hearing, but the tactic also worked with only partial information. The 1995 jan sunwai in Jawaja was held on the basis of

people's information without comparative government records but was still as powerful in mobilizing and sustaining public opinion as the earlier three jan sunwais. In fact, one of the important results of this public hearing was the series of demands for information from Bagmal, Asan Panchayat, taking the RTI campaign further and adding more members. In this case, many people who had been refused second instalments for housing grants were immediately given the money. There were many such incidents following each of the public hearings.

As a result of the hearing and the impact that the sit-ins were making, the chief minister who was touring and canvassing for votes in the forthcoming panchayat elections made election promises in Jawaja. He promised to make bills, vouchers, and muster rolls transparent by giving authenticated photocopies. He made a similar statement in the state legislative assembly, which was duly reported in the press by the *Dainik Navjyoti*, a Hindi daily published from Ajmer.[85]

**Thana (District Bhilwara) Jan Sunwai, 5 April 1995**

The context of this jan sunwai, which was almost after three months, was different from the previous ones. In one sense, it assimilated the experiences of the previous jan sunwais. It was the first hearing to be conducted jointly with the newly elected representatives of the panchayat. It was also the first jan sunwai to be held with official access to panchayat records, made possible through the order of the district collector.

The process of getting the information is very interesting. It revealed how the administration is not a monolith. Spaces need to be identified and used. The four jan sunwais had a significant impact on the public discourse and the CM's statement of access to public records in the assembly had been widely reported. The MKSS decided to use the CM's statement and approach the district administration to access the records of the panchayats under scrutiny.

Nikhil recalls:

> I went to meet the DC, Yeduvendra Mathur, to inform him of the MKSS' decision to hold a jan sunwai in Thana. I briefed him of the earlier jan sunwais and gave him a copy of the CM's statement in the Assembly, as reported in the *Dainik Navjyoti*.

He was enthusiastic and promised support. He also promised to attend the jan sunwai. He issued an order for information and copies of records to be furnished to the MKSS two days before the hearing. He asked me to go to the Mandal Panchayat Samiti office to collect them.

I arrived at the office in Mandal as it was opening. I was armed with the collector's order. As I went into the office, I realized that the officials were all congregated in the BDO's room and were discussing something loudly. I overheard them talking of the collector's order. One of them said, "How can we be ordered to give records to an 'aatankvadi sangathan' [terrorist organisation]!" The response from another person was, "It is the collector's order and we have to obey it." Pat came the retort, "Let us all disappear from this office so that when this Nikhil Dey turns up he can be informed that we are all out on work. Let's see how he gets the records. Who the hell is this Nikhil Dey?"

I was standing at the door. I stepped in, waving the collector's letter saying, "Here I am." The cat had walked in amongst the pigeons. All of them jumped up from their chairs and I got one to sit on, and a barrage of considerate hospitality poured out. "Tea, or perhaps milk? You must be hungry. Bring milk, grapes, etc." My response was, "Just give me copies of the records." The table was laden with milk, namkeen, grapes, and other goodies. As they were laying it on, a person walked in and said as he looked at the overlain table, "*Arre, JEn* [Junior Engineer] *Sahib, BDO sahib, aaj kounsi audit party aayi hai?* [Which audit party has arrived today?]"

The records were accessed in most part with the help of the collector, but the day before the jan sunwai, news came that the collector might not be able to come as promised. Later I learnt that he had, in his enthusiasm, called the Chief Minister's Office. The secretary to CM responded with severe admonishment. It was then that he realized that there was a contradiction between public statement in the assembly and administrative intent.

The jan sunwai in Thana was also held with partial information. But the fact that Ladu Singh, a member of the MKSS, was sarpanch obligated him to make information available. The jan sunwai attracted other sarpanches from elsewhere in Rajasthan and the campaign increased its spread.[86]

Ladu Singh Rawat, the sarpanch of Thana Panchayat, Bhilwara district, who was one of the core group members of the MKSS, decided to bring together five other sarpanches of his neighbouring panchayats and organize a hearing. The panchayats were Gyangarh, Nareli, Mota Kheda, Shivpur, and Kidimal, besides Thana. Earlier in the gram sabha organized in March 1995, Ladu Singh as sarpanch had disclosed bills, vouchers and muster rolls of the tasks done in the previous year, so that people could assess for themselves the extent of fraud committed then. This was the first time that a sarpanch had facilitated a social audit in the gram sabha.

In order to initiate a process that would get the public to audit the works of the last two or three years, Ladu Singh went ahead with the joint public hearing with six other sarpanches. The MKSS supported the exercise. The most essential ingredient of a social audit is the access to information related to development expenditure. Despite the public hearing being organized in the changed context of the CM's announcement, the sarpanch found that obtaining information on records of the last five years from the block office was an impossible task. This was despite a letter from the Bhilwara DC that the block officials should make information available for the period 1992–95. More than ten visits were made by the sarpanch and the members of the MKSS to the office of Mandal Panchyat Samiti. The block officials did not provide information, and this was reported to the DC and other district officials. After much effort, the information of only two panchayats – Thana and Gyangarh – was provided, that too a night before the public hearing. As a result, the public hearing was confined only to the works of Thana and Gyangarh panchayats.

Renuka Pamecha was an old hand at conducting public meetings. On 25 April 1996, she was chairperson of the fifth jan sunwai held at Thana village in Bhilwara district. Renuka, an efficient women's activist and college professor in Jaipur, had spent over twenty years fighting for the rights of women and helping other struggles for justice. Her family home was in Bhilwara. She had the credentials needed for a credible chairperson of a jan sunwai. Her manner was firm, if necessary even loud, but never harsh. She was thoroughly earnest and yet the inherent humour kept her from seeming intimidating. 'Yes, there is a lot here to make us angry', she said, 'but merely shouting will only make matters worse. Let us present all the details one by one and then decide what action should be taken. The jan sunwai is not a summary trial to be followed by instant punishment.' The BDO and gram sewaks who were present looked relieved by the reassurance. The officials had been ordered by their boss, an unusually sympathetic collector, to attend this jan sunwai. It was the first time that local government functionaries were in attendance. This was one of the several reasons why the jan sunwai at Thana evoked special excitement. About three weeks earlier, the chief minister of Rajasthan, Bhairon Singh Shekhawat, had made a statement in the state assembly that local government functionaries would have to make photocopies of all documents available to the people. That was partly why the BDO and his juniors were present. It also helped that the sarpanch of the Thana panchayat was Ladu Singh, an active member of the sangathan. Ladu Singh was the first sangathan activist who had successfully contested an election. This fifth jan sunwai also showed the maturity of the process. To a large extent the public hearings had been an experiment for the MKSS. But its foundational principles had been clear:

- the power, legitimacy and sanctity of the public hearings would emanate from the people, not from any judge or panel, and;
- the gathering would truly be a hearing and not a juridical or an agitational body. The priorities of the hearing would be set by the questions raised by the assembled collective. As Rajni Bakshi narrates:

> On both these counts, the sangathan could safely say it had succeeded. Yet, with the Thana Jan Sunwai the process also reached its limits in that particular phase. The five hearings had succeeded in attracting wide publicity, thanks to journalists who came from Jaipur, Udaipur and even Delhi and Mumbai. This was partly what compelled the chief minister to make that statement on the floor of the Assembly, But meanwhile, the local functionaries and bureaucrats at all levels also strengthened their resistance to this pressure to reveal documents. Even Ladu Singh, who as sarpanch was an elected representative of the village, could not get information from all functionaries in that Panchayat. Merely a chief minister's statement was not enough. A formal written order was essential before government functionaries at all levels would cooperate with information seekers. A year later, in April 1996, the Government of Rajasthan had still not issued this order. The dharna in Beawar followed.[87]

## A postscript to the Thana Jan Sunwai:

Why was audited information not being made available despite orders of a collector? Why the resistance to part with information, even to share it with elected representatives? The reasons were clearly revealed in the hearing in Thana. For the first time government officials were present in this hearing. The gram sewak and junior engineer were pointedly asked by a few villagers who came on stage about the bribes they had taken from them as beneficiaries of a programme. The people exposed the false bills and vouchers of material on record for the various construction works executed in the village in the previous years. Even government employees like the school teacher, the dispensary chaprasi and the patwari did not fear the consequences and openly validated the facts showing the misuse and misappropriation of development funds in the presence of the Block Development Officer.

Most interesting was the debate on so called "adjustments". The justification given by the officials for the now documented instances of corruption was that norms of labour–material ratio set by the government had to be met and therefore records were being fudged. It took the people only a single testimony to expose the fallacy of the argument. As the speaker pointed out, the false bills pertained to material and such falsification would only further destroy the laid down norms.

The gram sewak, when cornered, quietly conceded that "adjustments" were often made to pilfer money and that he had been party to the fraud. He offered to return whatever he had taken. In all the hearings a popular demand had been made that money stolen from the village or any individual be promptly returned.

This public hearing was different not only in terms of the organizers but it was the first where the block administration participated in full strength. The collector had shown an interest and written out a formal letter asking all block and PRI officials to participate in this effort. Apart from them, PRI elected representatives from Jawaja, Kishangarh, Arain of Ajmer district and Jaipur district participated in large numbers.[88]

### The Emerging Concept of Governance – Its Impact on Politics and Politicians

The villagers came not just from the local area but from far-flung villages to see what was happening. Aggrieved villagers testified. They were few initially, but the presence of an independent panel and the tremendous public response enthused many more to speak up. Members of the MKSS had organized big public meetings in the past, but these hearings were different. These were platforms created for free and responsible expression. It also created a general understanding and experience of democratic empowerment. The approach grew in popularity and growing numbers of villagers participated in the public hearings. With the findings from these five public hearings between December 1994 and the end of April 1995, it became increasingly clear that the disclosure of information and access to government records were absolutely necessary for realizing democratic rights. It also became apparent that without a legal entitlement and a campaign to get the draft ready and mandated, the issue would remain localized.

### Public Hearings – A Critical Review

Neelabh Misra writes:

> A series of public hearings or jan sunwais in villages demonstrated the power of information in fighting corruption and ensuring accountability from public functionaries and exposed entrenched opposition to information-sharing by the latter, the demand grew into a full-fledged mass agitation. As a result, the entitlement was included in the Rajasthan Panchayati Raj Act Rules in 1996. Since then the MKSS, and the villagers of Rajasthan have made extensive use of these provisions through a series of jan sunwais or public hearings, in fighting corruption, ensuring accountability from public functionaries and mobilizing people for effective participation in democratic governance. One lesson is clear from this experience. It is only with the help of agitation and pressure from people that these provisions have been implemented.
>
> The jan sunwais have demonstrated that when exercised collectively, the right to information can have an impact on development by plugging pilferage and it has the potential to

ensure people's control over Panchayati Raj Institutions, especially if the entitlement is institutionalized through processes like the Ward Sabhas and social audit. How does a typical jan sunwai unfold? During the run up, the sangathan and the villagers obtain photocopies of all the accounts relating to development works in a panchayat. For this they make use of the public right to inspect and obtain certified photocopies of all official records available at the panchayati raj level, as provided in the rules of the Rajasthan Panchayati Raj Rules section 321–328. These accounts are then carefully cross-checked through visits to the relevant sites, discussion with the villagers and enquiries from labourers employed on development works. This process generally uncovers many malpractices in different works that are subsequently described in detail in the general assembly of villagers. Then follow the testimonies from labourers employed on these works and other witnesses. Following this, there are questions and statements from the public and cross examination from the panellists. With the government officials also present sometimes, an attempt is made for the administrative and legal correctives of the irregularities identified. Some of the varieties of frauds usually discovered in the jan sunwais are: purchase overbilling, sale overbilling, fake muster rolls, underpayment of wages, and tinkering with labour–material ratio in the development works. The model, as we see, can easily be institutionalized as social audit through Ward Sabhas. Though the Rajasthan government has now given Ward Sabhas the power of social audit, the steps we witness in a typical MKSS jan sunwai need to be woven into the procedures of institutionalized social audit.[89]

CHAPTER TEN

# Political Promises and Accountability

## The Campaign Forces CM Bhairon Singh Shekhawat to Respond

The chief minister of Rajasthan was forced to respond to the series of jan sunwais and their findings because of a combination of factors. First among them was the emerging common understanding across central Rajasthan, backed by irrefutable proof that corruption existed because of a lack in transparency. The link between secrecy and denial of wages, livelihoods and access to development, became clear. The system had to respond to this powerful collective analysis from across a large cross section of people. People had found a simple but effective solution to combat corruption with the powerful tools of transparency and accountability. People's organizations, campaigns and those struggling to access constitutional fundamental rights in India understood that transparency in governance was necessary. The opaque government ruled by the Official Secrets Act and a colonial system of governance had to be dismantled.

The political system and the CM understood the power of the demand. But they were caught in their own dilemma. The government could neither accede nor deny a demand for transparency. It could not agree because of its own collusion in systemic corruption and the arbitrary use of power. It could not deny the demand because it would be seen as protecting its underbelly of corruption.

In the world of nepotism and corruption, a political statement reflecting people's demands is surprising. It provides an illusion of a working democracy. As the campaign moved on and popular understanding grew, the increase in volume of articulation by the power centres was surprising. It went beyond the modest expectations of the MKSS. In rural India, the buzz of local conversations often reflects topics of popular discourse. The jan sunwais brought up enough details for people to talk about and ponder for months. No politician who entered that area could avoid or evade the issue. The matter of transparency of records became the dominant political discourse in the four districts in central Rajasthan, where the MKSS worked. Chief Minister Bhairon Singh, while on the panchayat campaign trail, reluctant though he was, had to declare that he would give the people the right to information. In a meeting in Jawaja he declared that his government was committed to giving people access to records.

In her convocation address to the Asian College of Journalism, Aruna Roy says:

> People who attended the Jawaja Jan Sunwai went to hear him speak and came back with expectations of seeing the records sooner rather than later. Bhairon Singh continued to make declarations of his intent, the most important of which was his commitment in the Assembly through an assurance on the floor of the House. This was reported on the front page of the *Dainik Navjyoti*.... The fledgling campaign took copies of the text of the assurance from the newspaper and demanded its implementation.[90]

**Assurances, Promises, Statements by Bhairon Singh Shekhawat, CM, Rajasthan**

The debate on governance was magnified and disseminated far beyond its normal confines. As the extract from the B.V. Narayana Reddy memorial lecture elaborates:

> The discourse on governance was brought out of the closet and into the public domain. This time the discussion went far beyond the mere casting of a vote. The chief minister made the assurance confidently that he would make a dramatic gesture to appease people. He probably thought there would never be a need to put it into practice. But before long the MKSS and the fledgling Right to Information campaign began to demand compliance.

The concepts of transparency and accountability gathered momentum and became the subject of discourse in chai shops, buses and in public spaces in the four districts and even in Jaipur.

The casual and feudal dismissive nature of the ruling elite began to be questioned. Even civil servants who should have known better began to say, "It was *only* an assurance." The campaign believed that an assurance in the Assembly was sacred. It was completely unacceptable that an elected Chief Minister could make a statement in the Assembly and then refuse to honour it. The Chief Secretary and other bureaucrats reiterated their casual trivialization of democratic processes when they said they did not see why Assembly assurances should be of any concern to common citizens. So many assurances are made, and how many can actually be implemented anyway?

This demand was a leap forward for the common citizen's understanding of political and democratic accountability, and the linking of it to the arbitrary use of power. Arbitrary use of power and corruption are twin concepts; one must understand that they are interdependent, both conceptually and in practice. Corruption and arbitrary use of power corrode governance, and the administrative machinery created to deliver services. This is a moral obligation which went beyond financial integrity to define democratic responsibilities and accountability to Constitutional values. As the debate continued, it deepened into understanding of the mechanisms of governance.[91]

**Translation of the Chief Minister's Statement in the State Assembly**
5 April 1995: Declaration on the Right to Information by Chief Minister Bhairon Singh Shekhawat in the state assembly:

> There is one right that we could not give to the people of Rajasthan and that right is the Right to Information. It doesn't exist in any state in India, but I am thinking on it, and in the beginning of this thought, those who used to allege, from 1990 to 1994–95, till these elections, in these elections as the honourable members were saying VLW have siphoned off, patwaris have siphoned off, officers have siphoned off, panches and sarpanches have siphoned off. I want to state in this house today that from 1990 to 1995 in

> panchayats or in rural areas all the development works that have taken place, if anyone wants to take any information related with development from panch, sarpanch and panchayat, then they'll be able to get it after paying for the photo-copying charges. And also, if any discrepancies surface then those discrepancies will be enquired into by the state government or any agency set up by the state government. I believe no better opportunity is ever going to come [disturbance in the house].
>
> I am actually giving you an opportunity to find out how much money was siphoned off in panchayats, how much work was done, all that information I am giving you. And I am giving it to you so that you can see it, you can see the reality, and you report after seeing it, lodge cases, and tell those people that don't think "in 1990 if we siphoned off then nobody is going to catch us now". Give this impression to them, "Even if you siphoned off in 1990 then even in 1995 systems are being put in place to recover it from you." There is a need for it and that's why I believe that the honourable members ponder over it seriously.[92]

The local debate was straightforward, colourful and replete with anecdotes and stories. Mohanji recalled a popular local saying that the government's position was like the snake and the shrew. If a snake catches a shrew it's doomed. If it lets the shrew go, the shrew might kill it, and if the snake swallows the shrew it will die anyway. Rajasthan government's position was similar to that of the shrew.

Mohanji, an illiterate but educated Dalit bard of the MKSS, put his thoughts into powerful words:

*Pad gayo re Shekhawat chakkar mein*
*Baat hori yo sara Rajasthan mein,*
*Rajasthan mein, pura Bharat mein*
*Pehla pehla jhooth Jawaja mein bolyo,*
*Baat phaili pura gavan mein*
*Pad gayo re Shekhawat chakkar mein*
*Dooji wali jhooth mandir mein bolyo*
*Baat phail gayi pura Rajasthan mein*
*Pad gayo re Shekhawat chakkar mein*
*Meethalal ke chakkar mein*

*Bhairon Singh aayo*
*Dhool pad gayi dhola mein*
*Pad gayo re Shekhawat chakkar mein*

Mohanji's song, talking about how the government's lies had become the talk of the town, went 'viral'. Even before people had heard of the campaign, the song had established the context of the debate on accountability and transparency. It talks of empty promises and lies uttered by the CM and the chief secretary on several occasions.

Meanwhile meetings continued to be held. One of the most significant was the Rajasthan state-level meeting on the right to information, held in Beawar. In this public meeting, attended by K.R. Venugopal, former secretary, PMO, it was reiterated that the assurance given by the CM in the assembly in April 1985 be honoured. This meeting was widely reported in the local papers and drew the attention of a number of people including Ashok Gehlot, who subsequently became the chief minister of Rajasthan (Congress). In later years, he said that a former secretary to the prime minister's office giving unstinting support to this issue gave it immense credibility in his eyes. It is these small but significant interventions by eminent people across the board that boosted the importance and credibility of the discourse in the eyes of the powerful.

CHAPTER ELEVEN

# *Hamara Paisa Hamara Hisab*: Beawar and Jaipur Dharnas, 1996

A year after the promise made by the state chief minister in the assembly, the MKSS decided to go on an indefinite public protest in Beawar. The elected government and the bureaucracy had ignored the CM's assurance, or at best made light of it. A dharna was planned on the date that marked the completion of a year of waiting for the assurance in the assembly to be implemented.

The MKSS had made extensive preparations for the Beawar dharna. It was going to be a long haul. The groundwork included a pad yatra – a march – from village to village talking about the jan sunwais and the need for a right to information entitlement. Months before the sit-in, MKSS activists had visited approximately 300 villages to inform the people of their plans and to make two requests: first, people spend four days at the dharna; and second, each house donates at least a kilo and a half of grain. With this assurance the MKSS was prepared to wait out the government's response to their request.

Their preparations proved prophetic. For the next forty days, hundreds of people from all social and political classes, including professionals, trade unionists, and reporters, descended upon Beawar to join the dharna. They suffered the heat of the tent as they listened to speeches and joined in chanting slogans and songs. The people of Beawar donated food and money and opened their dharamshalas to the protestors so that they could bathe. Small vendors gave vegetables and milk, and farmers arrived from the adjacent villages with sacks of wheat. Volunteers offered to cook and serve water and even to take videos and photographs. Even the poorest villagers gave whatever money they could spare. The prevailing atmosphere was that of a fair, with political speeches, poetry readings and multiple forms of expression interspersed with discussions – with the persistent demand for a legislation enabling the right to information. Newspapers ran stories of ordinary citizens asking why they had been denied that right for so long and demanding action from the government.

The people of Beawar were puzzled that poor villagers were not demanding essentials like food, wages or land, but something as abstract as the right to information. Of course those were important issues. However, the years of struggle for immediate justice on issues of wages or land had led the MKSS to understand the shortcomings of not addressing the institutionalized mechanisms of injustice and governance. MKSS was located in the middle of the predicament, which had led to many discussions and arguments in Devdungri. Over a period of time the discussions became more focused. Mohanji, a small farmer, lyricist, singer and a Dalit, said, 'Till we get those documents out, we will always be liars.' Narayan, Lal Singh, Shankar, and the whole group were of the opinion that 'the muster roll, and bills and vouchers must be shown. How many dharnas and rallies can we organize? We get cheated every time we go to work. The local government official's response is predictable: "people do not work, and the record does not corroborate what you say."'

The decision to sit on dharna in Beawar marked a shift in scale and location. Beawar is 60 kilometres away from Devdungri. It is the nearest large town with institutions like hospitals, colleges and courts. It is a rail link to Jaipur, Ahmedabad, Mumbai, and Delhi. Many people visited the MKSS after the first set of jan sunwais. Among them was Harsh Mander, comrade, friend, and IAS officer, who was posted as course director at the IAS Academy in Mussoorie. He was interested in the jan sunwai as a mode and wanted to know what triggered off public participation. He had understood that RTI could be a breakthrough even for progressive and honest officials. In the day or two that he spent in Devdungri, the intense and exciting conversations were dotted with discussions that the campaign must shift its public protests to a place somewhat bigger than Bhim. Beawar was an obvious choice.

**The Dharna Begins in Beawar: April 1996**

Hundreds of villagers gathered at one end of the town of Beawar on 6 April 1996. Exactly one calendar year had passed waiting for the implementation of the CM's assurance. The numbers continued to swell, till it reached over a thousand. The MKSS rally made its way to the SDM's office and gave a notice that if the chief minister's promise was not implemented there would be an indefinite dharna. There had been a flurry of activity in distant Jaipur, which forced an emergency meeting with the chief secretary to be convened by the chief minister. The SDM in Beawar requested that the MKSS stay its dharna as the demands were going to be met. But it was clear from past experiences of the MKSS that the dharna would be lifted only after the government gave its order in writing.

There were reasons why the dharna strategically moved from the rather isolated office of the SDM to the crowded Chang Gate at the tri-junction of a busy marketplace. It pitched its tent on the spot where many previous struggles of the town had taken place, using a traditional space for communicating a new idea. Dharnas are both protests and a medium of communication. The MKSS decided to wait for the response of the government. It was late in the evening when the government's orders were despatched by fax. The SDM brought it to the dharna site, hoping that it would be called off immediately. But the orders only gave people the right to inspect documents, not obtain certified photocopies. The MKSS and those on dharna were not willing to accept any dilution of the CM's promise to give the people the right to information. They made it clear that anything less than authenticated photocopies would be unacceptable.

**Dharna for RTI: A People's Debate**

The dharna put mounting pressure on the state government to implement the CM's assurance, and drew the citizens of Beawar into a public debate. The critical relevance of access to information was understood and the campaign sowed its first seeds of popular approval and support. On the first three days, the dharna drew large numbers of bewildered onlookers.

They could not understand why a ragamuffin lot should come to ask for the right to information and not demand food, shelter or housing. There was a spate of derisive comments about the '*ghagra paltan*' (skirt platoon) and '*tatpunja*' (twits). But as the importance of the demand dawned on the people, the dharna became a platform for popular expression.

In the dharna pandal, Ambedkar Jayanti was celebrated jointly with the citizens of Beawar and other campaigners. All the trade unions and workers' organizations stood in solidarity to celebrate May Day. It made the MKSS realize that this could be the beginning of a major campaign for something more than even the right to information – a democratic claim for accountability of governance.

Nikhil Chakravarty[93] came with Kuldip Nayar[94] on the sixth day of the dharna. These two veterans, by their mere presence and words of encouragement, gave the issue elevated significance, and lent greater dignity to the demands of the poor. Swami Agnivesh also visited the dharna and had this to say:

> This fire of struggle, which has started from the villages of Rajasthan, will reach Delhi through Jaipur. The people will definitely be successful in recovering the money siphoned off in the name of development.[95]

The MKSS continued to use familiar stories to explain the human predicament. Shankar, in his gifted and masterly manner, took over the storytelling:

> There was a rich trader who was sleeping on the floor on a mat on a hot summer's night. Suddenly he felt sharp piercing movement on his ample stomach, and he got a quick glimpse of a rat running across it. He woke up and shouted loudly. The entire family woke up and ran in alarm, fearing that some calamity may have befallen the head of the family. They were afraid that he had been bitten by a snake. When they pelted anxious questions at him, he said, "It is really nothing, a rat just passed over my stomach." The family members were relieved and exasperated. They asked him to stop making a fuss and go to sleep. The trader said, "No, you don't understand. I have to learn to watch out. Who knows, it was a rat today, tomorrow, it could be a snake chasing the rat."[96]

Shankar then explained the relevance of the story to the audience. The MKSS and rural citizens had just looked at the accounts of the panchayat in the jan sunwais. They had found the rat but a snake of huge embezzlements threatened them – the rations, the housing, and employment denied on public works and huge scams were not far away. The people would do well when responding to the first alarm lest the greater danger, like the dreaded snakebite, took away their right to live.

After the visit of Nikhil Chakravarty, Kuldip Nayar and Swami Agnivesh, the MKSS heard that Prabhash Joshi,[97] editor emeritus of *Jansatta*, associated with the *Indian Express* for decades and one of the founder members of Hindi journalism, was going to pass through the town. After persistent efforts, they made contact with him and he agreed to stop at Beawar on his way back from Jodhpur to have dinner and listen to the story. Nikhil met him while Aruna and Shankar continued with the dharna.

Nikhil relates:

> Prabhashji was a very patient listener. While he continued to eat at Vinod Hotel, he only stopped me to clarify and to get more details. After he heard me out, he agreed to stay the night and address the gathering the next day. Medha Patkar was also due to arrive, and he said he would like to meet her as well. He, and later Medha, stayed in Guptaji's house. The house was an important space for the dharna, as a quiet space to plan and strategize for the dharna.[98]

Prabhashji went back to Delhi and wrote a seminal piece titled *Hum janenge, hum jiyenge* (we shall know, we shall live) in his column called 'Kagad Kare'. This became one of the defining slogans of the campaign.

In the words of Prabhash Joshi:

> The first dharna [sit-in] of the struggle for the right to information was organized here [Beawar].... Several public hearings took place in nearby villages and all the information buried in government offices, whose disclosure the officials used to refuse, came out in the open.... The dharna was helped by small-time vegetable vendors, grocery-store-owners and even well-off farmers. When the struggle intensified and the government turned a deaf ear to the demands, the dharna went to Jaipur and stayed there. Even there, the dharna was held by these resourceless labourers and peasants. Such

> participation and help came from these people because Aruna Roy, Shankar Singh, Nikhil Dey and all others live that very modest life as other labourers and peasants of the Rajsamand tehsil. As a part of the sangathan, these people don't fight their battles as leaders-volunteers of some union. These are not any organized workers of some firm or factory. They live like those for whom they fight.[99]

The MKSS could not have chosen a better spot for the sit-in than Chang Gate. It was a busy area. Thousands crossed the site every day. The passers-by who caught the words of a song would probably come back. But those who stopped to pick up a pamphlet or engage in conversation made it a daily habit to visit the dharna. The right to know eventually became a topic of incessant discussion among the people.

Watched over by the statue of Swami Kumaranand, popular CPI leader, and not far from the statues of Ambedkar and Gandhi, the dharna continued, changing the date every day on its board, crossing a dozen, two dozen days – eating, sleeping on the road, warding off predatory pigs at night.

There were pranks and fun as well. Chunni Singh and a few others slept on *thelas* or mobile handcarts used to sell wares, which were parked near the dharna every night. It was superior accommodation in comparison with the dusty road. Chunni Singh was a late riser. Fun-loving MKSS members, led by Shankar, once wheeled the sleeping Chunni Singh right into the busy street perpendicular to the dharna. Chunni Singh continued to sleep and woke up to find himself between vendors shouting; consternation spread over his face. He sheepishly defended his right to oversleep.

As people started understanding the issue, their spontaneous support grew through word, deed and action. There was a young boy called Ranjeet who studied in a school and also worked (for a few hours every day) at a medical store in front of the dharna spot. He used to earn Rs. 5 as his daily wage, and he donated Rs. 2 every day to the dharna. A disabled person from Fatehpuria would come and stay the whole day and donate 10 rupees every day. The safai karamchari – sweeper – swept the road, which was the sleeping and sitting area, and donated 10 rupees every day; the vegetable vendors gave free vegetables; the local merchants gave free water. The flower sellers gave donations; and the chaiwallah gave a standing subsidy on tea. Groups of people came from villages and brought their share of 2 kilos of wheat. The dharna received about 25 quintals of wheat, which covered the food consumption for the entire period of the dharna.

There was a sabzi mandi (vegetable market) nearby and the vendors there decided to help the dharna. A handcart was wheeled to the mandi and it brought vegetables every day. Initially the dharna got staple vegetables, like potatoes and onions, that lasted longer. One day Shankar made an announcement over the microphone with a request for green vegetables. The huge amounts sent by the vegetable market showed the concern the dharna had evoked.

Navalji Chauhan had a shop just in front of Chang Gate. He offered to pay for and organize drinking water for everybody for as long as the dharna lasted. Painter Hari Shankar made a board for the dharna to enable the MKSS to record its daily income and the number of days that had passed. A merchant allowed the MKSS to use his empty courtyard to cook food and eat; rest-houses and dharamshalas of all communities opened up for the women to bathe and use the washrooms; and water was paid for by a merchant in the edible oil business. The tentwallah put up tents for the dharna at a loss, despite the tents being the worst he had, and he continued to support the struggle.

Living on the road has logistical issues to be dealt with, as protestors in India know only too well. Guptaji happened to be at the pan shop, when Kavita and Aruna were coming back from the STD booth late one evening. He stopped them and, after the usual enquiries about the dharna, asked them what they did to sleep at night. He asked them to wait a while as he had something to give them. He returned with the keys to a vacant house he owned, and said they had full access to it while the dharna was on. A band from the Valmiki community came out in support and played for Ambedkar Jayanti.

The support was immense. In addition, there was a long and very important list of well-wishers. The dharna collected 86,000 rupees, which came in mostly as small contributions. There was a transparency board displaying income and expenditures. People from over 150 villages contributed grain, in quantum of 1 to 2 kilos each time. Everyone was invited to ask for details, if they so wished.

Om Mahawar, a popular communicator and poet in Beawar, narrated entertaining tales, and linked them with the RTI through interesting jokes and songs. Poet Surendranath Dubey wrote a poem on this movement. A famous bhajan toli (a group of religious singers) of Beawar came out in support of the demands and sang a bhajan, '*Kanudo makhan khagyo re*' for the dharnarthis or dharna participants. This became the tune for a very popular and somewhat contentious song '*Choriwado ghano hogyo re koi to munde bolo*'. Women, who had traditionally composed lyrics as they sang, contributed to some now well-known songs. Among them, Sushila, Shobha, Bhuri Bai, Chunni Bai, Koyali Bai, Seeta Bai and others composed songs for the struggle.

One very popular song that the dharna created was '*Main nahin manga*'. This was an interactive song. The entire audience generally gets drawn into the song, which has humour, political satire and topical allusions to which everyone responds. The singer also brings in theatre and acting in his interactions, lending more than the normal dimension to its content. This song has been translated into some other Indian languages. The song has simple lyrics, explaining why women have come to protest and what they want from the government. The lyrics of Mohan Ram (affectionately called Mohanji or Ba) were very powerful, the tunes simple. As a well-known Kabir singer of the area, he combined an ability to use music as a vehicle for the most profound statements. His songs became very popular. While the dharna continued as a focus of public life in Beawar, there was a growing bond between the dharnarthis and the people of the town.

Kamla Dagdi, a member of the municipality, came and said, 'You better win. I have a stake in it.' Surprised at her anxiety, MKSS members told her she should petition the CM, for they could not do more than protest. One of the MKSS group members asked her why she was so keen. Her answer was, 'We have played satta, and I have bet that you will win.' Some said the government would never give in. A lawyer who came to the dharna many times said, 'It's a valid issue. But which rotten system is going to pull its heart out in public interest?'

One of the strengths of a dharna, especially if organized by the MKSS, is its variety. At dharnas, you can find everything from a pitched tent with a few people playing cards to a big event in which people make speeches to the gathered audience. The MKSS consciously decided that each day of this sit-in would be different, and that an effort would be made to involve the people of the town from a cross section of society and get them interested in the issue.

Every day a *prabhat pheri* (morning march) from the dharna walked while it sang, '*Uth jag prashasan bhor bhayi, ab waqt kahan jo sowat hai*' (a song to wake up a sleeping administration) through different mohallas of the town. After every prabhat pheri, people came to the dharna from those mohallas and extended their support. The dharna became a hub where journalists, intellectuals, and activists all came to write, sing, and speak to strengthen the movement.

The news spread to other parts of India and captured the imagination of some eminent people, including activists like Medha Patkar, Swami Agnivesh, Khernar, and journalists like Nikhil Chakravarty, Kuldip Nayar, Prabhash Joshi, and Bharat Dogra. They supported and stood by the RTI campaign right from its inception, when it was just a small movement in rural Rajasthan. For those who were in Beawar that hot afternoon on 9 April, Nikhil Chakravarty's speech heralded a new beginning:

> I feel that this struggle in which you are involved is historic. This right to information is historic and extremely significant. Not only for your region or your state but for the entire country. It will be a huge struggle. That's why we have come here from Delhi. In the next few days, we hope that many others like us will come and join this struggle. As you know, I am quite old, but there are also some advantages of being old. In this long life I have seen several phases and several eras. I was witness to the era when the leaders of the nation had neither the army nor police nor any means of communication but still they had that power within themselves that they could galvanize people and could struggle against the mightiest power of the world. The secret behind this power was that the leaders of that time said that people of India have the right to know as to how the country is being looted. How much the British rulers are looting and how the people have the right to know. And as a result of that people said that we'll run our own administration and won't tolerate this looting.
>
> I have seen meetings of this very size, with these many people, when Gandhiji and other leaders organized such meetings in several small towns and then turned them into mass movements. The British rulers who were ruling the country had to ultimately leave. In the last fifty years whatever we have seen has saddened

us. Like Kuldip ji said, in the last fifty years it was our dream that the country be free of poverty but it's sad and indeed a shame that rather than alleviation of poverty, today there is so much corruption that entire government funds are siphoned off. It's such a shame that the government funds are pocketed by the middlemen/officials. The main thing is that it is all a secret, it's always hidden, it's never put in front of the people. Thus, this looting continues and the saddest part is that this money which is being pocketed by a few people, belongs to the poorest people of the country.

It is movements like these which can show us the way. This movement might appear very small today, but when small movements from small towns spread into peoples' movements then it is very difficult to crush them. They start spreading – from a small spark to a bigger one and then into a big flame. When we see such new courage, we can see the building of a new India where a people-based power gets ready. India will be a country where the administration will be clean, and people will participate in it.

I want to tell you that this movement we are seeing here in Beawar is an important movement not only for this town but for the entire country. And it is a matter of pride for us that we are here to participate at the inception of this movement.

We have come so far to join the start of this movement so that we can talk about it at several places, so that we can write about it. We are journalists. Today the country is in the throes of General Elections, but these elections have hardly any energy in them as some people will merely be replaced by some others similar to them. Important are movements like these where people themselves are saying that they'll find a way out. And we hope that we'll see this movement spreading. And we can say that when the seeds for a new India were sown, we were there, we also came as journalists, and we also took part. We salute you and this movement and we'll just say that carry on this struggle, we are with you.[100]

Harsh Mander, who had reinforced the MKSS resolve to come to Beawar, supported the dharna. When the dharna began, he was on a trip to China. He returned soon after to the LBSNAA Mussoorie. He took leave to attend the dharna. When he arrived we had also prepared a room for him near the protest site in case it would embarrass him. He volunteered to sit with the protestors and join the protest. A short while later he signed the register to endorse the demand. Unlike typical IAS officers who fight shy of public action, Harsh took leave from the government when he came and sat a full day in Beawar. It was a gesture that gave immense strength to the struggle. The biggest surprise was when he asked to speak on the microphone. The campaign expressed concerns that were brushed aside. He said, 'I have been asked how as a serving officer I can support this dharna. I want to make it clear that all of you are raising a demand that is constitutional and just. I am a public servant, therefore first of all I am a servant of the people, then the constitution and only thereafter a government servant.'

> With the right to information, it'll be possible to put an end to the corruption in the development works. This dharna should not be inferred as a move against the government. The government's policy is to remove corruption. When the details of the development works are shared with the people, people will be aware and corruption will automatically reduce.[101]

Medha Patkar's coming to the dharna was significant. She brought solidarity and approval for this demand from a sizeable portion of the movements in India. As a prominent activist, her support was invaluable. These were her words:

> The time has come when there is a need for fundamental changes to be brought in the country. It is only possible when the rural and urban people run their own politics as opposed to the politics run by a few politicians of the country. Otherwise, the corruption prevalent in the country cannot be wiped out. When people will ask for information everywhere – in villages, in *dhanis* [hamlets], in the *chaupal* [public place], in the bazaar – only then will we be able to get the right to information. The administration knows that if the papers of the tehsil, and the information hidden in them comes into the hands of the people, then the people will not only raise objections on the forged accounts but also protest it.[102]

**Role of Nirantar**

An entry in the MKSS Diary tells us:

> On the first few days, as we slept on the road and the noise and traffic dwindled, and an uneasy quiet descended on the market place, the dharna was visited by Ramprasad, the progressive editor of the local daily, *Nirantar*. The paper began its life at the same time as the MKSS and its committed editor sat up all night putting it together. The office and printing press was at the head of the market. A steep staircase made sure you were out of breath by the time you scaled the last step. The dharna attracted the attention of Ramprasad, and as it happens, he was one of the first converts to the RTI cause, along with Ashok Sain, the freelance photographer who still has some rare and fascinating photographs of the dharna. They became friends of the dharnarthis and offered critical support all the forty days the dharna was on. They still remain the best friends and critics of the MKSS and the RTI movement.[103]

But this was not restricted to *Nirantar* alone. Correspondents of major mainstream dailies were part of the reportage which carried the message to Rajasthan and outside. Siddharth Jain from *Rajasthan Patrika*, Vimal Chauhan from *Bhaskar*, and Rajendra Gunjail from *Dainik Navjyoti* made special contributions to the dissemination of information. The campaign owed a great deal to the responsible journalists who spread the message far and wide.

Retired judges, trade unions, and peoples' organizations also came. In all, 400 organizations signed up in support. The local newspapers played an important role in reporting on the event, with the reporters and stringers of bigger dailies not missing the dharna for even a day. Kavita Srivastava, now general secretary of the People's Union for Civil Liberties (PUCL) and well-known human rights defender in Rajasthan and then member of the MKSS, was a seminal part of the campaign and helped with the advocacy of the campaign.

To quote the MKSS Diary:

> One of MKSS's greatest lessons from the Beawar dharna was that public action needs a sustained, open, public forum, which elicits response, involvement and participation. Time and time again, ordinary citizens who came to the dharna said, "Why don't you stay on in Beawar, and sustain this platform? This forum has given us dignity and a voice." Initially we were looked down upon as a set of

> ragamuffin street fighters, and the elite turned up its nose at us. But later, as important public figures came to support the struggle, the issue got its context clearly defined; the forum expanded and got the enthusiastic support of many kinds of groups and individuals. It became the centre of all discourse in Beawar for those forty days.[104]

**Ajmer and Jaipur**

The dharna attracted a number of citizens from nearby Ajmer. The LIC union and its president, D.L. Tripathi, took on the responsibility of steering the RTI and the support to the dharna in Ajmer. The fact that *Dainik Navjyoti* published the only prominent extract from the CM's speech and assurance in the assembly acted as a bond with the paper and its owner, editor and correspondents. Dinabandu Chaudhary, the owner/editor, and the staff reporter, Rajendra Gunjail, were supporters. Vaid Vyas, friend and newsreader in the Akashvani in Jaipur, wrote most of his weekly columns on the demand for access to information. Kuldip Nayar also wrote a column for *Dainik Navjyoti*, and his articles also sustained the interest in the happenings in Beawar.

Meanwhile Khairnar, an anti-corruption protestor from Mumbai, came to lend support to the dharna. Like Anna Hazare, Khairnar espoused causes against corruption, and as an ex-employee of the Bombay Municipal Corporation, he drew huge support. He visited Jaipur and Beawar and addressed public meetings. Siddhiraj Dhadha, veteran Gandhian and Sarvodaya leader, chaired the meeting in Jaipur and joined the campaign. This is what Khairnar said:

> All the citizens have the right to know as to how the money given by them as taxes has been spent. The people also have the right to know as to what kind of development is being pursued by the state and why it is thrusting the poor people down the mouths of multinational companies and agencies. You should expand the scope and geographic reach of your struggle.[105]

On the thirtieth day or thereabout, the MKSS decided to take a part of the dharna to Ajmer, en route to Jaipur. The dharna in Ajmer was not at the traditional space outside the collector's office but at the marketplace – Madar Gate. The Ajmer dharna drew popular support and a cross section of its citizens came forward to acclaim the issue and support the demand.

After two days there, the mobile part of the dharna shifted to Jaipur.

The Jaipur dharna pitched its tent at Statue Circle, a few hundred yards away from the secretariat. On this picturesque spot, the crowd was perhaps different, but the proximity to the power centre made it difficult for the state to ignore the dharnarthis. Many prominent Jaipurians visited the dharna.[106] Professor V.S. Vyas, who headed the IDS, Jaipur, and was familiar with the MKSS since the days of its minimum wage battles, was an immense support as were the other luminaries in Jaipur. Justice Dave, Justice Dinkarlal Mehta and several others came to support the demand. Premkishen Sharma, well-known lawyer and member of the PUCL, was a constant supporter and adviser to the struggle. Mukulika Sen, friend of the campaign, offered us her home for all the meetings on strategy to take the demand further. The journalists, Sunny Sebastian, then with the *Hindu*, Rajan Mahan of NDTV, Narayan Bareth, Pal, Sam, Samsud Joh, Vijay Vidrohi, Anil Loda, Pradeep Loda, Shreeprakash ji, Lokpal Sethi of *Hindustan Times*, Govind Chaturvedi, Satish Sharma of UNI, Menan, H.K. Shastri of PTI, Rajendra Boda, Suresh Pareek, Abha Sharma, Prasanna Mohanti, Prakash Bhandari, Ramkumar Mishra, Anant Krishan of *Indian Express*, Rajesh Sinha, T.K. Singh, Vipul Mudgal, Piyush Mehta of *Aaj Tak*, Asha Patel, Mark Tully, Sandeep Shrivastav of *Indian Express*, Mohammad Iqbal of the *Hindu*, Vedvyasji, Anurag Vajpeyi, Vaimal Chouhan, Rajendra Gunjal, Pragya Paliwal, Om Thanvi, Shubhu Patva, Ramesh Vyas, Ashok Mathur, Gunjal, Rohit Parihar of *India Today*, Shikha Trivedi, Rajeev Malhotra, Bharat Dogra, Radhika Kaoulbatra, Rajni Baskhi, Sumit Chaturvedi, Seema Chishti, Raghu Rai, Pablo Barthelomew, Saba Naqvi, Vinod Mehta, Nirmala Lakshman, Malini Parthasarthi, Dinesh Shrimali, Tribhuvan, Ramprasad, Neelabh Mishra and many more reported and joined the demand in spirit.

Renuka Pamecha had this to say at the Beawar dharna:

> After the Beawar dharna we were assured that there will be a committee to investigate. The committee was formed and it worked but its report was neither made public nor was any attention given towards implementing its suggestions. Then a padyatra was organized and a dharna was staged in Jaipur. At that time Meetha Lal Mehta was the chief secretary and though he called himself progressive, he was also not in favour of it [disclosing information]. But when Ashok Gehlot came [as CM] he said that they'll make a

> law at the state level. For very long, consultations went on for it. One of the consultations was in fact held in the IDS. In a meeting Bhairon Singh ji was sitting right in front of me and he said, "I want transparency." When I heard it I said, "Why are you lying? You promise one thing and do something very different from it." Everybody was sitting there, I said it in front of all of them. I always used to say mere words are of no help, only if you do something concrete would they matter.[107]

The dharna was lifted when the CM promised that the assurance made to disclose public records would be honoured and set up a committee headed by Professor V.S. Vyas to look into it. To quote Dr. Vyas:

> In the last fifty years, billions and trillions of rupees have been spent on rural development, but the condition of our villages is the same. In such a situation, people have every right to ask what happened to that money. This is a religious battle. It will definitely be successful.[108]

Meanwhile in Delhi, public opinion was slowly being built with the articles written by Prabhash Joshi, Kuldip Nayar and Nikhil Chakravarty. Prabhash Joshi wrote:

> When a businessman starts some new work [of construction or something else], then he seeks its accounts from the *munim* [accountant] every evening. He does so because it is his money being spent in the work. Similarly, the works being done in every village of the country are being done with the money of the people. The people working on these works [government] are the ones employed by the people of the country. Then why can the people of this country not demand accountability from the government of the country?
>
> When a munim is supposed to give all the information to his owner then why should the government not give all the information to the common people of the country? If every common man of the country gets associated with this struggle for the Right to Information then that day is not too far when the "rule of the paper" becomes a "true rule [of the people]". [109]

Addressing a gathering in April 1996, Kuldip Nayar said:

> The whole country is trapped in corruption. The money sanctioned for development works often ends up in the pockets of officials. Bridges and roads are only made "on paper" and actually the money is siphoned off by the high and mighty. That's why, while the country has got Independence, the economic state of a common man hasn't improved. If we want to improve the state-of-affairs in the country then the right to information is a must. America changed its Constitution on the very first day after getting independence, under which the common person was given the right to demand any information from the government. In the Indo-China war, India lost. The government constituted an enquiry committee to investigate the reasons for this loss. The enquiry was done but the report hasn't been published till today. Once, in Delhi, an initiative to wipe out rats was started by the government. Purchases of cages and rat-killing drugs were shown "on paper", but, in reality, no such thing was done.[110]

The support of these doyens of journalism gave the issue political and moral credibility. The jigsaw of the history of efforts in post-Independent India was being pieced together because of the RTI campaign. The efforts of V.P. Singh as prime minister to bring in a law were scuttled. Various and varied judgements of the Supreme Court drew the attention of the people to the fact that the access to information derives from Article 19 of the Indian Constitution, and is basic to a sound and accountable democracy.

Beawar marked a significant shift from a local struggle to a state and national campaign. The shift was also deliberate as the MKSS had begun to realize the extraordinary implications of the RTI issue, as well as the limitations of fighting the battle within one geographical area. The year between the CM's assurance in the assembly and the beginning of the dharna gave the MKSS activists time to articulate the demands in ways relevant to local issues, while connecting them with the larger issues of transparency and accountability in India's democracy. It allowed the MKSS to demand the right to photocopies of bills, vouchers and muster rolls, as an illustration of the wider demand for the right to information law. The efforts during that year had demonstrated how important certified copies were for subsequent action. The obdurate resistance from the bureaucracy to give copies of the records had made us understand how important it was to procure a legal entitlement, and prepared us for a long battle ahead.

The Beawar dharna in 1996 made clear the three basic principles which defined the need for the right to know. The first was the right to transparency of accounts and records and the accountability of the government to its people. The slogan 'Our money, our accounts' sums up the demand for this right. The second was the recognition that the legal entitlement for the right should be drafted, framed and owned by the people after public debate. It is they, after all, who recognize the need for such an entitlement. The third and most important realization was the democratic accountability of an elected political government to its people. They have an obligation to fulfil the promises made, whether in electoral manifestos or on the floor of the house. This continuing pressure on political power to be accountable has made people understand the importance of their own participation in democracy, and their responsibility to work the system. It helped the issue that the Beawar dharna was taking place in the midst of a Lok Sabha election campaign, and that Chang Gate was a popular site for electoral meetings and speeches.

The forums of the three dharnas in Beawar, Ajmer and Jaipur were used to create a debate and initiate discussions on issues of corruption, the duty of the state, and the role of the citizen. The ordinary citizens got a public platform. The obvious loss of ethics in public life made the right to information universally important.

In Beawar, the notion of a campaign was born. The need for an entitlement, a law to set aside the Official Secrets Act, emerged. The involvement of people in the struggle and the campaign was further reinforced in the forty days. The movement for the RTI began from this dharna when people from all over the country came to express solidarity and support.

CHAPTER TWELVE

# The Formation of the NCPRI and the Making of the Law

**NCPRI: A National Campaign and Demand for Legislation**

The Beawar dharna put the RTI campaign on the national map. It also laid the foundation of a nationwide campaign demanding a strong legislation. The dharna was convened with a modest and immediate demand for transparency and political accountability to implement CM Shekhawat's assurance in the assembly that all panchayat records could be accessed by the people. In his words, 'photocopies of bills, vouchers and muster rolls' would be made available to people. But the dharna also brought into focus the implicit and critical need for a legislation to overrule the Official Secrets Act and guarantee transparency. By the time the Beawar dharna came to a close, it was clear that people would be able to universally access records only if there was legislation – state and/or central. The principles of an articulated RTI legislation had to become part of the demands of all people's struggles and campaigns. Prabhash Joshi and Ajit Bhattacharjea spearheaded the formation of the national campaign, along with the MKSS. The National Campaign for People's Right to Information (NCPRI) was conceived with the twin objectives of drafting legislation and starting a nationwide movement. Harsh Mander went back to Lal Bahadur Shastri National Academy of Administration (LBSNAA) when the director, N.C. Saxena, hosted a national-level consultation on the RTI law. Prabhash Joshi and Ajit Bhattacharjea spoke to Justice P.B. Sawant, ex-Supreme Court judge and chairperson, Press Council of India, in Delhi about hosting a national consultation to pilot the preparation of a model RTI legislation. The law was to be drafted after broad-based public consultation.

This resulted in three important developments in rapid succession. The first was the two-day consultation at the LBSNAA Mussoorie. The second was the meeting at the Press Council chaired by Justice Sawant. The third was the meeting at the Gandhi Peace Foundation (GPF), attended by a large number of prominent people from different movements and sectors who came together to constitute the NCPRI.

When Prabhash Joshi visited the Beawar dharna in 1996, he had suggested that access to information in India required a national support group to be created soon. He agreed with the popular opinion that the Official Secrets Act needed to be set aside or overruled by legislation as a first step to facilitate and define the legal battle for access to information. Harsh Mander had also underscored the need to define and work out a supporting legislative framework for overriding laws which prevented access to information.

The MKSS dharna in 1996 popularized the need for transparency in governance. It was in fact a massive citizen's education programme. It explained why information was necessary not only for fighting corruption and arbitrary use of power, but also to empower citizens to make democratic institutions work. People began to understand why the Official Secrets Act should be set aside or at least overruled. This made it possible to seek public support in campaigning for a law. All these various strains were interwoven in defining the emerging campaign to demand a legal framework for accessing information.

Laws have their limitations. But without them our rights cannot be defined and made accessible. Without a legal framework, constitutional rights can never be transformed into entitlements for justice.

## Formation of a National Campaign for the Right to Information

The first meeting for the formation of a national campaign was held in Mussoorie at the LBSNAA, and perhaps with good reason. Civil servants with integrity are best equipped to identify the nature of governance, its systemic failures and remedies. In fact, some of the suggestions made in that meeting became a part of the 2005 law. One of the critical inputs came from N.C. Saxena. His brilliant suggestion found its way into the law as the proviso to Section 8 of the RTI Act 2005: '...provided that the information, which cannot be denied to the parliament or a state legislature shall not be denied to any person.'

This was an invaluable insight which was further sharpened with the application of a good judicial mind when Justice Sawant redrafted it.

Looking back on the drafting process, Nitya Ramakrishnan, well-known lawyer and civil rights activist who attended the meeting, says:

> A group of people consisting of social activists, civil servants, lawyers and others met at the Lal Bahadur Shastri Academy of Administration in October '96 and set about making a draft of a Right to Information Act before it. With elements from both of these drafts a "slim draft of the Bill on Right to Information" was circulated by the Chairman of the Press Council for the deliberations of the drafting committee which was set up under the aegis of the Press Council. This greatly facilitated focused discussion and speedy progress towards the final version....[111]

Harsh Mander, also an integral part of the campaign, in his summary of the history of the process till then, writes:

> The movement...has touched the middle classes as well as the poor, because of the despair of their unending interface with a corrupt and unaccountable bureaucracy. It has also reached the middle classes through the consumer and environmental movements. The media have a major professional stake in the right to information because it would greatly aid the investigation of executive action.
>
> For sustained informed and vigilant advocacy for the passage of such a legislation, a National Campaign Committee for the People's Right to Information was constituted. The initiative for this initially came from the grassroots activists from Rajasthan, particularly the MKSS, who acutely felt the need both for powerful support at the national level for the local movement and for wider legislative backing. The initial group that came together comprised senior activists, press persons, academics and serving and retired civil servants, who were actively committed to a transparent, accountable and pro-people governance.

> Their major contribution as a group has been firstly to assist in preparing the Press Council draft, various versions of the proposed legislation for the right to information [which has been referred to earlier in this sub-section] and the detailed blueprint for its operationalisation. In this particularly, serving civil servants and activist lawyers played a central role. Senior press persons such as retired editors of national dailies who continue to write and who are read and heard with considerable respect, played a major role in building public opinion in the media around the issue and the local movement. Academics analysed the issue and placed it in the wider perspective of expanding democratic space. All of these varied groups helped in extending support for the grassroots movements, particularly of the MKSS, around the right to information.
>
> It is difficult to predict whether India is at last on the verge of the passage of a landmark law which would explicitly guarantee the people's right to information. However, an even greater challenge is to continue to anchor the movement and the application of this right in the struggles for survival and justice of the most dispossessed and wretched of the Indian earth, as an important part of a larger movement for equity and people's empowerment.[112]

Joshi and Bhattacharjea met Justice Sawant and persuaded him that the RTI legislation would benefit the media as much as it would the people of India. They argued that there was no other institution better equipped to anchor the framing of this law.

> The Press Council of India headed by Justice P.B. Sawant was persuaded to take the responsibility for the first formal draft of the law. The Press Council improved on a draft prepared by the Lal Bahadur Shastri National Academy of Administration, Mussoorie [referred to by Nitya earlier], and prepared the legislation after many consultations with law makers, activists, members of the bar and retired members of the bench and presented it to the government in September 1996.[113]

The definition of information in the draft bill was an inclusive one. There is no way one can exhaustively set down the kinds of information that can or should be accessed. The idea is that the policy should shift from secrecy to openness, excluding the minimum and allowing maximum disclosure. The definition is consciously not limited to records alone in the conservative and conventional sense. The maintenance of records properly catalogued is a precondition to accessing information. This information was circulated for neo-literates in Rajasthan, through *Ujala Chadi*, in an idiom that people understood and which evoked a lot of interest.

> It is said that information is power in itself. In our Constitution, the Right to Information is considered a Fundamental Right of the citizens. The Sanyukta Morcha Sarkar [NDA] has also announced the Right to Information in its common programme.
>
> There are two main objectives of this campaign:
>
> 1. Initiate drafting of a new law [for the RTI]. The National Campaign Committee has prepared a draft for this law in collaboration with the Press Council of India. For an open debate on this, it is being sent to various groups and organizations.
> 2. Public Hearings will be organized across the country to link people with this campaign. These hearings will be held on the issues of importance to the local people.
>
> The public hearings served as two-fold education. It propelled the campaign to reach out to different parts of the country and apply the right to know as a precursor for accessing rights on a range of different but equally important issues.
>
> The first two hearings were announced in *Ujala Chadi*: it will take place in Alwar on 26th September and the issue will be multinational companies and the interests of the common people. The second hearing will take place during 1–2 October in Bilaspur of Madhya Pradesh, and the issue will be the Public Distribution System.
>
> Apart from this, in the coming months, public hearings will take place in Bhopal [Bhopal Gas Disaster], Madhya Pradesh, and in Kashipur of Orissa.[114]

*Ujala Chadi* circulated the simple set of demands asking citizens to support the campaign. It requested readers to give their consent to the following declaration letter in support of the NCPRI:

> For enactment of this fundamental right, the National Campaign and the Press Council of India have taken an initiative of drafting a new

> law. We welcome this initiative. We believe that through this new law, transparency of information will increase in all the matters of public interest. The various dealings of the government and government agencies will be done keeping in mind the interest of the people and exchange of information will take place in these openly.
>
> We promise that we'll extend our support to the law. We'll put all efforts to achieve and enact this law. Understand it, discuss it and give your support to it. If you wish, you may cut it and paste it on a paper, sign it and get it signed by others as well.[115]

The people's campaign continued to disseminate information about policy and programme. The newsletter carried the details far and wide and was a very useful mode of communicating with Rajasthan's ordinary citizens:

> This campaign believes that democracy is a rule of the people. The elected representatives rule in the interest of those who elect them. The government's money belongs to the people. The people of the country have every right to be aware of all the decisions taken by the government. Then why are all accounts and decisions hidden from people? Today there are so many scams and corruptions in the country because all the decisions and wheeling-dealing take place behind closed doors. The people have the right to have access to all these records and to be able to take copies of these and question the government regarding these. When there is transparency in the functioning of the government work only then will the corruption end.
>
> A momentum is building up for running this campaign across the country. Many journalists, lawyers, activists and politicians have got associated with this campaign. Several political parties have included this right in their election manifestos as well.
>
> The Madhya Pradesh government has initiated the process of making an RTI law. In the Bilaspur division of this state, the government has given the Right to Information within the PDS system. Through this decision of the government, the black-marketing of sugar, wheat and kerosene in PDS shops has been controlled.
>
> The demands of this movement are:

- The Chief Minister of Rajasthan had made a declaration in the State Assembly on 5th April 1995, to give the Right to Information to the people. This should be immediately enacted.
- The report of the committee which was constituted by the Rajasthan government on the question of the enactment of RTI should be made public and it should also be enacted.
- The report of the tri-lateral committee which was constituted three years ago to index the minimum wages with inflation should also be made public and it should be enacted at the earliest.
- To rid the PDS of corruption and black-marketing, all the essential documents [ration cards, registers, etc.] and other information should be made accessible to people. The right to get copies of all the information should also be given to the people.[116]

The NCPRI was convened on 1 August 1996 in Delhi and the Press Council called a high-powered meeting to discuss the drafting of legislation for the RTI on 10 August 1996.

The process of drafting a law with people was itself a great learning. It involved ordinary citizens laying down principles and non-negotiables. The drafting of the law was done by a special group with legal expertise and skills. The Press Council held many consultations and meetings, but the final drafting was done directly under the chairmanship of Justice Sawant.[117] Nitya Ramakrishnan summed it up succinctly: 'To have a consensus emerge out of a gathering of individuals with markedly varying perceptions is a rare feat. Justice Sawant with his clarity, gentleness and determination has achieved this (in the formulation of the RTI Act).'[118]

The slim RTI draft bill called the 'Press Council Draft' was circulated by Justice Sawant on 30 September 1996, to Prime Minister H.D. Deve Gowda, his cabinet, the members of the Lok Sabha and Rajya Sabha, and to all state chief ministers. Justice Sawant also held a press conference releasing the draft act. On that important day, Sushila (MKSS) simply but powerfully articulated the notion of RTI. She was interviewed by the media, who were rather surprised to find a young rural woman advocating the Act. When she was asked how literate she was, she said she had cleared class 4. The derisive comment was, 'The sophisticated literate person has failed to understand its importance; what do you know, and do you think you will succeed?' Her now famous response was: When I send my son with 10 rupees to the marketplace, and he comes back I ask for accounts. The government spends billions of rupees in my name. Shouldn't I ask for my accounts?

She said in Hindi, '*Hamara paisa, hamara hisab*' ([It's] our money, our accounts).

Her logic cuts through to the essentials, brushing aside the miasma of layered and often contradictory understanding of access to information in a democracy. These four words have been translated into all Indian languages and many foreign scripts, because it is the shortest and most clear argument for democratic transparency and accountability. A thesis could be written around these four words.

The United Front government under H.D. Deve Gowda responded by setting up a committee under H.D. Shourie. The state governments and their response is a part of the following chapters. All subsequent drafts of the law by the NCPRI and many other campaigns were based on this excellent initial draft.

CHAPTER THIRTEEN

# The Process and the Campaign Travel: The Public Hearings

In Rajasthan, the forty-day dharna lifted on 16 May 1996, with an assurance by the state government that the chief minister's promise would be honoured. A committee headed by Arun Kumar, a senior civil servant, was set up to examine and propose methods of access to information and present its report in 60 days. Professor V.S. Vyas and Sushil Kumari Pradhan in Pali were the ex-officio members of this committee.

On 20 July 1996, the MKSS, with the Press Institute headed by Ajit Bhattacharjea (former editor of the *Indian Express*, the *Hindustan Times* and *Everyman*, a publication of the Sarvodaya movement under Jayaprakash Narayan) held a jan sunwai in Beawar on corruption in public works and delivery of services in Ajmer, Rajsamand, and Bhilwara. This was attended by media persons from Delhi and Nepal.

It was followed by a meeting called by the Pink City Press Club in Jaipur on the RTI. The meeting was chaired by Justice Sawant, where CM Bhairon Singh Shekhawat was a participant, as were many senior civil servants, senior journalists, activists and eminent citizens. In this meeting the CM had to acknowledge, at least for the time being, that the RTI was an inviolable right under the constitutional provisions and there could be no backtracking on the promise made by him in the assembly.

> In an extraordinary statement to present the hazards of transparency, the CM came out with a set of unacceptable arguments. When Justice Sawant reiterated in his inimitable dry judicial manner that the RTI was legitimate and there could be no theoretical or legal arguments against transparency, the CM stated his reservations. He said, that if there is a bridge in Barmer, a border district with Pakistan, and the records of the construction of that bridge are disclosed, and if there is proven corruption and bad construction it will be a threat to the security of the nation, as Pakistan may come to know of the weaknesses in our country. His case provoked derision and Renuka Pamecha broke out strongly critical of the statement. Justice Sawant dismissed it as irrelevant. But this story became a part of the folklore of the RTI in Rajasthan to show the absurdity and anxiety of a corrupt administration and government.

**Public Hearings Continue**

In Rajasthan, after the dharna in 1996, the Bharat Gyan Vigyan Samiti (BGVS) Rajasthan, MKSS, and the NCPRI organized a jan sunwai with the Mevs and other local communities in the village Sarekhurd, in Alwar district of Rajasthan on 25 September 1996. The issue was the forcible taking over of land by RIICO (Rajasthan Industrial and Investment Corporation) and Kedia Group (a major real estate group in the state). The process of acquisition was in violation of existing procedural requirements and entirely against the will of the people. The local residents here were already displaced during the partition and had been allotted land in Alwar. For them this double displacement was a penalty for existence itself. There was immense resentment and anger. The jan sunwai established the right of local citizens to claim their land.

Harsh Mander, the divisional commissioner, Bilaspur, in Madhya Pradesh, had visited the dharna in Beawar in 1996, and publicly supported the demand of the dharnarthis. Only a few members of the civil service have the courage to make an unambiguous public statement. It was therefore not much of a surprise when he took up the matter when he rejoined the state after a year at the IAS Academy in Mussoorie. The jan sunwai in Bilaspur by BGVS MP and the NCPRI began on 2 October 1996, with the support of the divisional commissioner. Harsh Mander invited the BGVS, the NCPRI and the MKSS to spend a week there to train and organize jan sunwais. S.R. Sankaran, an IAS officer and ex-secretary, MoRD, GoI, and Shekhar Singh, then teaching at the Indian Institute of Public Administration (IIPA), among others, came to Bilaspur to participate in the process. An MKSS report says:

> Through executive initiative in Bilaspur Division of Madhya Pradesh in 1996–97, the right to information was extended to the citizens of the local area in a number of contexts:
>
> **Public Distribution System [PDS]:** The PDS provides subsidised grains particularly in tribal regions. The significant gap in the PDS and market prices results typically in flourishing black markets in most regions so that the vast subsidies invested in PDS are actually diverted from food security of tribal people to unscrupulous traders and officials. In Bilaspur, this was selected as the first context in which to apply the people's Right to Information. All food grains diverted to the black market are shown usually in the records of PDS shops as having been distributed to poor consumers. The Bilaspur commissioner passed an administrative order enabling citizens to get copies of both the allotment and distribution register of all PDS sale outlets, thereby enabling PDS consumers for the first time, to have documentary evidence that grains were being distributed against the names which never reached them. The impact of this order was dramatic. The off-take in the PDS shops in Bilaspur in the months after this order dropped by half. This represented grain that was earlier being diverted to the black-market.
>
> **Employment:** For many young people in villages and towns, the ultimate dream is to get a government job. They register themselves with the employment exchange and await call-letters for interviews. These rarely come, and when they do they remain witness to the fact that nepotism and corruption rather than merit and qualification govern selection of candidates. The Bilaspur commissioner first passed orders that the copies of registers of candidates in employment exchanges can be received along with detailed rules about how candidates are selected [by a rotation system] from an interview call. For the first time, candidates were enabled to ensure that these selections were done fairly and with transparency.

The second order was that in any selection to a government job, anyone can ask for a list of candidates who applied with relevant qualifications and the procedure and criteria for selection. Once again, corrupt selections of less qualified candidates was controlled by people's intervention.

**Public Works:** For all public works implemented by local governments and officials in rural as well as urban context, citizens were entitled to seek copies of all relevant records. These included muster-rolls which indicate who was given wages against what quantity of recorded works. Likewise, bill and measurement-books and vouchers indicated details of purchase and use of materials.

**Public Contracts:** The significant right related to the award of contracts, which is another notorious area of settled corruption. Through administrative orders of Right to Information in contracts, citizens were empowered to seek lists of all applicants who applied for any contract with relevant details of their qualifications and bids. The public authority was also required to provide the basis and procedures for selections, for award of any contract. These rights to relevant information once again enabled citizens to control corruption in the award of public contracts.

**Pollution Control:** The Bilaspur divisional commissioner also took an important step to contain pollution levels in air and water caused by industrial installations in Korba township. The divisional commissioner's order made it mandatory for these industrial units to publish details of polluting effluents released into air and water by them in newspapers every day. The published details would mention the standard permissible limits of these effluents in air and water and the amounts actually released by these units.[119]

The MKSS was watching the process with great curiosity. The process followed was not very different, the people's reactions almost predictable in every case. Aruna writes that there was encouraging proof that it worked, when protests began from the lower bureaucracy, much like the protest of gram sewaks in Rajasthan. As they say in the local language, 'When you put down the fire and water meets the flames, the fire splutters!'

> I was curious about the responses in Bilaspur, where the initiative was being taken not by an activist group but by a senior IAS officer, divisional commissioner, well known for his sympathy for the downtrodden, his integrity and scrupulous attention to details. His reputation preceded him in every district posting. He was now divisional commissioner, in charge of four districts. The team that went from the NCPRI was composed of two ex-IAS officers, S.R. Sankaran, retired Secretary, MoRD, and me, I had resigned after 7 years in service. There was also Shekhar Singh, who took classes for IAS officers in the Indian Institute of Public Administration amongst others. Despite the powerful presence of all of us, the suspicion and wariness of the administration was palpable. The reaction of the system was an indication of the apprehension and fear of transparency, monitoring, and accountability. It emphasized the immense possibilities of using this process to establish factual truth, which had to be accepted, as it was supported both by testimony and records accessed from the government.[120]

These first set of official jan sunwais also contributed to the acceptance of this mode, which later transmuted itself as the social audit process. Social audit is now defined and accepted as a complement to the financial audits conducted by various agencies of the government, right up to the supreme audit agency, the Comptroller and Auditor General of India (CAG). It has become a mandatory part of the transparency and accountability process; for example, it is a part of the MGNREGA legislation.

However, the response of the collectors of the districts and the elected representatives was typical. They were apprehensive and wary of attempts to make the system transparent and accountable. It is ironic that the situation is called 'confrontational', while the demand for transparency is written into the word and spirit of the constitution and governance. The keepers of the system have become the owners of it. The sovereign people are seen as petitioners and every act as a concession to them. Opaqueness and secrecy are the fundamental reasons for corruption and the arbitrary use of power, and therefore the system is most resistant to transparency and accountability that threaten to dismantle oppressive misuse of power. The resistance proves the relevance and effectiveness of the process.

## Information Sharing in Rajasthan on Atrocities Against Women and Human Rights Violations

Apart from the Bilaspur feedback in the contexts mentioned above, the struggle for transparency was also linked to atrocities against women and general human rights violations. The Government of Rajasthan publicly denied the occurrence of increasing crimes against women. Women's rights and human rights groups found it very difficult to prove that there was often manipulation in investigation, delays or irregularities by the police in taking action relating to serious crimes like rape, sexual assault, battering, and domestic violence. There was no accountability of the police towards the people, including the complainant. The complainant had no right to know as to what was happening to her case. The police and the home department were not at all willing to have any dialogue on this issue.

Organizations working towards justice for women came under the banner of Mahila Atyachar Virodhi Jan Andolan, Rajasthan, in 1996. After much public agitation against this attitude, the state government set up a forum for dialogue- and information-sharing with the women's rights and human rights groups under the chairmanship of the home secretary. This forum met on a monthly basis. It was attended by the additional director general of police and the superintendent of police (women atrocities) and included junior officials. They sat with activists and relatives of the complainant to scrutinize irregularities or negligence at the level of the police on a case-by-case basis. The fact that this forum provided for openness and that any case could be subjected to public scrutiny led the police to become more accountable. An order was also issued by the home department that information regarding crimes against women be collated at the district level on a fortnightly basis and on a monthly basis at the state level. Apart from the fact that it resulted in each police station in charge and each district superintendent of police working hard to show that they were swift in responding to cases, it also got the activists information on a regular basis from the home commissioner's office and the SP's office.

> The success of this forum resulted in similar platforms being set up at the district level. Today the message is clear that the police and police stations have to be transparent, accountable and provide

information to the people. This has had a good impact and has resulted in improved police accountability even with regard to cases of general human rights violation and custodial crimes.[121]

The success of the process from central Rajasthan to Madhya Pradesh helped establish the consistency and relevance of the process. It was seen to impact the delivery system in Madhya Pradesh, and the results were as dramatic and indisputable as they had been miles away. The process also established its universal applicability, whether in rural issues of injustice or women's work with violence.

**Dams, Displacement: '*Jal, Jungle, Jameen*', Hunger and Drought**

There were different jan sunwais conducted on displacement: for the land oustees in the building of the Bisalpur Dam, Rajasthan, and one called in Bhopal by the Narmada Bachao Andolan for the oustees of the Maheshwar Dam. The Jal Jungle Jameen Andolan in Udaipur also held jan sunwais. The Akaal Sangharsh Samiti was born as a precursor to the Right to Food Campaign. People's movements and politics began to assert a right to participation in policymaking and governance. The jan sunwai allowed a coming together of the various perceptions of dealing with the malfunctioning of the system in implementation. The process allowed the administrative machinery to go beyond their smug satisfaction with rules and regulations to the more fundamental issues of justice, equality and ethics. Since the jan sunwai was organized in a public space, it emphasized the critical role of transparency and accountability in removing corruption and double-dealing. It established once again that people were right in their understanding that secrecy gives space for corruption, that corruption impacts the delivery system, (which was) created to address poverty. The role of RTI as a tool was understood and internalized in every set of jan sunwais. The ethical in the establishment became conscious of the need for legislation that would promote principled functioning of governments. The right to know was symbiotically linked with the right to life, livelihood, and expression.

CHAPTER FOURTEEN

# The Rajasthan Divisional Dharnas

The MKSS had a huge task ahead after the dharna in Beawar. The canvas of operations was not limited to the four districts where they worked but far beyond, not only geographically, but in terms of inviting participation and engagement of a very large number of sectors and people. The challenge was to evolve a process and a strategy that would take up the issue of transparency and accountability, and its inevitable link to better governance for the people in the state of Rajasthan. The energy and the creative seriousness of the dharna needed to be disseminated, heard, understood and felt by the people. Struggle also brings with it angst or anger against the double-speak and empty rhetoric of the government. This anger had to be channelized through an organized system. The MKSS Diary states:

> Accordingly, in February 1997, the MKSS set out to inform people in Rajasthan about the RTI campaign to demand transparency of information necessary for survival of the poor. The slogans "*Hum janenge, hum jiyenge*" and "*Hamara paisa, hamara hisab*" succinctly brought the essence of the demand to begin dialogues with people. Every grievance and non-performance led to an examination of the absence of democratic accountability. The state government, when it failed to implement its promise of transparency and access to records, was actually denying its citizens the promise of accountability. The fundamental issue was the abuse of the social contract between the

> citizen and the representative and the civil servant. Secrecy and opaqueness allowed this abuse; and corruption was its primary and visible manifestation. Politicians and governments pledge to work for the people under the Indian Constitution. This process of participation in democracy begins when we cast a vote to send representatives to panchayats, assemblies and parliament. People have to realize in a democracy the vote is a transfer of power – sovereignty, on a contract to a representative to deliver promises. If the CM made a promise, he had to fulfil it![122]

The Arun Kumar Committee was set up after the Beawar dharna to implement the assurance of the CM; in other words, to look at means for providing information to the people. It submitted its report on 30 August 1996. The information received informally by the campaign confirmed that the committee, whose members included the distinguished and well-known academician and economist Dr. V.S. Vyas, had endorsed the critical need for the transparency of panchayat records. In fact it had recommended systemic changes to ensure that this could be done. But the report on how transparency could be made functional became a secret document! The campaign guessed that the committee had come to conclusions unpalatable to the government. The government, in its arbitrary and arrogant style, had once again gone back on its promise of compliance.

The agenda of the proposed dharna in Jaipur beginning 26 May 1997 was to demand that the report of the committee instituted to examine the method of implementing the CM's promise of transparency be made public. Inherent was also the demand for accountability of political promises. A CM could not make empty promises; the concept of accountability was taking root. The actual demand was that records of panchayats be made transparent and that photocopies of these documents be supplied to people for a fee.

The MKSS believed that the common person had a stake in the decision-making process of the country, including deciding on the principles which outline policy and legislation. The Beawar dharna had proved conclusively that people understood the argument, and were willing to transform their understanding into support for public action. A part of the indifference of the ordinary citizen to public affairs can be attributed to the lack of information and comprehension of government functioning. The swelling campaign for the demand for the RTI law proved that once people understood, support would follow. The right to know how the government was using money and power began to be perceived as a fundamental democratic right, enabling every Indian voter to make an informed choice.

Beawar had proved that the struggle had excellent communication with the people, gauged by the support that followed. The MKSS re-established its understanding that modes must be culturally evocative and familiar; there must be enough time to discuss and exchange views on the issue, listen to dissent and state reservations. The language and idiom had to be the one most familiar to people. The slogans and songs with the colour and texture of humour, and stories, make immediate connections with larger numbers of people. A song or a chant can make a passer-by stop to listen to a catchy tune or a dialogue. The challenge is to define an issue with simplicity in a familiar mode without affecting the complexity of the thought. It often invites the listener to interpret the message in her or his own context. Communication across ever-changing cultural modes and idiom is always a formidable challenge.

However, this is not new knowledge. Cultural forms – of song, slogan and theatre – have proved to be excellent modes for carrying messages to people for centuries. Religion and faith have used it most effectively through the ages. Local folk storytellers and oral historians like the Bhatts in Rajasthan have done so too. Songs carry the message across long distances. Even when indifferent to its message, the singer and the listener, attracted by the lilt and rhythm, absorb the significance of the lyric. The modern advertising jingle continues in this tradition.

But this time the MKSS had to go beyond the familiar discourse – anger and angst raised by the injustice and corruption of the system that spurs poverty, deprivation and oppression. It had to introduce a legislative solution, link it to ordinary lives and provide a legal framework for citizens to monitor the state. It had to travel from the familiar area of grievances and denial of basic services to the unfamiliar domain of policy and legislation – usually left to a specialized group. It had been recognized that people's trust had been betrayed and the social contract, through the vote, violated. The logical continuity leading to pilferage, loot and the destruction of many lives was seen as a consequence of the misuse and arbitrary power in the hands of people who had no responsibility to answer questions or stand accountable for consequences. Even very literate friends were wont to ask, as one IAS officer in Odisha did, 'You should be talking of poverty, etc.; what relevance has information to the poor?'[123]

Talking about law and its principles through culture was a fresh challenge. The necessity for a law had to be grasped, basic principles of the law had to be understood and critiqued and transformed into simple lyrics and dialogue. In the case of the MKSS, Shankar's genius was the stimulus and the tethering point.

Rajasthan is a huge state. It has six divisions to oversee the work of a few districts each, headed by a divisional commissioner. The MKSS decided to go to all the divisions in Rajasthan – Ajmer, Jodhpur, Udaipur, Bikaner, Kota, and Jaipur.

The travel time to the farthest northern point of the state takes almost a day by rail and road. Travel, if it has to be within a time frame, could be long drawn. On the other hand, it had to facilitate reaching the remote as well as the most accessible places. After much discussion the MKSS decided to travel in a hired truck. The truck yatra began with the intention of popularizing the issues of transparency and accountability. The yatra carried focused messages to initiate a dialogue on participatory governance. These began with people's articulations, either against corruption or access to basic services prevented by corrupt practices, access withheld, hidden by lies, wrong information in documents, records, muster rolls, PDS registers, rations, medicines, absentee teachers from schools, and the much more fundamental aspects of access to decision-making processes in the panchayat and municipal bodies.

**Truck Yatra**

The yatra, jatha, and several other local words, describe a walk with a purpose. This is a part of the South Asian tradition of expression and communication, drawing people to listen, watch and respond to sentiments – religious, political or otherwise. In India this walk or yatra has been used by all kinds of formations and for different purposes. In Rajasthan it has been used traditionally for the famous annual celebration of Urs, at the Dargah of Khwaja Moinuddin Chisthi in Ajmer, and for the celebration at Ramdeoria in Bikaner. Thousands walk for days to reach their destination. Social activists all over the country have used the pad yatra to meet people, talk to them and mobilize them for a purpose. The MKSS has used it every year in its area to take many campaigns further.

> While the most effective mode has been the pad yatra [foot march] from village to village, we used a truck yatra to cover greater distance in a shorter time frame. A truck yatra is used to reach out, especially when time is short. Trucks remain the cheapest and most accessible mode of transport for the poor in rural India. The yatra vehicle in contrast to those commonly employed by politicians – the air-conditioned jeeps and trucks used for canvassing during elections – became a truck.
>
> The SWRC had an ordinary truck and was willing to loan it with someone to drive. Diesel and other costs were to be borne by the MKSS. Jeevan, who drove the truck, participated in all the events and was part of the extended RTI family. Forty campaigners piled into the truck and went from place to place to talk about the RTI.
>
> The cabin of the truck housed the driver and two others. The rest piled in at the back. There were old durries laid out to make it a little comfortable. The space was cramped as the provisions, the wood to cook, and the tent took their space with impunity. Nevertheless, it was the place where the real action was, and the fun! The occupants of the cabin were envious of the noises and sounds of enjoyment from the back. Shankar was, as always, the centre of the energy flow with his songs and wry political jokes. The roars of laughter and applause were infectious. He drew out the best in people. The journey was never tedious. Practical jokes heightened the giggles and laughter from the back of the truck.[124]

The canvas-covered open truck was a great success and a journey which promised adventure. It helped create a space for interacting with widespread public opinion and debate on the issues of transparency, accountability and ethics in governance.

Political yatras have become another genre – carried out on overly decorated vehicles, replete with noise, unnecessary spending of money, and a high degree of aggression. They are now popular with Indians, in a borrowed vocabulary, as 'road shows'. The 'Truck Yatra' was also an ironic comment on the many grand political yatras organized just before elections, or to incite communal passion. Political yatras are deeply embedded in Indian culture.

Walking for a purpose is an act given great sanctity and is also seen as a sign of commitment. As with Gandhi's salt march (Dandi Yatra), for example, it has been seen as a means of reaching out to people. The yatras the MKSS organized were not intended to be a one-way process. Rather, it was an essential part of learning from people. The yatra invited suggestions along the way, especially as there were not many ready-made solutions on which to pattern a demand for transparency. The MKSS has found yatras an effective tool of discovering new approaches or rediscovering those that have been used in the past but forgotten. Yatras are of course a very effective way to mobilize people to genuinely contribute to the movement.

The MKSS yatra tried and succeeded to some degree in redefining the nature of the political yatra. Instead of blaring pre-recorded music at high volume, there was street theatre, folk music and other forms of cultural expression. All of them creatively interpreted the debate about democracy and participatory governance to the people in their idiom. The MKSS Diary reports:

> Many such yatras have since been organized; one of them took the draft bill to the different Divisional Headquarters of the State a few years later.
>
> The formats for the dharnas were similar. In the three days the MKSS allotted to each division, there was time budgeted for different groups with multiple modes of communication. The MKSS skits and the songs from Beawar came very handy. There were long marches to the divisional commissioner's office, public protest, workshops with specialized groups, seminars, meetings to spell out the details of demanding accountability, all converging to emphasize the demand that the Arun Kumar Committee report be made accessible to the public.
>
> In Bikaner, the dharna was held at two places, the first outside the divisional headquarters and the more volatile one in Sadul Circle, where the cultural mode attracted the drummers from the Dholi community. The extraordinary percussion session was remarkable. In the article entitled "Footnotes to a Dharna",

published by *Lokayan*, Aruna and Nikhil presented a contemporary critique of the value of such happenings.[125]

Ramkaran[126] has been an excellent chronicler, a member of the Mazdoor Kisan Morcha set up in 1991. He goes back to his many diaries and corrects our failing memories. He recalls:

> The yatra began from the Ajmer Division, and this time the campaign had joint organizers – the MKSS and the NCPRI. Specifically, it was a demand to gain access to records of the ration shop [PDS] and all construction works from the Panchayat. From the hinterland of the city of Ajmer came supporters from the MKSS and the Rajasthan Mazdoor Kisan Morcha, Kishengarh Tehsil, in large numbers.
>
> Under the initiative of D.L. Tripathi, a well-known trade unionist, different trade unions had joined the protest in Beawar. D.L. Tripathi and his colleagues, the citizenry of Ajmer, including the editor of *Dainik Navjyoti*, Deenbandhu Chaudhary, welcomed the yatra. They were a part of the historic demand for the RTI in Beawar and pledged support to the dharna in Jaipur. The day was spent in talking to a variety of groups and in a protest outside the divisional headquarters demanding the disclosure of the Arun Kumar Committee report. The report of the committee set up to examine the disclosure of information promised by the CM of Rajasthan in the assembly became a secret document. The lack of intent of the Government of Rajasthan was clear. It was a determined and colourful flagging off for the journey ahead.
>
> The truck and its occupants then travelled to the newly created district of Baran, carved out of old Kota. Baran has a large population of Saheriyas, one of the most neglected tribal groups in Rajasthan. Moti, who sat on the minimum wage dharna in Bhim, was co-ordinating Sankalp, a strong organization which worked on schooling and education. Charu, who worked with Moti had organized the women and youth. Three very useful days from 12–14 April of sit-ins [dharnas] and rallies in Shahbad, Kishenganj tehsil, culminated with a dharna outside the collector's office.
>
> In Kota, Charu, the friends in Sankalp, and Moti who had sat on the hunger strike in Bhim in 1991, came from Mamoni, and helped establish the yatra's credentials. He had been a supporter of

the MKSS for many years. His participation in the hunger strike in 1991 had become a part of folk history. The MKSS continued to get his support on a range of issues. Well known in Kota, he established communication with a range of institutions and professional groups. The media too interacted with the people demanding the right to information.

The road and logistical necessities took us to Kota. In Kota new grounds had to be established, and the presence of Moti and Charu, and Sankalp Sansthan gave us the stamp of a serious and committed campaign. We went to schools and colleges and met journalist groups. We met politicians, academicians, and doctors. The open-ended discussions went a long way in establishing the grounds for the legislation. Apart from the Sankalp group, the LIC Union and other affiliates of the groups that had signed to join the Beawar dharna all gave their unstinting support.

When the truck entered Udaipur, the familiar organizations and faces of friends once again shaped the three days there. Ramesh Nandwana, lawyer and supporter since Sohangarh and with him the lawyer groups, Sewa Mandir, Astha and Ubeshwar Vikas Mandal, gave logistical and other support. Astha's independent tribal groups, too, joined the campaign. The organizations introduced us to the press, and we re-established connections with older acquaintances since we began work from Devdungri. Rajsamand was carved out of older Udaipur District in 1991.

In Udaipur the yatra stayed at Astha, and visited Sewa Mandir, Ubeshwar Vikas Mandal. All old friends supported the campaign in different ways. Sewa Mandir organized a meeting in its premises; Astha organized a public protest with support from citizenry and the media. Ramesh Nandwana joined and helped the protest in many ways.

Like Baran, the campaign went to the villages in Udaipur district, which ended with a dharna outside the divisional commissioner's office. Our assumptions that dharnas are great platforms to spread messages and ask for support were re-confirmed. We left Udaipur with the confidence that support would follow the campaign to Jaipur, for the long haul that was predicted.[127]

There was a break at that time for a week or more. The first public notice of impending strategies was evident from the public meeting held in Jaipur on 15 May 1997 at the statue circle. It was a notice to the state government to disclose the contents of the Arun Kumar report and table it in the public domain.

> The next destination was Bikaner. The truckload first went to Lunkaransar, where Urmul Jyoti had set up a Nagarik Sangathan struggling against corruption and corrupt practices. There were demonstrations and public meetings. [Like] as in all other districts, petitions were signed by the campaign along with people of that area, addressed to the CM.
>
> In Bikaner, Ashok Mathur and Sanjoy Ghosh, were our primary contacts. Ashok was a publisher of a small paper and Sanjoy, who changed Urmul Trust into a good development organization, were both our critical supporters. They helped establish contact and suggest places for public protest. The Ajit Foundation also helped with logistical and other support.[128]

It was in Sadul Singh Circle that Laxman Nilwa was accosted by a petty politician who wanted to know who the neta of this campaign was. Since the MKSS was a collective, Laxman said, 'I am!' The shocked and disbelieving response was:

> "Well endowed and established leaders have failed to fight corruption and change the system. What chance do a motley set of nincompoops [tatpunjia] like you have? Forget it, friend!" and arrogantly walked off. Months later in 1997, when this battle was won, the clarion call in Jaipur's Badi Chowpad was, "Tatpunjoon ki jeet" [The nincompoops have won!][129]

From Bikaner the yatra wended its way to Jodhpur. It was 22 May. The yatra stayed till the 24th, in the city and around, distributing pamphlets, talking to people, arguing, discussing, armed to cope with all exigencies; the truck stopped often to pitch its tent, cook, eat and proceed. The whole exercise was financed by public funding and sympathizers, many of whom were sympathetic NGOs who gave in kind – usually shelter and food. The spirit of the simplicity of a religious yatra combined with the Gandhian/socialist principles of identity with the most vulnerable, the poor, strengthened the argument for low-cost methods.

> In Jodhpur, Sushila Bora who ran a school for the blind and had become a friend through the Women's Development Programme run by the Government offered the school space. The tent was left in the truck and the school sheltered the truckers. Dr. Patwa helped with numerous details of logistics. All of them gave sound advice. The support of Mahesh Bora and Sumitra, supporters from the beginning since the Sohangarh days, was invaluable in connecting with social activism and their two professions – law and medicine. The support of Marudhar Mridul, the eminent lawyer; Komal Kothari, the distinguished and remarkable cultural historian; and of Vijaydan Detha, eminent writer, storyteller and friend, strengthened the campaign and placed the demand within the framework of social, legal and political acceptability. The protests at the divisional headquarters and on the street gathered public support and steadily increased the understanding of the need for the right to be informed and the proactive disclosure of information.[130]

The yatra ended in Jaipur to begin its historic fifty-three-day dharna. On 26 May 1997 the Jaipur dharna began in real earnest.

The most important part of political education in India is the determination to go to the people. The success of the RTI campaign was its concern with, and ability to, connect with people. The yatra was many things – it was a series of workshops, seminars, and meetings in public and specialized groups; it was protest; and also handing over memoranda to the authorities. It brought together the need for multiple kinds of democratic actions and education for successfully working a democracy with ethics, and equipping people to make well-informed choices.

CHAPTER FIFTEEN

# The Dharna in Jaipur: May–August, 1997

It would normally be assumed that the tumble and pace of travel in a truck would have exhausted and demotivated the campaigners. But the travellers came packed with the enthusiasm and unstinting support of the thousands of people they had met in the yatra. The hundreds who gathered at Statue Circle – the fashionable focal point in Jaipur for evening recreation, much like India Gate in Delhi – were a determined lot. Aruna Roy recalls:

> I was saying goodbye to the many who left that evening with a promise to return. Two women started a quarrel. As I was making peace between them, Galku Ma from Paner came and put an affectionate arm around me, and said, "Beta, I am going to stay with you as long as you are here. I will not abandon you or the issue." Galku Ma kept her word; she stayed all the fifty-three days we were there, barring the few days she had to go for an emergency. For me as for many others it was this kind of commitment that supported the demand for the RTI. If this fundamental foundation of struggle, street protest and continuum had not been there, the law making process and the negotiations would not have moved the political will to act the way it did.[131]

The Statue Circle in Jaipur was a popular city spot where people from all strata came to enjoy an outing. There were lush lawns, kept green and wet even in peak summers, when people in the city suffered from acute water shortages, and those around the desert state are parched for a few draughts of drinking water. In Rajasthan, women in the rural areas have to frequently walk miles for a couple of pots of drinking water, and drought is a perennial and accepted situation. The government's promise of hand pumps and water pipelines, and the millions of rupees sanctioned for it, disappear like a mirage in a desert. This was a constant irony and footnote on governance to the people who sat on these plush lawns, watching the rich circle the statue for their morning walks and evening jogs.

Many onlookers during the dharna were among those sitting in offices hearing the songs of protest, slogans and speeches over the microphone. They faced the daunting prospect of seeing the protestors in their offices during the day. The secretariat was about half a kilometre away. Close enough for the opaque system to worry about the demands, far enough to draw public participation of a large cross section of interested citizens.

The MKSS had waited over a year for the government to disclose the findings of the report of the Arun Kumar Committee, which was the culmination of the first dharna which began in Beawar. It was against this backdrop that the second long dharna began. The year 1997 was the golden jubilee year of India's Independence, and the protest demanding the citizens' right to know was an ironic comment and postscript on the proposed celebrations.

On 26 May 1997 the MKSS and the NCPRI began its dharna, with a state-level delegation to meet the CM, led by well-known journalist Kuldip Nayar. Kuldipji was optimistic that the man who had shared his days in prison with many of them during the Emergency would listen to reason. Our lack of faith in the government seemed misplaced to him. The CM promised that the order would be released for scrutiny of documents at the panchayat level in Rajasthan by 3 June. The delegation came back with mixed feelings. The members felt that the assurance was quite dubious; however, Kuldipji had faith in the promise. But, in spite of persuasion from many well-wishers, the dharna refused to lift till the orders were actually issued. The dharna continued, waiting sceptically for another assurance to be met on the promised date.

While the protests went on outside, much tension was building up within the government. The government could not justify its stand of secrecy on the basis of an act as outdated as the Official Secrets Act,

1923, a colonial legacy – one of the many left behind by the British. Independent India had not rescinded the Official Secrets Act, another footnote on the betrayal of promises of giving equal access made at the time of Independence. The Rajasthan government dug its heels in and continued to use the Act to suppress and deny information, in some cases even going to absurd lengths such as denying published information on the grounds of security of the state.

The 3rd of June came and went, and there was no sign of the order to meet the assurances given by the CM – nor was the committee report made public. The dharna organized the 'Vada Khilafi Divas' on 7 June. Kuldip Nayar, K.R. Venugopal, Hemlata Prabhu, Mukulika Sen, Sawai Singh, Premkrishen Sharma, Surendra Mohan, Wakar Bhai (CPI-M), Damodhar Thanvi, Marudhar Mridul, Than Singh, Ved Vyas, Siddhiraj Dhaddha, Pradeep Bhargava, Professor Bharatiya, Professor O.P. Mathur, Vikram Vyas, Professor V.S. Vyas, Renuka Pamecha, Mamta Jaitley, Sharada Jain, Lad Kumari, Sumitra Chopra, Radhakant Saxena, Prakash Chaturvedi, Sushmita Banerji, and many others attended the meeting. People with black bands tied around their arms gathered in thousands to protest and make the deaf government hear again.

Spontaneous lyrics and songs were created. Shankar and his friends sang:

*Jaipur ki sarkar tu bole kyon ni re, mundo khole kyun ni re.*

The song went on to add, 'You have ears like an elephant and huge eyes, but you choose not to see or hear,' the sentiments came from the heart and mind of an activist-lyricist and went straight to the centre of the issue. Like all other songs of that period, this too gained much popularity in Rajasthan.

The MKSS simultaneously used advocacy, dialogue and debate at various levels in the government. Delegates went to meet the ministers and secretaries almost every day. The police facilitated these appointments. Protestors stood at the barricade preventing them from going further towards the secretariat, singing an adaptation of the famous prayer of Gandhiji: '*Raghupati raghav raja ram, sarkar ko buddhi de bhagavan, CM ko akal de bhagavan, DM ko buddhi de bhagavan…*' to the accompaniment of drums and cymbals. The police were irritated as well as amused. The bureaucrats passing in their cars with red beacon lights were mostly angry, speculative, and derisive, while a few also looked amused. The protestors withdrew every day when the police promised an appointment with a minister and department of their choice.

*Yeh Panchayat hamare aap ki, Nahin kisi ke baap ki.*

A set of derivative slogans raised a crescendo at the pandal in the dharna – '*Yeh paisa hamare aap ka, Nahin kisi ke baap ka…Yeh desh hamare aap ka, Nahin kisi ke baap ka…Yeh sarkar hamare aap ki, Nahin kisi ke baap ki*'. Read together, these slogans expressed the emerging realization that the elected government was not master, but part of a system to serve and deliver. Sovereignty was vested with the people; these slogans underlined the fact that fundamental power flows from the people to those who govern.

As in Beawar, the growing popularity of the dharna drew in the media in Jaipur. The RTI campaign was reported widely, including newspaper reports both in the regional and national press; there was also consistent coverage by the electronic media. The state government was beginning to react to collective pressure from civil society and the media. Political circles and the state government found themselves incapable of dismissing the issue with customary arrogance and lies.

### The Ghotala Rath, or the 'Chariot of Scams': Lampooning Political Doublespeak and Hypocrisy

Poverty and corruption have been a constant concern for sensitive Indians from the beginning of remembered history. Whether it was Gautama Buddha, who left home and family, or the concern of great mystical poets like Kabir and many other Sufi saints, the verses of the subaltern poets of the south, or Subramanya Bharathi – deprivation and poverty remained a central concern.

The Bharatiya Janata Party (BJP) was the ruling party in Rajasthan in 1996 and was refusing to address the issue or amend the legislation to allow citizens to access information. It was ironic that at the central level the same party was preparing a grand rath yatra to be undertaken by their national leader L.K. Advani. The campaign was to highlight the prevalence of '*bhay, bhookh aur bhrastachar*' (fear, hunger and corruption), and suggest modes to lessen if not eradicate them.

The rath yatra was due to pass through the state of Rajasthan. The dharna decided to send its delegation to meet the yatra. They were refused an appointment, and wearing black bands and waving black flags they vented their frustration in Kota. The group came back furious. At that point Shankar, who had gone with the delegation, suggested that our campaign should precede the 'rath' to expose its lies and sham. But good counsel prevailed, and he along with other creative friends, including Bhanwar Gopal (Bhurji), Gajanand and many young women from all over Rajasthan, conceived and created the 'Ghotala Rath' and its yatra.

The fabrication of the rath itself was brilliant. It was a hand-propelled pushcart or handcart, known as 'thela'. Placed on the handcart was a garishly decorated chair topped with an umbrella. This served as the canopy from which hung several cardboard placards bearing names of the notorious scams of the last ten years. The people have to suffer from the torture inflicted upon them by the government and multinationals alike – companies like Enron and Union Carbide – and also from the various scams related to petrol pumps, urea, fodder, and so on.

A swashbuckling Kamdar reminiscent of the feudal past of Rajasthan marched at the head of the procession. The 'neta' sat on the chair, wearing a white kurta-pajama and a saffron scarf. The Ghotala Rath Yatra shocked, delighted, and finally stimulated people to think. This histrionic procession drew big crowds and, with songs, speeches and an accompanying skit, managed to convey the message.

The Ghotala Rath has been one of the most effective modes for spreading information and creating spaces for dialogue. The concept drew sharp satirical topical comparison in form and content to the religio-political rath yatras, as India celebrated the false promises of corrupt governments in its fifty years of independence. Cultural expression often encapsulates different forms of discontent. The Ghotala Rath Yatra brought different kinds of questions together. In doing so it became synonymous with the questioning of the government on its lack of transparency and accountability. The yatra became very popular, along with its songs and intrinsic theatre.

It was at this critical juncture that the activists of the MKSS decided to stage their own '*Svarna Jayanti ke Uplakshya mein Ghotala Rath Yatra*'. It was in sharp contrast to, and a political lampoon on, the hollow promises and campaigns of political parties and their air-conditioned raths. The political satire of the Ghotala Rath Yatra was evident in the thela itself. It was immensely popular and a great public performance.

Announcements were made for days at the sit-in that Shri Rajvani, popular leader of the masses, was coming to Jaipur from Delhi with his rath yatra, and was going to address the gathering. The Central Intelligence Department (CID) members, who were supposed to keep tabs on what was happening at the sit-in and give the administration daily updates, began to mention this in their reports, and people began to ask questions, 'Who was coming, from where, and why?' The MKSS capitalized on this and made frequent mention of this impending visit. Special announcements were made that since Shri Rajvani was to be a state guest, he would be staying at the VIP guest house. No one seemed able to figure out who this person was, and curiosity grew.

Finally, on the mentioned date, the MKSS announced that the guest had arrived and the procession of the chariot was about to begin. The entire team of the MKSS and other people at the sit-in began to line up behind the chariot. The state and the police had prepared well for the visitor, with two jail vans full of policemen and policewomen and many on motorcycles to go along with the cavalcade! Suddenly, Shankar emerged from behind the tent in the popular attire of the politician Rajvani and got on to the chariot, and the procession began. The police, who had been ordered to ensure adequate arrangements, also swung into action.

There were policemen on motorbikes on either side of the chariot, absolutely unaware of the sarcasm or the fact that the joke was on them. The chariot of scams had a song based on the tune of a popular Hindu bhajan, or hymn. Most of the people on the streets did not know what to make of the procession. Some joined thinking it was a religious procession, until they heard the words and looked closely at the procession. Some thought it was a political rally by some poor candidate. Most misconceptions were dispelled within a few minutes, when the procession stopped and Rajvani addressed the crowds. His speech, full of political satire and extraordinary wit, and based on the real condition of India, was a sell-out. People listened spellbound, and applauded, in most cases joining the procession, and often following it with a visit to the dharna. The Ghotala Rath also collected money in donation. The government found itself helpless to stop the spoof – it was not a roadblock, or a violent political protest breaking rules – what, after all, could they do?

The media loved the act, the common man was enthralled by it, and the administration was left seething, with no clue as to how to counter it, or how to stop its immense impact!

Rajvani (the voice of the state), the neta (Shankar acted out the absolute personification of a composite neta), celebrated the fiftieth year of scams, an endless list of remarkable achievements!

The politician on this rath was Shri Rajvani, who spoke the language of 'Raj' (administration/government). He described corruption as the soul of democracy and scams as his diet. On the rath, and on the umbrella above the head of the politician, the various scams (like urea, cement, cannons, tar, fodder, etc.) were described as 'achievements' of fifty years of independence.

Its magnificent success embarrassed the state government, not only in what it said, but the way it caught the imagination of the people and the press. The rath yatra was supported by the participation of other cultural groups and converted the forum of the dharna. It introduced a debate on the nature of information and democratic principles, and emphasized the role of people, ridiculing its doublespeak.

Unlike Beawar, Jaipur is a huge city; the dharna was near its official hub, but what about the common people? This chariot of scams could and did go to different localities every day. By the end of the fifty-three-day dharna, it had visited sixty-three enclaves and residential colonies of the poor, the rich, the middle class, the bustling old city, and the marketplaces.

The Ghotala Rath Yatra took the debate to the common people. All Indians are concerned and preoccupied by corruption and scams as they impact their lives. The access to simple and basic services is restrained and denied because of graft. This spoof on governance found a powerful response, intercepting the lives of ordinary citizens with a sharp commentary, and more importantly with an analytical and logical systemic solution. It helped start a dialogue on streets and street corners. Inspired as it was as a retort to immediate angst, it also critiqued, ridiculed and commented on the contemporary political rath yatras. It was a commentary on the interplay between religion and politics that many political rath yatras had used in a calculated manner to hegemonize and misuse traditional cultural symbols for gathering votes.

## The MKSS Diary

Wherever the yatra went, hundreds of people were at first curious, then surprised to see the parody and lampooning. Smiles spread as they got the meaning of the joke, which made them think hard. The dormant anger towards scams, scams-raj and corruption started getting articulated.

Rajvani would begin his speech with: 'Citizen friends! The scams (on the umbrella) which you see here are not scams, they are in fact the soul of democracy. This is the diet of the officers and politicians. Never let this diet reduce, in fact let it increase, so that the country becomes stronger. If the leaders of a country are weak, that country will also be weak, so keep feeding your leaders, don't let them get weak.'

A song that accompanied the rath was equally satirical and took the spirit of the religious overtones in the tune of the lyrics. The lyrics, however, were very different.

*Ghotala raj ki jai-jai bolo!*
*Jai-jai bolo, jai-jai bolo!*
*Bhrashtachar kar, hari-hari bolo!*

[Praise the corrupt state, sing praise to corruption]

The Ghotala Rath Yatra went to every part of Jaipur and toured all of Rajasthan and even other areas of the country, including Delhi, disseminating the message widely.

The parodying of topical political gimmicks like raths, yatras and false promises, establish immediate communication, and people feel an instant connect and respond with complete understanding. The common man has been taken for a ride and deprived of so many essential services and necessities because of corruption, nepotism, and misuse of democratic institutions. The rath drew an immediate response.

The rath yatra, the dharna, the media coverage, the large cross section that came and went, the huge banner which ran the length of the *shamiana* (tent) saying, '*Desh ki janta mang rahi sare paison ka hisab*', conceived by Sumir, brought increasing numbers of people to the dharna. The 'Pakhand Divas' or hypocrisy day was organized to condemn the government's doublespeak when CMs of the BJP-ruled states met in Jaipur to discuss governance. The RTI was also among its list of recommendations! It was a wonderful surprise for the thousands assembled on the day the dharna organized the 'Pakhand Divas' (25 June), to be fed by these chefs with mutter-paneer, in June! For the poor it is an expensive dish they can seldom eat. The MKSS area exports people to the 'dhabas'. Known as 'mistris', many are the 'chefs' of local cuisine. The 'chefs' decided that the workers were no less than the VIPs they served every day!

The identification of this method of communication and mobilization has been invaluable in the RTI campaign. As a tactic supporting our overall strategy, it has been a brilliant combination of many genres. The Ghotala Rath's ability to land anywhere and begin communication has given it a special place in the tactics used by the RTI campaign.

In the fifty-three days that the dharna sat in Jaipur, the public collection totalled Rs. 1,25,000 and contributions in kind, and a board displayed the exact amounts received and spent, and offered inspection and photocopies of all its accounts.

The relentless pursuit of asking for appointments continued. The aarti *Ragupati raghav* continued to be sung. The police continued to be belligerent and tolerant with the group. One day, the irate state secretariat issued orders for this to stop. The policemen on duty pushed the singers and tried to prevent the aarti. The protesters withdrew into the shamiana and sang and told stories to shame the policemen. Galku Ma was at her best. A day after, on Sunday morning, a huge posse of cops came to the shamiana. The people said, 'Lay off, the shamiana is our place, how dare you enter it?' The policemen folded their hands in namaste and began talking. The crowd shouted to say, 'Do not enter.' In response the policemen took off their belts, laid them on the grass and said, 'We have come to make peace and apologize. We have to obey orders. Please forgive us.'

Galku Ma, who appeared at the beginning of the chapter as a representative of the solid support of ordinary persons, was indeed extraordinary. She was a strong woman, progressive in her own context and a master storyteller. She must have told us a story every day – pithy, and sharp in its allegory and satire. The stories were of birds, mythical beasts and mostly those from the animal kingdom. Each story was a strong critique of contemporary politics. The oppressive chief minister, the chief secretary and the government made their appearance in the predatory animals like the crafty fox. She was a phenomenal success in generating the interest of the people. The policemen on duty, bored stiff, not only looked forward to her stories but began to request that she speak on the mike. Policemen and the dharnarthis shared a class and a common culture. Galku Ma became everyone's grandma and a mascot for the dharna.

Dhowba and Galku Ma, the kindly twosome, looked after everyone, to see that they were fed. The cooking took place behind the shamiana, well out of the sight of the passers-by. Dal and roti were cooked every day – the food was essential, the menu, a non-issue. Friends – Sharada Jain and Dr. Neelima Dhar, Kavita Srivastava's family, Sawai Singh and the Samagra Sewa Sangh, and numerous others – cushioned the dharnarthis in different ways, looking after their food and shelter.

Since the MKSS was protesting and could not be attacked on the usual grounds of foreign funds, Chief Secretary M.L. Mehta countered the protestors with veiled threats against the SWRC, a development voluntary organization, the director of which was Sanjit (Bunker) Roy, Aruna's husband.

> Renuka Pamecha had led a delegation to the chief secretary to demand that the assurance of disclosure of the Aruna Kumar Committee be honoured. He pointed to a three-foot pile of files and said, "Ask Aruna to lift the dharna; we are well equipped to proceed against the SWRC." Renuka said that this would not work to stop the demand and arm twisting tactics will be useless, in her typical forthright manner.
>
> When they came back to report on the mike this news startled and shocked everyone, to hear that such blatant threats could be used. Aruna went on the mike to say, "No one is above the law. If there is anything wrong, the law should take its course."[132]

The SWRC was visited by 'inspecting teams' three times that week. They responded by calling for a historic and courageous ethical exercise on 13 July 1997, what is now defined as a 'Transparency Mela or meeting'. SWRC's records of the ten years preceding 1996, including bank passbooks, accounts, files, Bunker Roy's personal and travel documents – all were set out in the panchayat of Buharu. A panel consisting of Justice Dinkarlal Mehta, MLA Gagdeep Dhankad, Dr. Sharada Jain, Bharat Dogra, L.C. Gupta, Sawai Singh, D.L. Tripathi, Ved Vyas, K.S. Subramanian, Marudhar Mridul, and many others heard the testimonies in front of thousands of villagers, who also testified. The government got its answer. The campaign evolved another mode with the SWRC in the holding of transparency meetings, where any organization that chose to be part of this ethical exercise could *suo motu* invite people to inspect their records. It was an important ethical win.

The significance of the RTI campaign is that, like all ethical campaigns, it demands of its proponents the same principles and practice that it demands of others. The Transparency Mela was a very important step, the first of its kind. The courage and honesty of the SWRC, a funded organization, was and continues to have a very important place in the history of the movement. It was an important occasion for everyone.

The dharna also organized a series of seminars and workshops, some in the dharna 'sthal' and others in different places. The Institute of Development Studies (IDS Jaipur) continually supported the theoretical and research needs of an issue of this importance. They organized many important seminars; one of the most significant was on the Maharashtra Rural Employment Guarantee Scheme and the need to extend it to the whole country. This began to place the articulation for work and wages, one of the predominant areas for seeking information, in the centre of another debate, and added to the already existing demand for the NREGA. They held seminars on rations, on the role of police, the environment, women's rights and labour.

The dharna decided to sit it out till 15 August if need be. The administration expected it to lift with the rains. But they did not bargain, thanks to the persistence of the protestors and the generosity of their supporters. John Singh of Anokhi generously donated a barsati tent which could outlast the monsoons and keep the protesters dry. As the storm clouds gathered, there was an interesting spectacle of rural protesters reconstructing the tent to make sure there would be no drainage. The AG provided shelter in the premises of his office, in the cycle stand and the use of its toilets for the women. In fact, the government press release was given to the protesters when they took shelter in the AG's office, as the photograph shows. There would be no better comment on the performance of the BJP-led Rajasthan government than the 'pandal' in Statue Circle.

This chronicle will not be fair unless it has a small comment on the role of civil servants. Friends in the civil service were afraid of being seen with the dharnarthis, including Aruna, an ex-IAS officer herself. Only a few came to the pandal. Bajrang Lal an old friend and supporter of ethics wherever he saw it in action and precept – and Sriniwas came in to stand with us in full visibility. Others invited Aruna to have ice cream on the opposite end to avoid being seen. This was not true of the Rajasthan subordinate service officers, who came and spent time in the pandal from time to time. Supported by the media, columns and reports raised the issue repeatedly with all its nuances. Ved Vyas wrote:

> **Jaipur's Government! Why don't you Speak?**
> The battle for getting the Right to Information did not start from any city or secretariat nor from the house of some writer, journalist or lawyer. It started from the small villages of a backward, illiterate and poor state like Rajasthan where the Bhagya Vidhata [Destiny Maker] of democracy toils hard day and night and carries the load of the sins of the panchayat contractors, officers and administration on his head. All the political parties talk of removing corruption and making it an electoral issue, but nobody wants to burn their hands to make up for making democracy believable. For the first time in the country, in Rajasthan, the rural movement for the Right to Information has risen with the slogan: "*Prashasan ki kya majboori, kyon nahin karte maang poori!*" [What is the administration's compulsion, why don't they fulfil our demands!] I found it all so meaningful that I am speechless. Among the labourers and peasants of villages when Bhanwar Gopal, Mohan ji, Chunni Bai, Gajanan, Balulal, Shankar Singh, Keli Bai and many others like them are singing just that one song on a ride in the capital – *Jaipur ki sarkar tu bole kyun ni re, mundo khole kyun ni re.*[133]

Delegations continued to meet the government and the pressure mounted. Harishankar Bhabra, the deputy chief minister, met a delegation in June. He called a meeting of the subcommittee and promised an order in July.

On 1 July in a surprising move, the deputy chief minister announced that the RTI was granted on 30 December 1996 with the amendment to the Panchayati Raj Act and rules. The government claimed that it had issued orders to more than fifty departments on the people's right to access documents. And on 13 July, the government fished out an older gazette notification to declare that the Panchayati Raj rules were indeed amended.

## The Gazette Extraordinary

As the MKSS moved into the 52nd day of its protest in Jaipur, the government conceded defeat. But it produced a six-month-old order amending Section 12 of the Panchayati Raj rules. This amendment ensured that people could inspect records from the panchayats and obtain photocopies within four days at Rs. 2 per page. The order was backdated, and the government tried to score points by stating that it had been passed before the MKSS dharna began, claiming that the sit-in was an attempt to discredit the government.

Quite unknown to everyone, there was an internal process to redo the rules in the Panchayati Raj Department. What did happen was that on 6 April 1996 an order of the chief secretary M.L. Mehta gave the right to inspect when the MKSS had sat in protest in Beawar, wanting photocopies of documents promised by the chief minister. But this order was incorporated into the Panchayati Raj rules, giving rights to copy – it was a gazette notification that no one saw or knew of. When the government was trying to address the issues of the dharna in Jaipur in 1997, the older gazette notification was discovered and the government declared that the campaign was feigning ignorance of a notification already in the public domain. The gazette notifications are a colonial gesture of informing the public at large. But they remain the most hidden of public notices and people, in this case even officers, remained ignorant of it! In fact, this notification was not seen by a majority of the people within or outside the government. It was like a party charade, to claim performance and yet not deliver.

The existing rules already allowed Panchayati Raj information to be accessed in four days. When this was read in conjunction with the newly incorporated amendments, it automatically applied to copies of documents in the public domain. This was an administrative mess and an ironic situation was born out of it. But the government could not ignore it, and had to retract from its position of denial. Not only did the government retract, but it placed the blame on the protesters, accusing them of prior knowledge of the notification and a deliberate attempt to gain political mileage, 'brownie points', by staging the dharna.

In hindsight, if this had happened earlier, the notification would have been a more limited one, allowing fewer concessions to the campaign. What the dharna forced the government to do was to extend the access to public documents and get copies in four days.

The campaign later came to know that Justice V.S. Dave, who headed the Law Commission in Rajasthan, was summoned by the chief minister late one evening to his residence. He was surprised to find a large number of vehicles Parked outside and found the cabinet assembled there. The CM asked one question, 'What is your opinion on the demand of the "dharnarthis" on the right to know and giving them photocopies of bills, vouchers and muster rolls?' As Justice Dave recounts that he unequivocally said, 'I support the dharna... RTI is inherent in the constitution'. (In a recorded conversation with Aruna Roy, Nikhil Dey on 11.6.2016)

**Press Conference on the Gazette Extraordinary**

The press conference held on 15 July was an exchange of comments and queries among all present. The mystery of the predated notification and its sudden appearance mystified everyone. But there was a general sense of jubilation as the demand had indeed been met. The Panchayati Raj rules were amended and papers could be accessed at the local level. The battle that began in 1994 reached the threshold of partial success. But even in the victory, future battles were clear. Tamil Nadu had passed an RTI legislation on April 1997, and Goa too had its legislation passed on 30 July 1997. However, the state that began the struggle was still battling and had managed to just get the Panchayati Raj rules amended. The road ahead was clearly mapped.

Vijay Diwas, 16 July, was a day of jubilation. The thousands who had been coming and going came once more to Jaipur to form a rally to Badi Chowpad, in the heart of the old city, and then to the Vidhan Sabha or assembly. The rallying call was that the 'tatpunjas' had won, answering the mocking comment of the neta in Bikaner. Harsh Mander and Justice Dinkarlal Mehta addressed the gathering at Badi Chowpad. The thela party wrote a special song and there was a sense of contentment that comes when logic prevails.

On a reflective and theoretical note, this phase established that the Indian democratic texture was capable at least of thinking about transparency and accountability and conceding under pressure to make it a part of governance.

This ended a major phase of the RTI campaign and movement. The fifty-three days in Jaipur again allowed the issue a focused attention. It was political education for the people in Rajasthan as well as other states. It offered a daily fare of stories and incidents for the media. It supported regular seminars and workshops on employment (the beginnings of the renewed NREGA demand), the discussions on drought (the birth of the Akaal Sangharsh Samiti, and the beginnings of the Right to Food Campaign), and many more. The fifty-three-day dharna fulfilled a major obligation of the campaign to educate itself and the people about the basic nature of the role of transparency and accountability in influencing policy, legislation, and governance in all its aspects. This echoed the call for RTI as the tool for real independence and sovereignty that began in Beawar, voiced by Nikhil Chakravarty, as the second war of real independence. In contemporary India the slogans of '*Hum bhook se mange azaadi, bhrashtachaar se mange azaadi,*' etc., have taken this into the popular folklore of slogans and people's struggles.

CHAPTER SIXTEEN

# NCPRI and the State Laws

The campaign grew organically, surprising even its members with its reach and the maturity of people's understanding of what could have been a complicated law. The songs and skits helped transfer this understanding into the language of the people.

This MKSS struggle gave birth to, defined and addressed a growing understanding of democratic governance among the poor. The most obvious takeaway from the struggle was that transparent governance had a direct link with the delivery of all services, that it would encourage democratic participation and help make informed choices. The other was the recognition that processes, through which legislative tools like laws are designed, also need to be scrutinized and evolved by citizens. Ordinary people see the law and the lawmaking process with respect and awe but feel alienated by it. The language and the idiom of the law are such that they keep commonsensical understanding at bay. The significance of the details of the law is incomprehensible to most lay people. The elite know its implication, acquire familiarity or hire skilled assistance to control the lawmaking process and define its content. The people, because of non-involvement, surrender control over its process and content, and remain very often at its mercy.

Aruna Roy recalls in the collective's diary:

> When I was young, I saw law as a boring necessity. My family of lawyers discussed issues that seemed too exclusive to draw the

> listener in. Three generations preceding mine were members of the profession. The "tomes" which contained "my rights" did not invite me to interact. The real importance of the law and the legal process slowly became clear when I began to work with people, first in government and then outside. When we began to ask for information, the web of laws, regulations, some inherited from British India, which were often quoted to deny us our rights. This made me realize that the times were very relevant and that my dismissal of them childish.
>
> The Official Secrets Act, for instance, has not been repealed by any government in independent India. I shared this understanding thereafter with all the persons I met. If this was the predicament of a person with literacy and access to the "best of education" – in the real sense of the term – how could the ordinary citizen be made a part of the process?[134]

In history, the demand for transparency and accountability in governance was not something new, nor was the MKSS discourse the first to table the issue. The contribution of the MKSS was in translating a somewhat esoteric issue into common idiom, and to make this demand the main and only focus of the campaign. It drew on and shaped the ordinary person's perception of a solution to the persistent twin evils of corruption and the arbitrary use of power. The MKSS with the help of Tripurari Sharma worked on a street play called *Khazana* in the latter half of 1997. The play was to expand on the theme introduced by the Ghotala Rath Yatra. It was an allegorical play on contemporary Indian governance.

*Khazana* – Treasure: As described in the MKSS Diary:

> The play is simple but very strong and successful in its message, and very good theatre, it attracts and holds people's attention throughout. A few persons discover a treasure chest. Their excitement knows no bounds as they start exploring it. Their greed and lack of ethics is the allegory of the story of governance. The treasure belongs to the people but the three knaves – the Responsible, the Informed and the Keeper, begin to loot and misappropriate the treasure of the people.
>
> Citizens come to demand help from the treasure in times of distress. The three knaves, now the ruling elite, define and create and recreate bunches of lies and deceit to ward them off. The people

> want to see the treasure. They also want to know the details of how this vast treasure was depleted. The machinations of the elected leaders and the bureaucracy are exposed. The citizens now mobilize to demand to know the truth, details hidden behind the miasma of words and statistics.
>
> The concluding part is a confrontation between the citizens and the power elite using the tug of war as motif. The question asking for what the government does is suppressed with, "You have no right." The people persist with, "We want information." The response is, "We will not disclose it." Citizens demand answers; the dogged response is, "Forget it, you will not get it." Finally, the citizens demand the Right to Information. The finale is "The Official Secrets Act forbids us". The actors turn to the audience and ask, "What do we want?" This led to some of the best interactive sessions with flash crowds gathered by the Ghotala Rath Yatra.[135]

Let us look into the debates that had been ongoing for years. During the 1960s, the government had also set up a committee to tackle corruption.

Lal Bahadur Shastri set up the Santhanam Committee on the Prevention of Corruption in 1962 and reiterated the 1950s' debates on the disclosure of income tax assessments and personal assets, extending it to the bureaucracy. The Committee recommended that in matters that are 'important to citizens in their day-to-day affairs', the government should make a clear distinction as to what information should be treated as 'secret' and what should be made freely available to citizens. However, it was during the Bihar Movement and the struggle for Total Revolution (1973–74) that the veteran Gandhian socialist, Jayaprakash Narayan, gave the clarion call to the nation to 'end corruption in day-to-day life and politics' (Bipin Chandra, 2003: 2). For the first time, the agenda of corruption and dysfunctional government gained national salience. Soon after, Indira Gandhi declared the Emergency.

Many judicial pronouncements talked about the right of common citizens to know. Apart from debates in the political and bureaucratic arenas, the Supreme Court in the mid-1970s interpreted the right to information as 'part of the right to free speech and expression under Article 19(1)(a)'.

While hearing a petition challenging the election of the then prime minister Indira Gandhi on account of electoral malpractices, Justice K.K. Mathew interpreted the 'fundamental right to speech and expression' in the following terms:

> The people of this country have a right to know every public act, everything that is done in a public way, by their functionaries.... The right to know...is derived from the concept of freedom of speech.

The Supreme Court, once again in 1982, while dealing with a case relating to judicial appointments, observed:

> The concept of an open government is the direct emanation from the right to know which seems to be implicit in the right to free speech and expression guaranteed under article 19[1][a]....

Fearing a similar incident in a fertilizer factory in Delhi in the aftermath of Bhopal, an environmental action group called Kalpavriksh moved the Supreme Court, 'asking the Court to lay down the right to information as a fundamental right'.

Following the Bhopal Gas Disaster in 1984, a growing concern over the lack of transparency in the regulation of risky industries led the environment movement in India to play a significant role in advocating for a public right to information. The anti-dam movement, working with the adivasi (tribal) communities, similarly failed to obtain information from the government regarding the impact of dam projects, such as the Sardar Sarovar, on the villages in the Narmada Valley. Likewise, workers on drought relief works were repeatedly denied access to government records.

In their fight against the state, various democratic struggles quickly discovered that this lack of access to information created a major hurdle. The relevance of and the need for government information became frustratingly apparent for the jan sunwais and other rights-based campaigns and grassroots struggles. Information – whether pertaining to minimum wages, the whereabouts of missing persons, or the dispossession and displacement by big dams – appeared integral to any struggle resisting the arbitrary exercise of coercive state power (symbolic and physical). Though the demand for a right to information law intrinsically linked the demands of all progressive campaigns for social justice and equality, the NCPRI finally articulated this demand and galvanized a campaign around it. In 1990, V.P. Singh as prime minister of the United Front Government stressed the importance of the right to information as a legislated right and initiated the process of drafting of the law.

## An Evolving Strategy: Advocacy and the Law

Over the years the MKSS had initiated creative tactics to engage citizens in a movement for RTI. The strategy of engaging and mobilizing interest at the grassroots provided the campaign with the legitimacy and strength to carry the movement forward. The MKSS knew from the very beginning that a national legislation alone could impact and bring real change in people's access to information and meet their demand for accountability. Prabhash Joshi, Harsh Mander, Ajit Bhattacharjea and many others in their several ways sought to push this agenda in urban India, where the centres of power were situated. The dialectic between the MKSS struggle and the NCPRI advocacy for the law was tangible and real, based on accepted principles and processes. As the movement gained momentum, this relationship became the basis for new strategic learning on understanding the fundamental process of lawmaking and relating it to the real concerns of people in a democracy, to make the law reflect and reason out their concerns. This was a crucial process, because the law was then owned by the people. This involvement with lawmaking fundamentally sustained people's participation in the many battles with the government to prevent the dilution of law.

The grassroots political struggle defined and spearheaded the RTI campaign. The struggle needed to take the leap from being a specific local engagement to demanding a law, an entitlement. In Rajasthan, the MKSS had worked to have the Panchayat Act amended. What about the rest of India? To make the transition from the specific to the universal required that the idiom, mode and involvement of the campaign become wider. The need for lawyers, draftspersons, legal assistance, media, and other groups became important.

The lawmakers and the grassroots struggle continued to dialogue in an innovative and creative manner. People could define the need for a law and its non-negotiables, but the skills of drafting the law needed some special expertise. Yet, there was an implicit understanding that people were the users of the law, and therefore needed to be involved in the making of it. The momentum and energy also came from the people. The MKSS campaign used the dharna and the street corner meeting to take the law to the people and get their feedback. In every town, the campaigners also met special groups equipped with skills - lawyers, academicians and others interested in the issue of transparency and corruption. The draft bill was discussed in detail and many amendments made to the provisions. It was then handed to the specialist groups, who put it together in the legal framework required for legislation.

### Introduction to the Law

As it has been recorded earlier, the NCPRI was created in 1996. One of its primary objectives was to draft the law. The NCPRI's mandate was to work towards drafting and campaigning for effective legislation to be passed at the Centre (in Parliament) and in the states. It was also committed to support people's struggles and groups agitating for accessing relevant information and records. From 1996 onwards, RTI laws were enacted in the states of Tamil Nadu (1996), Goa (1997) and Madhya Pradesh (1998).

### The Official Secrets Act

According to Suchi Pande's PhD thesis, *The right to know, the right to live: Grassroots struggle for information and work in India*:

> Thirty years after the 1962 China War, the OSA remained a significant tool in the hands of state functionaries at all levels to maintain secrecy. For example, at a workshop organised by the government on compensation for victims of the Bhopal gas disaster, "participants who took notes at the workshop were arrested under the provisions of the Official Secrets Act" (Laxman, Mander and Joshi). There were also cases of "disappearances" in insurgency-affected regions like Kashmir and Northeastern States. Family members of several missing persons, mostly young men – had no way to obtain information from the armed forces of the Indian state about the whereabouts of their family members.[136]

Most important of all, the campaign also realized that there was a need for an entitlement to set aside the Official Secrets Act after India obtained Independence in 1947. Each successive Indian government found the law useful in suppressing efforts at transparency. This process gave an opportunity to progressive and committed people in other parts of India and other paradigms to come together to form the NCPRI. The first effort to draft the law was made, ironically, at the Lal Bahadur Shastri National Institute for Administration, the training school for the bureaucrats. The effort to take the drafting process further was spearheaded by the Press Council of India, headed by an ex-justice of the Supreme Court, Justice P.B. Savant.

The Press Council bill sent to the state governments was met with different treatments. The states of Tamil Nadu and Goa passed acts. The Goa Act was much closer to the original draft of the Press Council and more people-oriented.

The Madhya Pradesh government presented its bill to the president of India for assent. Soli Sorabji, then attorney general, advised the president not to sign on the assertion that it was a central subject and therefore not within the purview of the state legislature.

In Rajasthan, the congress government, formed at the end of 1998, requested the campaign to draw up a draft bill. The campaign went to the divisional headquarters and spent two days in each place, discussing and amending the bill. The bill only dealt with state subjects and in the campaign's view it was therefore within the competence of the state government to pass its own bill. The debate about the attorney general's opinion continued.

In 1997, following the efforts of the divisional commissioner in Bilaspur, the Madhya Pradesh government implemented the right through a series of orders, still in force, whereby people could access information related to over forty departments. The collector of Sarguja district reported that in the public distribution system, for instance, the mere comparison of the register with the ration card had helped save black marketing and allowed the administration to double the consumers' ration quota.

## Push from International Financial Institution

> With a dramatic shift to open up the economy in 1991 came the added pressure for "good governance" from international financial institutions [IFIs] like the World Bank, the International Monetary Fund [IMF], and the Asian Development Bank [ADB]. The IFIs shaped the transparency agenda for many developing countries by making transparency and accountability mechanisms one of their

loan conditions. There was also an evolving international trend at this time to enact Freedom of Information laws [Florini, 2007; Banisar, 2006].[137]

## Implementing Access to Information Laws in the Early 1990s

An inter-ministerial task force was set up in 1991 to examine the feasibility of enacting a Right to Information Act. The task force visited the UK, Canada, Sweden and the USA to learn from their experiences with designing and implementing Freedom of Information laws. By the late 1990s, several state governments agreed to improve transparency in the functioning of government by passing right to information laws. By 1997, increasing pressure from loan agencies compelled state governments to enact right to information laws. For instance, according to NCPRI activists, the state of Karnataka received an unofficial communication from the ADB endorsing the creation of an RTI law.[138]

## Tamil Nadu

The state of Tamil Nadu was also under pressure from the Asian Development Bank [ADB] for bringing in the RTI law, and the ADB made the enactment of a transparency law a "precondition of loans for sector specific spending". In the case of Tamil Nadu, S. Guhan, from the Madras Institute of Development Studies, was an important advisor to the Tamil Nadu chief minister. He invited MKSS activists to Chennai after the Beawar dharna [in 1996] and said he "would try to ensure that a RTI law was passed". Tamil Nadu was the first state to enact a state Right to Information law but political opportunism resulted in a weak law. Despite efforts of concerned citizens such as S. Guhan, a statement made by the former state chief information commissioner for Tamil Nadu reveals the inefficacy of the laws springing from the state's limited transparency agenda. Referring to the Tamil Nadu RTI Law of 1996, he remarked:

"[the Act] became a secret almost as soon as it was passed [the law was not adequately and/or appropriately publicised by the state government]...besides the concerned Secretary to government

> could deny any request for information, deemed not in public interest, and sweep matters under the carpet."[139]

## Government of India

> The Central government, however, in line with the "good governance" agenda, thought it sufficient to introduce a few insubstantial measures. Even a request made by the Parliamentary Standing Committee discussing the Freedom of Information Bill in 2000 fell on deaf ears. With the international financial institutions advocating for the RTI laws, "transparency" and "accountability" had become the buzzwords within the corridors of the state. But the nature of transparency discourse arising from within the government was markedly different from the demands for accountability and transparency raised by the transparency struggles outside. While the state only echoed the neoliberal "good governance" agenda for public disclosure or "access" to information, the civil society demanded something as concrete as a legal right to information enshrined in law.[140]

## Definitions

Suchi Pande, who had worked as secretary, NCPRI, and lived through parts of the struggle for the RTI, went on to do a PhD, validating the process. This book draws from her experience and analysis.

> It is important to recognise that there was substantial conflict between the ineffectual "good governance" reforms pursued by the state at the advice of IFIs and the demands for a deeper and more social justice-oriented transparency emerging from civil society. NCPRI reflected the latter: it emerged to fulfil the growing public demand to guarantee all citizens the ability to hold public officials accountable in a meaningful way and on a daily basis. Thus, very different commitments grounded NCPRI's interesting in an RTI law. Indeed, as Baviskar [2007:20] argues, the World Bank and other IFI propagated "top down accountability" mechanisms did little to make the states accountable to its poorest citizens. The NCPRI leadership, she notes [2007:20], was "careful to distance itself from the neoliberal demand for transparency".[141]

It is important to put the emerging role of international financial institutions (IFIs) in context. The 1991 economic liberalization brought with it – among other things – the added pressure for 'good governance' led by IFIs like the World Bank, the International Monetary Fund, and the Asian Development Bank. While there was an evolving international trend to enact transparency laws, the transparency agenda for many developing countries was shaped by IFIs that made transparency and accountability mechanisms one of their loan conditions. Often these meant reducing the state's welfare role/function, and replacing vital functions and delivery of basic services with private, non-state actors.

But, while non-state actors were exempt from any public scrutiny, the IFIs also did not hold themselves up to the same standard of scrutiny that it required of sovereign national governments. The World Bank's disclosure policy was quite limited in breadth and scope of disclosure or access to information. Top-down accountability mechanisms pushed by IFIs manipulated policy processes of democratically elected governments in most developing countries, but they were also hypocritical – those same standards of transparency and accountability were absent from their own processes.

Though right to information appeared to be a universally desirable right, and with economic liberalization 'transparency' and 'accountability' had become buzzwords in the corridors of power, there was a fundamental and substantive difference in the demands for transparency inside the state, those pushed by IFIs, and those raised by grassroots struggles. While under pressure from IFIs the national and state governments began to value RTI as a means to 'good governance', NCPRI demanded something more concrete – a legal right to information. The NCPRI took the campaign into the arena of advocacy and framing of law. The bill, known as the Press Council Draft, was sent to the Lok Sabha (Parliament) and all the state governments for consideration.

The state laws, notwithstanding the pressures of the IFIs, managed to make India's RTI movement a homegrown battle for greater democratic participation in governance, and for people's right to monitor their own well-being. The slogans 'the right to know, the right to live', and 'our money, our accounts' called the bluff of the international agenda bent on pushing reform.

CHAPTER SEVENTEEN

# The Second Set of Jan Sunwais

The second set of jan sunwais were held after the limited success of access to information and the disclosure of government documents. It was time, in one sense, to come back to the actual and take matters in one's own hands.

These jan sunwais began in January 1998 in Rajasthan, with the significant success of the amended Panchayati Raj rules. This amendment made it possible for the ordinary citizens in the village to access information from the panchayat on all its work, including bills, vouchers and muster rolls of public works. In the jan sunwai held subsequent to the changes in the Panchayati Raj Act after the 1997 dharna, officers from the administration were present. The authenticated information was made available, though with difficulty, and there was a reluctant acceptance by the authorities that transparency had in fact come to stay.

Narayan of the MKSS and resident of Devdungri, whom we met in the initial chapters, played a significant role when the MKSS applied for information on public spending in three panchayats near Devdungri. He writes:

> I remember that we [the MKSS] applied for information from three panchayats – Kukarkheda, Barar and the newly formed panchayat of Kushalpura in which the village of Devdungri is located. We got the information quite easily. We went verifying or auditing physical and tangible details of works claimed to have been completed. In

Doothalav, Barar panchayat, we found that old stones near the site were used for an anicut or check dam, but there were false bills. We also found that the claim of having supplied forty bags of cement was not true. It was "farzi". In Hammalon ki Wer, we found that three students had been marked in the muster roll of a work on building a road, and also had been marked as attending school.

Kukarkheda had a personal issue with me. Basanta Devi, the Sarpanch, was my classmate. She also belonged to the same sub-caste, what we call "gothra", as me. We are both *apavath*, a sub-grouping of the Rawats. After failing to persuade and prevent me from accessing information and organizing the jan sunwai with the MKSS, she went to the *jati* panchayat, and made them hold a meeting at the "Challis Mil ka Chauraha" [a crossroad, at the milestone which marked 40 miles from Beawar], very close to Devdungri. About 400 people assembled there. The issue was to excommunicate me and Jait Singh, Shankar's cousin in whose house Shankar, Nikhil and Aruna lived, from the community. The attempt failed as the group split into two parts, with Kaletra supporting our participation. We had of course placed their embezzlements and non-performance before the panchayats.

In Kukarkheda there was a very interesting case. In the construction of channels or "naalis", a bullock cart was booked for transportation of sand and other building materials. In the verification we found that the person booked was away in Kathiawar [Gujarat] deepening wells for years. You can see his testimony in the film Anurag made and we showed it to the parliamentary standing committee. In Pavtia, the over-bridge was already constructed by people and it was cemented over but the whole work was billed. The RCC was not even there. In Kaletra, the missing work was alleged to have been buried by the sand storms. But there was no evidence either way. Neither we nor the anti-corruption department that came later to examine the case found any trace of it. Obviously, it was not built at all.[142]

All these testimonies were part of the Kukarkheda Jan Sunwai held on 9 January 1998.

Sarpanch Basanta Devi of Kukarkheda panchayat in Rajsamand district returned Rs. 50,000 against a fraud of rupees one lakh that the people confirmed when development works of the last three years were evaluated by them in the jan sunwai. She planned to return the other Rs. 50,000 in two instalments in the next two months.

The panel of distinguished people included Prof. V.S. Vyas, director, IDS (Jaipur); Dr. Narainmurty, eminent doctor from NIMHANS, Bangalore; Shekhar Singh, environmental activist and professor at IIPA, Delhi; and Sawai Singh, an eminent Sarvodaya activist.

In *Bapu Kuti*, Rajni Bakshi writes:

> Eventually, on 15 July 1997, after over two years of struggle, the Government of Rajasthan finally issued a notification granting people access to copies of panchayat level records. For several months after that, district officials denied receiving the notification. So the Mazdoor Kisan Shakti Sangathan waited another six months. In January 1998 it held two public meetings, one at Kukarkheda and the other at Surajpura.
>
> The sangathan's triumph lay not merely in the fact of these public hearings where people came armed with xerox copies of relevant development records. The true test of its success was the smooth, polite and non-vindictive nature of the proceedings. Even as various frauds came to the surface, the guilty sarpanches were allowed to respond without heckling. Basanta Devi was compelled to admit, and apologize for, a fraud of one lakh rupees. She agreed to return the money to the panchayat's kitty.[143]

The second jan sunwai was held in Shankar's panchayat of Lotiyana, where he was born and grew up. Surajpura, the village where a tent was pitched for the public hearing, was a mere 500 yards away from the school where he studied. Information on public works was accessed from the three panchayats of Lotiyana, Surajpura and Rawatmal. This jan sunwai was held with the nostalgia of the extraordinary Gandhian finale of the Kukarkheda hearing. Quoting the MKSS Diary:

> None of us had expected the jan sunwai to end the way it did. Considering the build up to it Kukarkheda could have become confrontational and violent. Instead of that it ended with an acceptance of guilt and a return of Rs. 50,000 – half the embezzled amount – by the sarpanch in public view. It was a Gandhian ending in January.[144]

The Surajpura Jan Sunwai drew a lot of attention and interest. Having heard of the earlier dharnas and struggle, people came from as far away as Mumbai to participate as panellists and many came to observe the process. Two IAS officers, Santosh Mathew and Harsh Mander, also attended the hearing. Along with Ajit Bhattacharjea, eminent academician and activist Pushpa Bhave, Dr. Sharada Jain from the IDS, Ved Vyas, writer and journalist, D.L. Tripathi, an activist from Ajmer, Beawar's Kesrimal, veteran trade unionist, and many others were present. Beawar citizens and many others from all over Rajasthan too came to observe the process. Jean Drèze and Bela Bhatia were also there during the hearing.

The MKSS for its part had become more skilful in accessing and collating information. Facts that the jan sunwai had unearthed recorded different methods used to defraud people of their right to development. The information sheets, for instance, of the muster rolls made no sense unless the rolls of all the neighbouring panchayats were compared for the names of persons working in the same period. It was discovered that six masons had their names in three different muster rolls in three panchayats for the same period and on the same days. This was an undeniable proof of fraud. The panchayats argued that the masons worked in eight-hour shifts and moved from one panchayat to the other. This was clearly an impossible task as what it implied was that the masons worked continuously for twenty-four hours. If it were not for the seriousness and the mal intent, here was a script for a farce.

In Rawatmal, the irrigation channel was constructed only on paper. The work was a complete fraud. Both the panchayat and the irrigation department quarrelled, each claiming that it was their work.

Like Kukarkheda, the sarpanch of Surajpura, Om Prakash Darzi, admitted defalcations and paid back 1,14,000 rupees. The Lotiyana sarpanch, Kanku Devi, the wife of a deputy superintendent of police (a distant relation of Shankar's whose actions he opposed) was debarred from standing for elections again. Chhaggan Singh, the sarpanch of Rawatmal, was proceeded against by the anti-corruption department. He agreed to return the embezzled money, an established fraud of 1.5 lakh rupees, to his panchayat in Ajmer district. The sarpanch of Surajpura in Ajmer also agreed to return the money – established fraud of 5 lakh rupees.

The process of public auditing kept improving and adding new dimensions in understanding the various ways in which people are defrauded. The British say that the devil lies in the details. So it does. But the way to its discovery needed an understanding of documents and papers, and to learn methods to read and collate them. The MKSS took this mechanism as a challenge and kept evolving and recording ways in which this process could be shared. Much later the social audit process gained from this understanding and meticulous recording of the process.

Nikhil and Kavita worked round the clock to get the participants from outside, and managed to get an impressive set of panellists. Shankar, Narayan, Lal Singh and all others in the MKSS orchestrated accessing information and the huge job of collating it. Among all the other eminent people who came was V.P. Singh, former prime minister of India. The MKSS got to know that he was actually in Rajsamand district visiting his 'sasural', i.e., in-laws. They also heard that on the 19th he would be driving to Ajmer, crossing, Surajpura where the public hearing was due to be held, on the NH-8 connecting Deogarh, where his in-laws lived, with Ajmer and further to Delhi.

V.P. Singh was the only prime minister to have attempted to bring in an Information Access or RTI law, and was of special interest to the MKSS and the NCPRI. It was decided that Aruna would call V.P. Singh's brother-in-law, Nahar Singh, to see whether the former prime minister could drop in, 'just for a few minutes'. To use the local idiom, the request was '*do minute ke liye padharein*'. And he agreed to drop in, adding another dimension to this jan sunwai. Over a period of time, he became an interested and strong supporter of the campaign, and was invaluable in the final negotiations for the law.

> As he descended from the Ambassador car leaving his wife to wait, he said, "*Jan Sunwai bahut accha naam hai. Is desh mein sunwai hi toh nahin hoti hai.*" When Sewa Ram, a supporter of the campaign since the 1996 Beawar dharna, tried to garland him, he refused and said these were unnecessary gestures. It made to the front page of the *Rajasthan Patrika*. He also said, "*Raja maharajaon ke time par, raja praja par nigrani rakhte the aur poochte the ki kaam kaisa hua aur kya hua. Aaj raj ka tareeqa badal gaya hai. Praja raja hai to karmchariyon se sawal karna hi padega.*"

Mamta Jaitley, long-time friend and comrade since the Sohangarh days, and editor of *Ujala Chadi* for the neo-literate, had this to say:

> A new history was written in the Magra region [Jawaja, Bhim] of Rajasthan. Two public hearings took place here on 9 and 19 January. The sarpanches themselves admitted the embezzlement of the money for developmental works. The sarpanches apologized to the people. Three sarpanches accepted their mistakes and returned the money. Basanta Devi of Kukarkheda deposited one lakh rupees in the panchayat funds during the public hearing. Chhaggan Singh, sarpanch of Rawatmal, deposited 1,50,000/- rupees in the panchayat funds a few days after the public hearing. Five lakh rupees were embezzled in Surajpura. Sarpanch Om Prakash Darzi accepted responsibility for scams in twelve construction works and deposited 1,14,000/- rupees in the panchayat funds.
>
> Scams have been taking place in development works for quite a while but last year the people waged a long struggle. Rajasthan government made transparency of bills, vouchers and muster rolls a legal entitlement by amending the Panchayati Raj Rules. Because of this entitlement evidence of scams surfaced for the first time. The MKSS representatives took photocopies of bills and vouchers by going to panchayats. After getting these, they verified all works, enquired from the workers, talked to the suppliers of the construction material and so on. They collected all the evidence, and that's why the sarpanches had to accept the scams.[145]

Apart from other significant learnings, these hearings challenged the assumption that identity politics is the biggest constraint to ethics in public life. Kesar Singh challenged this jati panchayat, as did Narayan. Both emerged unscathed and were able to present a basic ethical issue which overcame the role and pressure of jati or community. For Shankar it was not jati so much as family. The family of Kanku Devi and the deputy superintendent of police, the petty power elite of Lotiyana, continued to harass Shankar's family for some years.

Public hearing has become a common method for addressing larger issues of hunger, displacement, and other rights across the country. The dialectic is never a clean and tidy process, especially since those engaging in it use completely different paradigms. Facts help overcome more parochial interests. Yet there is a need to go beyond clearing the confusion, beyond information, towards participatory democracy.

CHAPTER EIGHTEEN

# The Rajasthan State Act – An Intermediate Success

In 1998, during the state elections, the Congress, then the opposition party in Rajasthan, promised in its election manifesto that if they came to power, they would enact a law on the right to information. As it happened, the Congress won the elections and the newly formed government assumed office in 1999. The MKSS and the NCPRI met the new chief minister, Ashok Gehlot, to demand implementation of its promise and to bring in an RTI law. Prabhash Joshi and Ajit Bhattacharjea, members of the NCPRI, came repeatedly to engage with the chief minister in pushing this demand.

On 11 January 1999, the NCPRI delegation met the new head of the state. He invited Prof. V.S. Vyas to head and set up a committee – an advisory group on the right to information. However, on 26 March, the government issued a notification constituting a committee of eight secretaries under the chairmanship of P.N. Bhandari, IAS and an additional chief secretary of the Rajasthan government, to draft a right to information law or rules. Professor Vyas was the only non-official member of this committee, and he declined.

The P.N. Bhandari Committee, included eleven members, all bureaucrats, was to examine the demand. On 29 March 1999, the NCPRI delegation met the chief minister again, demanding that the committee must also have public representatives and academics, movement activists and citizens. The chief minister refused to change the committee's composition but said that the government would ensure that the voice of the 'public' would be heard. On 6 April, the RTI committee issued a notice in all newspapers asking the public to send suggestions on the right to information.

The first term of reference for the committee was to decide whether the promise in the manifesto should be in the form of a law or an administrative order. The overwhelming unanimous response was for a law. During this period, Prabhash Joshi met the chief minister repeatedly to emphasize that the promise of a new law had to be met. When the Government Committee of Secretaries recommended that administrative orders would suffice and that a law was not necessary, there was loud protest both at the backtracking on the promise of a law (accountability) and at the committee's lack of transparency. The government reluctantly opened up the proceedings and included public consultation to discuss the draft. On 12 April 1999, the MKSS and NCPRI team was received as all bedraggled activists are – with contempt! The committee's opinion was that a law cannot be made by the state government as RTI falls in the Central government's ambit. They quoted Soli Sorabjee, attorney general, to this effect. The information levels of the scruffy group, as well as the thorough research and understanding of the background to the law, surprised the bureaucrats, who started seeing the bedraggled group with surprise and reluctant respect.

Two hours passed in debate. After the documents were laid out the secretaries had a separate conclave, and they came back with a suggestion that was astounding: 'You have more experience than we do. Why don't you prepare the first draft of an order?' They had formally asked the NCPRI to prepare a draft executive order, but this was not acceptable to the campaign. The MKSS and the campaign decided to take the matter up in the public domain. The MKSS and the NCPRI travelled once more on another truck yatra to all the divisional headquarters, all the districts where the MKSS worked as well as the remote districts of Ganganagar and Hanumangarh, bordering Punjab, with the draft law inviting responses and critique. This journey began on 19 April and the NCPRI (Rajasthan) agreed to conduct meetings all over the state and then present a draft law. It ended in May with the meeting in Jaipur when the NCPRI (Rajasthan) prepared a draft bill and gave it to the P.N. Bhandari Committee for consideration and comments.

> These consultations were varied and elicited interesting responses. For instance, in the meeting in Udaipur, a researcher who met the MKSS/NCPRI talked of the opaqueness in sharing ordinary information in accessing maps. Maps came under wraps prescribed for security documents. This was absurd as maps even then had become accessible through satellite imagery. The access to maps was basic to research. The highlight in the visit to Jodhpur was the meeting with the Bar Council. The two lawyers who helped with the organization of the meeting – Marudhar Mridul and Mahesh Bora – were supporters of the MKSS and the RTI, and had travelled the route with the campaign since 1994–95. The Bar Council unequivocally demanded a law and pledged to be a part of the struggle in case the state government withdrew from its promise of legislation. Komal Kothari had a special dinner for the yatris at his home with a discussion on the nature of governance and the impact on culture. His support to the campaign was important as he was an influential member of civil society in the city. He also facilitated discussions with *Rajasthan Patrika* in Jodhpur. Dr. Patwa helped with logistics and organized meetings with other concerned groups.
>
> The visit to Ganganagar and Hanumangarh was also stimulating. The culture of these two districts is highly influenced by Punjab; it was a more affluent part of Rajasthan. It had also organized worker groups that had to grapple with the demand for transparency and see it as integral to their demands for better working conditions and wages. It helped the campaign understand the other nuances of people's support for the RTI.
>
> In Bikaner, the discussions led to a greater understanding of Dalit issues and of their inability to access relevant information. The Valmikis fed the yatra and it was another step forward in breaking untouchability.[146]

This time the Ghotala Rath toured with the truck yatra. A collapsible thela was fabricated, and the props were packed in as well. Wherever the yatra went the Ghotala Rath managed to draw diverse groups of people into the debate. The street corner meetings and the interactions with people was supported by small discussions with people and the distribution of pamphlets to shopkeepers and bystanders. The message was spreading about the need for a law. The pace of the yatra gave people time to assimilate and question the draft, drawing them into the campaign.

Drawing on the input from these consultations, a draft civil society Right to Information bill was prepared, which was then submitted to the committee. The committee drew on the citizen's draft bill for its recommendations, but its final draft was weak and made it toothless. One of the major drawbacks was the absence of a penalty provision for non-furnishing of information. This echoed what happened in Delhi, when the H.D. Shourie Committee set up by the GoI diluted the Press Council draft.

*Ujala Chadi*, the newspaper run by Mamta Jaitley for the neo-literate, went into print:

> What we didn't get:
> Even after all this, there are many limitations in the law. Three issues are quite objectionable:
>
> - Information which adversely affects the relations between the Centre and the state/s can be denied.
> - How a decision was taken, which official of which department gave what comments [on a certain file], is written in the left of the files. These file notings have been kept out of the purview of disclosure. Corruption actually spreads by withholding such information.
> - The government can deny information on several grounds like the desired information is too general or too expensive to cull the information or too much time will be wasted in garnering information, etc.
> - Councils for RTI should have been established at the state and district levels to monitor and check the implementation of the law.
> - Those found guilty are to be punished as per the Service Rules. This method is too loose and time-consuming. There should have been a provision to fine errant officials [on a per day basis].
> - The provision of providing information within twenty-four hours on an issue concerning the right to life and liberty hasn't been openly accepted. It hasn't been made clear that the fee to get photocopies of the information should not be more than

the cost of photocopying. If the government wishes, it can charge a hefty fee for providing information and can prevent people by exercising this right.

Even despite all this, the enactment of this law is a huge achievement in itself, especially when there is no such law in the country.

Aruna Roy [MKSS] says, "This right is a mere station and not the destination. MKSS and NCPRI will examine the law in the coming days. They'll get information and find out the strengths and limitations of the law."[147]

The chief minister did not place the draft in the assembly for many months. It took the repeated pressure of the NCPRI members Prabhash Joshi and Ajit Bhattacharjea to push and make sure that the bill was tabled. The Rajasthan Right to Information Act 2000 was eventually passed on 1 May 2000 but came into force only on 26 January 2001 – after the rules were framed. The Act in its final form retained some of the suggestions of the RTI movement but diluted others. Activists in the state said it was stronger than some other state acts, like that of Tamil Nadu, but lagged behind those of Goa, Karnataka, and Delhi.

As reported in *Ujala Chadi:*

> The Rajasthan Assembly has ratified the law for a Right to Information. The people of the state have struggled for over five years to get this right. Enactment of this law is a victory of the people of the state. The Assembly has respected the rights and feelings of the people by enacting this law. The Governor is yet to give his assent to this law. This law is very important because:
>
> 1. Every citizen has been given the right to seek information regarding the work of any government or government-supported institution.
> 2. Photocopies of the desired information will be provided within thirty days [of applying for it]. The government has also assured on the floor of the house that in the case of exigencies information can also be provided within twenty-four or forty-eight hours.
> 3. Provisions have also been made in the law to punish the officials [as per the Service Rules] who deliberately conceal information.

4. An almost independent institution has been established to hear people's complaints at the state level which is called the Rajasthan Services Appellatory Tribunal.
5. The government has also accepted in-principle that they have to proactively disclose information in the areas of public interest.

   The MKSS, NCPRI and journalists had given many suggestions on the draft law that was presented in the Assembly. It is a matter of happiness that three out of these four suggestions have been incorporated in the law. The government has also assured to include the fourth one in the rules.[148]

Accountability, generally considered the next step to transparency, was seen as a parallel process by the campaign. It was therefore not addressed chronologically, but its concern went alongside. It was a dialectic which prepared and strengthened parallel concerns, feeding into and answering questions that were raised. It was clear that there was a fundamental connection between corruption and the arbitrary use of power. The campaign therefore did not delink corruption from other kinds of state misuse of power. This kept the campaign from succumbing to vulnerabilities in the internal debates on corruption or losing sight of other principles and values, like discrimination and misuse of authority to flout constitutional values.

The MKSS had lobbied hard for ward sabhas in the panchayats as the unit for planning and looking at the accounts of public works. The panchayat is often too large and spread out. The people know and can testify only about what they observe and know to be wrong. This was demonstrated in two experimental ward sabhas held in Kushalpura and in Bagmal, Rajsamand and Ajmer districts. The Kerala Shastra Sahitya Parishad (KSSP) had come on a visit to the MKSS to look at the method of monitoring works. The KSSP, with several other organizations from five states, among them SPS (Samaj Parivartan Sahyog) attended a special jan sunwai in Bhim. All this had educated the MKSS to feed the process (also used in the second set of jan sunwais) into the future sets of public hearings.

The assembly that passed the Rajasthan RTI Act in 2000 also amended the PRA to decentralize decision-making to the ward sabha as the unit for public audit/social audit. C.P. Joshi, then the minister for rural development, was convinced and supported this decentralized decision-making process.

The RTI campaign and the MKSS were now poised to use the new RTI law and put it to test.

CHAPTER NINETEEN

# The Challenge of Elections

**MKSS's Engagement with Panchayat Elections in Rajasthan**

Vijay Nagaraj joined the MKSS soon after his post-graduation from the Tata Institute of Social Sciences (TISS), Mumbai. In the three years he worked with the MKSS, he observed local elections and the complexity of its process. He writes:

> Elections to Panchayati Raj[149] bodies in India have not received the attention they merit despite their scale and significance. In sheer scale the elections to the three tiers of the Panchayati Raj system involve the participation of the largest number of people, both in terms of candidates and voters in this country. According to the Constitution of India's 73rd Amendment these local self-governments are the primary institutions through which people of India exercise their sovereign democratic power. That this significance is well appreciated by the people is evidenced by the fact that electoral turnout at level of the Panchayati Raj institutions across the country, in particular for elections to the village panchayats, is far higher than electoral turnouts for State Assembly or Parliamentary elections.[150]

Given the nature of corruption and misuse of power that the system responded to, it was inevitable that one way or the other people would begin to ask for transparency as an essential first step for an anti-corruption campaign. The uncomfortable question, 'Why don't you stand for elections?', and the more fundamental question, 'Whom should we vote for?' soon followed. These questions were addressed in part by the MKSS narrative and its engagement with elections. Some of those dilemmas still exist, notwithstanding the formation of the Aam Aadmi Party.

Folk stories are often used to encapsulate the complexity of political positions. The MKSS used the folk story of Kanda and Jooti, retold brilliantly by Vijaydan Detha, to explain the dilemma of an unethical political system. But the resolution was far away.

> Once upon a time there was a just Thakur [a chieftain] who believed that justice must be rendered transparently, and that even the criminal must be given a choice in the punishment meted out. One day a victim was brought and judged guilty. In his magnanimity the Thakur offered the person a choice. He could either eat 100 *kanda*s [onions] or be beaten 100 times on the head with a *jooti* [shoe] in the midst of the assembly. The man felt that eating the onions would be less demeaning in front of others. He ate a dozen onions and his mouth smarted and eyes watered. He thought he could not bear it any more. He asked to be beaten on the head. Half a dozen or more, and his scalp felt like pulp. He pleaded for a change back to the onions. In the end he was doubly punished. He ate the 100 onions and was hit on the head as many times!

The story is a telling narrative of the dilemma of electoral choices. Change occurs because of the causality of multiple interventions in a historical sense, plural in nature, affecting social change, legal entitlements and economic status. Writing of it, Vijay recalls:

> The MKSS first decided to engage with the Village Panchayat elections in a campaign mode in 1999 in response to critics who maintained that it was impossible to win panchayat elections and to administer a panchayat without engaging in some degree of moral trespass or corruption ubiquitously referred to as "adjustment". The MKSS fielded candidates for the post of sarpanch in three panchayats, two of whom won. The candidates spent less than rupees 1500 including their deposit amounts on the elections,

and campaigning on foot the candidates promised nothing except corruption free people's governance with total transparency, accountability, people's participation in decision making and social audit of their work. And true to their word that is exactly what they delivered. For instance, for the first time the people had the unique experience of having the muster rolls available for public display at the panchayat office to verify wage rates and attendance or of having meetings of the panchayat open to public or having meaningful Gram Sabhas.

**The Successive Engagement with Electoral Politics**

As elections approached, the MKSS was positioned like the victim in the folk tale – between the onions and the shoes! There was barely an apparent choice between the candidates who stood for the sarpanch elections. Almost all of them were rooted in the power elite, or were dummy candidates set up by them. Spending lavishly to win, and recovering money from the state coffers with impunity thereafter, was a pattern for which neither apology nor guilt followed as a logical corollary. The predicament was acutely felt by individuals and the community as a whole.

The MKSS, seen as a people's non-party political organization with integrity, was often asked to field a candidate. The intense discussions in Devdungri were mostly inconclusive because of the complexity of the ethical issue – intersected as it was by identity and money politics. The MKSS itself decided not to stand as an organization. Giving in to possibilities, the first set of candidates put up on an experimental basis by the MKSS were Lal Singh and Kalu in 1995. In 1999–2000, Narayan, Kalu and Tej Singh wanted to accept the challenge in what they felt was a changed scenario after the RTI struggle in Beawar and Jaipur and the formation of the NCPRI. The responses from the larger MKSS group were sceptical and ambivalent about possible success. Nevertheless, the candidates entered the arena. Thus, another chapter was added to the MKSS and the RTI, this time with reference to its engagement with electoral politics, to understand the complexity of the problems and the possibility of interventions. The narrative below takes the story further.

Before the RTI campaign had started full steam, the MKSS had, in 1995, persuaded Lal Singh as an experiment to contest for zila parishad member, Rajsamand, and Kalu for sarpanch from Vijaypura Panchayat, Rajsamand. Kalu, a Dalit, stood from a general seat and lost the elections by 125 votes, getting 460 votes and the second place. Kalu lost with dignity, because Vijaypura was grappling with the changing perception of leadership and controls through its understanding of transparency and accountability in land deals, and saw value in a different kind of leadership. Lal Singhji, who stood against a powerful lawyer, Shankarlal, lost his deposit. Lal Singhji went on his bicycle with pamphlets and covered his entire area. No more than 500 rupees on campaigning and no bribes! The zila parishad was still too remote for a village voter to comprehend its details. A contestant may be a familiar name, at best, but very often it was not even that. The party membership and its consequent politics also intervened in decision-making. The non-party contestant at the zila level had a distinct disadvantage. The power of money and the intrigue of caste and other identities were the frame of its realpolitik. Lal Singhji, who stood as a test case, lost and illustrated the point. Kalu stood in the area of his work and where he was well known. Lal Singh threw the net wide and had to struggle against identity, prejudice and anonymity. It spelt hope for panchayat elections but not for district-level representation.

What MKSS understood was simple and direct. Expectations from people and their perceptions are often boxed. The MKSS was an honest organization trying to change things around. It worked for rights-based action. The people were not quite sure, in fact dubious, whether it would indeed deliver in an electoral sense, where the system responded only to corruption and misuse of power.

> The elections to the village panchayat are particularly interesting in that they are not contested on a party basis.... This coupled with the localised nature of the elections means that there is an opportunity for individuals, the community, other interest groups and of course peoples' organisations like the MKSS to influence the process and the outcomes significantly. Being the foundation of the democratic polity of the country, an effective engagement with the political process at this level is also a logical first step for a peoples' organisation that is seeking a more substantive influence or role in other spheres of electoral politics.[151]

## The Second Round of Election Engagement, 1999–2000

In 1999–2000, the MKSS began to address the same questions again. But this was after it had consolidated its support in the area with the beginnings of the RTI campaign, the Beawar dharna, the drafting of the law, the truck yatras, and the formation of the NCPRI. After long discussions, the MKSS decided that the contestants would stand independently but would be supported by the organization. Strategically, the MKSS wanted to ensure the contestants were not disqualified because of their affiliation to it. And it wanted to maintain autonomy to continue the struggle despite members contesting elections to local government. The mandatory manifesto or *ghoshna patra*, promising transparency and accountability to the people, was laid down as non-negotiable. The MKSS manifesto, printed on one side of a flimsy yellow paper worth a mere 21 paisa each, on the one hand was perceived as a huge threat to the politics of wealth and inducement, and on the other broke through entrenched cynicism by forcing people to acknowledge that value-based politics and governance was possible, as was spending less than 1,000 rupees on their election campaigns. Some of the money was 'crowd funded', to borrow contemporary jargon.

> The "ghoshna patra" outlined an agenda for handing over the controls of the local government to the people. Prominent amongst the 24 points detailed in the agenda were issues relating to the payment of minimum wages, the people's right to information, accountability, participatory democracy, and finally a commitment to run an ethical and low budget election campaign.
>
> These were issues that had been popularly considered irrelevant, and impractical in a panchayat election campaign. If one looked at handbills that were put out by other candidates they would all ask for votes for the local "honest, hardworking, diligent, popular, pious, upright, capable...peoples candidates" ...a series of self-proclaimed adjectives. No issues, no agenda, no vision for the future. A few of the pamphlets might promise roads, handpumps, or schools, with the prior knowledge that the promises cannot be kept.

Narayan, from Kushalpura (Bhim, Block Rajsamand), Ram Singh (Badkochra, Jawaja Block, Ajmer), Teju (Todgarh, Ajmer), and Kesar Singh (Asan Panchayat, Jawaja Block) decided to contest for the post of sarpanch from their respective panchayats. Kalu contested for member panchayat (Vijaypura Panchayat, Deogarh, Rajsamand). Narayan spent 1,200 rupees on the elections and won by 200 votes. He became sarpanch for the panchayat in which Devdungri is located. From being a worker protesting for minimum wages in 1991, Narayan, a postgraduate degree holder, mature in his politics but young in his years, became sarpanch at the age of twenty-seven.

The campaigns were full of drama. Apart from the folklore around it, often discussed in the Devdungri kitchen and in the four districts where these elections heralded possibilities, the MKSS activists also wrote on it. Nikhil and Shankar recollect the campaigns, and in these stories lay the germs of future designs and the direction not only for the movement, but for local politics and governance. It detailed the mechanics of transparency and, therefore, the architecture of the legal framework. Fresh from campaigning for the MKSS candidates, they wrote:

> Ten kms apart in two radial directions were two…campaigns where MKSS workers were standing for elections. Kushalpura, in the neighbouring Rajsamand district, is the panchayat where the MKSS office at Devdungri is located. Here, a young full-time worker of the MKSS, Narayan, was taking on a former sarpanch, Tej Singh Rawat, and a recently retired official from the revenue department, Shanker Singh. There was a small but vociferous lobby of power brokers who were spreading the word that a vote for Narayan would be suicidal because the MKSS would not pay percentages at the BDOs and district offices, and therefore no work would be sanctioned. The MKSS and Narayan had during the last decade taken up issues of importance to the poor, through modes of struggle, but the people debated Narayan's efficacy in a corrupt and corrupting system, his frugal campaign style forced both the other candidates to maintain a level of decorum in their campaigning, but as the election date approached, it was the *katal ki raat*[152] that Narayan's supporters feared.

In Asan Panchayat of Ajmer district, another MKSS supporter, Kesar Singh, was battling to have the same manifesto make a strong impact on the traditional modes of dubious campaigning by the many other candidates in his panchayat. This was a panchayat where the MKSS had fought protracted battles to get access to panchayat records, and the sarpanch had been suspended on charges of misappropriation of funds. Yet, the former sarpanch and several other well-known petty crooks were distributing liquor and money, and the voters were being drawn into their paradigm. Kesar Singh was one of the eight candidates. Some had been paid to stand in order to cut Kesar Singh's votes.

The MKSS campaign was being watched in the whole area, but there were many panchayats where the lack of an alternative resulted in the old mix of traditional scenarios. Kukerkheda Panchayat, for instance, took on the ambience of a corrupted carnival as liquor was made available in unlimited quantities to whoever wanted it. As the polling date approached these kinds of measures grew more desperate.

In Badkochra Panchayat (Ajmer district), one of the leading candidates, Koop Singh, took a large group of people to the village temple under the pretext of providing a meal and got the priest to make everyone swear under religious oath that they would help Koop Singh win. In Sangawas, the former sarpanch Girdhari Singh set up a gateway in the main thoroughfare, got a pseudo-tantrik puja performed and advertised the fact that anyone walking through the gateway would be compelled by supernatural forces to vote for him.

Candidates anticipated symbols by looking up their names alphabetically and working out the symbol they would be awarded. Dummy candidates were put up to force someone else to get a bad symbol. The third and the fourth on the list – a cupboard and a radio – looked so similar they were bound to cause confusion. The sixth symbol – a boat – was quite alien to Rajasthan, and Bhanwar Singh, who was awarded the symbol in Jawaja, had to fish a boat out of the nearby talaab, mount it on a jeep, and drive it around day and night to ensure recognition.

The symbol is critical because it is awarded fifteen hours before voting at 4.00 p.m. The candidates have a couple of daylight hours and the night to wake up voters, including the large numbers of illiterate men and women, to explain to them where they must place their seal. Some voters are woken up several times by different candidates and the largest cash and liquor transactions are made at this time. This was the 'katal ki raat'.

As soon as the symbols were awarded in Todgarh, Nemi Chand's jeeps left for different directions sporting large banners of his symbol, the apple. Teju (Tej Singh) got a friend to take him on a motorcycle from village to village so that he could tell his supporters that his symbol was an aeroplane. He returned home at 8.30 p.m. to go to sleep, while Nemi Chand's vehicles continued to do the rounds. When the symbols had been awarded, Teju's supporters had used very graphic slogans – 'Teju will fly the aeroplane – the people will fill the fuel', 'Teju will become sarpanch – the people will rule the panchayat', and 'the battle is one of the rich vs the poor'. The question that night was whether this alliance of the poor would withstand and overcome the efforts of Nemi Chand's vehicles moving about all night.

The most difficult part of the MKSS campaign was to get voters to come on their own to the polling booth. Voters expect to be picked up and dropped. Some lived as far as 10 kilometres away. Nemi Chand's vehicles were plying, and Teju had made it clear that he had no money and no vehicle, and no intention of providing one. Many observers said this strategy would cost him dearly. This was perhaps the ultimate test of the voters' motivation and an occasion to gauge the extent of the impact of his campaign. Would the men and women come to vote on their own?

The crowd waiting for the election results was much bigger than before. The tension was also palpable as people kept repeating, 'Teju should win but will he win?' The results were announced just after 9.30 p.m. Teju was declared elected by what in panchayat elections is a comfortable margin of 175 votes – the crowd broke out into jubilant cries, and it was clear that most of those who had been anxiously waiting in the cold night for the election results were Teju's supporters. This had been a historic result. Teju in his short speech reiterated that in most matters he would function as a facilitator and would ensure that real power lay with the people.

Narayan also won his election in Kushalpura comprehensively, by over 200 votes. Kesar Singh lost in Asan Panchayat. Yet the real impact of these three candidates had been their ethical and extremely low-cost style of campaigning. Teju had spent a total of Rs. 850 on his campaign, and Narayan and Kesar Singh had spent just over a thousand rupees each on their campaigns. These were unbelievably low amounts of money in an election where several candidates end up spending over a lakh of rupees. The fact that two of them were elected showed that people were willing to support efforts where more ethical alternatives were provided. The MKSS electoral campaigns have had a tremendous impact in the entire area. However, there are as many questions as there are expectations.

A sympathetic electorate has provided support. But as many people in the area have asked, 'How will these sarpanches deal with the imminent battles with the more hostile and powerful people within the system? Will Narayan and Teju also get co-opted? Or is this the embryonic stage of the birth of a genuine alternative in panchayat and electoral politics in the area?'[153]

Vijay writes that the turnout for the 2000 panchayat elections in Rajasthan was about 71 per cent, compared to the turnouts of 58 and 51 per cent in the 2004 assembly and parliamentary elections respectively. The MKSS campaign focused on influencing the larger electoral political process rather than just seeking votes for the candidates that it was supporting. In keeping with this, the MKSS organized election meetings in places outside constituencies of its own candidates, and also sought to touch on a number of other issues. In contrast to others, the MKSS focused not on promises but on accountability. It sought to specifically spell out ways in which the candidates would be held accountable – making public and open all documents and decision-making, social audit, peoples' participation through ward sabhas, executing public works through people's committees, the formation of a vigilance committee and perhaps, most importantly, by spelling out the ethical standards that would be adhered to in the process. All this was then captured in a *janta ka ghoshna patra* (people's manifesto) that was publicly circulated in the form of pamphlets.

**The Third Round: 2005 (Post-Bori and Janawad Jan Sunwai)**

If the 1999 panchayat elections were an 'experiment' to prove a point, this time the MKSS engagement was more in the nature of a challenge both to the prevalent practice as well to popular perception regarding how elections are to be fought and contested/conducted.

Panchayat elections were due in Rajasthan in the last week of January and first week of February 2005. Voting for over 9,000 sarpanches and 1,10,000 ward panches was scheduled to take place on 31 January and 4 February 2005. Zila parishad and panchayat samiti elections were to be held on 29 January and 2 February. The MKSS had now been working in a few districts of central/southern Rajasthan for fifteen-odd years, where they had struggled to introduce transparency and accountability to make democratic institutions meaningful and effective for the poor and marginalized. These attempts were focused on their campaign for the right to information for a cleaner and accountable government. By contesting panchayat elections, on the basis of transparency and accountability, an attempt was being made to lay the foundations for ethical participation in the political process.

**On the Campaign Trail**

At a meeting in February 2004, the MKSS decided that it would further its previous attempts at participation in panchayat elections by fielding more candidates. This year some candidates who were MKSS workers and others who were being supported by them were contesting twelve posts for sarpanch in the districts of Rajsamand, Ajmer, Bhilwara, and Pali, and one panchayat samiti member in Ajmer district. It was also decided that these candidates would face the electorate with a 'people's manifesto' – a set of promises that had been arrived at collectively after a year of discussion on various issues of relevance in their region. This states the sangathan's stand on social issues such as child marriages, the custom of feeding the community after someone passes away, alcohol, and corruption. *The jan ghoshna patra* also stated that MKSS candidates and MKSS-supported candidates will not spend more than Rs. 2,000 on the campaign. The reason behind the MKSS keeping this expenditure limit, even though the official limit is Rs. 5,000, was to ensure that it is possible for the poor to participate in the elections. Their participation in local institutions is an essential step towards gaining control over the direction of development.

Kalu won with a substantial majority to become the sarpanch of Vijaypura, Deogarh Tehsil, Rajsamand district. Even more dramatic was the case of Vijayapura. Kaluram, a young Dalit supported by the MKSS, won this general seat securing a record 808 votes, spending a mere Rs. 695 on his entire election campaign. His nearest rival, who was reported to have spent at least Rs. 50,000, was a distant second with 441 votes.

In Vijayapura Panchayat, a day before the elections, the MKSS activists publicly challenged any candidate planning the usual pre-election night assault by announcing in village after village that full preparations had been made to ensure that their plans for the night were foiled. Large teams of young people were mobilized to keep vigil at night in some of the villages to ensure that liquor or agents with money did not enter. It was such public vigilance that ensured that in villages like Sangrampura (one of the largest in Vijayapura Panchayat) neither liquor nor money was distributed on pre-election night.

The assumptions made about the possibility of winning the elections, based on the victory of Narayan Singh (Sarpanch, Kushalpura) and Tej Singh (Sarpanch, Todgarh) in the previous panchayat elections in 2000, were only partially vindicated. The arithmetical progression did not take place. The setback came as a bit of a surprise, especially as in the last week preceding the elections it seemed as if the impact of the campaign had affected the liquor circulators, the money distributors and the trendsetters for campaigning who had held the populace to ransom for more than five decades. Many of the election campaigns had abandoned the jeep and tractor for 'pad yatras', challenging the MKSS's sole claim to keeping the campaign within the limit of Rs. 2,000 and abiding by the electoral code of conduct.

> What we now know for certain is that we need democratic education of a more fundamental nature. We need to nurture the ground for ethics and democratic debate in the context of electoral politics, coupled with the engagement with caste patterns for voting. This will definitely take us into social reform and addressing the issues of changing what have now become mainstream mores.
>
> There were three attempts made by the MKSS to contest elections. In the beginning, before the RTI, there was an experimental attempt which met with failure. In the second round, Narayan and Tej Singh became sarpanches of the Panchayats of Kushalpura and Todgarh respectively, and Kalu became ward panch in Vijaypura. In the third round, Kalu won as sarpanch in Vijaypura.
>
> Introducing modern electoral systems in older traditions of feudal and colonial structures need continual review. The Panchyati raj system was introduced in the '50s. But powerful feudal and other elite were elected year after year, almost in perpetuity, giving rise to a sardonic comment: "janam jati sarpanch" [a sarpanch in perpetuity] till the law was amended on 26.7.1994. In Rajasthan, seats for election to the panchayats are now reserved according a rotating quota system based on caste and gender. Fifty percent of the seats are reserved for women since 2000. In this roster system no one can be a sarpanch in perpetuity.[154]

A crucial aspect of the MKSS campaign was the stress on the importance of maintaining the integrity of the electoral process by ensuring that candidates do not resort to the use of any form of inducement, financial or otherwise, and calling on people to refuse such inducements individually and as a body (village, community or collective) and vote freely, fairly and fearlessly. The MKSS logic was clear. Every inducement offered by the candidates, whether liquor, food, meat, or arranging vehicles, is not a gift but a mortgage of the future, and is recovered from public money meant for the development of the village. The voters mortgage their future and this leads to corruption. Secondly, accepting any sort of inducement today, whether liquor, food or transport in exchange for one's vote, means bartering away the power to hold a sarpanch accountable tomorrow. The clear line of connection between an electoral campaign and the tenure of the elected representative and his corrupt practices was not only known but visible.

Secondly, a manifesto was not merely rhetoric but gave primacy to value-based people's governance. It clearly spelt out both the standards that would be adhered to, and the means by which values such as transparency, accountability, participation, and ethical conduct would be measured or realized, leaving a deep impression on the minds of people and also fundamentally altering the political discourse.

Thirdly, across all the panchayats the elections proved to be a rallying point for a large number of men and women, especially the youth, who responded to the MKSS call for ethical and accountable politics and came out in significant numbers to give time without any expectation of reward, only expecting a clean, accountable and effective panchayat. These people set aside work, including daily wage labour, domestic responsibilities and other commitments, and spent days walking around the villages campaigning without as much as a meal in return for their efforts. For a number of these people, the MKSS manifesto and the consistency in the method not only helped overcome their own cynicism regarding the electoral politics but also galvanized them into action. Even in defeat the MKSS gained new supporters and committed individuals in several panchayats.

In fact, the stress on ethical conduct, participation, transparency, and accountability did not appeal just to the poor. The universal nature of the MKSS appeal was perhaps best illustrated by the sight of a rich upper-caste woman, walking the whole day long with a large number of OBC/ Dalit men and women, campaigning for the first time in her life and that too for an OBC candidate. It provided a most telling story of how ethical politics can actually break down the most compelling barriers of caste, class and gender.

The fourth major gain was that of the successful mobilization of women. One common thread that ran through all election-related meetings was that of mobilizing women. Not just to cast their vote but to use the secrecy of ballot according to their independent free will and judgement rather than succumb to pressure from male family members or community leaders. In the context of electoral politics, they are at best treated as vote banks that can be encashed by distributing money or jaggery or as passive recipients of the benefits of reserved seats.

One of the key messages of the MKSS campaign had been to stress that the duty of the citizen begins after voting, in maintaining vigilance and ensuring the integrity of democracy by holding elected representatives accountable for the fulfilment of their duties and promises. As Kala Kot's Hukam Singh observed: 'Each one of us has to act like the sarpanch and control the panchayat'. Last but not the least, the biggest gains for the MKSS were the lessons learnt in terms of managing the electoral process and the complexity of the processes that shape electoral opinion.

**The Poor as Political Risk Bearers**

The role of transparency and possible accountability transferred some of the power of the local bodies to the people. The fact that the right to know is also the basis of the right to self-governance was visible. Minds of ordinary voters and people who were the flag-bearers of Indian democracy needed to have platforms and tools to exercise their right to democratic methods and processes.

Peoples' organizations like the MKSS made a strong impact in electoral politics with the introduction of a definitive set of norms. It was coupled with an effective implementation mechanism that could ensure a cleaner, more transparent electoral process in which candidates could be monitored. It led the movement, later, to a preoccupation with participatory governance. The RTI made a fundamental contribution to this understanding.

MKSS's electoral campaign and the RTI campaign were in a sense symbiotic – the possibilities and challenges of each fed into and shaped the other, allowing MKSS to break new ground. Despite the important victories, there is a long way to go to transform local panchayats into real institutions of participatory governance.

CHAPTER TWENTY

# The Public Hearings in Umarwas

**Public Hearing in Bori, Rajsamand District**

The MKSS had been working hard to convince the sarpanches about the need to have transparent and accountable panchayats. The gram sewak or secretary to the panchayat, as we have seen in the earlier chapters, was determined to fight against disclosure. This lowest rung of bureaucracy continues to be instrumental in first trapping the elected leaders into committing small deviations and then blackmailing them to sign on records; to swindle more from development expenditure. Since the signature is that of the sarpanch, she or he remains liable to prosecution. The gram sewak, at the lowest level of bureaucracy, goes scot-free, as do other functionaries.

In Rajasthan the sarpanches have been lulled into believing that the signing of the cheque determines their status and importance, though they have been repeatedly told that no minister or public representative signs cheques, and their importance is not reduced by not doing so. They continue to jealously want to protect the right to sign a cheque in which the decision is often taken by others, and expenditure is determined by the local mafia. Sunny Sebastian (special correspondent, the *Hindu*) who was a continual presence in the Rajasthan RTI struggle and campaign, in one of his reports in December 1999 writes:

UMARWAAS [RAJSAMAND], DEC, 23
...Where legislation has helped certain posts reserved for the Dalits and women, there are many ways for the upper castes to continue their hold over the villages as they did during the halcyon days of feudalism in Rajasthan.

What is perhaps sadder is the fact that now they can get things done through the "dummies" they make out of these Dalit sarpanches in panchayat samitis and play safe without the fear of ever getting caught by law enforcement agencies. A classic instance of the village tyrants and the feudal elements making a mockery of the much-hyped 73rd Amendment of the Constitution was brought to light this past weekend in front of a group of socially committed persons and a gathering of villagers at a jan sunwai [public hearing] initiated by the Mazdoor Kisan Shakti Sangathan [MKSS] at Bori village in Umarwaas Panchayat Samiti of Rajsamand district.[155]

Pyarji looked more like a poor seeker of information than a sarpanch, which he surprisingly was! He came timidly to the courtyard of the home in Devdungri and wanted to know if he could meet the 'mukhiya' (chief) of the sangathan. When he was asked what he wanted, he said he wanted a jan sunwai in his panchayat. Used to reluctant, fearful but aggressive sarpanches, the MKSS was rather amazed at this request!

Pyarji's story was typical and shocking; he was caught, as many of them are, in the abundant power of the local power elite in the intersected politics of caste and electoral democracy. Whatever the odds or the situation, the upper caste and powerful use it for their benefit. The panchayats have had reservation for Dalits, backward castes, and others in Rajasthan since 1994. In Umarwas, as in the rest of Rajasthan, elections to the panchayat were held in 1995, and the seat was reserved for Dalits [male]. Pyarchand Khatik was a Dalit. The traditional power elite did not want a Meghwal to contest as they were a sizeable majority and would have won, and probably worked independent of the traditional power elite. There was one Dalit khatik household, and Pyarji was working in Surat. Nain Singh, Rajput went all the way to Surat and brought him back to contest.[156]

Nain Singh Solanki, the thakur of the village, unchallenged feudal master even in those more democratic times, had consulted

> at length with his powerful coterie about how best to deal with the 73rd constitutional amendment. This amendment in 1995 had resulted in the reservation of the position of the sarpanch for the Scheduled Castes or ex-untouchables, so none of the coterie could stand for elections. But they could not afford to let power slip out of their hands, and even less submit to the ignominy of an ex-untouchable wielding power in the panchayat. The dominant Scheduled Castes of the village were the Meghwals, who spurred by the power of numbers, were assertive and confident. By contrast, there were only a few Khatik homes. The enquiries by Nain Singh and his band confirmed that the most timid, most submissive of the Khatik men, was Pyarji. They learnt that he had migrated several years earlier to distant Surat, and earned his living as a kerosene hawker. Their best bet then was to install Pyarji as the new sarpanch, and to retain their traditional stranglehold through him.
>
> A delegation was deputed to go to Surat forthwith to persuade him to fight the election. There were only a few days left for the filing of nomination papers, therefore there was little time to lose.[157]

Pyarji was a very simple person. When he protested and said he could not manage 'sarapanchai', he was told all he had to do was to win the elections that they would help him win.

> Pyarji was utterly confounded. Even in his wildest imagination, he had not thought of himself as being the village headman. He protested – I have studied no further than class four. I do not have the faintest idea about how the panchayat works. My kerosene business here in Surat is very small, but it gives me a steady income, and it has taken me several years of struggle to finally settle down. Elections cost a lot of money, and I have no money to spend.[158]
>
> Later on he was told that all he had to do was to stamp papers. In his words: "I was given a rubber stamp from time to time, and was told all you have to do is 'tapatup', that is stamp the papers and sign them, no questions asked. And that was what I did."[159] ...In the heady aftermath of the elections, Pyarji first tumbled down to earth when Lakshman Das gave him a bill of expenses that he claimed had been incurred for his election. Pyarji protested weakly that he had been assured that he would not have to bear

> these expenses. But now no one recalled the assurance. He was told that the expenses were 35,000 rupees for jeep hire charges, diesel, liquor. And, not to forget, repayment of 2400 rupees for an old loan which Pyarji had taken to purchase sheep, so that he could statutorily qualify as a candidate who had not defaulted on any bank loan. Pyarji had a total of 18,000 rupees saved up from so many years of lonely toil in Surat, and he paid these now to Lakshman Das, his heart breaking. But even after this, 17,000 rupees remained. To meet this, Lakshman Das said he would give him a loan. Pyarji agonised – How will I ever be able to repay this loan? But, Lakshman Das reassured him that there are many ways to earn money in the panchayat, and it would not be long before Pyarji would be able to repay his loan, and even have money left over on the side. Pyarji after all was the sarpanch.
>
> As the months passed, he signed and placed his seal on every paper peremptorily placed before him. Gradually, it dawned on him that the noose was being tightened around his own neck. He weakly and belatedly tried to resist, but was more nakedly terrorized and threatened by the coterie. Isolated and frightened, he continued to do as he was told.[160]
>
> But I now know that people are thieving and it is I who will get caught. So please organize a jan sunwai! Sumir Hinduja from the MKSS took on the responsibility of sending information. He also dealt with Pyarji's immense naiveté and his fallibility.[161]

The predicament was unusual and pathetic. The jan sunwai would go against Pyarji, but he was insistent that the jan sunwai be held. His persistence won the day, and finally the MKSS decided to go ahead with the public hearing. It had to deal with the unusual consequences, where the innocent would stand implicated for crimes not committed, but where the signature would bear evidence of complicity. The MKSS decided it would seek clemency for him, and continued with a perusal of the records and fixing the date for the public hearing.

Sunny Sebastian of the *Hindu* was a constant factor in reporting about the campaign for the RTI in Rajasthan. He was also a part of the process when journalist associations signed up as a part of the campaign to access information. His report of the public hearing in Bori begins with:

Now Pyarchand, for no crime of his, stood dismissed as sarpanch facing action for the recovery of Rs. 1.60 lakhs he had sanctioned unwittingly. Pyarchand approached the sangathan when he realized that funds had been withdrawn from banks in his name. Rejecting Pyarchand's clarification, the Chief Executive of the district suspended him in October 1998 and dismissed him in July 1999. Now Pyarchand faces forced liquidation in the form of recovery proceedings.

In a commendable case of thorough and painstaking investigation carried out over a period of eight months, the MKSS team led by Ms Aruna Roy, Mr Nikhil Dey, Mr Sameer and Mr Shankar Singh the pathetic saga of Pyarchand was unravelled in a six-hour long trial.

For the first time since the MKSS launched its jan sunwais as a part of its Right to Information campaign, the district collector, the superintendent of police, the SDO, the BDO and the tehsildar himself turned up at the programme. Nain Singh was also present to plead his case, at times noisily.

At the end, the collector, Mr Nirmal Wadwani, announced that an FIR would be filed against the guilty and a fresh investigation would be initiated into the case. The panel of judges, in their observations stressed upon the need for transparency and the granting of Right to Information for empowerment of masses. Ms Arundhati Roy, on her part, promised to return to the place after some time to see the outcome of the public hearing.[162]

Arundhati Roy (writer), Prashant Bhushan (lawyer), Madhu Kishwar (editor of *Manushi*), Amitabh Mukhopadhyaya (accountant general), Sanjeev Kumar, Mamta Jaitley (editor *Ujala Chadi*), Ravindra Shah (resident editor, *Bhaskar-Udaipur*) and Nirmal Wadhwani (collector, Rajsamand) were the panellists for the Umarwas Jan Sunwai, which was going to seal the fate of Pyarji.

Credit for Rajasthan's surprising response and commitment to RTI is shared by the role *Ujala Chadi* played to spread information in the idiom of people. It was a very significant and critical role. *Ujala Chadi* reported:

**The Fraud of Umarwas**

All the upper caste people of Umarwas Panchayat figured in this panchayat's BPL list, however, not even a single poor Bhil was included in this list. We got to know this in the Public Hearing in Bori village of this panchayat. In the Public Hearing, MKSS workers read out the records of the development works in the village and people testified in front of the panel. The truth came out in this open hearing easily and quite naturally following the reading of the documents. The majority of cases related to the allotment of Indira Awas or housing for the poor.[163]

The details that were reported in *Ujala Chadi* were familiar to rural inhabitants. Still, to see it in print and tracing the pattern of systemic loot was fascinating. One powerful member of the caste-class combine, Nain Singh, member of the panchayat, and who we may recall brought Pyarji to contest from Surat, was able to corner many of the benefits meant for the poor. He was brazen about the benefits and aggressive with the MKSS (these were borne out by the well-circulated film on the RTI presented to the Parliamentary Standing Committee).

**Indira Awas Yojana**

The ward panch Nain Singh [of village Basa] was given 12,300 rupees in his wife's name. Nain Singh has his ancestral Rawla [haveli] in the village. He is from a rich and powerful family. They built 2 rooms in their home and in fact, were not even the rightful beneficiaries of this scheme.

Nain Singh's brother [rich] Bhanwar Singh also took 10,800 rupees in his wife's name and even he didn't build any house from it. He has a house in the village and is quite rich.

Another brother, Ram Singh also took money twice in his wife's name [once in the name of Roop Kanwar and once in the name of Raj Kanwar]; one of them has died and never built a house.

Moti Bai [wife of businessman Lakshman Das], Kishan Das and Tulsi Das of Kitela village also took the funds fraudulently. They are all affluent and powerful.

Ward panch Prabhu Das [of village Umarwas] also took money in his wife's name.[164]

The British said that the devil lies in the details. Every public hearing was to prove this adage right. The *Ujala Chadi* went on to say:

The Bori Jan Sunwai traced 30 beneficiaries of this scheme in the

> village and all had got these funds fraudulently. Such a big fraud could only have taken place with the complicity of government functionaries and bank officials. The Junior Engineer had to verify the construction at several stages; the bank manager has to identify the account-holder who gets the benefit; and so on. When the house was never built how did it get verified in the records? And could a dead person have a bank account opened?[165]

Another block of corrupt practices was in the building of community centres and *chabootras* or platforms, which would be seen as a relatively small infrastructural contribution to village life by planners in Delhi and in Jaipur. But for the local elite it meant an additional space which they could build for their own benefit and enjoyment. The *Ujala Chadi* reported:

> **Community Centre**
> The community centre of Aasan village [of Umarwas panchayat] is actually built in the house of the panchayat samiti member, Kamla Bai! Its door opens in her house and she has locked it up and uses it as her own property! Similarly, in Basa village the community centre is in the ward panch Nain Singh's house.
>
> In Basa village a canal was made from a small pond. Two and a half lakh rupees were spent on this but this canal is used only by ward panch Nain Singh and his relatives. The tehsildar investigated the matter and found it to be true and submitted his report, yet, the practice has continued unabated.
>
> In Umarwas, thousands of rupees were siphoned off in the name of building chabootras. Several chabootras were already there. In several works, bogus bills and muster-rolls were used to get fraudulent payments.
>
> It was revealed in this Public Hearing that twenty-two lakh rupees were siphoned off in this panchayat.
>
> **Mockery of justice!**
> Once again, the entire responsibility for the frauds in this panchayat has been put on Pyarchand Khatik [the sarpanch]. The BDO of Kumbhalgarh…lodged an FIR on 7th January…heavy irregularities have taken place in the development works in the panchayat. False

attendances have been recorded.... In this sunwai, the collector of Rajsamand had referred to the CEO's report in which the sarpanch was found only partly responsible for the frauds by virtue of being the head of the panchayat. The collector had asked for a report on the evidence presented in the hearing and the MKSS had submitted the report [with all evidence] on 24th December.

It is clearly evident from the FIR that there has been an attempt to save the erring officials. Instead of a fraud of 4,71,000, the complaint only talks of 1,10,000 rupees. The fraud in the Indira Awas Yojana is missing entirely from the FIR.

Three gram sewaks – Gopilal Raigar, Moti Singh and Nirdesh Kumar Yadav – have all been identified as responsible for the fraud by the CEO [in his report] but they do not figure in the FIR. Junior Engineer V.K. Arora, BDO Bhanwar Lal Jain and the bank manager are all missing from this FIR. And no letter has been written by the district administration to institute enquiries against these [officials].

**The demands of the MKSS**

A new FIR should be lodged in the matter and all the irregularities should be included in this. There should not be any leniency towards the culprits whether they are government officials or others.

Within a time-limit strict action should be taken against all erring officials.

The report of the CEO must be given to the police for investigations.

All the money siphoned off by politicians and officials should be recovered from them.

Action must be taken against the powerful ward panches who threatened and warned the villagers who spoke against them.

Investigations should be constituted in the Indira Awas Yojana in Kumbhalgarh and action must be taken against all those who are involved in siphoning off the public money.[166]

Pyarji himself, caught between so many controversies still retained his poise and determination. He had this to say when asked about the jan sunwai.

I was feeling really good as our accounts were being scrutinized and verified. Irregularities worth lakhs of rupees were coming to light.

> I had never done any undue favour to anyone. Only if I have done something wrong then I'll have some fear....[167]

Sunny Sebastian reporting in the *Hindu* elaborated further:

> Through these Jan Sunwais the MKSS gives an opportunity to the people to demand accountability from the establishment, fight corruption, focus on certain aspects of decentralisation and build real democracy.
>
> *Bhains mange kakre, Sarkar mange akre* [the buffalo wants cotton seeds, the government wants figures], shouted Mr. Shankar Singh, star puppeteer and MKSS activist, introducing the theme of the public hearing: mere figures on paper are meaningless. It can satisfy only government departments, not the people.[168]

The jan sunwai in Bori was an education about how the system lays itself open to manipulation by dominant caste and class hierarchies.

> In December 1999, the MKSS made use of the limited access to official records that citizens enjoy under Rajasthan's Right to Information legislation, in order to lay bare the anatomy of corruption in public works in Umarwaas village of Udaipur district [*Frontline*, 17 March 2000]. The dubious role of the individuals who had dominated the local body, as also the connivance of contractors and government officials, was unravelled in a dramatic public hearing initiated by the MKSS with the enthusiastic participation of the poor and the landless. Although proven in the public mind, the corruption of the dominant coterie in Umarwaas is yet to elicit an official response.[169]

Pyarji resigned after the jan sunwai, declaring he was neither desirous nor competent enough to be the village sarpanch.

The battle for public ethics is a long road that the people of India have to learn to walk. To use the popular media phrase, we have to learn as a community, as a government, as media and as a nation, to walk the talk.

CHAPTER TWENTY-ONE

# Janawad Jan Sunwai

In close proximity to Bori Panchayat, there was another controversy raging in Janawad, Kumbalgarh Block, Rajsamand.

The Janawad public hearing happened at the critical juncture when the joint select committee of parliament (during the NDA regime) was examining the Freedom of Information (FOI) legislation. The hearing was also strengthened by the amended Panchayati Raj rules and the Rajasthan RTI law. But it equally showcased the weakness of the legislations, underlining the crucial need for a more meaningful entitlement. Chimanlal brought to the attention of the MKSS the Janawad case, just as Pyarji brought to light problems in Bori. He was supported by Lachhuba, a Dalit. These two elderly men led the vanguard of the Janawad struggle. Chimanba, as he was affectionately called, became a member of the MKSS and continues to work for transparency and accountability, despite his advanced years.

Chimanba was an important member of the panchayat of Janawad, and belonged to the same community as the sarpanch, Ramlal, he sought to expose. His determination to access information and pursue the case to its logical end marked the beginning of the process. Equally determined, the MKSS afforded Chimanba support and took this into the process of a jan sunwai. From there it travelled the route to policy and legislative demands. The widely known, reported and seen public hearing gave the demand public support, and its eminent panel underlined the veracity and authenticity of the information disclosed such that it prevailed on the decision makers. Janawad had the biggest and most eminent panel so far, with Justice Sawant, Justice Rajinder Sachar and Justice V.S. Dave, and eminent journalists Kalpana Sharma, Ajit Bhattacharjea, Prabhash Joshi, Bharat Dogra, Meena Menon, Sunny Sebatian, Radhika Kaul Batra, Narayan Barreth, Sukumar Muralidharan, Neelabh Misra, Prem Krishen Sharma, Vandana Shiva, Baba Adhav, M.P. Parameswaran, Surendra Mohan, and Nelson Fernandez.

The Janawad case was widely written about and drew and engaged the interest of the government and the political establishment, the media and those engaged in the incessant struggle against corruption and the arbitrary use of power.

Innumerable articles and reports were written on the Janawad Jan Sunwai. The MKSS kept a diary, but many of its members wrote and published articles. This chapter will not do justice if it fails to bring back some of those different voices together to form the narrative.

The Janawad public hearing occupies a central space in the logic of the RTI discourse. At the time it took place, the MKSS and the NCPRI Rajasthan had prevailed upon the government to put up transparency boards outside the panchayat office with details of work and expenditure incurred on them. The interest of the villagers and of Chimanba began with the reading of this board, which had details which they knew were fraudulent, making them indignant and wanting a thorough public enquiry. What appalled them even more were the 'corrections' that began to be made on the board, and there was loud protest. Even more shocking were the mushrooming efforts to finish incomplete or non-existent works by a scared and worried administration. For instance, the case of the veterinary hospital that suddenly got built on the existing panchayat building!

> After a three-year-long struggle, the citizens of Rajasthan gained in 1997 the right to obtain photocopies of all panchayati raj-related documents, including copies of muster rolls and vouchers of development expenditure, within four days of making an application. On 1 May 2000, the state assembly enacted amidst much fanfare a law that gave the people the right to information in all spheres of governance. In Janawad, despite sustained efforts and pressure, it took one year and a High Court directive to finally obtain the required information.[170]

The process (of acquiring the information), and not just the product (the actual information), is worth recounting here.

> Using the Rajasthan panchayati raj rules and inspired by the revelations at a public hearing held in December 1999 in the neighbouring panchayat of Umarwas, over 70 citizens of Janawad collectively decided to apply for copies of records of work executed in their panchayat in the previous five years. A…board painted on the wall of the panchayat indicating the total amount of money sanctioned and the amount spent on each item of work – had revealed shocking misappropriation. There were even cases of "ghost works" – where the only work that had actually taken place was the pocketing of money.
>
> In order to prove the fraud and pin down the guilty, copies of the records were needed. On 16 February 2000, the residents submitted the first application for information. When a month passed without any response from the panchayat sarpanch or secretary, the applicants approached the district collector.[171]

**The Story of the Right to Information in Janawad Panchayat**

In India it is not uncommon for theory to differ from practice. While information is to be given within four days of request under the Panchayati Raj Act, we got it after a year.

> Inspired by the public hearing held in December 1999 in Gram Panchayat Umarwaas and having seen the Information board in Gram Panchayat Janawad, the residents of Janawad filed an application information on 16 February 2000.
>
> The Panchayati Raj Act has the provisions for an Information board in Janawad, and when the board was painted, it was subsequently changed with different figures each time. We have still not received records that tally with the information painted on the board. While the information board in Janawad has created a flurry of activity, hardly any villages in Rajasthan have information boards, despite the law.

The information received was still not complete.

> To ascertain the total figures of development works expenditure the following documents are needed: sanction letters, technical sanction, muster rolls, bills, measurement book, utilisation certificate [UC], audit report. But after making photocopies of Janawad Panchayat's documents it was discovered that in most files if the muster rolls were present, the bills weren't. If bills were there, measurement books [MBs] were not, if MBs were there, then there were no Utilisation Certificate. This information was accessed after a lot of rounds to the panchayat office and we couldn't get the entire record till the last minute. Some records are still missing.
>
> The information being asked for was for the term of former sarpanch Sri Ram Lal. However, the present sarpanch, Bhuri Bai [Reserved Candidate – Scheduled Caste, Woman] also refused to part with information. We discovered that administrative officials were playing their own games with Bhuri Bai as their front [much as in the case of Pyarji] she was needed only for signatures. Her signatures were finally taken on blank papers and a petition filed in the high court.[172]

The Janawad case underlined and re-emphasized the need for a law to have a penalty provision in case information was denied. If one follows the chain of events manipulated and organized to delay information in Janawad, it graphically describes the shallowness of the 'iron frame' so often referred to as the basis of Indian bureaucratic management. The words conjure up the glitter of the premier service, the IAS; but the edifice stands on a layered and entrenched bureaucracy. This bureaucracy in cohorts with the petty political structure perverts the interests of the common person waiting to use the services of the government. This long excerpt from an article published at that time is an important document as it traces the denials step by step. This pattern – though changed by the RTI (2005) with the penalty clause – allows the readers to draw their own inferences about governance.

> The board showed large sums of money spent on development work supposed to have been undertaken in the village. But the works listed on the board did not exist in reality. Some of the citizens then applied for information in February 2000 u/s 321-328 of the Rajasthan Panchayati Raj Act Rules, 1996. In spite of a letter from

> the Chief Executive Officer, Panchayati Raj of the district to the Panchayat Secretary in May 2000 to give information it was not given to the people for three months. Although a new sarpanch took over in February, the panchayat secretary remained the same. The previous sarpanch managed to pressurise the new sarpanch into not giving information. He also got the gram sabha, which met only in name, and the gram panchayat to pass illegal resolutions that giving information would cause a law and order problem.[173]

MKSS reported this to the local administration and asked for the information again. The minister and the state Panchayati Raj department came in to get the illegal resolutions cancelled. The implementation of the law still remained.

> When the people of Janawad and the MKSS started an agitation about it, the pradhan of the block issued an order that information need not be given for another two months as a committee constituted by him under the BDO would enquire into the case. Incidentally, the BDO would be one of the accused if the fraud of that panchayat were to be exposed. The State Government once again issued orders in November 2000 to the BDO that information be given to the people. This was also violated by the panchayat secretary and instead he made a new interpretation of the law by saying that citizens had the right to inspection and not obtain copies. When the state government called for the records in order to give their copies to the MKSS, the gram sewak disappeared with the records and got a stay on the order from the Jodhpur High Court.[174]

The information was given to the people after a long struggle and a jan sunwai took place on 4 April 2001.

> On 17 May, when the MKSS first approached district officials seeking their intervention to have the law implemented in Janawad, letters were promptly issued ordering the panchayat to provide the copies. For the next three months the gram sewak, Balu Ram Saini, played a game of hide and seek, by giving dates but absenting himself, claiming that the records had gone for audit, and looking for technicalities and loopholes in the rules to deny the information.[175]

Sarpanch Ram Lal was in office from the year 1995–2000. When the public hearing took place, Bhuri Bai was the sarpanch. The records being asked for also belonged to that period. It seemed that Ram Lal was still trying to exert power and ensure that records were not shared, though he could not be re-elected as a ward member in the year 2000.

> Even the sincere and determined efforts of the secretary of the Panchayati Raj Department could not ensure the implementation of the law. The department issued orders annulling the alleged resolutions, called for an explanation from the gram sewak and the sarpanch, and ordered them to provide copies to the applicants immediately. When these orders reached the panchayat and block offices, the MKSS activists were given another date, in early November, to collect the required copies. One day before they were to collect the copies, the MKSS received a copy of an order passed by the pradhan of the block, Kishan Lal Gujjar, forming a "high-level enquiry committee" to go into possible corruption in Janawad panchayat. The committee was headed by the Block Development Officer [BDO] and was to be assisted by the junior engineer and the accountant. [In panchayat-related corruption cases it is mostly the persons holding these three posts who are accused of acting in collusion.] The order mentioned the persistent efforts of the MKSS to obtain copies of the records, and the pradhan endorsed the view of the gram sewak and the sarpanch that giving copies of these records would "disturb the peace".[176]

It seemed that the MKSS would have to return to Jaipur.

> As soon as the secretary of the department of Panchayati Raj issued orders to the BDO to ensure that records were provided, even block officials began avoiding MKSS activists and villagers. It was clear that the entitlement that had been obtained through a prolonged agitation would require another agitation for the people to benefit from it.
>
> On 22 November, the MKSS held a one-day dharna at the district headquarters of Rajsamand where over a thousand people gathered to demand that the law be implemented and the records of Janawad panchayat be provided. The district collector gave a public assurance that the records would be provided two days later and that the BDO, who was present, would ensure that this was done.

One would have thought that the collector's order would put a final seal of authority on the course of action the village-level officials had to take. But the end of the matter was not so close.

> ...there was a great deal of interest when the next day's newspapers carried a press statement by the gram sewak of Janawad that he had examined the law and according to his own interpretation he was not bound to provide copies of records. Issuing a press statement against the law and the collector's public assurance seemed a foolish thing to do. At the appointed time the entire village and the local press turned up at Panchayat Bhavan to see if the collector's assurance would be kept. Brimming with confidence, the gram sewak handed over a letter to the BDO, refusing to part with copies of the records.
>
> In his letter he sought further instructions from his superiors. However, in his conversation he made it clear that he had already received such instructions. The BDO had been making disapproving noises all through – issuing warnings to the gram sewak that he was doing something wrong by refusing to obey the collector's orders and follow the provisions of the law. However, as soon as the MKSS gave him a written representation to intervene and provide the copies of records as he was the gram sewak's superior and was present on the spot, he dictated a reply, which provided the finishing touches to the morning's charade. He said he would seek the advice of his superior officers and let the MKSS know in 15 days whether the gram sewak's new interpretation of the Panchayati Raj Rules was valid or not.[177]

The Congress government completed two years in Rajasthan in 2000.

> In several interviews the chief minister claimed that one of the outstanding achievements of the government had been the enactment of the law relating to the right to information. The time had come to let the people know how this translated at the field level.
>
> On 28 November, the MKSS held a press conference in Jaipur on the non-enforcement of the right to information law. It offered several well-documented examples of non-compliance with it.... But the extraordinary chain of events in Janawad became the focus of the press conference.[178]

The state government was perturbed by this and there was an order for the documents to be produced in Jaipur.

> The district administration promised to ensure that the copies were handed over, and MKSS activists were told that these would be delivered to their office by the time they returned. There was still, however, a long way to go.
>
> All through the next day, officials of Rajsamand district made calls and visits to the MKSS office to find out whether the records had arrived. Ironically, the officials kept asking the MKSS where their gram sewak was, and why the records they had sent with him to be delivered to the MKSS office hours earlier had still not reached. It transpired that the same gram sewak had been entrusted with not only the photocopies, but also the originals of the panchayat records, and both he and the records had vanished![179]

The MKSS was concerned over this disappearance but the district administration said he and the records were sure to return.

> There were rumours in Janawad village that he had gone to seek a stay order from the High Court Bench in Jodhpur. MKSS activists reassured Janawad's citizens that the courts had always insisted on transparency and that no court would grant a stay on orders to issue copies of the details of development expenditure, especially when there was a law that facilitates such provision. However, the assessment of the MKSS was wrong.
>
> The gram sewak returned after three days with the records – and a stay order from the High Court. The stay order continued to be in force from 29 November, until the case was disposed of on 20 February 2001. Despite the legal provisions under which affected parties can make an application to be heard within 14 days in cases where an ex-parte stay has been granted, a series of adjournments ensured that the stay order continued to be in force. The people of Janawad had to stand up to a variety of pressures from Ram Lal and this order left them wondering again about the institutions of justice.[180]

The people of Janawad were not ignorant of the ongoing corrupt practices. The right to information started seeming a way of generating proof of these open secrets.

> The board on the wall of the panchayat office was intended to present the facts about the development of the panchayat over the previous five years. However, it told the story of why there had been no development. Over Rs. 80 lakhs had been spent in five years and it was clear that substantial amounts had gone into the pockets of some people.
>
> There were details of works that simply did not exist.... There were other works on which a few thousands of rupees had been spent but several times the amount shown as the cost.... The successful getaway with the records by the gram sewak and the subsequent stay order were now being used by Ram Lal to prove his invincibility.[181]

But the gram sewak's method was not without loopholes.

> When the gram sewak left the panchayat office with the records, he hid one file among older papers and files. As the pressure to provide the copies mounted from an embarrassed state administration, a harassed additional collector of the district and the chief executive officer of the zila parishad turned up with copies of some of the old records the gram sewak had left behind. They insisted that the MKSS take these unasked for copies so that they could report that some documents had been handed over. Among these papers, inadvertently handed over, were photocopies of the papers in the concealed file pertaining to construction of a dispensary at Janawad in 1998 at a cost of Rs. 1,36,973.
>
> The MKSS took the file to the village on 10 December. An impromptu public hearing was organised some 100 metres from the Janawad dispensary. The dispensary had indeed been built, but over 30 years ago. Since then the nurse who worked there had approached the panchayat innumerable times for money, to undertake repairs to the building, but the panchayat repeatedly said that there was no money. In the seven years she had worked in Janawad, not a single rupee had come from the panchayat. And yet the papers showed a completed measurement book filled out by the junior engineer for this ghost work.[182]

There was now ample evidence against Ram Lal, the junior engineer, the BDO and the gram sewak.

> On the initiative of the MKSS, an official investigation was conducted, and on the confirmation of the fictitious work, a First Information Report [FIR] was filed in the police station by the BDO.... Finally, it seemed the proof was available. But no arrests were made.
>
> ...the court case continued. Five officials of the government and the MKSS were made parties by the panchayat and the sarpanch in the High Court. Bhuri Bai told a television journalist on record that she had no idea about any court case – she only signed where the BDO and the gram sewak asked her to. The state government promised to put all its efforts into having the stay vacated as soon as possible. Yet it chose to be constrained from top to bottom by a court stay on the order of the BDO.[183]

It was an opportunity for Ram Lal and his allies to do all the cover-up required.

> The criminal complaint lodged against him by the BDO, on the petition of the MKSS, relating to the sub PHC and several other fictitious works that came to light subsequently, is still under investigation and no arrests have been made. The SHO told the MKSS that he had confirmed the fact that the records had been forged, but he said that the forged muster rolls had to be sent for tests such as finger print tests and all that would take time.... But the tide has finally begun to turn in Janawad. On 26 January, in the social audit in the gram sabha held in the presence of the chief executive officer of the zila parishad, villagers identified seven ghost works, accounting for over Rs. 8 lakhs.
>
> The newly posted BDO lodged two more FIRs. Politicians and bureaucrats who were openly supporting Ram Lal are now distancing themselves from him. On 21 February, a day after the High Court decision was announced, the copies of the records were handed over to the MKSS. The MKSS promptly announced a Jan Sunwai [public hearing] in Janawad on 3 April 2001.[184]

The public hearing was held with the intention of putting pressure on the state government to take action on the basis of the evidence that had come up.

> The police have still not acted on the three FIRs. The MKSS has demanded that the administration immediately recover the defalcated funds and take firm action against all those whose job it was to prevent the embezzlement.... After 3 April Janawad is likely to be remembered for the detailed exposure of corruption in the development machinery. If people want to find solutions, however, Janawad must also be remembered for the struggle it had to wage to expose corruption....
>
> ...the story of Janawad offers us some lessons. The first is that the right to information will encounter strong resistance from the bureaucracy. Only stiff penalties for non-compliance will give the Act the teeth it requires....
>
> The second lesson is that the bureaucracy will use any excuse to deny information, and therefore the exemption clauses must be extremely restricted and must not give any room for misinterpretation.
>
> The third lesson is that if any information is denied by an official, it is quite likely that the official will get support from his superiors. The only safeguard is to allow at least one independent appeal.
>
> Finally, as the board in the panchayat of Janawad has illustrated, there is a lot of critically important information that can be easily provided even without it being asked for. If such information is given to citizens, it can truly create the basis for citizens' participation in a range of democratic activities. Suo motu display and dissemination of information must be mandated by the Act, so that the term "transparent governance" is not allowed to become another empty slogan.[185]

The importance of Section 4 of the RTI Act was embedded in this important experience. That is perhaps why the RTI (2005) was framed with transparency provisions, information to be supplied within a time frame, and with an independent appeal mechanism. This also traces the relationship between public action and the framing of a relevant and responsible piece of legislation. The fact that the struggle of the MKSS and the campaigning and advocacy of the NCPRI was a dialectical relationship contributed to the framing of a better law.

In jan sunwais held in the past the MKSS has been looking at

> percentage of fraud in a particular work. What is most startling about the Janawad Panchayat is that there are over 35 works that are ghost works [i.e. they exist only on paper].
>
> This reveals a complete breakdown of the development machinery and raises questions about the executive, implementation, monitoring and evaluation that should have been carried out.
>
> It would be wrong to blame only the panchayat and panchayat level authorities for what has happened. It was clearly possible only because of collusion with higher authorities, both administrative and political.
>
> There have been audit reports, utilisation certificates, measurement books, muster rolls, bills and vouchers, all duly filled out, signed and countersigned by higher authorities and yet no work. The people of Janawad have suffered and this gives us an indication of why our poverty alleviation programmes have failed despite massive expenditure.
>
> We hope this jan sunwai will help break the nexus and empower people to plan, implement and monitor development on their own terms.[186]

These repeated experiences of fraud after financial audit had cleared the accounts, kept re-emphasizing the need for a public audit mandated by law. The social audit then became a concept the campaign fought for, and was put into practice. Never more so obviously necessary than in rural public works, and therefore a part of the NREGA law. The corruption exposed by the NREGA actually proves how much more was siphoned off when everything disappeared into the jaws of the predatory system. Far from criticizing the NREGA, anti-poverty campaigns should recognize its significance.

Prakash Sharma was a well-known Hindi journalist who started supporting the campaign. When he left the mainstream to start publishing his own paper, *Raj Drishti*, he advised the RTI campaign on advocacy. Writing in colourful and powerful Hindi, he says, in 'Manoeuvrings of the Crocodiles in the Sea of Development':

> To measure how the river of development is flowing in the state, we have also chosen a village to measure/examine it and the name of the village is Janawad…

> We chose this village because the junior engineer working in this village [who oversees the development works] was awarded by the government on Republic Day for his honesty, integrity, patriotism, and dutifulness…
>
> We also chose Janawad because its Sarpanch Shri Ramlal is considered a close aide of influential leader and former chief minister Heeralal Devpura sarpanch…[187]

The struggle in Janawad and the spectacular revelation of corruption and scandal gave birth to many reports. One report said:

> The story of the arduous Janawad struggle for the Right to Information had become such a legend in the area, as well as outside, that the grounds for the Jan Sunwai were backed with more than 3000 people on 3 April 2001.[188]

Another report stated the following:

> Inside the large colourful pandal, at Gomti Chauraha in Janawad [90 kms from Udaipur], villagers drew attention to several "ghost works" – projects that were supposed to have been completed but which existed only on paper. Government officials, activists, the press and locals listened in awe at the scale of corruption unfolding before their eyes….
>
> In Janawad, of the 98 development works undertaken since 1994, 38 turned out to be ghost works, according to Nikhil Dey, an MKSS activist. He says works worth Rs. 1.33 crore were reportedly carried out in the panchayat but MKSS had scrutinised only Rs. 65 lakh expenditure. Some records were missing and investigations by MKSS and the people revealed corruption to the tune of Rs. 45 lakhs. The then sarpanch, Ramlal, roams scot-free even today. Under the free housing scheme for the poor, sanctions were made in 1994–1995 and the money was even deposited, according to records, but the people did not even know of it. Amar Singh, who applied for a loan under the housing scheme for the poor [Indira Awas Yojana], did not get a house.[189]

The joint select committee was meeting in the parliament to look at the legislation as the Janawad Jan Sunwai was in process. Aruna and Nikhil recall (in a report published in *Frontline*):

> While the Central Bill on the Right to Information is being examined by the Joint Select Committee of Parliament, it is necessary to highlight some of the experiences in States in which laws relating to the right to information have been enacted. The experience in Janawad panchayat in Rajsamand district of Rajasthan illustrates graphically and dramatically the critical need for strong and enforceable legislation on the right to information if there is to be any hope of giving the ordinary people any real entitlement through this law.[190]

Janawad contributed in a fundamental way by helping the ordinary citizen understand governance. It stripped the veneer of respectability of status to demonstrate in full view of the people how corruption took place. It clearly showed how laws and rules made with the consent of the people and mandated in the parliament and assemblies are twisted and rendered meaningless when implemented by a corrupt system. The sequence of events was transparent and participatory. This trajectory led to two different learnings for public action. First, a law must be overseen by people, and second, the implementation of a law, or as Aruna and Nikhil called it in their article, 'Chasing a Right', was a part of this continuum. Many people understood that democratic governance, if it was to mean anything at all in terms of real development, has to be a shared process. The system alone could not and would not allow scrutiny and accountability. Finally, the reactions that Bori and Janawad elicited were anger and chagrin that the people who govern have the audacity and impunity to fool honest citizens of their due share of development benefits!

An article in *Frontline* had this to say:

> ...the Janawad jan sunwai was categorical about who should be held culpable for this state of affairs in their panchayat.
>
> On 9 April, three of the individuals identified at the public hearing were arrested by the State police and booked for criminal conspiracy, fraud and corruption. Ram Lal, sarpanch of Janawad for much of the six-year period for which the MKSS managed to audit the official record, was the most notable catch. Also booked were two State government functionaries – Ata Mohammad, who functioned as secretary of the panchayat for a two-year period when it was directly under the administration of the State

government, and Savanchand Chandel, a junior engineer with the State Panchayati Raj Department. The MKSS believes that the action, although belated, against the three will serve as a deterrent for others who have been engaged in similar pursuits.[191]

CHAPTER TWENTY-TWO

# Government Enquiry Endorses Janawad Public Hearings

The MKSS, since the days of the first jan sunwai in 1994, had been demanding that transparency and accountability were twin processes of a democracy. The demand for transparency exposed the huge scam in Janawad that also lead to a systemic and transparent accountability process. The high-profile jury, the record attendance of thousands of people despite former Sarpanch Ramlal's threats, and the cross section of civil society that attended the hearing was appalled at the brazen siphoning of funds.[192] The detailed report of this also reached the then chief minister Ashok Gehlot. He was compelled to set something in motion to address state accountability. In a typical response he said he would set up a 'committee'. The MKSS was not willing to see the setting up of a committee as a solution, unless it was headed by a person of integrity and competence. The collective experience of movements and campaigns including the MKSS had made the organization understand that the setting up of a committee was often merely postponing decision making, or in simple lay language delaying the process and passing the buck.

Sri Prakashji, editor of *Raj Drishti,* writes:

> After a struggle for almost a year, finally, truth was triumphant. The administration had to provide information to the people [however incomplete] related with development works. On the basis of the

> available documents, a Public Hearing was organised in Janawad on 3rd April, 2001. And it came to light that works only worth 65 lakhs had taken place, 44 lakh rupees had been siphoned off. The CM of Rajasthan constituted a special enquiry looking at the seriousness of the matter. An investigative team headed by Deputy Secretary of the Finance Department Bannalal and an officer of the Rajasthan Audit Service) physically verified the 141 development works conducted between 1994 and 2000. After this verification, the corruption that came to light was shocking and also shameful, especially for those who claim that no corruption has taken place in the Famine Relief or Development works. In a small panchayat, if 1.25 crore rupees are shown to be spent [in six years] and the actual expenditure is 55 lakhs and the rest [70 lakhs] is gobbled by the politicians, officers and contractors then what would you call this?
>
> The people of the state should applaud the CM who appointed a special investigative team and ordered the investigation.[193]

The appointment of Bannalal, a Rajasthan state audit service official, was a salutary beginning to the process of enquiry. Well respected for his integrity and thoroughness, his appointment was received with relief by the MKSS and the campaign. The report published in *Raj Drishti* continues:

> The people should also applaud Bannalalji and all others of his team who worked without any fear or favour and conducted their duties with utmost honesty. They supported the truth. In our eyes, they lit a candle of hope in the darkness of hopelessness.[194]

Bannalal spent about a month in the Kumbalgarh block and Janawad. He was hardworking, assiduous and thorough in his investigation. Many interesting instances of audacious corruption are illustrated in the following anecdotes or vignettes, as noted in the MKSS Diary:

> Bannalalji went to see the check dams or anicuts. Chimanba, Shankar, Sowmya, Narayan and others from the MKSS went with him, as did the entourage of engineers and other staff from the panchayat samiti and panchayat. They had to see three anicuts. They were the Jadon ka Kheth anicut [under the Employment Assurance Scheme], Amartya Anicut under the Famine Relief works] and

the Aadavala Anicut [Irrigation department i.e., Jeevan dhara], all located in the revenue village of Amartya. First one department, the next and then the last led Bannalal to the same anicut by three separate routes, and all claimed that they constructed it! The tragedy of it, besides the irony and humour, was that these were supposedly audited and accounted for! The suspicions of the villagers were confirmed in the extraordinary sequence of events.

This became rich material for a very powerful play called *Dastak* created by Tripurari Sharma with the MKSS and the NCPRI, which is very popular and has been enacted in Delhi and Rajasthan many times.

The news about these anicuts booked in the name of the irrigation, the panchayat and famine departments, and the absolute effrontery of the government officials spread like wild fire. The Gomti Chauraha, the meeting place for political gossip outdid itself with the numbers of people who collected to hear the news and register their protest.

But there was more to come. There was the case of a well in Janawad, claimed once again by three contenders! It was built under the Sarvajanik New Well programme under Famine relief. All claimed that the work was done by them. In Gomti Chauraha the well claimed to have been dug was nowhere to be found. It was a ghost work, entirely missing on ground!

The panchayat built a Gram Panchayat Bhavan. It was visible and the people could see it being built and in all innocence they thought it was all that had been claimed. As soon as the transparency board went up there was deep suspicion, when the veterinary hospital, sub-PHC were nowhere to be located. Actually there was an older sub-PHC building that had been inaugurated with pomp and show 20 years before when Mohan Lal Sukhadia, then the chief minister had visited Janawad.

Bannalalji uncovered the fraud. The veterinary hospital was sanctioned under the MPLAD scheme and the United Funds scheme. The sub-PHC was sanctioned under the Untied Funds scheme. For all three budgets presented and claimed, there was only one gram panchayat building on the ground!

The veterinary hospital was subsequently built on the panchayat building, while the enquiry was on! It gave rise to the famous lyric sung by the Hela:

*In a fake democracy, fake leaders are making*
*fake speeches,*
*They do not show people the accounts*
*The work they have done has no parallel on earth*
*They open a veterinary hospital on the second floor*
*How will the cattle climb up to get treated?!*
*What kind of hollow rule do we bear with in*
*Rajasthan!*[195]

The interest of the media continued as the issue did not end with the public hearing. Many accounts of it demanding that there should be a rational response continued to be reported in the media. *Raj Drishti*, in its issue of 15 August 2001, reported:

> But what to do with those who sat on the report for 20 days even after it was submitted on 24th July. Not even a word has been said by the government yet [on this matter]. How will they speak? They must be all tongue-tied! After all, not one or two, but forty-nine officers are involved in this matter! This is the matter of former CM Devpura's close aide Ramlal! All of them are linked to the high and mighty [somehow or the other]. This nexus spreads till Jaipur. Now we have to see what a transparent and sensitive government does with this report or where this report ends up![196]

In another article, 'Right to Know – Right to Decide', it was reported:

> Year 2001: A public hearing led by MKSS in Janawad village panchayat exposed an unimaginable extent and kinds of corruption in rural development works. The public outcry against it led the government to launch a thorough probe by a committee headed by Bannalal, Deputy Secretary of Audit in the Rajasthan government. The Bannalal committee unearthed an embezzlement of Rs. 70 lakhs out of a total development expenditure of Rs. 1.25 crore in the panchayat in five years. Most of the works executed by the panchayat were ghost works and most of the muster rolls had ghost entries. The Bannalal Committee Report stated clearly that:

> The total fraud confirmed and proved was 70,44000.00 rupees, 55.19 per cent of the total expenditure in the Panchayat.[197]

Neelabh Misra in 'The Right to Information Discourse in India' writes:

> The Jan Sunwai exposed a huge amount of fraud and embezzlement in government work. A subsequent government enquiry established corruption worth Rs. 70 lakhs out of development works of Rs. 1.25 crores over five years. A total of nine FIRs have been lodged with the police against the government officials and the public representatives concerned by the state government. Let us see how long the course of justice takes.[198]

Soon enough, the state government under pressure after the submission of the Bannalal Committee Report took a comparatively early action.

> Action taken on Bannalal's recommendations: [50 names featured in his list on whom action must be taken. The government took action in the following cases]
>
> 1. Ramlal Gujjar: Former Sarpanch, arrested, debarred from contesting elections
> 2. Bhuri Bai: Sarpanch, process on to declare her unfit to hold office
> 3. Jamunalal Lavati: Former Development officer, suspended, departmental action initiated
> 4. Danvir Singh: Former Development officer, departmental action initiated
> 5. Atta Mohammad: Former Gram Sewak, arrested, suspended
> 6. Balu Ram Saini: Former Gram Sewak, suspended departmental action initiated
> 7. Hemant Kr. Paliwal: Former Gram Sewak, suspended, departmental action initiated
> 8. Sawar Lal Chandel: Former Junior Engineer, arrested, departmental action initiated
> 9. Vinod Arora: Former Junior Engineer, departmental action initiated.[199]

The government was apparently shocked at the lopsided allocation of funds to panchayats within a panchayat samiti and the quantum of fraud, not to mention the shameless flouting of propriety, good sense and ethics in execution. They ordered special audits of the highest-spending panchayats in each of the development blocks or panchayat samitis in Rajasthan. As for the MKSS, the Janawad Jan Sunwai became a landmark in many ways.

Following is a postscript that points the way forward. The importance of a participatory audit process was underlined by all the jan sunwais and transparency exercises. It culminated with Janawad, which brought together and tied the various threads to make a strong statement about governance, corruption and a denial of development, life and livelihood to people. It exposed the arbitrary use of power to corner undue benefits and the opaqueness that led to acts of corruption that induced a sense of shame at the brazenness of people entrusted with the constitutional obligation to deliver.

The MKSS–NCPRI combine did a singular service in not only exposing corruption, but also tying in each of these individual actions with an analysis of the systemic flaws and suggesting remedies. The democratic process was indeed coming of age, and Chimanba and Lachuba, who began a battle with the collective conscience of the people, remain the pioneers of this great achievement. The chain of human effort and the great collective of voices and people, including Bannalal, a government servant, underscored yet again the need to work across categories if this country is really serious about public ethics.

Janawad remains an incident, a happening and a process that touched and changed each one who was a part of it. Social audit began to be seen as necessary, and found its way into the NREGA with the logic of theory and practice, backed by the sum of these experiences.

MKSS homes and office in Devdungri.

Anil Bordia in Sohangarh 1989, Mahila Van Vikas Evam Anusandhan Samiti.

Chunni Singh delivering a speech in Bhim, 1989.

Van Utsav – Rally in Sohangarh to claim the allotted land.

The women who won the battle for land.

5

गांव का मनोहारी दृश्य

# सोहनगढ़:— महिलाओं की अहम भूमिका

महिलाओं की कई जगह अहम भूमिका रहती है और जहां कहीं भी महिलाएं आगे आती है वहा पुरुष भी अपने आप आगे आ जाते हैं और कंधे से कंधा मिलाकर उस काम को पूरा करने तथा कराने की कोशिश करते हैं। समाज में भी यह देखा गया है कि जिस किसी काम को महिलाएं हाथ में ले लेती हैं वह काम चर्चाओं के दौरान ही पूरी हो जाती है।

राजस्थान के राजसमन्द जिले में देवगढ़ पंचायत समिति के अधीन एक गांव है "सोहनगढ़"। इस गांव में महिलाओं की जागरुकता सुनने को मिली है। अगर शहर की महिलाएं जागरुक हों तो इतना महत्व नहीं रखता जितना कि गांव की महिलाओं का जागरुक होना काम रखता है। क्योंकि गांव में इतना अधिक पर्दा होता है कि कोई किसी से बात तक नहीं कर सकता है। कई गांवों में महिलाएं आज भी पंचों के सामने पांव में जूते चप्पल पहनकर नहीं निकलती। ऐसी स्थिति में ग्रामीण महिलाएं बगावत की तरह आगे आये तो यह काबिल - एक तारीफ है।

गांव वाले बताते हैं कि इस गांव में तथा आसपास की भूमि पर कुछ लोगों ने कब्जा कर रखा था। इस कब्जे को हटाने के लिए तथा जमीन को गांव में लिये जाने के लिए ग्रामीण महिलाओं ने एक जुट होकर वृक्षारोपण का काम हाथ में लिया और देखते ही देखते वृक्षारोपण के नाम पर उस जमीन को काफी हद तक मुक्त करा लिया। इस कार्य के लिए महिलाओं ने बाकायदा एक कमेटी का गठन किया और उस गठन के अंतर्गत वृक्षारोपण संबंधी कार्य किया। इस तमाम कार्य के पीछे प्रेरणा भी एक महिला अफसर की ही रही। यह महिला अफसर आई.ए.एस. अरुणा राय ही थी। उन्होंने जिस समय वृक्षारोपण का कार्य शुरु करवाया उस दौरान कई अफसरों ने भी वृक्षारोपण में हाथ बटाया तथा गांव के काफी लोगों ने सहयोग दिया। इस गांव की भूमि में आज भी उस योगदान के वृक्ष पनप रहे हैं।

**शहर से दूर - जिला राजसमन्द**

देवगढ़ तहसील का यह गांव भीतरी भाग में बसा हुआ है तथा गांव में रावत, राजपूत, अधिक रहते हैं। अन्य जातियों में अनुसूचित जाति के लोग हैं। ग्रामीणों का मुख्य धंधा खेती ही है। यहां पर सरसों, तिल, तेल, रायड़ा, ज्वार, बाजरा आदि फसल होती है। इस क्षेत्र में पानी अच्छा होने के कारण फसल भी काफी अच्छी बैठती है। अन्य गांवों की अपेक्षा इस गांव में पानी की कमी नहीं है। पानी के लिए तालाब है तथा आसपास में एनिकट बने हुए है। गांव के लोग पशुपालक है। यहां पर काफी पशु है। इन्हें शिकायत है कि कुछ जमीन ऐसी है जिस पर गांव वालों का हक बनता है उन्हें उस जमीन पर पशुओं को चराने दिया जाना चाहिए पर नहीं चराने दिया जाता बल्कि कुछ व्यक्तियों ने उस पर अधिकार कर रखा है। इसके अलावा बाहर के पशुपालकों के पशुओं को चरने दिया जाता है। और इसके बदले उनसे पैसे वसूल किये जाते हैं जो लोग अपने पशुओं को लेकर आते हैं वे भीलवाड़ा क्षेत्र के पशुपालक है।

गांव कच्चा पक्का बना हुआ है। गांव में काफी मकान पक्के है तथा और मकान पक्के बनते जा रहे हैं। यहां पर भी जमीन की कीमत काफी बढ़ती जा रही है। गांव के लोग सभ्य तथा समझदार हैं। काफी लोग साक्षर है। पढ़े-लिखे भी हैं। अपना कह जानते तथा समझते हैं। पहनावे में धीरे धीरे शहरीपन आता जा रहा है। इस क्षेत्र में पुरुष के सिर पर साफे नजर नहीं आते हैं। बहुत ही कम लोग या नहीं के बराबर पगड़ीधारी दीख पड़ते हैं। वह भी ढूंढने पर नजर आते हैं। भाषा यहां की उदयपुर से मिलती जुलती है। गांव वाले अपनी नई पीढ़ी को पढ़ी लिखी देखना चाहते हैं। काफी लोगों का ध्यान खेती की तरफ ही है पर थोड़ा बहुत पढ़ा-लिखा ग्रामीण भी अब यह महसूस कर रहा है कि उसकी संतान खेती की बजाय नौकरी करे या बाबूजी बन जाये तो ज्यादा ठीक है क्योंकि नौकरी में अब दम नहीं है।

सोहनगढ़ में पशुचिकित्सा नहीं है और ना ही आसपास है। इंसानों के इलाज की भी व्यवस्था नहीं है। जानवरों और इंसानों के इलाज के लिए देवगढ़ ही है। दोनों ही इलाज के लिए देवगढ़ ही आते हैं। कुछ पशुपालक केगढ़ भी अपने पशुओं को ले जाते हैं। ग्रामीणों का सुझाव है कि दस गांवों के लिए भी अगर पशु चिकित्सा या किसी कम्पाउंडर की नियुक्ति कर दी जाये और वो दो माह में एक बार भी पशुओं की जांच कर चला जाये तो ग्रामीणों को काफी राहत मिलेगी क्योंकि ग्रामीणों के लिए एक तरह से कमाई का साधन जानवर ही है। सारी दुनिया कहती है कि जानवर इंसान को पालता है। अगर जानवर दूध देना बंद कर दे तो इंसान को छठी का दूध याद आ जाये। ग्रामीणों को अफसोस है कि सरकार गांवों पर ध्यान नहीं देती है।

विवरण व छाया- महावीरसिंह चौहान

Newspaper report in *Dainik Navjyoti*, 1992.

# Udaipur village tense over land allotment

By USHA RAI

The Times of India News Service

NEW DELHI, August 6.

TERROR stalks Sohangarh village in Devgarh tehsil of Udaipur district since July 15 when 120 bighas (25 hectares) of scrub land that a rich Rajput zamindar had appropriated was allotted to a cooperative body of economically backward Rawat women.

Till recently, the villagers of Sohangarh were paying the zamindar, a former jagirdar, grazing rights of Rs. 5 for a goat and Rs. 10 for a buffalo for the season. The women were finding it increasingly difficult to get grass and fodder for their cattle and fuel wood for their home fires though there was a large chunk of unoccupied government land adjacent to their village because the former jagirdar, Mr. Hari Singh, was controlling it.

When the villagers heard of land distribution for social forestry programme they decided to apply for it. First the men tried for individual allotments and when this proved difficult the women formed a collective body and applied at every stage. Mr. Hari Singh, the known leader of the area, thwarted their efforts.

It is for the first time that these women have shown political maturity and come out of their purdah. Fully backed by their men-folk they ultimately succeeded in acquiring land for social forestry. But the 120 bighas was from the 429 bighas (khasra no 1331) being controlled by Mr. Hari Singh, and he has not been able to forget it. "I will die or will get killed but I will not leave this land", he announced when the women first started filling forms to acquire the land.

The very evening the women, under the banner of Shramik Mahila Van Vikas Evam Anusandham Samiti, got possession of the land. Four of their menfolk, all leaders who were in consultation in a hut, were attacked by Hari Singh's men. They were terrorised with swirling swords and lathis while one of Hari Singh's men, mounted guard with a gun, Sholay-style, sitting on top of the gateway to the house.

When a cry went out that Banwar, a Rawat leader, was injured, men and women came out with axes. Kitchen knives and whatever implements they could get hold of, they literally chased away the intruders.

The very night a complaint was lodged at the Devgarh police station by the villagers. The five attackers, who were identified in the complaint, included Methu Singh and Balwant Singh, two brothers of Hari Singh, a son of Hari Singh and two other relatives. Earlier the villagers had given an application for protection fearing breach of peace.

Mrs Aruna Roy, Mr. Nikhil Dey, Mr. Shankar Singh and Mrs Anchi Singh, who have been working among the villagers and doing research on anti-poverty programmes in the area for the last two years, are equally apprehensive. Since they are seen as the force behind the villagers efforts to assert themselves, they too have been threatened by Hari Singh in the presence of the SDO, the deputy superintendent of police, the tehsildar and the SHO.

Mrs Aruna Roy is afraid that the great strides made by the women in Sohangarh may come to nought, if the tension is not dispelled.

In a bid to defuse tension and express solidarity with the villagers of Sohangarh, Mrs Roy said that a meeting was held there on July 29. Representatives of voluntary organisations from Jaipur, Udaipur, Ajmer and Tilonia as well as those of all political parties and even some bureaucrats attended the meeting. A Van Mahotsav function was also organised and some 50 samplings were planted. But every night the saplings were uprooted. Neither Hari Singh nor the local MLA, Mr. Laxman Singh, who was recently involved in a mines scandal, attended the meeting.

Now that the VIPs have left leaving trails of dust, the villagers are feeling insecure again.

Newspaper report in *Times of India*, 1989.

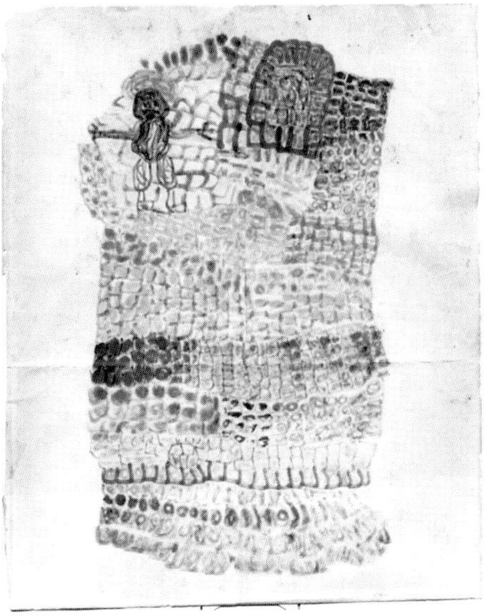

Hari Singh, drawing by six-year-old Vikas.

Tej Singh, Sohangarh, founder member of the MKSS.

The first MKSS May Day meeting in the market place at Bhim.

एक मई १९९० को भीम में मजदूर एवं किसानों की

विशाल रैली

स्थान– पाटीयों का चौड़ा

समय– दिन को १२ बजे

सभी मजदूर किसानों को सादर आमन्त्रण

संयोजक–
मजदूर किसान शक्ति संगठन

श्री लखकार प्रिन्टिंग प्रेस, भीम

The first pamphlet of the newly formed MKSS, 1990.

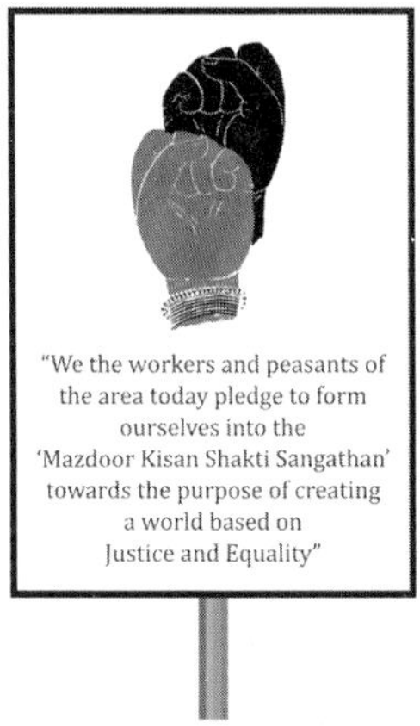


May Day placard announcing the birth of the MKSS, 1990.

People gathered on May Day, 1990.

A play being performed that travelled announcing the formation of the MKSS.

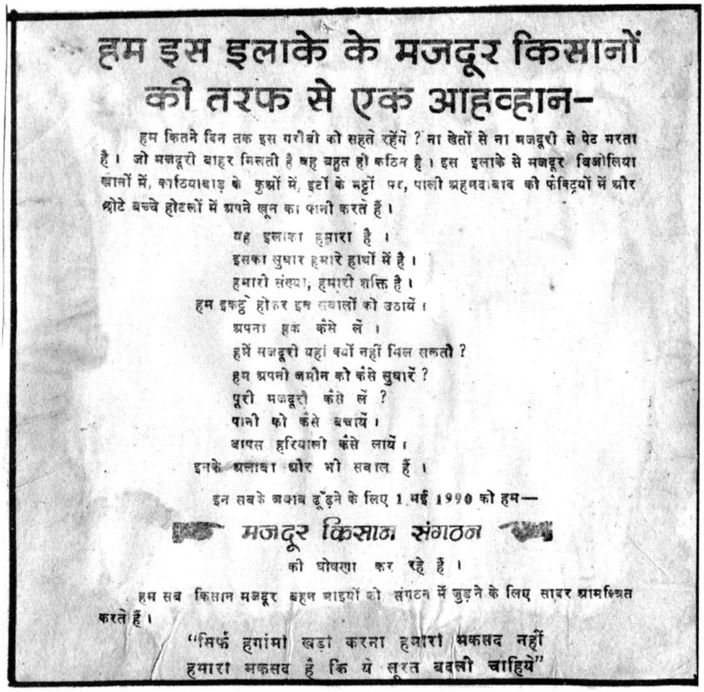

हम इस इलाके के मजदूर किसानों की तरफ से एक आहृवान–

हम कितने दिन तक इस गरीबी को सहते रहेंगे ? ना खेतों से ना मजदूरी से पेट भरता है। जो मजदूरी बाहर मिलती है वह बहुत ही कठिन है। इस इलाके से मजदूर बिजोलिया खानों में, काठियावाड़ के कुओं में, ईटों के भट्टों पर, पाली अहमदाबाद की फैक्ट्रियों में और छोटे बच्चे होटलों में अपने खून का पानी करते हैं।

यह इलाका हमारा है।
इसका सुधार हमारे हाथों में है।
हमारी संख्या, हमारी शक्ति है।
हम इकट्ठे होकर इन सवालों को उठायें।
अपना हक कैसे लें।
हमें मजदूरी यहां क्यों नहीं मिल सकती ?
हम अपनी जमीन को कैसे सुधारें ?
पूरी मजदूरी कैसे लें ?
पानी को कैसे बचायें।
वापस हरियाली कैसे लायें।
इनके अलावा और भी सवाल हैं।

इन सबके जवाब ढूंढने के लिए 1 मई 1990 को हम—

मजदूर किसान संगठन

की घोषणा कर रहे हैं।

हम सब किसान मजदूर बहन भाइयों को संगठन में जुड़ने के लिए सादर आमन्त्रित करते हैं।

"सिर्फ हंगामा खड़ा करना हमारा मकसद नहीं
हमारा मकसद है कि ये सूरत बदली चाहिये"

Pamphlet announcing the agenda for the newly formed MKSS.

First hunger strike to demand minimum wages, 1990.

Breaking the fast – first hunger strike, 1990.

*Left and Right*: Bhim convention, 1990.

# Rajasthan Govt flouting minimum wage lav

**Express News Service**
JAIPUR, Aug 15

The rustic stubborness shown last month by a few hundred villagers of Jal Panchayat in Bheem tehsil of Udaipur district, who refused to accept anything less than the minimum wages for work done under the famine relief programmes. Nineteen of them even sat on a hunger strike for six days at the SDM's office.

By doing so, they have exposed the hollow claims of the government regarding the functioning of relief works. Also nailed in the event was the government's unwillingness to give the villagers the minimum wage of Rs 14 even after the hunger strike.

What is, however, a major cause for concern is the fact that, though villagers elsewhere in the State may not have protested like those of Bheem tehsil, similar conditions of non-payment of minimum wages may well be existing in other parts of the State. At least a fair number of activists involved in development work, including Ms Aruna Bunker Roy, who has been working in Bheem area for the last four years and played a key role in organising villagers there, and the state general secretary of the Bhartiya Mazdoor Sangh (BMS), Mr Rishab Chand Jain also hold a similar view.

Another disturbing element in the Bheem case is the manner in which the district authorities and the local MLA, Mr Mandhata Singh, who is also the brother-in-law of the Prime Minister, Mr V. P. Singh, alternately cajoled and threatened the villagers against taking recourse to agitational methods. First, an attempt was made to dissuade the villagers by giving assurances which was followed by a not too discreet attempt to dub the recently formed villagers' body–the Mazdoor Kisan Shakti Sanghthan (MKSS) as some kind of a Naxalite movement. Finally, when the villagers started the hunger strike, the local MLA, Mr Singh, is reported to have told the villagers that "not a paisa" would be increased.

According to government sources, it is usually the Public Works Department (PWD) which refuses to pay the prescribed minimum wages to labourers engaged in relief works. Even in Bheem, it was the PWD and the Irrigation Department which refused to oblige by paying minimum wages even though the Forest Department had paid minimum wages in the same area. The overall scenario offers an explanation to the statement by the State Relief Minister, Ms Pushpa Jain, in a press conference about two months back, that the department was unable to meet the "employment targets" under relief works in all but one district of the State because the labourers were getting better wages elsewhere. She could have well added that the government was falling short of the target because of its inability to offer even minimum wages. Observers wonder on how various government departments would hedge the new minimum wage prescribed by the State cabinet (Rs 22), when they try all the tricks in their bag to avoid paying the earlier minimum wage of Rs 14.

In fact, there are many who feel that it is the government's greed for "numbers" which is responsible for the present state of affairs in which the trend is to employ as many people as possible irrespective of the amount sanctioned for the work which ultimately results in labourers getting less than the minimum wage. Another scourge for those employed in relief works is that the government, in contravention of the Supreme Court judgement, computes the labourer's wage on both the time and task rate simultaneously. Another irritant, which, according to Ms Aruna Bunker Roy, also results in a loss of productivity for the State, is the novel method of computing wages by which the entire group at a site–whether they all work actively or not–get an even share from the sanctioned amo Thus there is a negative bonus sorts with the result that nobou really works.

Talking to ENS here on Sunday, another activist working in Bheem tehsil–who, incidentally, was bashed up by goons of a local jagirdar recently–pointed out that there was need for a drastic change in the mentality of those manning relief agencies and works. "If only they would stop treating this as dole and rigorously demand work, the labour on relief works could truly help in building national resources," he said.

Thinking in political circles also seems to be veering around to this viewpoint. According to Ms Roy, the Chief Minister, Mr Bhairon Singh Shekhawat, had recently told a delegation of activists that the government was contemplating a review of the famine relief works in consultation with various organisa tions engaged in development work

*Indian Express* report on the hunger strike, August 1990.

Second hunger strike, 1991.

दैनिक नवज्योति

अजमेर दिनांक 9 मई 1991 पृष्ठ सं. (10)

न्यूनतम मजदूरी आन्दोलन

# श्रमिकों का आमरण अनशन पुलिस ने जबरन तुड़वाया

(कार्यालय संवाददाता)

अजमेर, 8 मई। मजदूर किसान शक्ति संगठन के तत्वावधान में न्यूनतम मजदूरी की मांग को लेकर ग्राम [illegible] में पिछले चार दिनों से जारी मजदूरों के आमरण अनशन को कल देर रात पुलिस और प्रशासन ने बल पूर्वक तुड़वा दिया। मजदूर [illegible] मई से पुनः धरना देंगे।

जानकारी के अनुसार 7 मई की रात को बारह बजे के करीब अचानक आए अनेक पुलिस कर्मियों ने सोते हुए [illegible] धरना व अनशनकारियों को घेर लिया। ए.एस.पी. ने मेडिकल जांच के लिये अनशनकारियों को तहसील भेजने के लिए कहा। संगठन के लोगों ने इस बात का विरोध करते हुए पहले पुलिस को हटाए जाने की मांग की। साथ ही एस.डी.ओ. द्वारा अनशनकारियों से पहले बातचीत करने का प्रस्ताव रखा गया।

प्रशासन ने इस बात को न मानते हुए अनशनकारियों के धरनास्थल पर बलपूर्वक तोड़फोड़ शुरू कर दी। धरने पर सो रही औरतों को घसीटा गया, लाठी मारी गई, कई मजदूरनियों के कपड़े फाड़ दिए गए। अनशनकारियों जिनमें मोतीलाल, किशोर सेन, गंगासिंह, रुकमा बाई, केली बाई, शंकर सिंह, नौरती बाई और हरीसिंह को पुलिस जबरन अपने साथ ले गई।

घटना को लेकर ग्रामवासियों में गहरा रोष व्याप्त हो गया। ग्रामीणों ने सैकड़ों की संख्या में एकत्रित होकर मौन जुलूस निकाला व घटना की कड़ी निंदा की।

मजदूरों ने इस अन्यायपूर्ण अमानवीय व्यवहार की न्यायिक जांच की मांग की है।

*Dainik Navjyoti* report on the second hunger strike, May 1991.

Negotiating with the representatives of the Government of India – second hunger strike.

India's largest selling daily newspaper

ESTABLISHED 1838

THE TIMES OF INDA

NO. 111 VOL. CLIV. CITY II — NEW DELHI: FRIDAY, MAY 10 1991 — Rs. 1.80

JAWAHAR ROZGAR YOJANA

# Aid to Rajasthan may be cut

By USHA RAI
The Times of India News Service

NEW DELHI, May 9: THE Central rural development department has threatened to cut off the Rs. 100-crore grant due to Rajasthan during the current financial year under the Jawahar Rozgar Yojana, provided the state fails to adhere to the regulations on payment of a minimum wage of Rs. 22 under the JRY.

The tough stand has been taken by the Centre after a team of the ministry visited Bhim, Rajsamand district, where some 300 workers from five districts have been agitating for the last three months for minimum wages under the Mazdoor Kisan Shakti Sangathan. Since May 2 there has been a fast-unto-death. Telegram after telegrams from the Centre, using the harshest language possible to adhere to the guidelines have gone unheeded.

On May 7 there was a lathi-charge on the hunger-strikers and three women were injured. Five of those on hunger strike were forcibly moved to a hospital.

**Ironically enough, when all political parties are wooing the people and making all kinds of promises from "roti" to "naukari", in Rajasthan, a demand for implementing the promised minimum wages, backed by a fiat from the Centre, is being ignored. When the chief minister, Mr Bhairon Singh Shekhawat, visited Bhim this week hopes were high that the workers would get their due.**

Now the Centre feels compelled to invoke section 26.10 for non-payment of the minimum wages, which is withholding the Central grant.

MOST RECALCITRANT STATE: Though there have been several violations of the minimum wages guidelines under the JRY by U.P., Gujarat and Rajasthan governments, when the Centre intervened the minimum wages were paid. But Rajasthan has been the most "recalcitrant" state. and

For well-over a year now the workers of Rajasthan who survive on famine relief work, JRY and the other government programmes have been agitating for minimum wages and in last November the Institute of Development Studies, Jaipur, brought together policy-makers and legal experts to thrash out the issues relating to the minimum wages in the government-sponsored rural employment programme. The secretary, rural development, Mr Shankaran, participated in the deliberations. It was decided that the minimum wages must be paid on all government works, including the famine relief works and, in general, the time-rate, (payment on the hours of work put in) basis should govern the payment. Exceptions could only be made where the labourers themselves took a decision for a different rate of payment.

In January this year, the Rajasthan government issued guidelines for the conduct of JRY works incorporating the decisions taken at the workshop.

For about 20 days from December 25 last year, 400 people were provided employment at 13 sites of Barar Gram Panchayat, 10 kms from Bhim under the JRY. On December 26, the workers pointed out to the authorities concerned that their work was neither being assigned nor measured at the end of the day as stipulated in the JRY guidelines.

But on January 23 the Barar Gram Panchayat passed a resolution for interim payment of Rs. 11 as daily wages to the JRY workers. Tweleve workers refused payment and demanded to know how the wage was being determined. Then the agitation spread and led to the dharna and hunger strike.

As a matter of fact in February, after measuring the work done, the Panchayat felt only Rs. 7.80 should be paid as daily wages.

The Central team, which visited Bhim, found that there was no mention in the muster roll that the workers absented themselves. If the workers were shirking this should have been noted. Nor was there any clue as to whether

Continued on page 16, col. 4

Continued from page 1, col. 4

enough work was being assigned. The Central team report, however, indicates that for a large number of people employed less work was done.

But legally the workers have to be paid the minimum wages, the rural development department has pointed out. The piece rate wages are invariably higher than the minimum wages. Even if the workers were given less work they have to be paid the minimum wage of Rs. 22.

WAGE RATE: The Centre has pointed out that "wage rate is not subject to panchayat resolutions. It is inconceivable that wages should be paid at the rate of Rs. 11 and Rs. 7 while the minimum wage is Rs. 22."

Quoting paragraph 26.8 of the JRY guidelines, the Centre has pointed out that it is the responsibility of the state government to ensure payment of prescribed wages to JRY workers. Instead, the state government chose not to extend minimum wages of Rs. 22 up to November 1990 even though it was notified in June.

The lengthy telegram states that the Minimum Wages Act does not permit the treatment of relief work and employment programmes distinct from other works. Similar works whether in PWD (public works department) or Forest departments or in relief work or employment programmes have to be treated on a par for wage entitlements. The JRY wage payment is governed by clear-cut guidelines and should not be mixed with other issues which are not of any concern to the government of India.

The state has fixed time rate wages in its notification of June 1990 and this should be honoured, says the Centre. The JRY guidelines mention the piece rate wage as one of the methods to prescribe the wages. Guidelines also stipulate that piece has to be notified with a fall-back wage. Fall-back wage, or irreducible minimum wage rate, will be the wage rate, the Centre has said.

"Payment of wages is governed by sections 3, 14 and 15 of the minimum wages Act. If the workers were present for normal hours of duty and none of the infirmities specified in provisions to section 15 of the Act have been established, the payment will have to be at the rate of Rs. 22 for each day of work put by them, irrespective of so called output of work."

*Times of India* front page news on the hunger strike, May 1991.

पत्रिका — उदयपुर, 5 मई, 1991

# भीम में न्यूनतम मजदूरी की मांग पर आमरण अनशन

[कार्यालय संवाददाता]

उदयपुर, 4 मई। जिले की भीम तहसील में न्यूनतम मजदूरी की मांग को लेकर राजस्थान किसान मजदूर शक्ति संगठन द्वारा शनिवार को भीम पंचायत समिति मुख्यालय पर 5 श्रमिकों ने आमरण अनशन आरंभ कर दिया। अनशनकारियों में 2 महिलाएं व 3 पुरुष हैं।

संगठन के प्रवक्ता शंकरसिंह के अनुसार आमरण अनशन दोपहर 12 बजे शुरू किया गया। संगठन जवाहर रोजगार योजना व अन्य विभागीय निर्माण कार्यों के श्रमिकों को न्यूनतम मजदूरी 22 रुपए प्रति दिन दिए जाने की मांग कर रहे हैं तथा गत 29 अप्रेल से पंचायत समिति मुख्यालय पर अनिश्चितकालीन धरना दे रहे थे। संगठन ने अपनी मांगों के लिए गुरुवार को प्रशासन को 48 घंटे का समय दिया था वरना अनशन आरंभ करने की चेतावनी दी थी।

इस बीच संगठन का एक शिष्टमंडल शनिवार को उदयपुर में मुख्य सचिव से मिला व उन्हें ज्ञापन दिया। मुख्य सचिव ने आश्वासन दिया कि वे उनकी मांगों पर शीघ्र निर्णय करवाएंगे।

—

भोपाल, 4 मई [वार्ता]। भारतीय कम्युनिस्ट पार्टी के राष्ट्रीय सचिव होमी दाजी ने शनिवार को यहां कहां कि वामपंथी मोर्चे ने कांग्रेस [इ] के लिए मैत्री के द्वार सदैव के लिए बंद नहीं किए हैं, मगर भारतीय जनता पार्टी के साथ हाथ मिलाने का कोई प्रश्न ही नहीं है।

*Rajasthan Patrika* reporting on the hunger strike, May 1991.

Inauguration of the Mazdoor Kisan Kirana Store, 1992.

Inaugurating the PDS run by the Devdungri Samiti in Devdungri, 1992.

Inaugurating the PDS run by the Devdungri Samiti in Devdungri, 1992.

# Fighting inflation at the grassroots

RECENTLY, a peasants and workers organisation based in Rajasthan demonstrated an important but neglected aspect of the fight against inflation—that citizen's initiatives are as important as macro-economic policies.

This organisation—Mazdoor Kisan Shakti Sangathan—had earlier attracted attention for its work in ensuring the timely payment of minimum wages at drought relief work sites. While doing this, the Sangathan had for the first time opened up a new from in protecting the livelihood of the people by taking up anti-inflation work.

While the Sanghatan's work encompasses parts of four districts in Rajasthan, the semi-rural town of Bhim (Rajsamand district) is the centre of its work and struggles. It is here that this organisation has recently opened a co-operative shop called Mazdoor Kisan Kirana store to supply a wide range of essential commodities. The local MKSS members initially contributed Rs 10 each towards this venture which was backed by a few interest-free loans from well-wishers.

The effort concentrated on reduced retail margins and quality control to provide goods at lower prices. It was decided that since those who run the shop were dedicated MKSS activists, they would take no more than the legal minimum wage of Rs 22. Incidentally, the senior-most member of MKSS also gets the same wage.

Other members of the MKSS also helped to ensure that high quality was maintained by personal supervision of the grinding and cleaning work. For example, while getting the coriander seeds and turmeric ground, they were asked how much haldi should be mixed in the dhaniya and how much salt mixed in the haldi, the activists, unlike other shopkeepers, insisted on absolute purity.

Predictably, the response of the consumers has been very favourable. The news of the good quality and low prices spread rapidly, first among MKSS sympathisers, and then among other people as well. A high turnover within a short time enabled the new venture to meet its target of being able to function at a margin of just one per cent. Till mid-April this small shop had already chalked up daily sales of about Rs7,000. During the marriage season of late April-May, however, the sales peaked to nearly double this amount—about Rs14,000 a day.

The new shop not only sold products at a cheaper rate, it also announced its low prices over the microphone. Thus in a market where many buyers were illiterate, the shop's low rates were communicated to potential customers. This was greatly resented by other traders who then petitioned the collector to take action against the new shop. When they failed to evoke a satisfactory response from officialdom, they set up a loud music system near the shop, to drown out the announcements of the rate-list.

This however, had the opposite effect. Several shoppers, attracted by the loud music came closer and eventually found out about the new shop next door as well.

The result was that the MKSS venture succeeded in bringing down the market rates to some extent as other retailers were forced to cut their high margins to compete with them. This had a favourable impact on inflationary trends far beyond the items sold directly by the new shop.

Lakshman Singh, who buys spices worth Rs20 daily for his dhaba, says that he not only saves Rs5 a day now by going to the new shop, but the quality of these spices are much better too. Lal Singh, a peasant says that even people from villages nearly 10 km away, prefer to buy their groceries from the new shop. Nikhil Dey, a leading MKSS activist says that prices have come down by about 15 per cent since this experiment began about five months ago.

Crucial to this success have been persons such as Latu Singh and Tulsa Singh, who manage the daily affairs of the Mazdoor Kisan Kirana Store. They are not only honest and sincere MKSS members they are experienced as well, having worked earlier in big grocery stores. As they know the nitty-gritty of buying and selling, they cannot be duped easily. Little wonder then that the bigger traders are now trying to entice them away with higher salaries. But they have resisted all such offers. As Latu Singh says, "The feeling that we are the links in an important part of our own people's welfare is that keeps us here."

**The Sangathan has managed to bring down the market rates by forcing other retailers to cut their high margins**

Apart from handling the work of their own shop, Latu Singh and Tulsa Singh are also training new colleagues such as Madho and Dhanna Singh so that they can take set up more such ventures. The next shop is scheduled to open at another semi-rural town Jawaza.

Meanwhile, the traders of Bhim have stepped up their campaign against the new shop. They have exerted pressure on the local wholesalers and dealers to stop suppeying provisions to the shop. They have even attempted to stop a transporter from carrying their supplies. These patentlyunfair moves against a small and low-resource competitor, have certainly created some problems for the MKSS store. However, they have also worked out their own solution by obtaining supplies from other towns or asking friends to get local supplies on their behalf. Once some traders also tried to force them to close down in support of communal demands; but were forced to beat a shamefaced retreat when all their threats had no effect.

The Mazdoor Kisan Kirana Store at Bhim is a pioneering effort at proving how careful planning backed by honest, dedicated work can defeat inflation at the grass roots and also improve quality. Hopefully, the local administration will do their utmost to protect this effort (and similar ventures in other areas) from the local vested interests.

■ Bharat Dogra

*Economic Times* report on the opening of Mazdoor Kisan Kirana Store, May 1993.

# नवभारत टाइम्स

निर्बन्ध

## एक दुकान जो महँगाई से लड़ रही है

भारत डोगरा

*Navbharat Times* report on the Mazdoor Kisan Kirana Store, 1993.

First Jan Sunwai at Kotkirana, 2 December 1994.

Fourth Jan Sunwai at Jawaja, 7 January 1995.

*Left and right*: Beawar Dharna, the first big prolonged demand for the RTI, Beawar, 1996.

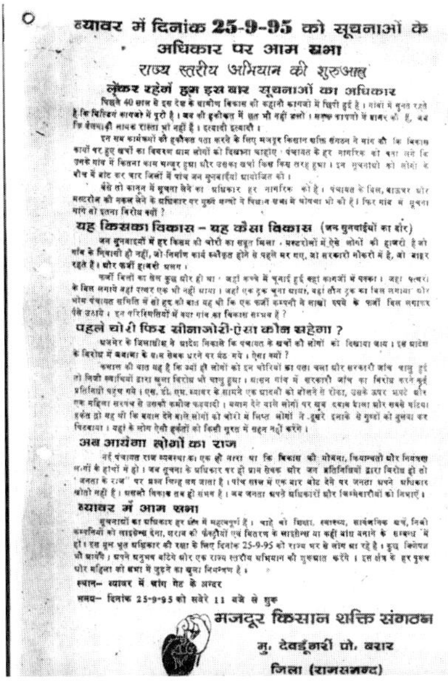

ब्यावर में दिनांक 25-9-95 को सूचनाओं के अधिकार पर आम सभा

राज्य स्तरीय अभियान की शुरुआत

यह किसका विकास – यह कैसा विकास

पहले चोरी फिर सीनाजोरी-ऐसा कौन सहेगा?

अब आयेगा लोगों का राज

ब्यावर में आम सभा

मजदूर किसान शक्ति संगठन

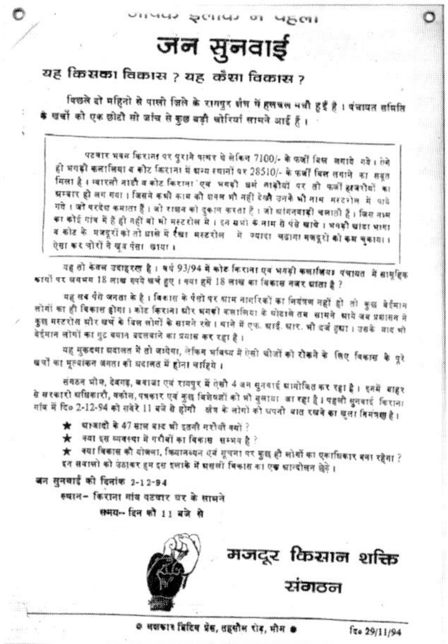

जन सुनवाई

यह किसका विकास ? यह कैसा विकास ?

जन सुनवाई की दिनांक 2-12-94

स्थान– किराना गांव पटवार घर के सामने

समय– दिन को 11 बजे से

मजदूर किसान शक्ति संगठन

दि० 29/11/94

Pamphlets were important tools to communicate with people: (*Left*) announcing an 'Aam Sabha' in Beawar, 1995; (*right*) announcing the first Jan Sunwai at Kotkirana, 1994.

भीम में जन सुनवाई आज, 'विकास' की पोल खुलेगी

दैनिक नवज्योति

विधानसभा में शेखावत की घोषणा

पंचायत विकास कार्यों में गड़बड़ी करने वालों को दंडित किया जाएगा

The first newspaper report of the Jan Sunwai, *Navbharat Times,* 1994.

*Dainik Navjyoti* announcing Rajasthan CM's statement in the Assembly promising transparency and copies of bills, vouchers and muster rolls.

Medha Patkar at a dharna in Beawar, 1996.

Aruna addressing a rally at Chang Gate, Beawar 1996.

Jaipur Dharna, a demand for the RTI at Statue Circle, Jaipur, 1997.

The dharna concludes with victory – the right to access records under the amended Panchayat Raj Act, 1997.

The second round of Jan Sunwais – Kukarkheda, 1998.

पहले चोरी, फिर सीना जोरी ।
जनता के पैसों का, लूट - बन्द करो ॥

भीम में **21/7/98** को भ्रष्टाचार के खिलाफ रैली औरधरना
हर नागरिक को इस आन्दोलन में जुड़ने का आव्हान्

पिछले पांच सालों मे इस क्षेत्र में हो रहे विकास कार्यों में भ्रष्टाचार को रोकने का प्रयास चल रहा है। यहो से जन्मा सूचना के जन अधिकार का अभियान अब पूरे देश में भ्रष्टाचार के खिलाफ लड़ने के लिए आशा की किरण बनी हुई है। अब लोकसभा में भी इसका कानून बनने जा रहा है। 1997 में राजस्थान सरकार ने विकास कार्यों में हर नागरिक को सूचना के जन अधिकार का आदेश पारित किया। इस क्षेत्र में भी विकास के बिल, वाउचर और मस्टरोलों की नकल (सत्य प्रतिलिपी) लेने के बाद चोरी के सबूत मिले हैं। चोरी करने वालों का पता चला है। कुछ पंचायतों में गबन किये हुए पैसे वापस पंचायत कोष में जमा भी हुए हैं। ऐसे लग रहा था कि कम से कम कुछ पंचायतों में एक नया ईमानदारी का रास्ता खुलेगा और गरीबी हटाने का असली प्रयास किया जायेगा।

**यह कैसी व्यवस्था ?**

लेकिन भ्रष्टाचार करने वालों के गिरोह को इन प्रयासों से खतरा लग रहा है। वे सुधार के रास्ते अपनाने की जगह चोरी जारी रखने के रास्ते ढूंढने लगे हैं। प्रशासन, राजनैतिक दलों, और गांव में बिछी उनकी जाल सक्रिय होने लगी है। इस पूरे आन्दोलन को असफल करने का प्रयास चल रहा है। कालादेह समेलिया, कुकरखेड़ा बरार, सांगावास और विजयपुरा [illegible] पंचायतों में चोरी के सबूत मिलने के बाद भी प्रशासन निष्क्रियता दिखा रही है। कुकरखेड़ा पंचायत की श्रीमती [illegible] ने अपनी पंचायत में हुए भ्रष्टाचार की नैतिक जिम्मेदारी को खुले आम कबूलते हुए एक लाख रुपये पंचायत [illegible] में जमा कराने की घोषणा की। इस वादे से मुकरने के पीछे किन-किन लोगों के हाथ हैं? पंचायती करके ईमानदार [illegible] को दबाने के प्रयास करने वालों से हम पूछना चाहते हैं कि क्या असली पंचायती का यही अर्थ है? अपने दिल पर हाथ रख कर बतायें कि दिनांक **4/7/98** को कुकरखेड़ा में हुई पंचायती क्या न्याय और सच्चाई की थी?

पंचायत विजयपुरा में 1994 में एस. डी. एम. की जांच रिपोर्ट में साफ पाया गया था कि फर्जी निलामी करके प्रभावशाली लोगों को कौड़ियों के भाव पंचायत की कीमती जमीन सौंप दी गई। फिर भी जिला कलेक्टर राजसमन्द, ने इन प्रभावशाली लोगों के पक्ष में निर्णय कैसे दिये? हम पूछना चाहते हैं [illegible] क्या इस ग्राम पंचायत, उसके नागरिक, सरकार की सम्पत्ति, और गरीब लोगों के साथ न्याय है?

"हमारे इरादे--हमारा संकल्प"

हमारे इरादे बहुत साफ हैं। हमारा संकल्प बहुत पक्का। इस देश के नागरिक भ्रष्टाचार के [illegible] फैलाने वालों और गरीबों का शोषण करने वालों से तंग आ चुके हैं। आजादी के पचास साल की [illegible] हम असली आजादी की लड़ाई लड़ेंगे। हम गलती करने वालों के सामने बिल्कुल नहीं झुकेंगे, चाहे भी प्रभावशाली हो।

दिनांक 21/7/98 को भीम में होने वाला भ्रष्टाचार विरोधी प्रदर्शन एक [illegible] सुथरी व्यवस्था रचने की दिशा में एक कदम होगा। हम मांग करेंगे कि हर ना[illegible] आसानी से सूचना उपलब्ध हो। भ्रष्ट लोगों के खिलाफ कठोर कानूनी कार्यवाही ह[illegible] किये हुए पैसे उनसे वसूले जाएँ। और उन्हें पद से बर्खास्त किया जाएँ। इस क्षे[illegible] नागरिक को इस रैली और धरना में शामिल होने का खुला निमन्त्रण है।

कमाने वाला - खायेगा ।
लूटने वाला - जायेगा ।
अब नया जमाना - आयेगा ।

दिनांक : 21/7/98, मंगलवार
स्थान : रैली भीम डाक बंगले के सामने से प्रातः 10 बजे प्रारम्भ होगी ।

और से-

मजदूर किसान शक्ति संगठन
देवडूंगरी (बरार) जिला-राजसमन्द

✲ मुद्रक-जगदम्बा प्रिंटिंग प्रेस, हॉस्पीटल के पास, भीम ✲

Pamphlet announcing a rally in Bhim for RTI, July 1998.

Jan Sunwai in Umarwas, 1999.

Pyarji, sarpanch of Umarwas 1999.

## हमारे गांव में हमारा राज

### दिनांक 4-4-2000 को टाडगढ़ रंगमंच (स्टेडीयम) मे पंचायती राज व्यवस्था और लोक सशक्तिकरण पर खुली चर्चा

- अकाल राहत और विकास कार्यों में पूरा काम पूरा दाम ।
- सरकारी तंत्र और कर्मचारियों पर जनता का नियत्रण।
- ग्राम सभा और वार्ड सभा को वास्तविक रुप से ताकतवर बनाना ।
- पंचायतों में पर्याप्त धन की व्यवस्था हो। हर पंचायत में एक सचिव हो। सरपंचों को न्यूनतम मजदूरी से मानदेय मिले ।
- भ्रष्टाचार रोकने की पुख्ता व्यवस्था हो। सूचना का अधिकार और वार्ड सभा के माध्यम से हर काम का हिसाब किताब लेना।
- ग्राम सभा और वार्ड सभा ही विकास की योजनाऐं बनाये ।

इन मुद्दों पर हम चर्चा करे। समस्याओं और सम्भावनाओं को समझे । और वास्तविक तोर पर सत्ता को लगाम आम लोगों के हाथों में पहुंचाये इस उद्देश्य के साथ मजदूर किसान शक्ति संगठन ने टॉडगढ़ ग्राम पंचायत के साथ मिलकर इस क्षेत्र की जनता, जन प्रतिनिधि, सरकारी अधिकारी और अन्य विशेषज्ञों के साथ एक खुली चर्चा रखी हैं।

इस मौके पर केरल, कर्नाटका, महाराष्ट्रा, आंध्र प्रदेश, मध्य प्रदेश, और दिल्ली से देश के जाने माने संगठनों के प्रतिनिधि भी अपने विचार रखेगें।

आप इस खुली चर्चा में ज्यादा से ज्यादा संख्या में आये और इस आंदोलन को ताकत दे ।

**सिर्फ हंगामा खड़ा करना हमारा मकसद नहीं ।**
**हमारा मकसद हैं कि यह सूरत बदलनी चाहीये ।।**

दिनांक : 4-4-2000
स्थान ; टाटगढ़ रंगमंच [स्टेड़ीयम]
समय : सवेरे 10 बजे से साय 3 बजे तक

**मजदूर किसान शक्ति संगठन**
**गांव देवडूंगरी पो. बरार**
**जिला-राजसमंद (राज.) 313341**

— लक्षकार प्रिंटिंग प्रेस, तहसील रोड़, भीम —

A pamphlet inviting people for an open discussion on Pachayati Raj and people's empowerment in Todgarh, 2000.

Janawad and its frauds, an incomplete water tank billed and paid for, 2001.

Gopi, a poor worker defrauded of minimum wages, showing the dots that she used to maintain record of her days of work.

Jan Sunwai in Janawad, 2001.

The first NCPRI Convention Public Meeting in Beawar, 2001.

Government initiated Jan Sunwais of the highest-spending panchayats in each block.

*Above and below*: Government initiated Jan Sunwais of the highest-spending panchayats in each block.

Jan Niti Abhiyan Truck Yatra, 2003.

Ghotala Rath Yatra with Shankar as Rajvani, 2003.

The truck for the Jan Niti Abhiyan Yatra with its banners.

The second NCPRI Convention –
Vinay and Charul, singing *Janne ka haq* at the convention.

Former prime minister, late V.P. Singh addressing the second NCPRI Convention.

Surendra Mohan addressing the second NCPRI Convention.

Senior journalist Kuldip Nayyar, addressing the second NCPRI Convention.

Lal Singh of the MKSS addressing the second NCPRI Convention.

Harsh Mander addressing the second NCPRI Convention.

Protesting against the RTI amendments, 2006.

*Urgent call for action!!*

**CAMPAIGN TO SAVE THE RIGHT TO INFORMATION ACT**

*Indefinite Dharna at Jantar Mantar from 7th August 2006*

A series of activities is being planned to put pressure not to allow any dilutions in the RTI act 2005. The activities include:

**INDEFINITE DHARNA**
At Jantar Mantar from 7TH August 2006 with representation from as many States as possible. The dharna will draw people from all walks of life including mazdoors, kisans, professionals, Students, Artists and people from the administrative and political community who believe that real transparency is essential for the running of our Democracy.

**PERFORMANCES *by groups like***

- Euphoria performance – 7th August, 2pm
- Charul and Vinay of Loknad – 7th/8th August
- Ghotala Rath Yatra – 8th August onwards
- Hela party Rajasthan – 10th-12th August
- Street play/Puppets/Masks performances – everyday
- And others

**EXHIBITIONS**

- On the Use of Right to Information
- Of Banners and Slogans
- Of Photographs and cartoons
- Art for Democracy

**MEETINGS *with members of Parliament***

**MEDIA BRIEFING**

**REFERENDUM *on the proposed amendments***

**SIGNATURE CAMPAIGN *in support of saving RTI***

**FILM SCREENING *and daily* PRODUCTION *of "Radio RTI"***

**SEMINARS *and* WORKSHOP, PUBLIC LECTURES *on RTI*** *(many will be held in conjunction with the Dharna)*

***"Fighting Corruption through the Peoples Right to Information-The Indian Experience"*** on August 10th and 11th at YMCA Jai Sing Road, New Delhi

***"Campaign to Save the Right to Information Act"***
*supported by NCPRI,NAPM,Drive against Bribe, Parivartan,MKSS,Josh,Kabir and many other individuals and organisations*
Open call to all to come and join the campaign and contribute in any way to save the RTI Act

***For more details contact : 9868875898,9818782996,011-20507339,011205015,011-20033988***

Pamphlet urging people to join the campaign to 'Save RTI', 2006.

CHAPTER TWENTY-THREE

# NCPRI Convention, Beawar 2001

For the MKSS, conventions had become a useful platform for deliberation with varied and multiple social groupings. It was also a useful space for collective reflection. What was significant about the Beawar convention in 2001, and what made it somewhat different, was the fact that the citizens of Beawar were an integral part of the management. Bharat Dogra, convener, NCPRI notes:

> When after five years the National Convention of the NCPRI was organised in Beawar in 2001, the friends of the campaign took part in various programmes and cemented their friendship. The way the citizens of Beawar [shopkeepers, traders, labourers, teachers, students, managers of dharamshalas, journalists, etc.] supported the convention, really touched and moved the guests who had come from different parts of the country. A representative from Delhi was heard saying, "We have come from the national capital, but we might not be able to organise such a [fantastic] convention in the capital!"
>
> The way in which scholars and activists working on various issues [in different parts of the country] have come here, it seems in a very short span of time, they all have realised the importance of this right in their own spheres and also for social awareness in general.[200]

The MKSS struggle strengthened the argument for a transition from representative democracy to one in which representation would be reinforced and monitored by people's engagement and participation in governance. It held great promise as a value and was understood as a part of the structure of democratic governance.

One of the reasons why the concepts of transparency and accountability were accepted so naturally could be traced back to the early days of the MKSS struggle, which persistently and consistently involved people at every stage, in thinking, in strategizing and in action. The demand for RTI germinated from a people's articulation of continued denial and lack of access to services and resources. It logically followed that such people should be part of those seeking solutions.

> Prior to the celebrations a "Jan Sunwai" is scheduled to be held at Janawad panchayat of Kumbalgarh block in Rajsamand district, near Beawar on 3 April. "The Janawad Jan Sunwai would critically examine the efficacy of the act in Rajasthan and present the findings at the Beawar convention", notes Nikhil Dey of the MKSS.[201]

The convention was planned to follow the public hearing in Janawad on 3 April. Action is often another idiom through which people convey their analysis of policy and performance. The public hearing provided irrefutable data and a logical structure to frame the argument for the law. It also underscored the demand for participation of people in planning for policy and legislation. After all, as implementers of the law, they had the complete and pragmatic appreciation of its relevance. It therefore followed that their experience should form the foundation of a robust law.

For instance, Janawad proved absolutely that if the law did not provide for a penalty for wilful prevention of access to information, it would nullify the entire entitlement. It took the collective efforts of the MKSS and the Janawad group led by Chimanba a year to access information. The demand for penalty on a public servant for wilfully preventing access to public information had to be fought all the way to the parliament.

It is interesting that one of the most important sources of information about happenings in Beawar is the local daily newspaper *Nirantar*. Going back to its archives has been both nostalgic and informative for the MKSS. As noted in the MKSS Diary:

The convention was organized in Beawar: the scene of the 1996 forty-day dharna, and the first big protest that shaped the RTI Campaign that gave birth to the NCPRI. It was only appropriate that the city that got symbiotically involved with that struggle should host the first convention of the NCPRI. It re-lived the days of community support when the daily newspaper *Nirantar* was an important daily commentator; it inevitably became the source for the documentation of the forty days of street struggle. *Nirantar* also covered the convention in detail every day. Ramprasad Kumawat, the editor of the paper, personally wrote the edit pieces that strung together the first narrative of the convention.[202]

The following are translations from *Nirantar*, published in April 2001.

Beawar will see two chief ministers and others visiting the MKSS/NCPRI convention, with almost 400 personalities who will grace the occasion. There will be dignitaries from all walks of life including two chief ministers from Rajasthan and Madhya Pradesh. Justice Sawant, retired judge of the Supreme Court of India, and chairperson of the Press Council, will chair the convention. There will be an RTI mela in Subhash Udhyan on the 6th evening, of the two-day Convention on 5 and 6 April, exactly five years after the struggle began in Beawar.

The fourth day of April 2001 saw Chang Gate lit with oil lamps [diyas] and eminent invitees at the same place where the dharnarthis had sat on dharna for forty days in 1996 to demand legislation. It was a symbolic pledge to spread the campaign and the determination to force the government to enact a law to disclose documents relating to governance to the people.

Diwali came to Beawar twice this year and candles and diyas were lit in Chang Gate on the 3rd of April 2001, to mark the beginning of the first Convention of the National Campaign of People's Right to Information [NCPRI].[203]

The NCPRI was created with the objective of formulating an effective legislation. Its aim was also to encourage and support grassroots-level initiatives, for its demand and use.

Laws had been enacted in the states of Tamil Nadu, Goa, Rajasthan, Karnataka, and Maharashtra. But there were critical lacunae in all the acts and resistance from the bureaucracy. There had been a number of efforts by different groups to use the RTI as part of their own struggle. It was important to share these experiences and arrive at a common agenda for action.

The presence of Justice Sawant, chairperson of the Press Council of India, underscored the importance of the convention. His address at Chang Gate on the eve of the convention was powerful, balanced and echoed the determination to get the legislation through parliament. There was an emerging acceptance of its fundamental importance in a democracy. Addressing the gathering, he said:

> In a democracy, the citizen is sovereign and no one can prevent his access to information.... The political representative and the civil servant should serve the people. They are obliged to listen and work for people. It is their obligation to do so. People for their part must understand that their rights become possible to achieve only after they understand what they are.[204]

He further added:

> Information is people's wealth and their capital. The government is just a trustee. In a colonial order, when people were not free, rules and laws were different. But we have been free for 50 years, it is necessary therefore for us to change our mindsets. People need to educate themselves and in turn educate their political representatives, who will then make sure that the civil servant places people first in democratic governance.
>
> If people come together, the government will have to bow before their will. People are unaware of their own power. And see themselves as subjects. They have to realize their own power; the showing of solidarity and collective strength will shame the system to deliver. We have forgotten to struggle in post-independent India. In a democracy, no individual should feel helpless. The RTI is a right enshrined in the fundamental rights of the Indian Constitution.[205]

He also emphasized the role of the Press Council and its efforts to provide a good RTI law for the people of the country. His statement that RTI would be the means of protecting democracy in India was like a refrain. Calling the FOI Act prepared by the NDA a weak law, he made a scathing remark on the government.

Baba Adhav, a socialist trade union leader from Pune,[206] also addressed the meeting at Chang Gate, and linked hunger to RTI. He drew parallels between a corrupt system and endemic hunger. Self-preservation of office and officers cannot be used as an excuse for not disclosing information which would impact the lives of people.

Reporting on the event in the *Hindu*, Sunny Sebastian wrote:

> The people behind the transparency movement and right to information in the country will get together at the relatively unknown town of Beawar in Rajasthan for two days from April 5 to celebrate the fifth anniversary of the struggle. The dusty Chang Gate area in Beawar, once known for its trade union activities, will provide the venue for the stocktaking and jubilation.
>
> It was at Chang Gate in 1996 that a 40-day dharna launched by a disparate group of villagers under the banner of the Mazdoor Kisan Shakti Sangathan [MKSS] transformed an elite sounding expression, "the right to information" into a slogan, "the right to know is the right to live".[207]

Inaugurated by Digvijay Singh, chief minister of Madhya Pradesh on, 5 April, the convention began its formal sessions in the premises of Government Senior Girls School, Chavni Road. The inaugural session had Bharat Dogra, Justice Sawant, Prabhash Joshi, and Ajit Bhattacharjea.

Bharat Dogra as the convener of the NCPRI introduced the theme of the convention resolution to empower democracy through a people's RTI. He began with acknowledging the strength the campaign had derived from the support of the city:

> We have congregated here [from different parts of the country] in Beawar on 5th–6th April, 2001, the fifth anniversary of the National Campaign for People's Right to Information. This is the historical movement for transparency and accountability to which the people of Beawar gave their resolute support, and which led to the birth of the NCPRI. People are the masters in a true democracy. But, in reality, they exercise their sovereignty only once in five years [while voting]. The challenge in front of people is for them to find ways of exercising their sovereignty on a regular basis.

> Alongside the unseen reality of a severe famine and widespread hunger, we could clearly see the limitations and possibilities of our democracy. When the public is struggling to barely survive, the government of India is sitting on 50 lakh quintals of food-grains. The system for famine relief has been neglected and left to die its own death. Not only the state, even the media and the civil society seem to be a part of a conspiratorial silence. It is in such a state of silence that a state is obstinate enough to abdicate its responsibilities. In this system of misuse and abuse, the public is angry over the deep-rooted and rampant corruption but often finds itself helpless in changing the situation. But India's strength can be seen in the life of its ordinary people and in its democratic institutions. The challenge before us is to save this power and the right to information is an important tool in making space for democracy despite all the odds.
>
> The Right to Information is not only important in itself but it also helps in getting other rights, which are necessary for people to gain some semblance of control over their lives. It was in these diverse contexts that the wide possibilities of using the RTI were discussed in the convention.
>
> The convention resolves to carry ahead the struggle for the following issues using the right to information – famine and hunger; health and education; human rights; displacement; electoral politics; judicial accountability; media; voluntary organisations and civil society; nuclear and defence establishment; globalisation and economic growth; women and laws related with people's Right to Information.[208]

Digvijay Singh, in his inaugural address, made two important points: 'People's representatives should begin their political career as ministers with taking an oath to transparency rather than to secrecy.' He also said, 'In a democracy, accountability to people cannot be questioned. My power lies in sharing information.' He argued that sharing information through transparency will give people less cause to complain. It follows logically that fewer problems will arise and if there are no problems, people will not be angry, which will enable governments to act efficiently with ethics.

Following the plenary, the participants panned out the sessions. These were varied and held in different parts of the small city. Public and private buildings opened their doors to the convention. A very distinguished set of specialists in their fields sat down with workers and peasants, activists, community workers, citizens of Beawar, politicians and journalists to discuss and debate the relevance of RTI in each of their specific and special areas. These workshops began with the experiences from different struggles and activities across the country regarding the need to access information. The bottlenecks and constraints shaped the formulations necessary to make the entitlement relevant and usable.

> The issues/themes of these workshops will make it evident as to how broad the context of deliberation was. The issues were – health, education, labour and wages, voluntary organisations, human rights, women development programmes, electoral processes, famine and food security, accountability of the judiciary, mass communication, displacement and rehabilitation, energy, rural development and management of natural resources, globalisation, industrial pollution, information technology, nuclear power and laws related with the right to information. Several experts of various fields had reached Beawar to coordinate all these workshops. The participants of the convention divided themselves in these different workshops for a while and the summary of all the discussions was read out in the convention and eventually a "Beawar Declaration" was prepared on the basis of the major conclusions/resolutions of the eighteen workshops.[209]

The workshops on almost eighteen different issues laid the concrete structure of what the law must address. They focused on the importance and relevance of the specific information critical for their survival and dignity. People speak of entitlement in the context of the difficulties they face in accessing services and basic rights.

The second day began with the Ghotala Rath Yatra and the Hela – a large choir of men from different walks of life who come together to sing. They come from Gangapur city, Sawai Madhopur, where the Hela has been a part of the conscious and critical commentary of contemporary politics. Sung to the accompaniment of a *naupat*, a large traditional drum, and cymbals, they have enriched every campaign. Hela has been a part of most of the important protests of the MKSS. After Hela's performance, the procession which began at Chang Gate made its way down the main market street to a huge park which opened up to house the public meeting.[210] The Information Mela recapitulated briefly the conclusions of the previous day and underscored the determination to get a relevant and rigorous legislation.

> The Beawar convention was an observance of the five years of the right to information movement, at the precise venue where it had been launched in April 1996. During this period, the movement has successfully pressured the state government to enact an enabling legislation, that nevertheless remains weak in several respects. The Rajasthan Act, for instance, provides for no punitive action against officials who wilfully delay or deny access to information. A toothless Act, various speakers at Beawar pointed out, is perhaps of as much value as no Act at all. But the MKSS's Janawad operation proves that with sufficient diligence, even a deeply flawed law could serve an important public function.
>
> Humour and irreverence are two other powerful propaganda tools that the right to information movement has deployed. The public at Beawar, for instance, were induced to participate in the convention by a Ghotala Rath Yatra, an ironical celebration of the spirit of corruption, with the MKSS's Shankar Singh playing the archetypal politician revelling in his power and his exemption from all forms of accountability. Satire may seem out of place in the grim circumstances prevalent in Rajasthan but in conjunction with agitation and the systematic pursuit and scrutiny of information, it is galvanizing the poor and the deprived into an awareness of their rights.[211]

Through this convention it was hoped that it would send a strong message for an effective central legislation on the RTI to be tabled in the Lok Sabha. The convention was also expected to express a collective resolve to do away with the prevailing culture of secrecy and break the nexus in governance between the political and bureaucratic establishments, which results in the arbitrary exercise of power.

The public meeting on the second day, too, drew a huge crowd, expecting the state Chief Minister Ashok Gehlot to make some important announcement. Prabhash Joshi, speaking at Chang Gate earlier, on the evening of 4 April, had given a call to the citizens of Beawar that the town that gave birth to the RTI should also get to fight for its implementation.

Among various political leaders present on the second day was A.B. Bardhan, general secretary, CPI. He congratulated the MKSS for pushing the law and argued that its implementation alone could prevent corruption. Ashok Gehlot, addressing the gathering, said:

> To bring transparency to people in ordinary life, fundamental changes are required. If we mean business when we talk against corruption and black money, the political establishment will have to take strong decisions. To gain people's confidence, one must stop scams. If we have to retain the trust of the people, RTI is an important entitlement and the government is committed to take the process to its conclusion. It is necessary to take this campaign to the villages in Rajasthan…how a government has kept the promises made in the manifesto like a passage of the RTI law in 2000… Poverty and illiteracy may prevent access to information. The Anti-Corruption Bureau must be strengthened. Implementation of the RTI is critical to its success.

In an exhaustive and detailed report of the Beawar convention, Sukumar Muralidharan, who participated and reported on the convention in *Frontline*, wrote:

> In Rajasthan, the right to information becomes almost synonymous with the right to life.
>
> As guest of honour at a convention on the right to information, Rajasthan Chief Minister Ashok Gehlot was perhaps keen to maintain an image of transparency and candour. The early-April gathering of activists, campaigners and political workers at Beawar in Ajmer district of Rajasthan took place under the shadow of a third successive year of deficient rainfall in parts of the State. This has in turn caused acute livelihood stresses and raised the prospect of famine-like conditions. Deaths from food deprivation and its attendant diseases have already been reported from parts of the State.
>
> For this reason, the deliberations at Beawar tended to focus on the government's effort to cope with the looming humanitarian emergency. The assembly was convinced that the affected people would be able to contribute to the efficacy of the relief effort if they were equipped with the knowledge of their entitlements

under established law and custom and if they were aware of the special measures being initiated to cope with scarcity conditions. Without the wide dissemination of such information, development administrators would be sluggish in responding to people's needs and relief measures would prove of limited utility and benefit.

Believing that the Chief Minister would be receptive, the assembly put a number of questions to him, some on the contingency measures being initiated to cope with famine-like conditions, others on the legislation introduced by his government to provide citizens with the right to information. Specifically, Gehlot was asked whether the famine code had been invoked in the state and how the government proposed to meet the obligations that stemmed from it. Under the code, every person willing to work in scarcity-hit areas is entitled to obtain employment under special public works, while those incapable of work would be eligible for gratuitous relief.

A further question was posed about the quite arbitrary figure of 800,000 that had been fixed as the maximum prospective number of beneficiaries of emergency employment programmes. When scarcity conditions were known to be afflicting a population of over 20 million, the Chief Minister was told, a ceiling of this nature did little to mitigate suffering.

Certain irrationalities in the administration of the employment programme were highlighted, all to do with inadequacies of information dissemination. The allocation of employment targets between development blocks, for instance, is announced after a totally avoidable delay. On this account, the prospective beneficiaries are kept in the dark till the day the muster rolls are drawn up for labour employment. This leads to many eligible individuals being left out and a less than optimal distribution of the benefits of the special relief programmes.

The Chief Minister was also told that wage rates paid in public works programmes effectively work out to a figure well below the statutory minimum. And finally, at the root of all the inadequacies in the implementation of anti-poverty programmes is a default by the State government: of its total entitlement of foodgrain for people below the poverty line [BPL] it lifts a mere 60 per cent from the Central pool.

Responding to these queries, Gehlot spoke at length about how his party had always supported the right to information. This commitment was consummated in his government's very early legislative initiative to inscribe the right in the statute book. As for the specific concerns that had been articulated about famine conditions in parts of the State, the government's records were always open for inspection, said Gehlot. The National Campaign for the Peoples' Right to Information, the umbrella organisation that was the sponsor of the Beawar convention, could nominate any individual of its choice to examine the records if that would serve to assuage public misgivings.

With these remarks – long on political posture but perfunctory on matters of detail – Gehlot took leave of the gathering. Activists of the Mazdoor Kisan Shakti Sangathan [MKSS], which hosted and organised the convention, made repeated appeals to him to return and deal with the specific concerns that had been placed before him. But Gehlot had to rush off to other engagements and as a politician he was not going to depart from the practised policy of giving nothing away unless compelled to.

Aruna Roy, founder of the MKSS... came up with the appropriate response. Since the administration has proven that it is not amenable to a discussion about a matter involving the lives and livelihoods of millions, she said, the agitational programmes would have to be stepped up. The MKSS would begin laying siege to the warehouses of the Food Corporation of India [FCI], where the burgeoning stocks of food with the Central government were beginning to waste away. The agitation would continue till the government opened up the granaries and began a welfare programme that would relieve the suffering of the most vulnerable sections, said Roy.[212]

## The Beawar Declaration

The convention decided to end with a declaration. Declarations are a way of sharing collective decisions with people and also become a benchmark for accountability.

The Beawar Declaration placed the RTI in its democratic context. Access to information was necessary to fight and win the battle against poverty, injustice and inequality. It was also to realize fundamental and other basic rights enshrined in the constitution, including the elusive sovereignty guaranteed. The declaration, in seeing the RTI in the context of specific needs, underlined its importance as a 'transformatory' law, one that would enable the realization of other rights under the constitution. The declaration covered the specific areas of drought and chronic hunger, displacement, health, education, human rights, electoral politics, judicial accountability, media, NGOs/civil society organizations, nuclear and defence establishments, globalization and economic development, women, and laws on people's right to information. (For the complete draft of the Beawar Declaration, see Annexure I, pg. 339.)[213]

**An Important Footnote**

A few days later, a demonstration against the paradox of apparent plenty amidst poverty took place in Udaipur. The tribal areas of Udaipur are among the worst affected by the drought conditions prevailing in Rajasthan and have witnessed a number of deaths from the diseases that spread in times of deprivation. The two main Left parties and the Janata Dal [Secular] had planned their raid on the godowns well before Gehlot's public display of reticence in Beawar. Following that event, the Udaipur demonstration drew in a substantial contingent from the MKSS.

On 12 April, a large crowd assembled in the vicinity of the Udaipur District Collectorate to listen to former Prime Minister V.P. Singh, Communist Party of India [Marxist] Polit Bureau member Sitaram Yechury and CPI State Secretary Tara Singh Sidhu. With V.P. Singh and Yechury symbolically equipping themselves with hammers to break the locks that were perceived obstacles to food security, the crowd set out in procession for the FCI warehouse. Stopped a kilometer before their destination, the demonstrators broke through police barricades and courted arrest. As they dispersed, they held out the promise that this would not be the last action of its kind.

The slogan raised in Udaipur was that the youth needed opportunities to work. Eight hours of work a day could be compensated with an appropriate quantum of food that would help a deprived family retain its tenuous hold on subsistence.

But the State government pleads inability on grounds of financial stringency. And the Central government merely argues that it is doing its bit in allocating grain to the State, only to find that the State government seemingly has no use for it.

A glance at the Central government's outlay in rural employment programmes would show that the scandal of 50 million tonnes of grain wasting away in warehouses as scarcity conditions grip large numbers of people will continue to haunt the country. In 1999–2000, the total outlay in rural employment programmes was Rs. 3,729 crores – marginally lower than the budgetary target. When the Budget proposals for 2000–01 were presented, ample evidence was available that the preceding monsoon had been deficient in certain regions. Yet, Finance Minister Yashwant Sinha chose to cut the outlay in rural employment sharply, to Rs. 2,655 crores. At the same time, he held the allocation for rural water supply programmes at the preceding year's level of Rs. 1,890 crores.

Less than two months later the government seemingly encountered the flash of revelation. Although it was always apparent that the onset of the summer months would sharply increase pressure on livelihoods in the rainfall deficient areas, the government waited till the blazing heat had set in to begin to reckon with the magnitude of human suffering. A huge public spectacle ensued with ministers scaling new rhetorical peaks in seeking to mobilise public support for the relief effort.

Yet in concrete terms the response was abysmal. The outlay on rural employment and water supply programmes remained unchanged. All additional financial allocations went through the special contingency funds that have been created to cope with natural calamities. And these special allocations, it is known, have a tendency to flow through channels less open to public scrutiny, finally to end up enriching those who least deserve any kind of relief.

True to form, the Central government has been niggardly about rural employment and water supply programmes this year, the magnitudes of the increase in allocation being just over 10 per cent for both. With this level of reluctance at the Centre, it is no surprise that State governments should prove incapable of lifting the allocation of foodgrain they are entitled to for BPL populations.

And though a large part of the problem may lie in the aggregate volumes of expenditure in rural works, the core issue really is their poor execution and the chronic lack of accountability and transparency of development administrations.

Underlying the current scarcity conditions in Rajasthan is the unsavoury reality that years of budgetary spending in rural works have done little but enrich dominant coteries of contractors, middlemen and the landed elites. This denial of the legitimate entitlements of the rural poor is another consistent focus of the right to information campaign, particularly as articulated by the MKSS.[214]

CHAPTER TWENTY-FOUR

# Post-Janawad and the Response of the Government of Rajasthan

The Janawad public hearing was a turning point in Rajasthan not only for the RTI but also for the government. It shook the complacent attitude of the state government. The disclosure and proof of mismanagement, fraud and brazen corruption forced the government to sit up and take stock. The disproportionate budget allocations to the Janawad panchayats posed a disturbing set of questions for the district and state administrations and their slackness in supervision. It was unthinkable that a sarpanch could get away with such embezzlement of funds. The fact that the collector and the superintendent of police were not present at the public hearing in Janawad despite the presence of eminent people in the panel raised questions not only on them but also on the state government. It was an attempt to turn a blind eye and gloss over gross irregularities and corruption by the system.

Though Janawad was one among thirty-seven panchayats in Kumbalgarh block, Rajsamand district, it managed to corner roughly a third of the budget of the block or panchayat samiti. The district authorities and the state government were either ignorant of this, or party to it. Either way it was a deliberate misuse of public money.

**From Public Hearing to Public Audit**

The Rajasthan state government had no choice but to take stock of the findings of the public hearing. The wrongdoings were factually proven, through an unconventional audit process, and validated. It was like constructing an argument block by block, case by case. It was impossible to refute the logic and the truth of the series of disclosures, with the usual bogus arguments and myths. The official disclosure of data proved conclusively that fake documents and records could not stand public scrutiny. The rationality and tangibility of factual proof destroyed the nexus of corrupt practices.

In deciding to conduct government public hearings, the Rajasthan government in fact acceded to the concept of collaboration between the citizens and the government, to both monitor and hold the system accountable. The state government issued orders that the highest-spending panchayat in each panchayat samiti or block would organize a public hearing/audit. This was, as expected, received with fear and misgiving by the corrupt system and people.

These jan sunwais also established the power and acceptance of public audit to address and resolve the blatant abuse of power. They brought in a cross section of eminent Indians as panellists – with the NCPRI – to witness the jan sunwai or public audit. It showcased the strength of people's participation in combating corruption and their ability to shape systemic reform and impact governance.

It was a far cry from the initial days of the MKSS, when the BDO in Bhim was petrified to hand over a published BPL list. It was also now irrefutably proven that the mystification of disappearing muster rolls – a series of fantastic stories, of goats eating them up, or getting blown away in the wind – were of course, fabricated. The repeated reasoning of local people about methods of siphoning of funds was proven.

These hearings were significant because they pushed the system from passive collusion to transparent participation. The process of public audit became an important mode for administrative accountability, and had to be recognized and given due credit and place in the system. Transparency was acknowledged as the important first step to stop corruption, and the platform of the emerging social audit process was acknowledged as a means of establishing accountability.

The huge proportion of fake assets and claims continued to be demolished by peoples' testimony and physical verification, in the series of government audits done by the Government of Rajasthan following the jan sunwai in Janawad. The assumption that information was power remained unchallenged, and was accepted as a part of the popular public discourse. The connection between corruption and poverty, and corrupt oppressive processes within the structure that perpetuated it, could not be deconstructed without transparency.

The people's right to know derived from Article 19 of the Indian Constitution. The legal entitlement was a necessary precondition to empower people's resolve to expose these scams and empower people to control their own lives and future. So far, the attempts to 'improve and reform' the delivery system from within corrupt governments – in camera – had failed to a large extent. At best, what remained was a wish list of the 'good civil servants' within the system. The only solution was to ensure that these processes were transparent and accountable, and under the scrutiny of the beneficiaries. This alone would ensure the delivery of democratic promises of access to basic services.

*Yeh panchayat hamare aapki*
*nahin kisike baap ki*
*Yeh paise hamare aapke*
*nahin kisi ke baap ke*

These two slogans were a call to people to reclaim democratic institutions and the state from corruption, and the unilateral and arbitrary control by the political representative and the bureaucrat. When the MKSS was invited to participate in these government-propelled hearings and engagement with the process, the invitation was accepted to reclaim and monitor whatever was feasible from the malfunctioning system.

'The devil was in the details' demanded the continuing scrutiny of people. It obligated the government to provide platforms to present and examine the information. Scrutiny in turn demanded that the tools be continually honed and revised to make them relevant. In other words, struggle and advocacy logically led to engagement with implementation and scrutiny of methods of delivery as well.

## Factual Truth and the Public Hearings

In recalling the events that unfolded during the series of government-organized public hearings/audits, this chronicle draws on newspaper reports published by the local media.

> The MKSS participated in eight out of the many public hearings organized by the government. They were gram panchayat [Kumbhalgarh Panchayat Samiti, district Rajsamand] on 16 February 2002, Panotiya Gram Panchayat [Railmagra Gram Panchayat] on 18 February 2002, Lasani Gram Panchayat [Deogarh Panchayat Samiti] on 20 February 2002, Jhalon Ki Madar Gram Panchayat [Khamnor Panchayat Samiti] on 25 February 2002, Farara Gram Panchayat [Rajsamand Panchayat Samiti] on 26 February 2002, and Baghana Gram Panchayat [Bhim Panchayat Samiti] on 27 February 2002. Hearings were also organised in Bagor Gram Panchayat [Mandal Panchayat Samiti, Bhilwara] on 24 February, and in Panchu Gram Panchayat [Nokha Panchayat Samiti, Bikaner] on 4 March 2002.[215]

## The Hearings: The Devil in the Details and the Manufacturing of Consent

The quality of jan sunwais was defined by the character of the local administration. The Reeched Jan Sunwai was held on 16 February 2002. It went well because the usual reticence and antagonism was not obvious. The BDO participated quite enthusiastically. The MKSS also contributed to the general ambience of the hearing by working with beneficiary groups earlier, by disseminating information. The beneficiaries were aware of the details of the irregularities, which motivated participation and articulation.

One of the popular songs of the MKSS on corruption was '*Choriwado ghano hogyo re, koyito munde bolo*' (enough of scams, speak out now). This song, often sung by Shankar, commented through the lyrics on the enormity and irony of the all-consuming hunger of the greedy – swallowing even toilets, roads, sand and cement – where else could they have gone, because they were not to be seen anywhere. In this list Reeched added another impossibility – an engine to pump water. The sarpanch here had swallowed the engine; it was only on a piece of paper!

The emerging stories of cheating, thieving and defrauding were tragic tales of callousness and heartbreak. But strangely enough the pathos of narrating these tales brought in black humour and irony, often the powerful tools of expression and critique of the poor. For them it provides a kind of catharsis.

Janawad had shown how the disproportionate allocation of funds to a panchayat was fatal. These jan sunwais added details to the understanding of corruption and corrupt practices. For instance, they underscored and proved that contractors accelerated unaccountable fraud and corruption. Though denied by the rules, it transferred the power to cheat and fraud with impunity to an entity outside the government and therefore not under regular scrutiny. The contractor becomes a single window for corrupt practices and is controlled much more easily by the political and bureaucratic nexus. The irony was that during the public hearings, the contractor himself was often forced to narrate the story of how he (dishonestly) got the contracts!

The Panotiya Jan Sunwai was held at Railmagra Panchayat Samiti of Rajsamand district on 18 February 2002. The panchayat had spent Rs. 28,53,084 on 42 developmental works.

There were clear government orders that panchayat works could not be contracted. In contracting work through the local contractor, the panchayat lays itself open to illegalities, clever manipulation and corruption. When works are managed by the panchayat, the worker has a right to claim minimum wages, and the government has an obligation to provide it. However, when the work is implemented through a contractor, the minimum wage is the first violation, as the worker is hired and fired by him. The quality of work is also affected; bad material and over-billing often leads to disaster, impacting the whole village.

Corruption is used as the reason for rubbishing pro-poor policies. But those who benefit from corruption are the middlemen, the real parasites on society. They just switch to other means of exploitation. By suspending poverty reduction programmes, the victims are punished with denial of benefits for crimes they did not commit in the first place.

The Lassani Jan Sunwai was held on 20 February 2002. Lassani is a panchayat of the Deogarh Panchayat Samiti, Rajsamand district. In the five years preceding the jan sunwai, more than 39 lakh rupees had been spent on 70 developmental works. A number of irregularities surfaced in the public hearing. As usual, most of the work had been contracted out and the poorest, for whom these works were opened in the first place, hardly got any benefits of wages. As reported in *Ujala Chadi*:

> The BDO was obstructive and tried to stop people from testifying during the public hearing. His interjections roused the anger of the people. District collector Kunjilal Meena was also present in this sunwai. Despite his presence, the BDO was trying to shield the corrupt officials. Neither the sarpanch nor the gram panchayat were supportive.
>
> Interesting highlights of this jan sunwai were the minor sensation occasioned by the allegation of forgery by a former sarpanch. But this was dismissed after matching his signature with the documents. The administration is forever trying to cover up its failures and biases. The surprising defence of corrupt practices came from a senior official, the Divisional Commissioner who tried to justify the "Contract System" and the labour-material ratio of [60 for labour and 40 for materials in all budget allocations].[216]

**Bagaur**

In every panchayat, the discrepancy between market and sanctioned rates for masons, and the inability to get outdated structures of payment revised, legitimized corruption. Every panchayat had either false muster rolls or exaggerated bills for material to cover up for the shortfall in wages. This falsification of accounts with the blessing of the system supported corruption. The MKSS has argued that government rates and payment methods have to be rationalized in the public works programmes if the system has to fight corruption.

The Jhalon Ki Madar Jan Sunwai was held on 25 February 2002 with engineered disruption. Amidst the hullabaloo, the BDO read out details of all the 77 developmental works and affirmed their propriety. The people were too scared to speak; it was only the MKSS that presented its findings. Rowdy misbehaviour and bullying tactics were used to hide corruption!

**Hectoring by Sarpanches!**

The brouhaha took place because a tribal boy, Kalu (s/o Teka), rose and said that 7,000 rupees were siphoned off by filling his name fraudulently in the muster rolls. The upper castes and the privileged were in a rage because a poor person from a scheduled tribe had the gumption to speak. Also covered by *Ujala Chadi*, the report elaborated:

> At showing this courage to speak the truth, five to seven people abused him in the presence of Rohit Kumar, the programme director, District Rural Development Council, and said that they'll settle scores with him later.
>
> All hell broke loose in the hearing organised in Jhalon Ki Madar Panchayat [of Khamnor Panchayat Samiti in Rajsamand district]. Sarpanches of forty-one panchayats gathered here and tried to hush up the people from speaking out.
>
> C.P. Joshi, the minister for rural development, had to use his authority to calm the situation. He said, "Whether you like it or not, this hearing will certainly take place. If anyone is troubled by it, they are free to refrain from it, but, these social audits [of the expenditure on developmental works] will certainly happen and it is not possible to stop these now."
>
> During the period under examination, 77 works had taken place in the panchayat and 86,05,464 rupees were spent on them. Mangilal was the sarpanch of this panchayat for 22 years. People are scared to even speak against him, leave alone opposing him. At least half of the population of this panchayat is tribal. They come from one of the most oppressed of communities, not aware of their rights, and terrified of retribution if they should speak out.[217]

**Farara Public Hearing**

Farara is a panchayat in Rajsamand Panchayat Samiti of Rajsamand district. The jan sunwai here was held on 26 February 2002. In the series of MKSS-attended panchayats, this one was significant for its veiled threats and intimidation.

For years it has been under feudal dominance. The MKSS team, which was there to assist the administration, was not provided any information in the first place. When the information was shared under orders, the local panchayat threatened that they were not responsible for any deterioration of law and order or any untoward incident caused by its dissemination – dangers of destruction of records or looting. As reported in *Ujala Chadi*:

> The Sarpanch Bahadur Singh was uncooperative. He declared, "There is no space in the Panchayat Bhawan. My secretary will not come to help you. He will only come on the day of the hearing." It was a warning not to disseminate information or stay in the village. When the information wasn't provided, the MKSS decided not to participate in this hearing but sent two observers and also videographed the hearing.[218]

**Disruptive Tactics**

> At the place of the hearing, film songs were played at a very high pitch to drown the proceedings. When the BDO started reading the details of the developmental works, objections were raised about some of the details. The questions related to the quality of the works and the material. When a road-work was discussed, Mohan Singh testified that he had worked on this road but never received payments. Money was siphoned by forging his signatures. The sarpanch used traditional pressure tactics and asked Mohan to swear in the name of Kunteshwar Mahadev, the local deity, which he did![219]

The Baghana Jan Sunwai was held on 27 February 2002. This jan sunwai attracted a large number of women; they were more than half of the participants. The whole pandal was jam-packed. As the large turnout of articulate women testified, it was part of the MKSS work area. It also explained why the women stayed for the entire proceedings and voiced their concerns.

> During the hearing, the junior engineer of the panchayat samiti read out the details of the developmental works. When the quality of Peethaguda hathai-work was being audited, the residents objected and said that this work had not taken place, only some cement had been put on the older hathai. The junior engineer contradicted their testimony and stated, "The work has taken place, in fact I have myself seen it." The people challenged his assertion and said if the work has taken place then workers would have been employed, they challenged him to read out their names from the muster rolls! Eventually the engineer had to admit that the work had not taken

> place and that fake muster rolls had been filled. It was a vindication of reason and courage. In the public confrontation, people's political understanding and intelligence prevailed.[220]

**Delayed Wage Payment**

Non-payment of wages is a crime against the poor; it impacts health, life and livelihood. In Baghana panchayat, wages were outstanding in some works for almost four years . Women workers vociferously raised the issue of non-payment of wages for the Hanuman anicut work. Even workers at the primary school in Kaniyana had not been paid. Laluram had not been paid for the room he had built at the Veeramguda School.

One positive outcome of this hearing was that a very poor tribal, Mana Bhil, was included in the Annapurna scheme, which provides food to the most deprived.

The Paanchu Jan Sunwai was held on 4 March 2002. The hearing began among assertions that all was well in this panchayat. 'Everything is okay!' However, there was an undercurrent of simmering anger and discontent against such a blatant cover-up.

This hearing took place in Paanchu panchayat of Nokha Panchayat Samiti of Bikaner district. Not many people from the village participated in this hearing because they were afraid of being victimized or ostracized. Outsiders and police personnel far outnumbered the villagers. It was under heavy police protection that the hearing took place.

All the sarpanches of the district had registered their protest against this hearing. Many sarpanches from outside the panchayat came to lend support to the Nokha sarpanch. They opposed the involvement of non-governmental organizations in the audit process, alleging that to maintain the required ratio of labour and material (60:40), they were forced to fudge records and fill bogus muster rolls, etc. They liberally cursed the jan sunwai and the organizations involved.

In the presence of the programme director of the District Rural Development Council, M.L. Kheenchi, and district council member Ashok Yadav, the BDO Hanuman Chaudhary presented the records of the developmental works that had taken place in the panchayat. The question of missing measurement books and fake muster rolls were repeatedly raised, but not countered or answered.

Despite all the anger and the plan to disrupt, when confronted by the deputy inspector general (corruption) and the additional magistrate (development), the pradhans of Nokha and Bikaner accepted that there were irregularities, but claimed it was due to the compulsion of adhering to the unrealistic rules. They threatened the government with boycott if the public representatives continued to be made accountable.

> Rajsamand's District Collector had ironically enough asked the MKSS to train the team which conducted the public hearings. The sangathan was expected to be involved in the entire process [from preparations before the hearing to the actual organisation] of public hearings. The sangathan had decided that it will participate in every hearing conducted in Rajsamand, Bhilwara, Ajmer and Bikaner districts.[221]

The local residents demanded to know what was happening in the name of development in their panchayat. It was a democracy, and their right to know had to be recognized and details furnished.

The leanings from the auditing of the highest-spending panchayats effectively changed the social and public policy of the Rajasthan state government.

These public hearings displayed and proved that the questioning of impunity had to be in the public domain with participation of the people who knew the details. Every fake muster roll and the falsification of record, essential for siphoning off money, could not stand when countered with the simple testimony of people. The campaign for transparency became a logical and natural corollary to the demand for delivery of services and the struggle against hunger, poverty, unemployment, badly run schools and hospitals, and the insolent impunity of the administrative machinery. The system played a smart game between being the colonial authority vested in the bureaucracy and the traditional feudal authority of caste and gender.

The concept of people's audit being absorbed as a part of the systemic efforts of government to address corruption in the form of a 'social audit' began from these very thorough and committed efforts. The state government was besought by pressures, but it did carry on and go ahead. It demonstrated political will in responding to people's demands. The villagers for their part grew in understanding the democratic process of using their power with responsibility.

The grounds for rationality in addressing poverty-related programmes began to emerge along with the need for transparency and accountability.

The MKSS's commitment to the RTI, understanding the critical needs for an entitlement and the non-negotiables of the MGNREGA (Mahatma Gandhi National Rural Employment Guarantee Act) can be traced to these series of events, which presented a sum of understanding the interface between the people and the government. These audits also established the power of people's action, and the immense courage of people like Chimnaram and hundreds of others, who are the pillars of Indian democracy.

**A Postscript**

The MGNREGA and the perfidy of corruption is a persistent news item in contemporary India. But the fact that corruption is disclosed is a sea change. Transparency and information have enabled monitoring of public expenditure. Before the RTI, the rural population knew nothing about allocations to their panchayats. It is because of basic transparency that corruption has been exposed. The availability of information enables the ordinary citizen to track every rupee to know how much is missing. Where they got 1, 2 or at the most 10 paise of every rupee sent down for them, now they get 50, and are aware that the rest has been swindled. MGNREGA also introduced the concept of people's planning to make sure that people could define the nature of development and also be aware of what might actually be sent down, and later, monitor its expenditure.

CHAPTER TWENTY-FIVE

# Jan Niti Abhiyan

Being a local organization with a strong belief in local democracy and local self-government, the MKSS naturally wanted to work with panchayats and their elected representatives. However, it became clear that the dominant power structure had ensured that panchayats would only be implementing agencies, and Panchayat Raj would be more 'Sarpanch Raj' than '*hamare gaon mein hamara raj*'. Many battles against oppression would see the sarpanch take the side of the established power structure. As far as development works and corruption is concerned, such unreasonable restrictions were placed on the executive heads of the panchayat, i.e, the sarpanches, that they amounted to a framework where the sarpanches could engage in corruption with impunity but had no space to question the system or even adhere to the completely unreasonable norms set from above. The sarpanch became a vote bank manager for MLAs and MPs and was given protection against inquiries and investigations in return. The provision for caste- and gender-based reservations has been a major positive step in increasing participation of social groups who were completely marginalized in the social process. However, if the individual from the marginalized community were to choose to challenge the existing hierarchy and power structures, there are more than enough legal traps to see to it that they fall in line.

The Ghotala Rath Yatra had proved itself as a potent instrument to expose corruption and the relationship of the political class with systems of corruption. Through satire and lampooning, transparency had been presented as the antidote that could not only fight elections but prevent it. Even this was a limited articulation of what transparency and the right to information could achieve. As the MKSS and others started to put the provisions of the RTI to use, it became clear that information was the first vital step towards peoples' participation in the entire gamut of governance. It was not just about poor implementation or corruption. Often the policy/law itself was flawed and it helped build a more unequal and exploitative society. If people could not participate in every stage of governance, it was obvious that the ruling elite would enact laws and put in place policies that benefitted themselves even at the cost of others.

It was clear that the discourse had to expand beyond corruption to the role of an informed citizenry in a democracy. The idea of doing a Jan Niti Yatra, i.e., a Peoples' Policy Yatra, was born. The communication content of the Ghotala Rath Yatra was changed to draw people in a larger conversation on development and participatory democracy. Concrete examples of empowerment came from the growing experience of using the RTI to make people in power accountable. The yatra travelled across the state, once again in a truck and as before stopping in different divisions and districts. Only this time the message was much broader and rather than just asking for a single law there was a demand for legitimizing the participation of people in every stage of governance. Discussions about employment and the right to work, state of schools and the right to education, people's health and the health of the medical establishment, agriculture policy and the state of farmers, drought and drought proofing, gender, caste, marginalization of minorities in our democracy...all began to take place.

Although there was no attempt to directly put up candidates in the state assembly and the parliament, there was a conscious decision to engage with the political parties and the electoral process in this manner. The Jan Niti Abhiyan was followed by an election watch Truck Yatra during the 2004 elections, attempting to build a people's manifesto that could be used as a basis of discussion with parties and their leaders.

We will cover here three yatras: Jan Niti Yatra, Election Watch Yatra and Rozgar Adhikar Yatra. The Ghotala Rath became a part of the Truck

Yatra to draw spontaneous flash crowds, when the truck stopped at crowded street corners to communicate its messages and elicit responses. The campaigns for the RTI and the Right to Employment decided that a yatra would be the best way to get support for both a better RTI legislation in India, and the demand for employment on the manifestos of the political parties. General elections to the Rajasthan state assembly as well as the parliament (Lok Sabha) were due in 2004.

The first fortnight of July 2003, the districts in the south and western parts of Rajasthan saw some special activities, along with relief from a prolonged drought. Heavy rains marked an end to a four-year drought. The reprieve notwithstanding, people were drawn to the Truck Yatra that focused on the fundamental issues of livelihood.

In geographic terms, Rajasthan is a very large state. To walk the length and breadth of the state would have taken months, if not years. The MKSS decided once again to hire a truck and take a cross section of people along to spread the message and create a demand for the issues which were of critical importance to everyone.

Meanwhile, many members of the various campaigns were forming the School for Democracy (Loktantrashala), a growing definition of the need for people to fill in the gaps in information, understanding and critique of democracy. It was conceived as a place for eclectic democratic education. The institution was registered in April 2003 with Jean Dréze as president and Aruna Roy as vice president. The four bighas of land which belonged to the MKSS and was bought in the early 1990s for 5,000 rupees was later transferred to the Loktantrashala to locate the school. The nascent Loktantrashala decided to join the yatra and contribute in learning and reflecting on the process. The Jan Niti Abhiyan was underway to make NREGA a demand for the upcoming Lok Sabha elections.

> Making use of different modes of expression and awareness generation such as political speeches, press conferences, street plays, people's assemblies, workshops and the ghotala rath yatra, the demand for a legal guarantee for work was being articulated with renewed vigour and passion alongside mobilizing public opinion for a renewed focus on people-oriented policies and laws. With the aim of promoting people's participation in democratic processes and policy formulation, the MKSS along with other rights-based struggles and organizations had initiated the Jan Niti Abhiyan.

> Aruna Roy inaugurated the truck yatra. She noted the purpose of the yatra was to submit a memorandum that contained policy action points that came from the people rather than some agenda that was forced by bureaucrats and policy makers from above. The Jan Niti Abhiyan focused on two issues: 1) passage of the National Rural Employment Guarantee Act [now MGNREGA], and 2) ensuring implementation of the Supreme Court ruling on electoral reform, which would be the responsibility of the newly established Rajasthan Election Watch. The yatra also asked people to be vigilant against any kind of attack on democracy, religious tolerance and freedom, the right to information and corruption. Participants of the yatra noted the frustration of the ordinary women and men with politicians, but due to lack of credible alternative candidates they felt helpless. However, based on the support extended by women and men from all classes to the Jan Niti Yatra, it is hoped they will overcome their frustration and take action.[222]

The MKSS, as part of the many campaigns, was beginning to feel reassured about the processes it had initiated with the struggle for the RTI. The RTI campaign had opened up the discourse on the nature of political engagement. It reviewed older positions, particularly the stark polarity of being either pro- or anti-state, by placing public interest in governance as the bridge between people's needs and their government's constitutional obligations to deliver. This powerful and basic empowerment opened up varied stages and places for direct engagement with governance, including policy and legislation. The struggle became more hopeful of achieving its ends, and the control of the power elite less sure of its ability to manipulate people, their vote and their aspirations. The discourse was edging towards a larger parabola of electoral commitments.

CHAPTER TWENTY-SIX

# Freedom of Information Bill, 2002

**Between Government, Parliament, and the People's Movement**

The struggle to get the law in place in Delhi continued and its legal trajectory is well documented through articles and reports. But the details of the stories of negotiations and the ups and downs – its spicy bits – are in the tales of the campaigners. They ferried the comments of the people in power – the North Block and the South Block – and the parliamentarians. The dialectic continued between the sovereign people and the keepers of the constitution, obliged to make the system work for the larger common good.

The immediate provocation for the passage of the weak and ineffective legislation in 2002 included the role played by Ram Jethmalani, who was at that time the minister for urban development. He issued orders for placing some of the documents of the ministry in the public domain. There was an immediate furore and the cabinet secretary rushed to the ministry and the minister over the weekend to stop the process. The conflict that ensued between the minister and the senior-most of bureaucrats opened up spaces for public action. There was speculation, as there usually is at times like this. But, more interestingly, the NCPRI found enough legal loopholes to approach the court.

The process of litigation in the Supreme Court pushed the Government of India to declare its intent, which according to them was honourable. To demonstrate that it was there, the government hastened the passage of the FOI Act in the Parliament. The Supreme Court was satisfied with the assurance that the law would be passed soon, and it was. But the law fell short of expectations in many ways. It did not notify the law – a ruse used by the government to prevent the use of it, toothless as it was. When the campaigners demanded its notification, they were told, 'The UK took four years and more to notify their law, wait…there are many more years…one day it will be notified.' The demand for revisions and a better law continued. There were examples of better state laws, such as the second Maharashtra RTI law, which was reformulated by Madhav Godbole as key draughtsman, after protests led by Anna Hazare demanding revisions in the first law passed by the Maharashtra assembly were useless. The Goa Act too was closer to the Press Council Draft. But none of them had a penalty provision to ensure time-bound delivery.

The FOI vs the RTI gained popularity in the Indian discourse on transparency and accountability. The Indian campaign for the transparency of the government, unlike its East European counterparts, already had a guarantee for the freedom of expression under Article 19 of the Indian Constitution. What they wanted to address, therefore, was the denial of their right to access their rights because of misgovernance, in which corruption, the arbitrary use of power, and the lack of political and bureaucratic will played oppressive roles. It followed logically that their demand was for an RTI legislation and not an FOI Act. The NDA government, by giving them an FOI Act, indicated its unwillingness to address the more fundamental relationship between the government and its people, that of accountability.

It is perhaps important to quote contemporary comments to trace the history of the campaign for the RTI Act and to address every shortcoming of the FOI Act.

## The Central Law: Filling the Holes and Expanding Spaces

Constitutionally, the RTI flows from our right to equality before the law and lack of arbitrariness (Article 14), our freedom of speech and expression (Article 19 [1] [a]) and our right to life and liberty (Article 21). Often at cross-purposes with laws like the Official Secrets Act, the struggle for RTI, emerging as it did from people's struggles for empowerment and justice, has firmly established the significance of access to information in the functioning of a genuinely democratic polity. The Supreme Court has underlined this right for citizens through many of its rulings. While the FOI Bill has existed since the post-Emergency scenario in the country, it was conceived specifically with regard to the freedom of the press, which was severely curtailed during the Emergency.

The first draft articulating the RTI for citizens was prepared by the Press Council of India under the chairmanship of Justice Sawant and the NCPRI in 1996. This was later revised at an NIRD-organized workshop. In the same year, the H.D. Shourie Committee was set up, which made amendments to the Press Council Draft, diluting its provisions considerably, and drafted and recommended the FOI Bill in 2000. This Bill was referred to the Parliamentary Standing Committee on Home Affairs, which in turn invited suggestions from various non-government and government representatives, including the NCPRI, in 2001. Very few of the committee's recommendations, however, found their way into the FOI Bill, which was passed by the Lok Sabha in December 2002 (see Annexure II, pg. 346).

However, this Bill remained only on paper; and it was never notified, which was a prerequisite for it to become a law. Significantly, it suffered from serious limitations. According to the NCPRI report, some of these limitations were:

> The request for information by an individual could be rejected on the following grounds:
>
> 1. Information likely to affect the sovereignty and integrity of India, security of the state or strategic scientific information and conduct of international relations.
> 2. Information likely to prejudicially affect the detection and investigation of an offence.
> 3. Information likely to affect Centre-State relations.
> 4. Information regarding records of deliberations of the Council of Ministers, Secretaries and other officers.
> 5. Information that may result in the breach of privileges of Parliament or the Legislature of a State, or contravention of a lawful order of a court.[223]

There was no independent appellate mechanism, i.e., no commission, and all matters of appeal were within the government.

The most blatant exemptions in FOI Bill 2002 are the list of defence and security tagged in the end that keeps them out of the purview of the law, while these are the very organisations most often accused of illegally violating civil liberties and human rights, including the right to life. Moreover, excluding such organisations as vigilance and anti-corruption bureaus and revenue enforcement agencies from the purview of the proposed Act would only protect the course of various corruption cases by affording them secrecy. Additionally, the clause that any "competent authority" can withhold any information on the ground that it interferes with the work of a government office or involves a disproportionate expenditure in providing it also affords blanket exemption [Mishra 2003].

A critical omission is the exclusion of private bodies like Corporations, Companies, NGOs, etc. from the purview of the Bill. Given increasing privatization and cases of violations of environmental laws, community and human rights violations, these bodies must be made transparent and accountable to the citizens of the country.

Apart from the factors of exemptions and applicability, the Bill does not provide for any penalties in case of non-compliance, nor does it have an independent appeal mechanism. The first appeal is to the next higher authority and the second appeal to the central or state government, as the case may be, and the courts have been barred from intervening, entrenching the right in a system already ridden with a culture of secrecy and wide-scale corruption. The Bill would have much to gain with penalties on non-complying officials amounting to portion of salary [since a fixed amount of money loses its value over a period of time], along with disciplinary action and an independent appellate mechanism.

While incorporating the provision for suo moto or proactive information sharing on the part of public authorities, the Bill is silent on the manner of publication of information, which must be understandable in easy to understand idiom and local languages. Also, the Act should provide a more extensive and illustrative list of items to be published suo moto leaving room for additions emerging from problems encountered by people at the implementation end of the Law.

> Information relating to the life and liberty of a person must be made available within 24 hours and not 48 as the Bill stipulates.
>
> Apart from information stored on paper and electronically, the definition of "record" must include materials and samples [say, of food grains] also. [This was addressed in detail later in the RTI Act 2005.]
>
> A set format for applying for information must be provided with all possible assistance to people applying for information. All applications should be recorded on a specified register with a mandatory acknowledgement receipt of the application given to the applicant.
>
> The right to inspect documents must also be provided.
>
> The fees for providing information must not exceed the cost of reproducing/supplying the record.
>
> If information is not provided within the specified time frame, it must be deemed to be a refusal and appeal must be allowed, even if the request is not explicitly rejected.
>
> The senior officer of the department from which the information is demanded must also be made liable for not providing requested information. [This later converted to the penalty imposed for non-furnishing of information within the stipulated period.]
>
> No information that is available to the Members of Parliament or state legislatures should be denied to any citizen. [This was reflected in the over ride to section 8 of the RTI Act 2005.]
>
> The nomenclature of the Bill itself is problematic as the law ought to secure the people's right to information and not just the freedom of access to information and hence the Law should be called the Right to Information Law.[224]

The petition filed by the NCPRI in the Supreme Court, before Ram Jethmalani resigned as minister, continued to press for transparency and accountability. The court's pressure finally took shape in the passage of the Act. To sum up, the campaign got a poor FOI law, with no independent commission of appeal – meaning no real accountability and redress – no penalty provision for not furnishing information in time, very poor suo moto disclosure, and a very inadequate definition of information, both narrow and restrictive.

The MKSS, as part of the larger campaign in NCPRI, saw its strategy of struggle, advocacy and engagement merge with the politics of people's movement. The scope of the RTI as a tool to fight injustice in its multiple manifestations was more commonly understood. The nature of the demand, the RTI, which was later defined as a 'transformatory' law – an enabling legal tool for realizing many more constitutional guarantees – was comprehended. The older argument, of the ineffectiveness of an RTI law for the poor and those suffering from injustice, was proven wrong.

CHAPTER TWENTY-SEVEN

# Friends and Colleagues in Delhi

Campaigning for a good Central law was only one of the reasons for the MKSS coming to Delhi. Ever since the Beawar dharna of 1996, Prabhash Joshi, Ajit Bhattacharjea, Kuldip Nayar, and Nikhil Chakravarty had invited the MKSS to Delhi, to advocate nationally for an RTI law and take the campaign to all Indian states.

Senior journalists and public intellectuals had made an enormous effort to support the MKSS during its unequal battle against the colonial administrative structures in Beawar and Jaipur. They played an important role in forcing the MKSS to realize that it was more than a localized and state-level battle, and had enormous national implications. They had knowledge of, and capacities to draw media attention to the Rajasthan movement. They knew politicians from across the spectrum who appreciated the fact that the campaigners were advocating a cause which was beyond partisan calculations. These senior journalists and opinion makers offered to be a part of the campaign and regularly attended meetings. They made a consistent effort to identify and build alliances. Their extensive contacts with people from all walks of life helped the RTI campaign grow in depth and vision. Many of these activities were coordinated from Delhi, and it meant that some of the MKSS members had to spend much more time in Delhi than before. Some of the activities were local to Delhi, and some had much wider applicability.

One strong ally made in 1996 was Justice P.B. Sawant, who was the Chairperson of the Press Council of India (PCI). He recognized the opportunity provided by this fledgling movement to combine grass-root peoples' movements with legal entitlements to establish a more transparent democracy. He immediately offered to anchor an initiative to hold widespread public consultations and draft an appropriate and effective model right to information bill. Most importantly, he made it clear that he was happy to bring his offices as chairperson of the PCI to work together with the NCPRI to prepare this draft. He was a former judge of the Supreme Court, with a sharp understanding of constitutional principles. His statutory position as a kind of mentor of interests of the press gave him a mandate with statutory rights. Justice Sawant made sure a strong peoples' draft formed the basis for all subsequent discussions on the RTI legislation when he sent the final bill to the prime minister, all the members of parliament, all chief ministers, and other relevant people in authority. In fact, even the watered-down version presented by the H.D. Shourie Committee, which formed the basis for the FOI Bill, was critiqued as ineffective when compared with the NCPRI/Press Council Draft.

While drafting the bill, Justice Sawant travelled to Rajasthan, Goa, Andhra Pradesh, and Maharashtra to learn further from experiences on the ground. Activists like Shekhar Singh, and Prashant Bhushan from the NCPRI kept working on the first model bill right through the time when the RTI Act 2005 was enacted and the FOI legislation was repealed. Justice Sawant, along with Shekhar Singh, Prashant Bhushan, Aruna Roy, Bharat Dogra, Prabhash Joshi, Ajit Bhattacharjea and many others were the panellists in the first public hearing on development works organized by Parivartan in Sundernagari in Delhi.

**Sundernagari Public Hearing**

Arvind Kejriwal, on sabbatical from the IRS, began Parivartan in Delhi and came to visit the MKSS to learn about the RTI campaign. Parivartan was a voluntary organization active in Delhi against corruption that affected the ordinary person. It had run a campaign against bribing officials in the income tax and the electricity departments. Kejriwal was part of the group of people who met to discuss transparency and accountability issues. He had also started coming to NCPRI meetings. He had heard of the demand for the RTI being raised by the MKSS and the mode of the jan sunwai and was curious to see its effectiveness.

In 2001, he came to observe a public hearing at Beawar Khas Panchayat, just outside Beawar, where it was being held as a part of the government-organized social audits following Janawad. This was the beginning of a close interaction between the MKSS and Parivartan, and later with other groups that worked on social sector issues in Delhi. It began with a decision to hold the first jan sunwai in urban areas looking at development and infrastructure expenditure. Parivartan also worked to address citizens' grievances related to the Public Distribution System (PDS), public works, social welfare schemes, income tax and electricity.

The MKSS was keen to take the jan sunwai to the metropolis to see the effectiveness of this process. The Delhi Right to Information Act, which came into effect on 2 October 2001, empowered citizens to access government files by simply filling out a form and submitting it to the concerned department. Parivartan soon realized that it provided immediate relief to people by taking up their issues on their behalf, but this intervention neither empowered citizens to resolve their grievances directly, nor helped bring about permanent systemic changes. The organization began to use the Delhi Right to Information Act 2001 to involve citizens in resolving public grievances.

Impressed by what the MKSS jan sunwais had achieved, Parivartan planned a jan sunwai on development works and infrastructure in Sundernagari. Shankar, Kheema Ram, Lakshmi, Sowmya Kidambi, Kamayani Swami, Mohanji, Nikhil and some others from the MKSS joined in the planning, preparation, publicity, and conducting of this public hearing in Delhi. The MKSS team camped in Sundernagari and along with Arvind, Anjali Bharadwaj, Panini Anand, Rajiv, Santosh, Rekha and others from Parivartan, did the preliminary work, performed the play *Khazana*, and helped with the collation and formatting.

Sundernagari was a resettlement colony in Delhi, and the objective of the jan sunwai was to force the Municipal Corporation of Delhi (MCD) to account for money spent on civic/public works. There were eleven blocks in Sundernagari, and seven in New Seemapuri. In each block, Parivartan and MKSS workers sang songs, performed small puppet skits, and held meetings at street corners. Panini Anand had a song that lamented the prevalence of corruption called *Gandhi tere desh mein...* Arvind Kejriwal used the example of taxes at each street corner meeting to point out that the poorest people paid taxes and should ask for accounts. People were informed about the construction and repair work claimed to have been done by the MCD in their block, and the amount spent on each of them. It emerged that a number of projects hadn't even begun, or that they were incomplete, or that their quality was very substandard. The residents went on site visits to see for themselves lapses between what was written in the contracts and the reality.

On 14 December 2002, a public hearing was organized in Sundernagari by Parivartan along with the NCPRI and the MKSS of Rajasthan to publicly discuss the works and their accounts. The contract for each project was read out and residents testified as to their current status. Of the sixty-eight works publicly audited that day, an estimation of the misappropriation of funds was done for sixty-four works. The total amount of misappropriation was approximately Rs. 70 lakhs. It was also revealed at the jan sunwai that often it was not inadequate funds that impeded development but so-called 'leakages'. Almost a thousand people attended the meeting, including local residents, journalists and eminent personalities. For the first time, the people felt that the government could be held accountable under full public scrutiny. A panel of eminent people and media representatives, including Justice Sawant, Ajit Bhattacharjea and Prabhash Joshi, watched the rather stormy proceedings.

The preparatory phase had already led to high drama. In one instance, the slum and jhuggi-jhopdi department of the MCD began laying a street in the jhuggi area of Sundernagari in late February 2003. The citizens noted that the sand being used in the construction was of poor quality. And the cement was not being mixed in the right proportion. They stopped the work and informed Parivartan as well as the junior engineer at the MCD. The latter admitted the deficiencies and offered to rectify them. But the people insisted on disciplinary action against the responsible MCD officials.

About thirty people, along with Parivartan staff, went to the office of the executive engineer for the region and demanded the suspension of the junior engineer. The executive engineer assured them that the engineer would be transferred, the material replaced and the lane redone. All three promises were carried out.

While the jan sunwai had a dramatic effect on the development administration, each issue and its legal implications based on the findings were barely acted upon. Later on, out of frustration the organization was left with no choice but try to take the issues to court.

Parivartan's next initiative was to look into the documents of ration shops in the Sundernagari area. Following complaints from residents about foul play. Triveni, a poor woman, complained to Parivartan that whenever she visited the ration shop the shopkeeper would always say, "No stock". She had not been given her rice entitlements for a number of months. The public grievance commission directed the Delhi food and civil supplies department to share the records of all eighteen ration shops in Sundernagari, Welcome and New Seemapuri over four months, with Parivartan. However, on an application moved by the ration shopkeepers of Sundernagari, on 22 July the Delhi High Court put a stay on the disclosure of the records. No valid reasons were given.

The prevalent system of secrecy bred corruption. Parivartan began demanding transparency in the operation of the Public Distribution System (PDS). Representatives from the organization along with other RTI supporters and activists met the then Delhi chief minister, Sheila Dixit, who in turn asked the food commissioner to show her the records to ascertain facts. One of the options with the government was to file for a vacation of the stay.

In 2003, Parivartan exposed a PDS scam, in which ration shop dealers were siphoning off subsidized foodgrains in collusion with civic officials.

> Information accessed under RTI – from daily sale registers, stock position registers, and copies of cash memos – were analysed, collated and a verification exercise was undertaken. Out of the 182 families surveyed, 142 families did not receive a single grain of wheat and 167 families did not receive rice during the month of June 2003. A total of 87 per cent of wheat and 94 per cent of rice under the PDS had been diverted and sold in the open market [Pande, S. 2008. The Right to Information and Societal Accountability: The Case of the Delhi PDS Campaign. *IDS Bulleting 38[6]*. Pp 47-55]

**Satark Nagarik Sangathan (SNS)**

In 2003, Anjali Bharadwaj, along with Seema Mishra and some others, had started working in the slum settlements of Malviya Nagar and formed the

Satark Nagarik Sangathan (SNS). They had also started accessing records of development expenditure but focused more on issues of transparency and accountability related to ration expenditure. The MKSS also found an urban echo in their work, as they began to demand proactive disclosure and wall paintings of MLA constituency fund expenditure, and hold very effective community-level jan sunwais on rations. SNS decided to use the Delhi Right to Information Act to access records and improve delivery of public entitlements.

As the SNS website states:

> For years, ration shopkeepers in Malviya Nagar had denied people their ration on the pretext that they did not get any ration supplies from the government. If cardholders asked for their share of ration, shopkeepers misbehaved with them. Repeated complaints to the Food department fell on deaf ears. When in 2003, SNS workers distributed pamphlets in slum settlements giving information about people's rightful entitlements under the PDS including the quantity and price of ration they are entitled to every month, it stirred up a storm. The Soochna Ghar of SNS became a scene of hectic activity with local ration cardholders meeting to decide how they could set about seeking their legal entitlements under the PDS.

In February 2004, people took the help of SNS to file RTI applications under the Delhi Right to Information Act seeking records of their ration shops – including the stock and sale registers of the shops. Records obtained revealed that the shops had been regularly withdrawing wheat, rice and sugar every month at highly subsidized prices under the PDS but had not been selling the commodities to the intended beneficiaries. The entries made in the daily sale registers of the shops showed that the commodities had been sold to fictitious cardholders. When members of SNS deciphered and disseminated the information obtained to slum dwellers through street-corner meetings and discussions, people demanded a forum where they could openly question ration shopkeepers and the concerned officials about the pilferage. The idea of holding a jan sunwai was mooted. A jan sunwai was organized by SNS on 25 July 2004. It was the first of its kind to be held in Delhi for the PDS, and for the first time, a forum was provided to cardholders to publicly demand accountability from government officials and fair-price shop owners. The hearing was attended by about five-hundred people including local ration card holders, representatives of the Food and Supplies (F&S) Department, media persons and interested citizens. The sunwai was presided over by a panel consisting of eminent personalities. At the public hearing, records of ration shops in the area obtained by SNS and local ration cardholders were scrutinized. Ration cardholders of the area publicly testified about the numerous problems faced by them in accessing their quota of ration.

The *Hindu* of 26 July 2004 reported:

> At the hearing, records of two ration shops in the area obtained by the Sangathan using the Delhi Right to Information Act were scrutinised. The two shops have denied ration to their cardholders for over five years on the pretext that they have not been receiving any ration under the PDS. The records obtained reveal that both the ration shops have regularly claimed wheat, rice and sugar every month at highly subsidised rates from the Government godowns but have not sold the commodities to the intended beneficiaries.
>
> The entries made in the daily sale registers of the shops show that the commodities have been sold to fictitious cardholders. The shopkeeper, who was unable to explain the discrepancy, attended the Jan Sunwai and offered a public apology. But people said he had not been offering ration to them even in the past one month and wanted action to be taken against him.
>
> The hearing was presided by a panel of eminent personalities including Harsh Mander, Senior Advisor to the Food Commissioners of the Supreme Court; Shekhar Singh, formerly Member of the Delhi State Council for Right to Information and founding member of NCPRI and Bharat Dogra, its convener.
>
> The functioning of the PDS was examined in detail at the hearing which provided a forum to the cardholders to publicly demand accountability from government officials and fair price shop owners. After the hearing, a resolution was passed demanding that the Government should revoke the licenses of the two shops, file a case against the FPS owner under Section 7 and 12 AA of the Essential Commodities Act, initiate action against the concerned officials and make available publicly the records of all fair price shops at the office of the Assistant Commissioner.
>
> It was also demanded boards with ration details should be

> displayed at the shops besides displaying the list of card holders publicly at the circle offices. Grain sample should be prominently displayed at the ration office and a system of local monitoring and vigilance.[225]

These episodic jan sunwais in Rajasthan and other parts of the country were demonstrating to the MKSS and other groups just how effective and empowering such a platform could be for the ordinary citizen. It was not just a question of examining records but also having an effect in terms of action taken, and affecting policy – especially related to transparency and accountability issues.

From the SNS website once again:

> The jan sunwai was a prime example of people's empowerment – the first step in shaking up systemic corruption that has been taking place in the PDS, a scheme meant to ensure food security for the poor. As a result of the jan sunwai, show cause notices were served to several ration shopkeepers, their security money was forfeited and licences suspended. Disciplinary action was also initiated against the concerned officials. The pressure created and sustained after the sunwai through regular use of the RTI, resulted in a marked improvement in the functioning of the PDS in the area – ration shops started supplying most cardholders their full quota of grains and oil and opening their shops more regularly.
>
> These efforts have had a systemic impact upon PDS delivery not only in the Malviya Nagar area but in the rest of the capital as well. This is evident by the fact that as a result of such efforts, the Food and Supplies department decided to throw open all PDS records for public audit on designated days of the month – a step that enhanced transparency in the PDS and acted as a deterrent to corruption in the system.

The RTI connection with issues of public delivery, livelihood, and survival therefore was built into the fabric of its implementation in rural and urban areas. It was also a campaign where its parameters were being defined by peoples' organizations working with poor and marginalized communities.

In the meantime, the MKSS had to keep planning and making trips to the national capital to join with other groups and put pressure on the

Central government and other political party leaders to support a strong national legislation. Performances of the Ghotala Rath Yatra and mini-demonstrations were held in many places in Delhi: at the Bikaner House where the Rajasthan government's resident commissioner's office was located; at the India Gate lawns; on Bahadur Shah Zafar Marg, where the major newspapers had their offices; in Central Park, Connaught Place. As the neta atop the handcart, Shri Rajvani, waved to the passers-by, the pamphlets of the movement were picked up and read with interest. The Hela singers came from Sawai Madhopur, performed in their inimical satirical style and sang songs on corruption and placed the story of the RTI in a local cultural mode and context. People from Rajasthan as well as Delhi participated in these events, creating innovative platforms of communication. The message of the RTI began to spread within the national capital, and across the country.

Delhi also had a special significance in drawing connections between the local, and the global. The stakes in bagging development contracts were high, and the concentration of corporate houses in the capital area was dense. Another solidarity issue the MKSS got involved in related to the supply of drinking water in Delhi. In 2004, Parivartan used the Delhi RTI Act to access communication between the Delhi Jal Board, the state government, and the World Bank (WB), regarding a project to privatize Delhi's water distribution and supply. Parivartan decided to file a series of RTI applications with the Delhi Jal Board to investigate rumours and a news report that there were plans to privatize water supply in the city. Madhu Bhaduri, who had retired a short while earlier from the foreign service, decided to file the RTI on behalf of Parivartan, and a Pandora's box opened. It became clear from the records that there was a lot of pressure to first have an evaluation done of Delhi's water supply by Price Waterhouse Coopers (PWC), and then use its report to proceed with a privatization plan. So keen were the funders of the study, including the World Bank, to have PWC and no one else do the study that the terms of the competition and bidding were changed twice, after it became clear that PWC was not going to bag the contract.

The communication between the Delhi government, the Jal Board, and the World Bank brought papers out that had never been accessible to people before. The WB country director in India was stung by the allegations and called all the activists to his office to 'explain' the World

Bank's position. The dramatic meeting opened with a demand from Parivartan to the WB that they disclose all the communication between them, and the government, and the Jal Board. They refused because they said they were bound by their disclosure policy that did not allow it. The Parivartan activists said they had already procured the information under the Delhi RTI Act, and all the activists then walked out, making it clear that there could be no discussions with the WB without full disclosure.

Kejriwal and other activists questioned the design and huge expenditure on the project, as well as the proposal to distribute Delhi's water zones to four multinational corporations with poor track records internationally. The Delhi Water Campaign with the help of professors from prestigious institutions such as IIT Delhi and IIM Ahmedabad and Bangalore argued that the government's proposal for privatization would hike water tariffs by at least ten-fold, thus effectively cutting off the water supply to the city's poor, and not ensuring 24x7 water supply for middle-class households. The project was finally stalled as a result of the campaign's efforts.

This struggle had also given a chance to the MKSS to analyze the WB disclosure policy and compare it to the Indian RTI Act. In a paper written by Suchi Pande and Nikhil Dey, it became clear that the WB had tried to hold the high moral ground lecturing to countries about their lack of transparency while it itself practiced opaqueness and there was blatant lack of transparency.

The MKSS along with other organizations like the Centre for Equity Studies the Commonwealth Human Rights Initiative, and individuals like Shekhar Singh and Harsh Mander, continued their discussions with the Delhi government on the Delhi Right to Information Act, and Delhi's appellate body under the act – public grievance commission. All these interactions allowed the MKSS and the NCPRI to learn the nuts and bolts of how a new law would work or face challenges of implementation. Shekhar Singh, along with his computer, and his house, served as a constant resource centre for working on incorporating these lessons into the many draft versions of the model act constantly being improved upon.

Thanks to senior journalists like Nikhil Chakravarty, Prabhash Joshi, Ajit Bhattacharjea and Kuldip Nayar, the MKSS negotiated the hostile spaces of power in Delhi with greater ease and effectiveness. For all of them ethical issues were non-negotiable, and therefore MKSS learnt to deal with the media and national political leadership in an organic and straightforward manner. They were all part of print media and had been editors who understood the politics of journalism and the journalism of politics. They taught us not to shy away from, or grow dependent on the media.

As Prabhash Joshi repeatedly pointed out, the poor peasants and workers of Rajasthan were fighting a battle that the media should have fought decades ago. He said that RTI was a bread-and-butter issue for the media, and therefore it was one issue on which the media should be both reporter and participant. The importance of the RTI to the media became clearer with time, but it also allowed the MKSS to continually dialogue with journalists, whether or not stories were being published, or editorials being written. Delhi provided that place for the MKSS to understand politics, journalism, and the struggle to find space for the stories of the poor and the marginalized. These were vital lessons to keep in mind while campaigning in the distant villages and towns where India lived but rarely got reported about.

CHAPTER TWENTY-EIGHT

# Second NCPRI, 2004

The 2001 Beawar Convention laid the foundation of a successful and appropriate platform for communication on the RTI law. A huge number of issues across the board were perceived through the lens of the RTI and its potential. This representative cross section of people understood why the national law – a legal instrument for transparency – was relevant for each one of these specific groups. A law to enable transparency of government had to be useful to every citizen and yet be universally relevant. The simple yet effective slogan – '*Hamara Paisa, Hamara Hisab!*' – was logically expanded to cover a range of issues. Enacted state laws had actually provided people a practical base for understanding the nature and scope of the law. The defects in the law pointed out remedies that had to be addressed in the national law.

In the second convention of the NCPRI in October 2004, a thousand participants assembled in the Arts Faculty of the University of Delhi to discuss the position, the legal entitlement and its application after a gap of two years. This convention was attended by 250 organizations from twenty states.

The convention critiqued the FOI Act passed in 2002 and demanded a strong RTI Act promised by the UPA I stated in the National Common Minimum Programme.

> As advocacy and networking on the issue of RTI grew, Tamil Nadu and Goa became the first two states to legislate on the subject in

> 1997. In Madhya Pradesh, and upon its formation Chhattisgarh [as it retained the legal set-up of Madhya Pradesh], more than 50 government departments passed orders for providing access to information. However, while the bill was passed by the state legislature, it failed to get Presidential assent and become law.
>
> In Maharashtra, as a result of the efforts of several NGOs, an RTI law was formulated which was very weak. The demand for a new law by citizen's groups was then launched, but although a more comprehensive new law was passed, it was not being implemented. When Anna Hazare sat on a hunger strike in August 2003 demanding its implementation, it was finally put into place. Journalists and concerned citizens groups also brought pressure to bear on the government, as a result of which the RTI is being widely used by people's organisations and individuals in the state now.
>
> In Delhi, the RTI Act was enacted in 2001 as a result of citizens' pressure but even after a couple of months of the Act being notified, activists encountered serious difficulties in gaining access to information. Parivartan and other citizens groups staged demonstrations for the "system" to be put into place effectively and were using the RTI in many bastis, including residents' welfare associations, to uncover anomalies and corruption in public services like the PDS, health services, urban development schemes, and civic functions like garbage disposal etc. Public hearings have also been effectively used to uncover embezzlement of public funds and food grains. However, users of the law and activists have had to face the political mafia, without adequate protection. Protection of activists and whistleblowers becomes paramount in the access to the RTI in such a scenario.
>
> Assam and Jammu and Kashmir were the new entrants to the list of states with RTI legislation in place. Citizens' groups are attempting to use the RTI against very difficult odds.[226]

As in Beawar, the precursor to the convention was a jan sunwai, organized by Parivartan and the Satark Nagarik Sangathan (SNS) and attended by many of the participants of the convention. The issue was the public distribution system, it was held at Ekta Vihar, in R.K. Puram. As in Janawad, this hands-on experience did not fail to connect reflection and theory to ground realities.

Setting the Stage: Public Hearing on PDS in RK Puram

> A symbolic and fitting start to the Delhi convention was a jan sunwai [public hearing] on the public distribution system [PDS]. Despite an elaborate PDS apparatus in the country, food security for the poorest [the PDS catered to the Below Poverty Level citizens of the country] was a distant dream, kept blatantly out of their reach by the nexus between politicians, bureaucrats and ration dealers.
>
> There were specific testimonies by residents of Ekta Vihar in the R.K. Puram area of Delhi and from other parts of Delhi as well. There were testimonies from Orissa, Chhattisgarh, Jharkhand, Karnataka, Andhra Pradesh, Maharashtra and other parts of the country. The presentations were divided broadly along four issues: accountability, Dalits' access to the PDS, urban migrants and homeless and their access to the PDS, and alternative approaches to distribution.
>
> The testimonies from Bolangir in Orissa highlighted the plight of migrant workers. They cannot access either health care or food, handicapped by their inability to speak the local language and powerlessness to negotiate the system. Similarly, the homeless have no ration cards despite being one of the most marginalized groups in the country, and no access to basic facilities like the PDS.[227]

The case study of a 75-year-old grandmother with four grandchildren who had not been able to get a ration card despite trying for four years offered a vivid example of the kind of problems people face in getting basic entitlements. Users of the PDS brought samples of food grain distributed in PDS shops to demonstrate how rotten and inedible it was. Women from the bastis[228] complained that the PDS shop owners sold at inflated rates and charged them for 7 litres of oil against 5 litres. The most common complaints voiced by the people were that the PDS shops remained closed and rations were not available. The testimonies covered cheating on the amount of rations dispensed, apathy of the MCD officials in helping citizens with requests for change of address, add/delete names on the ration cards, as well as non-issuance of ration cards. The success of the public hearing was the prompt cancellation of licenses of three PDS shops with established records of cheating and non-delivery.

The PDS occupies a central space in the lives of families that live from day to day on the edge of hunger and starvation. It is also important for families dependent on daily wages and precarious employment.

## Plenary Session

> The plenary session was attended by a thousand people from all over the country who raised issues of policy and implementation as people of many states already had a state law in place. The formal proceedings of the convention began on 9 October 2004, at the Arts Faculty Convocation Hall, University of Delhi [North Campus]. The first session was chaired by veteran journalist, member of Parliament, and founder member of the NCPRI, Kuldip Nayar, who welcomed the representatives of various people's organisations. There were group introductions of the participants from various states and campaigns, and Rajasthani folk singers from Gangapur city inaugurated the convention with a contemporary political satire in the traditional "Hela" style. A choir from Gangapur city, Sawai Madhopur district, Rajasthan recounted the history of the people's struggle for the RTI. The convention was designed to have a series of plenaries which looked at the larger democratic relevance of the right to know and therefore to act in a participatory way, and judiciously to strengthen and deepen democracy for the people.[229]

## Inaugural Session

'When you see something wrong happening, and if you do not speak up, that's the day you start dying.' Inaugurating the convention, Kuldip Nayar began his speech with this quote by an American poet. He drew the attention of the convention to the potential of the RTI not only to question government expenditure on public works in remote villages and neighbourhoods that affect people directly, but to ask broader policy questions, such as waging war, whether there is consensus, the expenditure and the legitimacy of this expenditure. When we cast the vote, we become victims of identity politics. The potential of the RTI lies in its promise to enable us to make informed choices.

Bharat Dogra, also senior journalist and convenor of the NCPRI, reading out the Beawar Declaration (see Annexure I, pg. 339) said that, though the RTI campaign in the media has been projected as a struggle against corruption, a closer look shows its fundamental role is in strengthening democracy at the grass roots.

Slogans in different languages from all the states were then raised: 'The right to know! The right to live!'

The inaugural plenary, on democracy and RTI, formally began with representatives from grass roots organizations and campaigns drawing the connections between democracy and RTI from a wide range of experiences and context. The speakers included Sushila from MKSS in Rajasthan, Santosh from Parivartan in Delhi, Shivaji Rao from Maharashtra, Anjana from the Dalit Network in Andhra Pradesh, Ram Sagar from Asha in Uttar Pradesh, and Prabhash Joshi, senior journalist and member of the NCPRI.

The sessions were lively, dotted with stories of the strength the right gave each one of them, through access to information. This cut across geographic areas, varied issues and diverse communities. There was continuous reference to the significance of how the RTI originated from a small localized struggle and transformed itself into a campaign in Beawar, strengthening not only the movement that had reached Delhi, but also giving confidence to small groups.

Anecdotes and analysis continually drew the attention to the critical role of the RTI in the survival of the poor, which was India's insight into the international discourse on information access and legal entitlements. Despite the sporadic cynical and derisive comment of, 'What do illiterate peasants, workers and women know of the right to information?', speakers reiterated how central they and their understanding were to the formation of the struggle and even contributing principles to the legal entitlement.

Every speaker, no matter where they were located, agreed that concerted people's action alone could make a big difference to root out corruption from the political system. Linking RTI to voluntary disclosure of government records, i.e., suo motu transparency, is the logical first step towards its eradication. Speakers also spoke of transparency and accountability of the movement itself, as a non-negotiable first principle in demanding transparency, accountability and ethics in governance. The scope of the RTI to address contentious issues like untouchability, violence against women, and assaults on children, was illustrated.

Another important takeaway from the convention was the critical role of collective action. It was accepted as part of the process, as a principle and a goal to be achieved. It fundamentally alters the balance of power in favour of the marginalized.

The fact that the weak FOI Bill had not yet been notified was seen as an advantage, allowing people to make and sustain a demand for a better law.

Prabhash Joshi, editor emeritus *Jansatta*, *Indian Express*, and member of the NCPRI working committee, traced the spread of the movement through the familiar slogans chanted at the plenary. The slogans were raised in all major Indian languages. An independent government could not refuse to be transparent. Independence and the right to know were inextricably linked.

The session ended with Kuldip Nayar reading out a pledge (taken by all participants) to use the RTI for shaping a more participatory and meaningful democracy.

**Plenary on the Right to Information and People's Campaigns and Democracy**

The speakers included leaders and representatives of many of the people's campaigns in the country who underscored the critical significance from different perspectives of the RTI in a democratic framework.

> The second plenary on RTI and Campaigns, had representatives from several broad-based campaigns across a diverse range of people's rights and entitlements. The speakers included Jean Drèze from the Right to Food campaign, Prakash Kardalay of the RTI campaign in Maharashtra, P.V. Rajagopal of Ekta Parishad, Harivansh Bhai of *Prabhat Khabar*, Ranchi, an independent newspaper in Jharkhand, Suman Sahai of the Gene Campaign. Harsh Mander represented access to justice in a communal context and also for the disabled, Pradeep Prabhu raised questions regarding adivasi evictions, M.P. Parmeswaran represented the KSSP in Kerala and Medha Patkar of the Narmada Bachao Andolan also came.[230]

**Plenary on Agriculture, Right to Food, Land & RTI**

Speaking on the close connection between the right to food and the RTI, Jean Drèze, development economist and activist, emphasized that hunger prevents people from participation in democratic processes. He argued for the 'immediate enactment' of the Employment Guarantee Act promised by the UPA government's Common Minimum Programme. According to the NCPRI report on the plenary:

> P.V. Rajagopal lamented the fact that after 57 years of independence, land issues of 70 per cent of the Indian population have not been addressed. It was an area where RTI intervention was urgently required, he pointed out. Echoing these sentiments, Suman Sahai pointed out how the import of seeds has devastated Indian farmers. She added that RTI could be used to delve into WTO related issues. This was an urgent requirement, because once indigenous agriculture is destroyed, the country will lose its identity.
>
> The diversity of campaigns pointed out the close relationship of survival of the poor to RTI and concerted, collective people's action. Without transparency and accountability in all the mechanisms in place to deliver these rights, these cannot be realised. Questions also need to be asked about false or partial information circulated by government. If there is no land for displacement, how is it available to give away to MNCs and companies? What has happened to land donated for distribution under the call for Bhoodan and the land acquired under the Ceiling Act?
>
> The disastrous effects of biotech seeds need to be understood. The country's survival is dependent on agriculture and people's control over it is crucial.[231]

**Plenary on Good Governance, Communalism, Disability Rights & RTI**

Prakash Kardaley, as a journalist committed to transparency, drew attention to the fact that people and the reporter have an equal stake in transparency, citing the example of the RTI law in Maharashtra. Harivansh Bhai, editor of *Prabhat Khabar*, Ranchi, argued for the use of the law for the fourth estate.

Pradip Prabhu, as an activist with tribal people and a campaigner, stated unequivocally that for tribal people the right to life remained notional, confined within the tomes of the law and the constitution. In the case of adivasis, the eviction of 15 lakh families as a result of a Supreme Court order is a denial of their right to life. There were over sixty police firings in Madhya Pradesh in 2002 and 2003 and Chenchu villages were declared national parks, making these adivasis beggars on the highway. Why do colonial laws like the Indian Forest Act and the Land Acquisition Act still have currency in the country?

M.P. Parameswaran went further and argued that 'no one will give us the right to information. We will have to take it. Not providing information is a crime against people.'

> RTI is also an important tool in the context of denial of justice by the state. In the context of Gujarat, the complicity of the state both in the genocidal violence and in the denial of justice thereafter have meant the use of POTA in Gujarat against more than 300 Muslims and not a single Hindu. Of the 4,000 cases filed, 2,000 were withdrawn. By using the RTI, the state can be held accountable to maintain the secular fabric of the nation as enshrined by the Constitution. In this context, Harsh Mander described how RTI had been successfully used against government indifference in Gujarat after the 2002 carnage. In the case of marginalized groups like the disabled, even the basic figures of how many people suffer from disability are not clear, leave alone the issue of accountability in the case of the entitlements of the disabled vis-a-vis the state.
>
> Medha Patkar distinguished between the right to information and the right to know. She remarked that knowledge for the sake of knowledge was not enough. She cited the example of female foeticide as an instance where information should not be given. Knowledge and information must be used for people's survival and distinctions must be made between desirable and undesirable information.
>
> Dalits have asked for the right to knowledge for generations and have been denied the right for centuries.[232]

**Plenary on Right to Information and Law and Implementation**

Many of the participants were users of the law already in place, and had personal and/or first-hand experience of its efficacy. The plenary on the RTI, law and implementation, was addressed by people from various states where the RTI laws had been enacted, and from states where efforts were underway to enact a law. The session was chaired by Supreme Court lawyer Prashant Bhushan. Prakash Kumar, secretary, Delhi Government, spoke about the experience of RTI in Delhi. Some of the new elements of the Delhi Act included the introduction of penalty provisions and use of social audits. He complained that only 90–100 applications were received and that the RTI Act was not used enough. Anjali Bhardwaj of SNS India spoke about the many bottlenecks in accessing information and the excuses of officials not to give information. However, she emphasized that even the suggestion that an application for RTI was going to be filed was enough to move the government machinery into action. Anu Rao from Karnataka too reiterated this point, stating that now not only organizations but individuals were able to get information.

Biraj Patnaik from Chhattisgarh pointed out that the work on PDS in Chhattisgarh in the context of right to food trying to implement Supreme Court orders has delivered results. He said that twenty-six food inspectors audited 1,200 shops in Chhattisgarh. The audit exposed malpractice in 1,100 shops and the licenses of all these were suspended. Licenses around 3,000 to 3,500 fair-price shops were cancelled in tribal areas on the basis of this survey.

While agreeing with the speakers before him, Keval Semlani cautioned that the system was already overloaded and therefore there was a need to make very specific requests for information to prevent further deterioration. Onkarnath Tripathi from Orissa and Amitabh Chaudhary from West Bengal highlighted the problems with implementation and the inconsistent impact of the Act in many parts of the country.

Ajit Bhattacharjea, former editor of the *Times of India* and member of the NCPRI working committee, rounded up the discussion by highlighting the role of media in spreading awareness about the Act while finding media wanting in its involvement. Aruna Roy called upon everyone to observe 16 October as a 'day of action' and submit applications under the RTI Act all over the country. She also invited everyone to the convention on the Employment Guarantee Act on 19 October.

**Concluding Plenary**

The concluding plenary took place in two phases. In the first phase some of the plans and visions for future action were discussed by Aruna Roy, Arvind Kejriwal, Prashant Bhushan and Lal Singh. Many resolutions were also passed.

The second session was chaired by the former prime minister V.P. Singh. The highlight was the convention song *Janne ka Haq*, composed by Charul and Vinay, now one of the most popular songs of the movement. It encapsulated the different ways in which RTI is relevant to the common person. V.P. Singh continued to give support to the campaign and spoke eloquently about the right to know.

**Right to Information**

*My dreams have the right to know*
*Why for centuries they keep getting shattered, never get fulfilled!*

*My hands have the right to know*
*Why for years they have remained unemployed – have no work even today!*

*My feet have the right to know*
*Why they have to walk from village to village – why no sign of a bus!*

*My hunger has the right to know*
*Why grains rot in godowns and not a fistful for me!*

*My old mother has the right to know*
*Why no pills, no needle, no clinic - nothing for bandages, for stitches!*

*My children have the right to know*
*Why they have to toil day and night, why no school in the village!*

*My fields have the right to know*
*Why the huge dams are built and yet my crops are lifeless!*

*My rivers have the right to know*
*Why factories pour poisons, as if rivers have no life!*

*My forests have the right to know*
*Where are the branches, leaves, stem and soil gone, why not a spring in sight!*

*My village has the right to know*
*Why no power, no roads, no water, why no ration shop open!*

*My settlement has the right to know*
*Why our homes are razed and ruined without a trace!*

*My votes have the right to know*
*Why big promises one fine day, no work for five years!*

*My Ram has the right to know,*
*Rahman has the right to know*
*Why the blood flows in the streets, are we all not humans!*

*My life has the right to live*
*What is life without rights – it's no life!**

**Workshops**

A glance at the variety of well-attended workshops demonstrates the interest generated in the use of the RTI. Some looked at constitutional rights and systemic issues, land, social audit, WTO and World Bank, industrial pollution, and urban evictions, constitutional and legal rights and developments, human rights, combating communal violence and discrimination, health, employment guarantee for the rural poor, evictions (forests), civic activism, knowing power – the politics and political economy of information, market, food security, the politics of difference, and access to information in areas where the Armed Forces (Special Powers) Act was in force.

On the following day there were workshops on urban services for the poor on biodiversity, environment and water, disappearances, education, social movements, media, disability rights and mental health, budgets, social sciences, PDS, economic globalization today – finding spaces for informed action, nuclear issues, project (dams) displacement, labour, elections, access to information in the context of criminal justice, and whistle-blowers.

---

*Translation by Suresh Desai

**Common Threads**

The breadth of issues covered during the convention workshops served to emphasise the role of citizens' access to information in areas as diverse as human rights abuses by the state, rural and urban development expenditures, social audit processes, military expenditures, the criminal justice system, or social movements. There were several points of convergence emerging from each of these workshops despite the diversity of issues, some of which are discussed below.

Socially marginalized groups like women, Dalits and adivasis, apart from suffering poverty, are also denied access to public spaces due to the social mores of their particular contexts, even if they happen to be literate. This calls for expanding the vision of RTI-related activism to include social change processes and internal democracy, and information sharing within people's movements and organizations without which citizenship of a democratic state is impossible to realize. Furthermore, the use of a local, easily comprehensible form of language in which information is provided is inherent to the issue of access. This was clearly borne out in the discussions emerging from the workshops on the Politics of Difference and Access to Information, Social Movements and Forest Evictions.

The law is also often used by the elite to suppress the marginalized further in favour of policies and projects that serve their own interests. For instance, the workshop on Urban Evictions pointed out that the elite, using the RTI, often get urban development policies sanctioned that evict slum-dwellers without consideration for their lives and livelihoods because slums pose an 'eyesore' to the urban elite. If the slant of the RTI legislation is not overtly in favour of the poor, the nexus between the elite and politicians will only be further strengthened.

While many laws are made to monitor citizens, the RTI is an effective tool in the hands of citizens to monitor government and private actors and hold them accountable. However, it is possible only if there is awareness among the people of their rights. For this reason, each workshop underlined the role of social movements in empowering the poor and marginalized to access rights through increasing awareness and struggle.

The accountability of private bodies – whether corporations, NGOs or media organizations – to the citizens of the country cannot be ignored. In view of the increasing emphasis on privatization as well as the impunity with which powerful international and national corporations violate the rights of the people, this has become extremely important. The increasingly profit-driven nature of media organizations aligns itself with the elite rather than the marginalized, colouring the information they provide. Similarly, many NGOs, through misguided market- and profit-oriented or communal ideologies, end up hurting the interests of the poor and the marginalized and need to be held accountable. These issues were discussed in detail in the workshops on industrial pollution, food security, health, environment, urban evictions, and media. A comprehensive RTI legislation has to bring private bodies within its purview, otherwise it will remain severely handicapped.

A good RTI law needs to ensure that information is provided by the government and private bodies in a timely manner in order for it to be effectively used. The significance of timeliness of information to securing life, security and justice of citizens was especially brought out in the workshops on disappearances, criminal justice and communalism. Penalty provisions for late and/or incomplete and/or misleading information will greatly serve to enhance the RTI.

An effective legislation also needs to take into account protection of whistle-blowers within public and private institutions from harassment and life threats. Similar protection needs to be extended to all citizens demanding their right to know. The workshops on whistle-blowers, urban services and civic activism discussed this aspect in detail.

Each department and public and private institution has to have a list of suo moto disclosures through relevant information channels clearly distinguished. Information officers and commissioners can aid this process greatly. Care has to be taken that suo moto information is widely and comprehensively disseminated, through public notice boards, wide pamphlet distribution and involvement of the media.

Information is not just for passive acceptance by the citizens; the state must actively seek information from the people in order to function effectively in their interests. Apart from ensuring systems wherein people's experiences influence state activities, the RTI must ensure that there is space for expanding and/or altering the practice of governance and access to justice based on people's experience. The law cannot be conceived of as complete when formulated as such, and must be seen as continually evolving through insights from implementation efforts and the struggles of the citizens in accessing their rights.

The convention ended with the enthusiastic adoption of the Delhi Convention by all participants.

## The Delhi Declaration

The first NCPRI declaration in Beawar was a milestone for the campaign for peoples' right to information. It set the pattern for subsequent conventions. The convention in Delhi in 2004 went further in expanding the scope of the RTI, with more specific demands for the law. The understanding of participatory democracy underscored people's assertion for transparency and accountability. It was a mere three years between Beawar and Delhi. But in this short interval the campaign had spread to numerous states, significantly through the passage of state laws and their use. Localized struggles to access acted as broad platforms to communicate about the law and its potential. As a result, the RTI movement and the national campaign has been greatly strengthened and the fundamental relationship between the RTI and democracy has emerged with clarity.

The participants of this convention from twenty states and two-hundred organizations and movements demanded in one voice that the National RTI Act should replace the FOI Act, a toothless apology of an act lying to be notified. The demands were for an inclusive definition of information, with punitive measures against non-complying officials. Without these entitlements the Act would remain a paper tiger. The right to vote is exercised once in five years. But the persistent demand for accountability from the elected representative, during and after those five years in office, will be empowered by the RTI. The questions were multiple. They asked of the state why in spite of stated intent and money spent, many working hands do not have the opportunity to work, where there is no appropriate wage, lives of people are still not secure, and children remain hungry, while grains rot in godowns, where all resources are being sold to the rich. The answer lies in disclosing information and exposing corruption and the arbitrary use of power.

## Resolutions

In one of the workshops, on the right to information and labour, some students from the University of Delhi raised the issue of the working and living conditions of the construction workers employed on various construction projects on the university's premises. They do not meet the minimum standards prescribed by the Government of India. Subsequently, this matter was raised at the concluding plenary of the convention and the nearly 800 delegates present passed the following resolution:

> The National Convention in its plenary session on the 10th of October, 2004, unanimously appreciates the efforts of the students of Delhi University in highlighting the plight of wage labour working on the university campus on construction works in violation of their right to minimum wages, other rights as workers and even their Right to Information. Those attending this convention urge the Delhi University authorities, and Labour Department, Government of Delhi, to take immediate steps to ensure that the fundamental rights of the labour concerned are protected and that immediate redressal and accountability is ensured.[233]

Subsequently a letter (dated 24 November 2004) was submitted to Deepak Nayyar, vice chancellor of Delhi University, and to S. Regunathan, chief secretary of Delhi, to urgently look into this matter and ensure that all necessary action be taken at the earliest.

**Workshop Resolution**
**RTI & Disappearances Workshop**

After hearing narratives of affected persons from Kashmir and Manipur and after much discussion, the workshop on RTI and disappearances suggested that NCPRI pass a resolution supporting access to information in states such as Jammu & Kashmir, Manipur, Nagaland and Assam, where the Armed Forces (Special Powers) Act, 1958, holds sway. It was felt that NCPRI should also support the creation of an independent judicial commission constituted to investigate into all cases of 'disappearances' in Kashmir, northeastern states and Punjab, and information about the 'missing' or 'disappeared' persons be made public and available to the affected families; and thus the following resolution was proposed.

> The National Convention in its Right to Information and Disappearances workshop on the 10th of October, 2004, noted that in states such as Jammu & Kashmir, Manipur, Nagaland and Assam, where the Armed Forces [Special Powers] Act, 1958, holds sway and

grants wide powers to the security forces, people cannot exercise or enjoy the Right to Information. It was, therefore, resolved to demand of the government that the National Right to Information Law, with the recommended amendments, be immediately passed and that it ensure that, notwithstanding any other law in force, information relating to the life and liberty of individuals, to alleged abuses of human rights and to allegations regarding corruption, must in the interest of democracy, be accessible and made available to the public, even if such information relates to any of the security forces. Further the Right to Information Act, passed by any State, must also be amended to provide all information relating to the life and liberty of people, even if such information relates to any of the security forces.

It was further resolved to demand from the government that they immediately constitute an independent Judicial Commission to investigate into all cases of "disappearances" in Jammu & Kashmir, the Northeastern states and Punjab, within a time bound period. All information about the "missing" or "disappeared" persons be made public and suo moto be made available to the affected families.

The NCPRI convention as a platform was established and accepted by the RTI community that attended it. The (NCPRI) campaign functioned effectively as an anchor to collaborate and coordinate with other entities to bring in the national law in 2005.

CHAPTER TWENTY-NINE

# RTI Law 2005 and the NAC

The evolution of the National Right to Information Law (2005) is a story of the success of Indian democracy and a celebration of its people, who understood and struggled to make constitutional principles come alive in practice. This is a short recapitulation of a long and fascinating journey.

The NCPRI and the MKSS used modes of struggle, advocacy and campaign to form the movement for the RTI. The emerging dialectic between the state and the central law and the un-notified Freedom of Information Act (2002), which later became the Right to Information Act (2005), drew the citizens into an informed debate. This incremental process educated the people about the necessity to build mutual solidarity networks among each other as well as engage with the government and the parliament to formulate policy and legislation.

In a democracy, there are multiple stakeholders whose rights cannot be set aside. It is never a straight route to the objective. Among the campaigners there is every possibility of different priorities and perspectives, even in what seems to be an issue of consensus. The struggle, the campaign, its advocacy and the movement had to define and act to make this complex engagement possible.

The demand for a national RTI law therefore also had to negotiate with the state and central framework, deal with questions of India's federal structure, while using the strength and weakness of law in each state, to finally illustrate the need for a strong and effective national law. When the law was drafted by Justice Sawant as the Chair of the Press Council, it was sent to the parliament and the state chief ministers. Some progressive states passed their own laws. The first states to pass the law were Tamil Nadu (1997) and Goa (1997). Some other states passed it later: Rajasthan (2000), Maharashtra (2000), Karnataka (2000), Delhi (2001), Assam (2002), and Jammu and Kashmir (2003). Political education was one of the interesting fallouts of the state campaign. The experience put forward the argument for the need for a national law. In using the state laws, citizens critiqued their shortcomings and through this emerged the non-negotiables for inclusion in the central law.

The Goa law incorporated much of the Sawant draft, including the override – what the MP or MLA could see, the citizen could also see. The revised second RTI law in Maharashtra was drafted by Madhav Godbole, in response to Anna Hazare's protest against the first Maharashtra Act. The experience of failing to access information in Janawad for a year in central Rajasthan under the Rajasthan RTI Act 2000, underscored the need for specific provisions on timeline for providing information and penalty for non-compliance. There were both negative and positive lessons learnt from various state laws. The drafting of the central RTI law gained from these efforts.

Insofar as the campaigns and the people were concerned, they had to deal with a mind shift. Traditional mobilization and demands came from a context of inequality – discrimination and economic divides – where the state was seen as an adversary, manipulated by the caste and class power elite. Reclaiming the state through the expression of constitutional rights and regaining democratic institutions was an important first shift. This dealt with the primary step of engaging with parts of the state, and understanding this engagement not as a co-option but asserting the right to be part of the process of decision-making. The slogans, '*Yeh panchayat hamare aap ki, nahin kisi ke baap ki, yeh desh hamare aapka nahin kisi ke baap ka, yeh paise hamare aap ke, nahin kisi ke baap ke,*' trace a growth in understanding that democracy had to shift more dramatically towards participation. Representative democracy had to a great extent betrayed its promise to deliver. Though necessary, its failure to be accountable to people – beyond the vote – was underscored again and again. In the now-famous song of Vinay and Charul, *Janne Ka*

*Haq*: '*Mere vote ko yeh janne ka haq re, kyo ek din bade-bade wade, aur paanch saal kaam nahin?*'

The debate on the national bill gained momentum with voices raised from many quarters.

> The Urban Development Minister Ram Jethmalani issued an order using the Supreme Court Constitution bench decisions that held that the citizens have the right to get information about all aspects of government functioning. He had also insisted that anything available to Members of Parliament must be available to citizens. It was the same clause that N.C. Saxena, an IAS official, had suggested in 1995 at a meeting at the IAS academy in Mussoorie.[234]

The Sawant draft was put through many committees in and outside the government. The H.D. Shourie Committee, with one non-government person who was named the chair, sent its watered-down recommendations. Justice Sawant, Ajit Bhattacharjea and others from the first group of drafters of the bill, as well as political representatives, participated in a conference in the National Institute of Rural Development (NIRD), Hyderabad. As pressure grew with a writ filed in the Supreme Court, the bill was hastily placed in parliament in June 2000. It was passed as the FOI Act in 2002 under duress, and was weak and watered down . The law was not even notified, without which it cannot be used by the citizens.

**The State Laws**

The passage of the state laws and their usage did two things. It educated people about the right to access information. It was a demand that resonated across the country in its principles, but the legal formulation and the tool it provided had to be understood. The fact that the state laws came before the central law made it possible to know where the fault lines existed in the different state laws formulated across India. People came up with sound suggestions and a good critique of the law from across the country.

One important critique that led to the strengthening of the RTI Act (2005) was that without a penalty provision, information would be delayed indefinitely or at times even denied. The case of Janawad in Rajasthan is a case in point. However, there were innumerable examples across India to support this argument.

> Apart from the factors of exemptions and applicability, the proposed Freedom of Information Bill, 2000, falters on the significant counts of penalties for non-compliance and an independent appeal mechanism. Our grassroots experience in seeking information under the Rajasthan Panchayati Raj Act Rules, 1996, convinces us that a law without penalty provisions for non-compliance and an independent appeal mechanism outside of the government/bureaucratic apparatus would not have enough teeth to ensure compliance from an obstinate system. It is a pity that like the Tamil Nadu and the Maharashtra state Right to Information Acts the draft FOI bill provides no penalty at all.... All the other state Acts like Goa, Karnataka and Rajasthan provide for some penalty. The Rajasthan RTI Act provides for disciplinary action under service rules, whereas Goa and Karnataka subject the erring official to discretionary monetary fines apart from disciplinary action under service rules. We propose that mere disciplinary action under service rules would not be effective enough against an erring official as demonstrated repeatedly in the case of other kinds of routine dereliction of duty by the government staff. And we suggest that fines too should not be a fixed sum but a portion of the erring person's salary, say half a day's salary for per day of delay in giving information beyond the stipulated limit. This is because a fixed amount would lose its value after some time as money tends to lose value over a period of time. Besides, a fixed amount as fine would mean an uneven burden for officials drawing different levels of salary.

The second glaring lacuna was the absence of an independent appeal mechanism. It should have been obvious that no one in a ministry or department would overrule another colleague to share information in the normal course. This appeal had to lie outside the formal government structure. Suo moto, i.e., voluntary disclosure, is a vital part of the transparency mechanisms. There are many aspects to transparency in governance. But the two important perspectives come from, firstly, the obligation to disclose, and, secondly, the right to know and demand information. If the first obligation had been a part of governance since 1947, the nature of governance in India would have been very different. But the new independent India adopted the British colonial system in toto. In conclusion, summarizing and abbreviating a huge body of work and public opinion, one can only say that the process of drawing up legislation itself was placed in the public domain in a prolonged and diverse manner for the first time. Each stakeholder group played its role. The examination of records, a complicated business, had to be learnt and then critiqued. The bottlenecks of the bureaucratic congenital desire to hide information became apparent. The remedies too were defined and debated, giving people ample opportunity and time to consider alternatives. Ultimately many of the vital non-negotiables of the law were defined by them.

The enlightened part of the bureaucracy began to see in the law its own liberation from being forced to go against the law because of diktat, either from within the bureaucracy or from the political establishment. Sympathizers to the transparency debate swelled even within the system. Though small, this group played a very significant part in the engagement. N.C. Saxena, Harsh Mander, K.B. Saxena, to mention a few, and many other serving officers, still in government, played important roles in shaping the Act. This made the law popular in a real sense and the usage of it later was very widespread. In popular terms, 'the law was owned by the people'; it shifted from government legislation to 'our law'. This shift in popular diction is an important indicator of its universal appeal and acceptance.

In the midst of this there was a collapse of the NDA government's India Shining promises. The country voted in the UPA 1 under the leadership of Dr. Manmohan Singh. The electoral promises of the UPA were encapsulated in a document called the National Common Minimum Programme (NCMP). The promise of a better and stronger RTI was one of the promises made in the NCMP to the people of India.

The government set up the National Advisory Council (NAC) to monitor and ensure that the promises made in the NCMP were fulfilled. It was an encouraging attempt to ensure participation and accountability by the new government. It brought in the campaigners for the RTI and the right to work or NREGA. The NCMP guaranteed:

> The UPA government will immediately enact a National Employment Guarantee Act. This will provide a legal guarantee for at least 100 days of employment to begin with on asset-creating public works programmes every year at minimum wages for at least one able-bodied person in every rural, urban poor and lower

> middle-class household. In the interim, a massive food-for-work programme will be started.[235]

In response to the protest that the FOI Act (2002) was weak and ineffective, the UPA government promised a better law under its Common Minimum Programme.

> **NCMP Administrative Reforms**
> The UPA will set up an Administrative Reforms Commission to prepare a detailed blueprint for revamping the public administration system. E-governance will be promoted on a massive scale. The Right to Information Act will be made more progressive, participatory and meaningful. The Lok Pal Bill will be enacted into law.[236]

Despite bureaucratic subterfuge, and resistance from various quarters, vigilance and advocacy by citizens groups helped ensure that a strong RTI law was passed by the Indian parliament in June 2005. The RTI Act 2005 came into effect on 12 October 2005. Since then citizens have been using the law in different parts of the country with varying degrees of success.

## The NAC and the RTI

When the UPA promised a better RTI in the NCMP and set up the NAC to monitor its promises, the advisory council became a focus for RTI campaigners. It was an opportunity to engage with the government in the process of framing legislation before it went in for formal approval. In fact, the NAC was a platform of official consultation with the political establishment as well as the bureaucracy. Perhaps this unique coming together of power structures made it a powerful institutional base.

In the words of Bharat Dogra, convenor, NCPRI:

> Without a continuing campaign till the very last stages the achievement of a strong and effective RTI law would not have been possible. Many individuals and organisations made important contributions to this long process. It was a joint democratic effort involving many people and groups spent over the vast area of India. In all this the contribution of MKSS and the NCPRI was particularly significant. The MKSS also brought to the national effort the moral force of demand for right to information being

rooted in the struggles of workers and drought-affected small and marginal farmers.[237]

The NAC's singular contribution was the creation of a consultative mechanism for looking at legislations with people during the drafting of a law. The non-compromising political will of Sonia Gandhi, chairperson, NAC, support from members – Jairam Ramesh, Jai Prakash Narain, N.C. Saxena, A.K. Shiva Kumar, Professor Hanumantha Rao, and Jean Drèze – and the presence of a fairly powerful political lobby outside the government, also helped push the law. Repeated meetings between Prime Minister Manmohan Singh and NCPRI members, the presence of MPs in the Rajya Sabha like Kuldip Nayar, the powerful support of the Left parties and of former Prime Minister V.P. Singh, sustained the demand of the RTI campaign. The campaign, for its part, with the help of Shekhar Singh, Nikhil Dey, Prashant Bhushan and other members of the NCPRI, Charmaine Rodrigues, Arvind Kejriwal and others helped in the continual drafting process needed to change the FOI Act 2002 back to the original draft of the Press Council, with inputs from the state laws. V.P. Singh, commenting on the backtracking of the government on the NREGA and the RTI, said, '*Ek mein money nahin hai, aur doosre mein mann nahin hai*' (For one there is no money and for the other there is no will)!

The draft was modified by the government before it was sent to the parliament. The campaign continued to be vigilant to monitor changes. The Parliamentary Standing Committee made 158 changes in the draft sent to it after listening to the testimonies of the people. The law, eventually passed in May 2005, was surprisingly much better than any indication of its content in the year preceding it. We thought that the parliament and Indian democracy had come of age.

CHAPTER THIRTY

# RTI Amendments, 2006

**Cold Feet Ten Months After the RTI was Passed in Parliament**

The RTI law was unanimously passed by the Indian Parliament in May 2005. It was notified and became effective on 13 October 2005. The NAC, which had been convened in 2004 to oversee the implementation of the National Common Minimum Programme, forwarded its draft of the RTI to the government in a few months. The efficiency and quickness of its passage from the campaign to the NAC and then to the government showcased possibilities of quick and efficient disposal if political will and the will of the people could come together to ensure bureaucratic compliance. But within ten months of its passage, the government developed cold feet.

The Indian RTI law defined information exhaustively. One of the fears of a secretive system was the transparency of the decision-making process, which in bureaucratic jargon is called 'file notings'. When the draft bill went to the cabinet, they deleted file notings from under the definition of 'information' and thought that their fear had been well addressed. However, as soon as the implementation of the law began, there was an appeal in the court of the Central Information Commissioner (CIC) asking to see file notings as they were covered by Section 2(f) in its definition of information: 'records, documents, memos, e-mails, opinions, advices, press releases, circulars, orders…' The CIC, Wajahat

Habibullah, ruled that file notings were covered by the definition and should therefore be made available. The government was furious and reacted immediately by coming up with the idea of amending the law further to prevent disclosure of the process of decision-making.

**What is a File Noting?**

A file noting is a separate (normally green) sheet on the left side of files. While the right side of a file contains the proposal, the left-hand side gives an officer's considered comments on the issue. Comments are made on the proposal suggesting possible decisions to be taken. This note is sent to senior officers and they too record their opinions. In short, the dynamics of the decision-making process is contained on this page. We all know that the real expression of power and control is exercised through decisions. If decision-making is under wraps, the citizen could be a victim of manipulation and lies. It was therefore a vital area for disclosure and accountability.

When it became clear that the government was about to introduce regressive amendments in the right to information law, the NCPRI with the help of other organizations launched a strong and successful campaign to oppose and check this. (Bharat Dogra, 2011).

In July 2006, the Union Cabinet approved a set of amendments, some of which would crucially damage the scope and power of the Act. The most critical of these related to barring the disclosure of 'file notings'. Also, cabinet papers that had been hitherto made available after decision-making were to be now barred from disclosure even after the decision had been taken. As a result, the process of decision-making would have been kept out of the public domain, making it far more difficult for the citizens to participate in the process.

The fear of being exposed gripped the bureaucratic apparatus, especially after the CIC's ruling that file notings should be disclosed under the RTI law. That is why the central cabinet of ministers hastened to ring in the amendments. Within a year of it being notified, the government strategized to weaken and dilute the law. However, people gathered in large numbers across the country in Maharashtra, Rajasthan, Madhya Pradesh, Meghalaya, Andhra Pradesh, Orissa, Karnataka, Tamil Nadu, Gujarat, Uttar Pradesh and, of course, at the Jantar Mantar in Delhi to protest against the amendments. Ordinary people used different strategies to protest – some sat on hunger strikes, others organized a referendum, press releases were issued, songs written and sung, street plays performed in several corners across the country, protesting against the government's intent.

A historic dharna began at Delhi's Jantar Mantar on 7 August 2006. With the help of Joint Action for Social Help (JOSH), the famous rock band Euphoria performed to a packed crowd of young people who had came out to save the RTI.

The Supreme Court justices such as the Late Krishan Iyer and J.S. Verma, along with Justice Sawant, issued a strong statement against the proposed amendments.

These statements in support recorded that the strength in a democracy lay in people's participation and, therefore, the proposed amendments to the RTI were seen as unconstitutional.

The referendum quickly revealed an overwhelming victory for the people, as several cast their vote against the amendments. Eminent journalists, writers, and artists joined hands with activists and sat at the dharna to express solidarity. Sandeep Pandey and Anna Hazare went on hunger strikes at two different locations, and Amnesty International expressed concern over the amendments.

Former prime minister V.P. Singh, with all the prominent leaders of the left – CPI, CPI-M, Forward Bloc, etc. – came to the dharna and used their collective pressure to prevent the amendments. The media supported the protest and almost all the print media published strong editorials. The electronic media also gave space and supported the demand to withdraw the amendments.

In the end, collective pressure – public anger and protest – prevailed, and the Government of India withdrew its proposed amendments bill. The minister for Public Grievances and Pensions, Suresh Pachuri, reassured the public that the amendments bill would not be introduced in the parliament.

When the department of personnel and training still failed to remove the misinformation from their official website that file notings could not be accessed or disclosed, there was a huge uproar. This inaccuracy persisted even after repeated directions from the CIC to remove the clause.

There was a plethora of reactions from people from diverse backgrounds. A vast cross section of society came out strongly to protest against this backdoor attempt to dilute this hard-won right to citizens.

The uproar was not just limited to the common person, social activists or only information-seekers, but compelled certain eminent people to add their voice to the protest.

Union Home Secretary Madhav Godbole wrote in his letter to the president, 'The decision of the GoI to amend the RTI Act is highly retrograde and would totally defeat the very purpose of the Act.' C.G. Somiah, former Comptroller and Auditor General (CAG) of India, had said:

> When I was invited by the joint select committee of Parliament to appear before it and comment on one such Bill a few years ago, I had strongly pleaded that the people must have a right to see the notings on the file, including the notes put up to the committee of secretaries and the cabinet and its committees, after a decision is taken on a case. The only exceptions could be matters pertaining to national security, defence, external relations etc. but they must be much more narrowly defined than is the case at present.

P.S. Appu, former director of LBSNAA, stated, 'The correspondence side of a file contains little relevant information. The interesting details are in the notings. Denying access to the notes takes the life out of the law.' E.A.S. Sarma, IAS, former secretary, Power, also wrote to the prime minister. In response to letters from Anna Hazare and V.P. Singh asking the prime minister not to be swayed by vested interest, the PMO incomprehensibly sent a letter and a press note justifying the proposed amendments as a progressive move to ensure greater transparency. For the energetic and rapidly growing RTI movement in India, this was a major challenge to see whether they could protect this nascent fundamental democratic right from being undermined.

In many cases it has been seen that it is opinions of public servants contained in file notings and letters that uncover the corruption in a deal. In the Panna Mukta Oilfields deal, the disclosure of the file noting of the S.P. Anti-Corruption Unit, CBI, Mumbai, was critical to understanding how power had been misused in making the deal. It revealed how the oilfields of ONGC were sold to a consortium of Reliance/Enron for a song. The S.P. had recorded that the deal had caused a loss of at least 10,000 crore to the public exchequer.

As Dr. P.C. Alexander, who was the governor of Tamil Nadu and Maharashtra and a Rajya Sabha MP, said:

> The argument that civil servants will feel inhibited in expressing their views frankly or freely on the file if they are likely to be disclosed does not fairly reflect the view held by the overwhelming majority of civil servants who are strongly committed to the principles of honesty and transparency in decision making. In fact, the persons more likely to feel embarrassed by disclosure of file notings will be the dishonest among the ministers.

The editorials for their part did a fair critique of the absurdity of the government's regressive reaction to progressive legislation passed unanimously by the parliament. The *Times of India* wrote, 'The UPA government often reminds one of a batsman who is unsure of his footwork. It is uncertain when to go forward and drive or to defend off the back foot… The only plausible explanation for the fear among babus is their unwillingness to work in an environment of transparency… That the government is willing to bend before them exposes a lack of courage in pushing reforms it has pledged to citizens.'

This attempt to amend the RTI has been a continual threat. As we write this chronicle in 2017, the MPs in the Rajya Sabha have again brought up the baseless fears and allegations of blackmail, alleging that it is a grossly misused law. All the allegations have been raised and proven wrong repeatedly. It is estimated that between 60 and 80 lakh people use the law every year. Studies of the RTI including the RTI and Analysis Group (RaaG) study have proved that these allegations don't cover more than a small percentage of users of the law. What has been proven, however, is that the RTI has managed to address a wide-ranging spectrum of grievances and cases of corruption – from the ration shop in a small hamlet to the Adarsh scam, and the Vyapam scam to the 2G scam. The fear voiced by the Rajya Sabha members arises from fear of transparency, accountability and justice.

For the citizens of India it is a reminder that the RTI has enabled us to experience our sovereignty and dignity. In an unequal and iniquitous society, any demand for equality and participation, when it's effective, will always be seen as a threat. Since the users of the law are in such large numbers, periodic shows of strength will act as a deterrent to this threatened abuse of basic constitutional rights.

In contemporary India, in the early months of 2017, plagued by a plethora of non-participatory and unexplained policy and other decisions, the Indian government is using empty rhetoric in exchange for dialogue and consultation. There are no platforms for informed debate and dissent. Many serious questions concerning India's economic and social ills remain unanswered. When questions are asked, users of RTI are annihilated; the number of martyrs to truth, the seekers of information, totals fifty-six. On 29 January 2017, Gopalkrishna Gandhi, former governor of West Bengal, delivered the Justice Krishna Iyer memorial lecture in Thiruvananthapuram. The question he addressed was, 'Who rules India, the parliament, the assembly, the panchayat or NOTA?' His conclusion was that 'fear, mistrust, money' were the real rulers. To fight this triumvirate, the community of RTI users and activists pledge their determination and commitment to realize the dream of a free and equal India promised by the Constitution.

# In Conclusion

*'Log judte rahe caaravan badhta gaya'.*

**A Footnote**

The journey of eighteen years from 1987–2005, captured in this chronicle, paused to gather more people and continued its struggle. In 2005, the first journey ended with celebration and wonder. The energy, tenacity, cheerfulness, determination, and confidence that carried the MKSS through, has not flagged. It has been shared with the 6 to 8 lakh users of the RTI who reportedly use the law every year. From 1987 to 2005 the MKSS knew that it was struggling, drafting, thinking, planning, talking, and singing its way with the NCPRI to the passage of a law. The MKSS has always acknowledged, and asserted that the RTI was much more than a tool to fight corruption. It became increasingly clear it was a fundamental and transformatory right against the arbitrary use of power. Huge energy flowed through the years of struggle and campaigning, and thousands of people contributed to keep it going.

Whenever we travel we are accosted by many who come to engage in conversation because the RTI law has empowered them. The right to know is so fundamental a part of life. As Prabhash Joshi said in his editorial in *Jansatta* (1996), 'the right to know is the right to live'. It goes beyond just governance. It proceeds logically to democratic rights, to peace, and to many issues that know no national boundaries. A step further and it relates to the quest for reasons of existence itself.

The end of this journey marked the beginning of the next, raising questions and challenges for what was to follow. It was clear that there would be another protracted struggle to battle the negatives yet again. This time the vested interests and power elite would attempt to defeat in implementation what they could not in legislation. The 'right to question' should have found sanctity in this subcontinent, which gave birth to thinkers like the Buddha – who questioned inequality and promoted rationality above all. But it is in the nature of hegemony and power to control. All institutions fall victim to concentration of power unless they are continually challenged. Democratic institutions are no exception. The adage 'power corrupts and absolute power corrupts absolutely' is a reflection born from generations of observation directed by common sense and people's knowledge. Controls over information and hegemony of knowledge are also absolute power. The right to question is sacrilege for despots, dictators and those who believe in inequality and control concentration of power.

Our country knows this condition well. Democracy, like all other institutions, has to make sure that its stated principles of equality, fraternity and liberty are not narrowed down to sectarian interests. The RTI is a powerful tool to use in the constant vigilance that democracy requires to function with efficiency and justice. The right to question implicitly demands a share of power, in the context of normative principles mutually agreed upon. In this case, they are the universal principles of justice, and public ethics defined by the Indian Constitution.

Questions about governance, once accepted, have to be answered. They are therefore viewed with fear. If answers have to be logical and in the context of principles, the process has to be rational. As a corollary, the need for truth must be established in the immediate sense of implementation of state and legal guarantees. The logic of questioning has been accepted across all cultures universally. It is ironic then that at this point in civilization one has to argue the case for the legitimacy of questioning. Romila Thapar, delivering the Nikhil Chakravarty memorial lecture in 2014 titled 'To question or not to question? That is the question', addressed the restrictive nature of the growing hegemony of unaccountable power. The RTI is a powerful tool that asserts the right to do so – every single time it is put to use.

The last word is that of Lal Singh, who walked the journey from

Sohangarh to Devdungri and further, and stayed close to the earth. In early 2000, Aruna, Shankar and Nikhil were invited as part of the MKSS to the HCM institute of public administration to talk to civil servants about corruption and the RTI. As usual the MKSS went with a larger and more representative group. Lal Singh and Narayan also came. When the time came to speak, the 'more important' people were given ten minutes each. Lal Singh and Narayan were asked impatiently to finish in three minutes as the lunch break was a few minutes away. This is what Lal Singh said:

> *'Mujhe teen minit nahin chahiye. Mai apni baat ek minit me rakh dunga... Hum sochthe hain ki suchna ka adhikar hume nahin mile to kya hum jeeyenge, ya nahin jeeyenge.... Aap sochthe hain ki suchna ka adhikar mil jaye tho aapki kursi rahegi, ya nahin rahegi. Magar doston, hum subko milkar sochna chahiye, ki kya ye desh rahega ya nahi rahega.'*
>
> ['I do not need three; I can make my point in just one minute... If we are denied the right to information we wonder whether we will survive. You are probably worried that if the right to information becomes a law whether your centres of power will survive. But friends, what we should collectively be concerned about is whether our country will survive or not.']

The sharing of power is always contested space. Almost sixty information seekers have lost their lives as they questioned corruption and the arbitrary use of power. They were killed to silence the truth they disclosed based on documents and evidence. The battles continue. But the RTI lives on as an established democratic guarantee.

The international Global RTI Rating placed the Indian law on the third place; we have slid down to the fourth place as more recent legislations of different countries learn from experience to create better laws. Yet the Indian experience of a collective peoples' movement for the RTI remains without parallel. No matter how resistant power structures may be, it is impossible today to think of governance architecture without transparency and accountability. Another set of building blocks, the Whistleblowers' Act, Grievance Redressal, and Accountability laws beckon us on to another set of marches across India. Increasing brutal violations of constitutional guarantees of equality and freedom of expression undermine the rule of law itself and threaten basic democratic guarantees.

The quest for truth is equally tenacious, and questioning will survive. The voices of truth will find every possible avenue to be felt and heard. Some of them are much stronger through the use of the RTI. All peoples' campaigns in India use the RTI. All demand more, not less transparency. The tool was fashioned after all by intelligent ordinary Indians to expose deceit and the denial of rights.

Satyameva jayate?

# Notes

1. Ajit Bhattacaharjea, former editor *Indian Express* and *Hindustan Times*, founder member NCPRI. Unfinished writings, posthumous manuscript.
2. *Ibid.*
3. Rajni Bakshi, *Bapu Kuti: Journeys in Rediscovery of Gandhi*, pg. 23
4. Ajit Bhattacharjea, unfinished writings, posthumous manuscript
5. Prabhash Joshi, *Diamond India*, May 2005
6. Shankar, *Diamond India*, May 2005
7. Living with Dignity and Social Justice
8. MKSS Diary
9. Rajasthani folk tale
10. Report on Delivery Systems of Poverty Alleviation Programmes for the Rural Poor: 1991, pg. 16
11. Rajni Bakshi, *Bapu Kuti*
12. Devdungri Notes & MKSS Diary
13. MKSS Diary
14. *Ibid.*
15. Rajni Bakshi, *Bapu Kuti*, pg. 47
16. Report on Delivery Systems of Poverty Alleviation Programmes for the Rural Poor: 1991, pgs. 28, 37
17. Lal Singh talking to Bhanwar Meghwanshi
18. Chunni Bai talking to Bhanwar Meghwanshi

19. Report on Delivery Systems of Poverty Alleviation Programmes for the Rural Poor: 1991, pg. 38
20. Supreme Court of India; Sanjit Roy vs the GOR 1983 AIR 328, 1983 SCR (2) 271
21. Report on Delivery Systems of Poverty Alleviation Programmes for the Rural Poor: 1991, pg. 57
22. MKSS Diary: Aruna Roy
23. MKSS Diary: Aruna's notes
24. Report on Delivery Systems of Poverty Alleviation Programmes for the Rural Poor: 1991, pg. 60
25. MKSS Diary
26. *Diamond India*, May 2005, pg. 6
27. MKSS Diary: Aruna's notes
28. Report on Delivery Systems of Poverty Alleviation Programmes for the Rural Poor: 1991, pg. 111
29. *Ibid.*
30. MKSS Diary
31. Report on Delivery Systems of Poverty Alleviation Programmes for the Rural Poor: 1991, pg 11
32. Rajni Bakshi, *Bapu Kuti*, pg. 54
33. When Rajasthan had princely states before Independence
34. MKSS Diary: Shankar
35. *Ibid.*
36. Naurti, Sarpanch of Harmara, 2010 to 2015
37. Supreme Court of India; Sanjit Roy vs the Government of Rajasthan 1983 Air 328; 1983 SCR (2) 271, 1983 SCC (1) 525 1983 Scale (1)38 Date of Judgement 20/01/1983
38. Report on Delivery Systems of Poverty Alleviation Programmes for the Rural Poor: 1991, pg. 72
39. MKSS Diary: The Rawats are a militant people They are small in stature but fearless. They used to waylay people between Marawar and Mewar, for a living. They did not accept the British either. Raju Rawat is a legendary hero, he fought the British and was hanged for his protests."
40. MKSS Diary
41. MKSS Diary. They filed a case in the Jodhpur High Court, which they won twelve years later. They won in principle, but the amount paid at 1990 rates did not compensate for the financial loss.

42. Rajni Bakshi, *Bapu Kuti*, pg. 57
43. MKSS Diary
44. Excerpt from the report "Background of the Issue of Minimum Wages in Government Employment Programmes" prepared by the Institute for Development Studies, Jaipur.
45. MKSS Diary
46. Report on Delivery Systems of Poverty Alleviation Programmes for the Rural Poor: 1991, pg. 119
47. *Ibid.*, pg. 121
48. *Ibid.*, pg. 76
49. Narayan to Bhanwar Meghwanshi in an interview
50. *Ibid.*
51. Common sense politics and the RTI
52. This song was written by Mohan Ba during the Bhim dharna. In which it is said: These times belong to the thieves and bribe-seekers, earlier, thieves lived in forests, now they live in bungalows; earlier, they used to kill by rifles, but now they kill with a stroke of pen; earlier, they used to travel on camels, and now they travel in cars; earlier, they used to rob us in the night, now, they rob us in the bazaar (in broad daylight).
53. MKSS Diary
54. Naurti Bai
55. Mamta Jaitley (Vividha Features) and *Ujala Chadi*, woman's activist and alternative journalist, wrote and supported the MKSS since Sohangarh and the campaigns for RTI, MGNREGA and Food etc
56. 'Living with Dignity and Social Justice', pg. 36
57. MKSS Diary
58. *Ibid.*
59. Rajani Bakshi, *Bapu Kuti*, pg. 60
60. Shankar Singh, *Diamond India*, January 2007
61. *The Economics Times*, 30 May 1993
62. MKSS Diary
63. *Ibid.*
64. Nikhil Dey, *Diamond India*, January 2007
65. MKSS Diary, Nikhil Dey & Shankar Singh
66. Nikhil Dey, *Diamond India*, January 2007
67. MKSS Diary
68. *Ibid.*

69. *Ibid.*
70. Neelabh Misra: 'The Right to Information Discourse in India' (Experiences of the MKSS and other Organizations)
71. MKSS Diary
72. The Problem Seminar, July 2004
73. Rajni Bakshi, *Bapu Kuti*, pg. 56
74. MKSS Diary
75. *Ibid.*
76. B.V. Narayana Reddy Memorial Lecture, 1 February 2000
77. *Ibid.*
78. MKSS Diary: Shankar
79. Renuka Pamecha, Panellist, Kot Kirana
80. A Study for Exploring Non-Formal Modes of Learning for Youth and Adults in Remote Rural Milieu, 1995
81. Sawai Singh, Panellist, Kot Kirana
82. MKSS Diary
83. *Ibid.*
84. A Study for Exploring Non-formal Modes of Learning for Youth and Adults in Remote Rural Milieu, 1995
85. *Diamond India*, Feb–March 2011, pg. 39
86. MKSS Diary: Nikhil Dey
87. Rajni Bakshi, *Bapu Kuti*, pg. 76
88. A Study for Exploring Non-Formal Modes of Learning for Youth and Adults in Remote Rural Milieu, 1995, pg. 147
89. Neelabh Misra: The Right to Information Discourse in India (Experiences of the MKSS and other organizations)
90. Asian College of Journalism, Aruna Roy, pg. 13
91. B.V. Narayana Reddy Memorial Lecture
92. The Right to Know, The Right to Live, pg. 106
93. Nikhil Chakravarty was the head of Prasar Bharati and editor of *Mainstream*. He became a touchstone for ethics in journalism. He refused an honour from the state, to maintain his independence from the government. He remained an icon for generations of people involved in struggles for rights.
94. Kuldip Nayar, a well known journalist, was arrested towards the end of the Indian Emergency (1975–77). He was also a human rights activist and a peace activist. He was a member of India's delegation

to the United Nations in 1996. He was appointed high commissioner to Great Britain in 1990 and nominated to the upper house of Indian Parliament, Rajya Sabha in August 1997.

95. Swami Agnivesh (Bandhua Mukti Morcha)
96. From the collection *Batan Ri Phulwari* by Vijaydan Detha
97. Prabhash Joshi began his career with *Nayi Duniya*, and was the founder editor of the Hindi daily *Jansatta* in 1983. A publication of the *Indian Express* group. He changed the definition of Hindi journalism with the publication of *Jansatta*. He edited the Hindi version of *Everyman's*, a journal devoted to advocating Jayaprakash's views and sponsored by Ramnath Goenka. This journal campaigned for JP's movement for purity in public life.
98. MKSS Diary
99. Prabhash Joshi, *Diamond India*, May 2005, pg. 12
100. Nikhil Chakravarty's speech in Beawar 1996
101. Harsh Mander, *Rajasthan Patrika*, 19 April 1996
102. Medha Patkar, Narmada Bachao Andolan, *Dainik Navjyoti*, 22 April 1996
103. MKSS Diary
104. *Ibid.*
105. G.R. Khairnar (former deputy commissioner, Mumbai Nagar Mahapalika) *Dainik Navjyoti*, 11 May 1996
106. Complete list as credits
107. Renuka Pamecha, audio interview by Suchi Pande
108. Dr. V.S. Vyas (renowned economist), Ex-Director IIM Ahmedabad, *Ujala Chadi*, May 1996, Member Economic Advisory Council to the prime minister
109. Prabhash Joshi, *Dainik Navjyoti*, 22 April 1996
110. Kuldip Nayar's speech in Beawar, 11 April 1996
111. Nitya Ramakrishnan, Civil and human rights lawyer. A postscript to the two meetings where the RTI law was drafted in Mussoorie and the Press Council, both in 1996.
112. *The Movements for RTI in India*, Harsh Mander and Abha Joshi, Selective Writings, Sec. A, Article 4, pg. 22
113. Aruna Roy, B.V. Narayana Reddy Memorial Lecture, 1 February 2000, pg. 28
114. *Ujala Chadi*, September 1996

115. *Ibid.*
116. *Ibid.*, February 1997
117. Justice P.B. Sawant was appointed justice in the Supreme Court from 1989 to 1995, he has been active in public affairs, including being chairperson of the Press Council from 1997 to 2001.
118. Nitya Ramakrishnan as a postscript to the two meetings where the RTI law was drafted in Mussoorie and by the Press Council, both in 1996.
119. MKSS article – Article 17 in Selected Writings, CD distributed and sold
120. MKSS Diary
121. *Ibid.*
122. *Ibid.*
123. *Ibid.*
124. *Ibid.*
125. *Ibid.*, http://www.righttofoodindia.org/data/truckyatra.pdf
126. Ramkaran, SWRC Tilonia, has been a supporter of the MKSS since its inception and Aruna's colleague from 1979 to 1983. When all organizations concerned with workers rights set up RMKM, Rajasthan Mazdoor Kisan Morcha, he was very active in the Kishengarh area and a primary participant in the RTI struggle and campaign.
127. MKSS Diary
128. *Ibid.*
129. *Ibid.*
130. *Ibid.*
131. *Ibid.*
132. *Ibid.*
133. Ved Vyas (former president, Rajasthan Sahitya Akademi), *Diamond India*, June–July 2005
134. MKSS Diary
135. MKSS Diary: Shankar
136. Suchi Pande's PhD thesis
137. *Ibid.*
138. *Ibid.*
139. *Ibid.*
140. *Ibid.*
141. *Ibid.*
142. MKSS Diary
143. Rajni Bakshi, *Bapu Kuti*, pg. 81

144. MKSS Diary
145. *Ujala Chadi*, February, 1998
146. MKSS Diary
147. *Ujala Chadi*, 10 May 2000
148. *Ibid.*
149. Vijay Nagaraj: The rural local self-government system consisting of three tiers namely the village, the block (agglomeration of villages) and the district (agglomeration of blocks).
150. Vijay Nagraj
151. *Ibid.*
152. Literally 'the night of murder' – the night before voting when money changes hands and final decisions are made to support candidates
153. Clean elections; Shankar and Nikhil MKSS and RTI clean candidate elected sarpanch in Rajasthan
154. 'Panchayat elections: An insight', Sowmya
155. Sunny Sebastian, *The Hindu*, 23 December 1999
156. MKSS Diary
157. Harsh Mander, *The Seal of the Sarpanch: Unheard Voices,* Penguin 2001
158. *Ibid.*
159. MKSS Diary
160. Harsh Mander, *The Seal of the Sarpanch: Unheard Voices,* Penguin 2001
161. MKSS Diary
162. Sunny Sebastian, *The Hindu*, 23 December 1999
163. *Ujala Chadi*, 10 January 2000
164. *Ibid.*
165. *Ibid.*
166. *Ibid.*
167. Interview by Suchi Pande
168. Sunny Sebastian, *The Hindu*, 23 December 1999
169. 'Campaigns: A forceful assertion', *Frontline*, Sukumar Murlidharan, 28 April 2001
170. 'Chasing a Right', *Frontline*: Aruna Roy and Nikhil Dey, April 2002
171. *Ibid.*
172. Selective Writings, Section B, Document 4, Janawad Jan Sunwai on 3 April 2001
173. 'Chasing a Right', *Frontline*, Aruna Roy and Nikhil Dey, April 2002
174. *Ibid.*

175. *Ibid.*
176. *Ibid.*
177. *Ibid.*
178. *Ibid.*
179. *Ibid.*
180. *Ibid.*
181. *Ibid.*
182. *Ibid.*
183. *Ibid.*
184. *Ibid.*
185. *Ibid.*
186. MKSS Diary
187. Experiences born out of the Janawad Scam Enquiry Report Shri Prakash Sharma, *Raj Drishti*, 15 August 2001
188. Neelabh Mishra, People's Right to Information Movement: Lessons from Rajasthan, 2003
189. 'Taking the bull by its horns', *The Hindu Business Line*, Meena Menon, 23 April 2001
190. 'Chasing a Right', *Frontline*, Aruna Roy and Nikhil Dey, 13 April 2001
191. 'Campaigns: A forceful assertion', *Frontline*, Sukumar Murlidharan, 28 April 2001
192. Radhika Kaul Batra's film on *Janawad: Accounts and Accountability*, 2001
193. Prakash Sharma, *Rajdrishti*, 15 August 2001
194. *Ibid.*
195. MKSS Diary
196. Prakash Sharma, *Rajdrishti*, 15 August 2001
197. Selective Writings, Section A, ART-13, Right to Know – Right to Decide
198. 'The Right to Information Discourse in India' (Experiences of the MKSS and other organizations), Neelabh Misra, pg. 4
199. Radhika Kaul Batra's Film
200. Bharat Dogra
201. *The Hindu*
202. MKSS Diary
203. *Nirantar,* Beawar, 3 April 2001
204. Justice Sawant's address in Chang Gate, reported *Nirantar*
205. *Ibid.*

206. Baba Adhav, Hamal Panchayat, eminent sociopolitical activist and socialist trade unionist from Pune.
207. 'Commemorating transparency movement', *Hindu*, Sunny Sebastian, 2 April
208. Bharat Dogra, *Apna Panna*, October, 2004
209. *Ibid.*
210. See *Accounts and Accountability*, Radhika Kaul Batra (https://www.youtube.com/watch?v=Vfg4LCkYxQo)
211. 'Campaigns: A forceful assertion', *Frontline*, Sukumar Murlidharan, April-May, 2001.
212. 'Campaigns: A forceful assertion', *Frontline*, Sukumar Murlidharan, April-May, 2001.
213. Please see annexure for the Beawar Declaration
214. 'Campaigns: A forceful assertion', *Frontline*, Sukumar Murlidharan, 28 April 2001
215. *Ujala Chadi*, 10 March 2002
216. *Ibid.*
217. *Ibid.*
218. *Ibid.*
219. *Ibid.*
220. *Ibid.*
221. *Ibid.*
222. *Diamond India*, September 2003, pg. 6
223. NCPRI report
224. *Ibid.*
225. 'Jan Sunwai takes erring shopkeepers to task', *The Hindu* (online edition), 26 July 2004
226. NCPRI report
227. Ibid.
228. Slums and resettlement colonies
229. NCPRI Report, edited by Manini
230. *Ibid.*
231. *Ibid.*
232. *Ibid.*
233. Venkatesh Nayak CHRI and member, NCPRI Working Committee, in an interview with Suchi Pande, 11 November 2010.
234. "The Centre for Public Interest Litigation and Common Cause, two

non-government organisations, filed a public interest litigation in the Supreme Court asking the court to declare unconstitutional the actions of the cabinet secretary as well as Section 5 of the OSA that prevents public officials from disclosing official information. It further asked the court to direct the government to issue administrative directives based on the Press Council of India draft RTI Bill." Shekhar Singh, former Convenor and founder member NCPRI, interview with author, New Delhi, 29 May 2007.

235. NCMP
236. NCMP
237. Bharat Dogra

# The Beawar Declaration

**Introduction**

We have gathered from many parts of the country, at Beawar, on 5 and 6 April 2001, to mark five years of the national campaign for the people's right to information. This campaign arose from a landmark movement for transparency and accountability, resolutely supported by the people of Beawar. In this gathering, we considered ways of taking this movement further to deepen democracy. In a true democracy, people are sovereign, but in practice today, they exercise this sovereignty at best only when they cast their vote. The challenge for people, therefore, is to find ways to exercise their sovereignty on an ongoing basis. Both the limitations of our democracy and its possibilities came in sharp focus as we gathered in Beawar in the shadow of severe drought and widespread, unaddressed hunger. As people are struggling to survive, 50 million tons of food grains are stored away by the Indian state. The time-tested system of drought relief has been quietly abandoned. This dismal abdication of state responsibility thrives on a conspiracy of silence that engulfs not only the state but even the media and civil society. People are outraged but often feel disempowered to change a situation of chronic and all-pervasive corruption, all at levels from the defence seam exposed by the Tehelka tapes to the misuse of local development funds, revealed by the recent jan sunwai at the village Janawad, not far from Beawar. The strength of India is in the spirit of its people and the resilience of its democratic institutions. The challenge is to build on these strengths to consolidate and expand democratic space against great odds. This also involves confronting growing anti-democratic tendencies, including state repression, sectarian movements, corporate influence and the defense establishment. The right to information is a crucial means of action in this struggle for democratic space. It is important in its own right as well as for securing the other rights that enable people to survive and take control of their own lives.

The convention considered wide-ranging possibilities for furthering the application of the right to information in different contexts.

**1. Drought and Chronic Hunger:**
In a situation of widespread hunger amidst plenty, people do not know why such a situation has arisen. What resources are available with the state? Why are these not being made available to the people? What are the state's responsibilities under the famine code? What are the state's plans and what has actually been done to provide food and generate employment every week, every month for every village, every district and in every state?

**2. Displacement:**
Millions of internal refugees have been displaced by large projects and urban development plans. This large-scale violation of rights has been facilitated by the denial of relevant information, and active dissemination of wrong information. The nature of the public purpose, the details of acquisition and rehabilitation should be actually shared with affected people, to enable their informed written consent. Transparency of land record management for both rural areas and urban slums is imperative.

**3. Health:**
Democratization of health, people's control over their own health and people's health in people's hands. Current status – vicious cycle of poverty and poor health, stress on female sterilization, vertical programmes rather than preventive and promotional health, huge inequity in quality and access to services, corruption and complete lack of accountability of the health administration, compounded by mystification by health professionals.

The right to information is crucial to enable people to regain control. Disaggregated, demystified information for health services at village, block and district levels, also budget analysis and social audits.

**4. Education:**
Likewise, the deep structured inequities in the education system are enabled also by a lack of information and accountability. People should both know the performance of the state, and be able to hold it responsible.

**5. Human Rights:**
Most human rights violations, especially against poor and marginalized women and men, and Dalits, tribal people and minorities, occur behind resolutely opaque walls of police stations and jails. The entire criminal justice system has been constructed along colonial lines to be the most opaque and unaccountable wings of the state, which foster the most extreme forms of repression and arbitrariness, and protect the oppressors. These are strengthened further by draconian laws, arbitrary arrests and detention. These bastions, like jails, in any real democracy, need to be thrown open to public scrutiny and accountability. Information is crucial to a person in police or jails to their family members, and to human rights defenders.

**6. Electoral Politics:**
The strengthening of real democratic spaces through information requires the radical reform of crucial democratic institutions, such as the electoral system, the legal system and the media. For instance, the assets and criminal cases filed against all candidates seeking election to public office should be made available to the Election Commission to the people, in order to make representative democracy truly representative.

**7. Judicial Accountability:**
Even the judiciary needs to have in-built systems of public accountability and accessibility to poor people. The performance of courts at all levels, including speed of disposal of cases and the assets of judges, should be made available to people, and the language and systems of the legal system demystified.

### 8. Media:

No less than other institutions, the assets, business linkages, land and other facilities received from government and political affiliations of media houses and individual journalists, utilization of newsprint and circulation figures should be given to the people. This would enable people to make informed judgements about the probity and impartiality of the media; there should be a regular interaction between media practitioners and representatives of grass-root organizations work in the field of right to information.

### 9. NGOs/Civil Society Organizations

It is important for civil society organizations, including mass organizations and citizens bodies, to be genuinely accountable to the communities they work with. They should place disaggregated accounts, assets of board and staff members, as well as the performance reports before the people, to enable them to assess the work and polity of the organization.

### 10. Nuclear and Defence Establishments:

The defence and nuclear establishment in India, as elsewhere, is one of the most anti-democratic institutions, which thrives on secrecy, propaganda and jingoism. Budget allocations and expenditures, purchase decisions, military and nuclear strategy, health impacts and safety standards should be brought resolutely into the public domain, for informed and free debate. This is utterly vital because these decisions impinge on the survival of the human race and resources from crucial social and survival sectors, and the adherence to the values of peace and humanism.

### 11. Globalization and Economic Development:

The livelihoods of poor people, especially in the countryside, have been critically compromised by a series of international agreements, which have been reached with absolutely no public debate or even information. Similarly, large public assets, including in the power sector, are being sold and restructured without even minimal public scrutiny.

### 12. Women:

The suppressed situation of women is related to many denials, of which denial of information is critical. It should be the state's responsibility to actively inform women about their land rights, reproduction and health rights, right to information development and other vital entitlements.

The women's development programme was a successful effort to inform women about their rights and it should be strengthened.

**13. Laws on the People's Right to Information:**
Whereas the people's right to information is inherent in the fundamental rights to life, liberty and expression, the convention seeks the passage of strong laws by central and state governments to further safeguard the right to information. These laws should cover not only the state, but also the corporate sector, the judiciary and NGOs. They should have minimal exemption clauses, penal provisions for wanton default and independent appeal mechanisms. In addition, the state should have not only an obligation to inform people when they so demand it, but to positively share information which is used for their survival and well-being.*

**The Beawar Declaration** was then read out. It expresses the questions that need to be answered in the minds of the people on issues below:

- **Drought and Chronic Hunger:**
  In a situation of widespread hunger amidst plenty, people do not know why such a situation has arisen. What resources are available with the state? Why are these not being made available to the people? What are the state's responsibilities under the famine code? What are the state's plans and what has been actually done to provide food and generate employment?
- **Displacement:**
  Millions of internal refugees have been displaced by large projects and urban development plans. The nature of the public purpose, the details of acquisition and rehabilitation should be actually shared with affected people.
- **Health:**
  There is huge inequity in quality and access to health services, corruption and complete lack of accountability of the health administration compounded by mystification by health professionals. Information for health services needs to be available at village, block and district levels.

**Selective Writings, Section B, 1-Beawar Convention (4th to 6th April 2001).*

- **Education:**
  Deep structured inequities in the education system are enabled also by lack of information and accountability. People need to know the performance of the state.
- **Human Rights:**
  Most human rights violations, especially against poor and marginalised women, men, dalits, tribal people and minorities, occurs behind opaque walls of police stations and jails. These bastions need to be thrown open to public scrutiny and accountability.
- **Electoral Politics:**
  The electoral system needs to have information and provide this to the public. For instance, the assets and criminal cases filed against all candidates seeking election to public office should be available to the people.
- **Judicial Accountability:**
  The judiciary's language and legal system need to be people-oriented. The performance of courts at all levels including speedy disposal of cases and assets held by the judges should be made available to people.
- **Media:**
  The assets, business linkages, land and other facilities received from the government or corporates, political affiliations of media houses, journalists, utilization of newsprint and circulation figures should be given to people.
- **NGOs/Civil Society Organisations:**
  The NGOs need to be genuinely accountable to the communities they work with. For instance they have to place accounts, assets of Board and staff members and performance reports.
- **Nuclear and Defence Establishment:**
  Budget allocation, expenditures, purchase decisions, military and nuclear strategy, health impacts and safety standards should be brought into public domain.
- **Globalisation and Economic Development:**
  The livelihoods of poor people, especially in the countryside have been critically compromised by a series of international agreements, which have been reached with absolutely no public debate or even information. Similarly, large public assets including in the power

sector are being sold and restructured without even minimal public scrutiny.

- **Women:**
  It is the State's responsibility to actively inform women about their land rights, reproduction, health rights, right to information and other vital entitlements. Women have to be informed about their rights and rights need to be strengthened.
- **Laws on the People's Right to Information:**
  The central and state governments should further safeguard the Right to Information, by enacting strong laws. These laws should not only cover the State, but also the corporate sector, the judiciary and NGOs. They should have minimal exemption clauses, penal provisions for wanton default and independent appeal mechanisms. In addition, the State should have not only have an obligation to inform people when they so demand it, but must positively share information which is used for their survival and well-being.

On April 9, after the jan sunwai and the convention, three of the culprits were arrested: the ex-sarpanch, the gram panchayat sevak and one of the junior engineers. **This is the first time that such action has been taken immediately after a public hearing**. The Rajasthan government has since assured the MKSS that a special team will be constituted to do a detailed investigation.

ANNEXURE II

# The Freedom of Information Bill, 2000

**A BILL**

*to provide for freedom to every citizen to secure access to information under the control of public authorities, consistent with public interest, in order to promote openness, transparency and accountability in administration and in relation to matters connected therewith or incidental thereto.*

BE it enacted by Parliament in the Fifty-first Year of the Republic of India as follows:—

**CHAPTER I**
**PRELIMINARY**

1. Short title, extent and commencement.-(1) This Act may be called the Freedom of Information Act, 2000.
   (2) It extends to the whole of India except the State of Jammu and Kashmir.
   (3) It shall come into force on such date as the Central Government may, by notification in the Official Gazette, appoint.
2. Definitions. In this Act, unless the context otherwise requires,—
   (a) "appropriate Government" means in relation to a public

authority established, constituted, owned, substantially financed by funds provided directly or indirectly or controlled—

(i) by the Central Government, the Central Government;

(ii) by the State Government, the State Government;

(b) "competent authority" means—

(i) the Speaker in the case of the House of the People or the Legislative Assembly and the Chairman in the case of the Council of States or the Legislative Council;

(ii) the Chief Justice of India in the case of the Supreme Court;

(iii) the Chief Justice of the High Court in the case of a High Court;

(iv) the President or the Governor, as the case may be, in case of other authorities created by or under the Constitution;

(c) "freedom of information" means the right to obtain information from any public authority by means of,—

(i) inspection, taking of extracts and notes;

(ii) certified copies of any records of such public authority;

(iii) disketts, floppies or in any other electronic mode or through print-outs where such information is stored in a computer or in any other device;

(d) "information" means any material in any form relating to the administration, operations or decisions of a public authority;

(e) "prescribed" means prescribed by rules made under this Act by the appropriate Government or the competent authority, as the case may be;

(f) "public authority" means any authority or body established or constituted,—

(i) by or under the Constitution;

(ii) by any law made by the appropriate Government, and includes any other body owned, controlled or substantially financed by funds provided directly or indirectly by the appropriate Government;

(g) "Public Information Officer" means the Public Information Officer appointed under sub-section (*1*) of section 5;

(h) "record" includes—

(i) any document, manuscript and file;

(ii) any microfilm, microfiche and facsimile copy of a document;

(iii) any reproduction of image or images embodied in such microfilm (whether enlarged or not); and

(iv) any other material produced by a computer or by any other device;

(i) "third party" means a person other than the person making a request for information and includes a public authority.

## CHAPTER II
## FREEDOM OF INFORMATION AND OBLIGATIONS OF PUBLIC AUTHORITIES

3. Freedom of Information. Subject to the provisions of this Act, all citizens shall have freedom of information.

4. Obligations on public authorities. Every public authority shall—

(a) maintain all its records, in such manner and form as is consistent with its operational requirements duly catalogued and indexed;

(b) publish at such intervals as may be prescribed by the appropriate Government or competent authority,

(i) the particulars of its organisation, functions and duties;

(ii) the powers and duties of its officers and employees and the procedure followed by them in the decision making process;

(iii) the norms set by the public authority for the discharge of its functions;

(iv) rules, regulations, instructions, manuals and other categories of records under its control used by its employees for discharging its functions;

(v) the details of facilities available to citizens for obtaining information; and

(vi) the name, designation and other particulars of the Public Information Officer.

(c) publish all relevant facts concerning important decisions and policies that affect the public while announcing such decisions and policies;

(d) give reasons for its decisions, whether administrative or quasi-judicial to those affected by such decisions;

(e) before initiating any project, publish or communicate to the public generally or to the persons affected or likely to be affected by the project in particular, the facts available to it or to which it has reasonable access which in its opinion should be known to them in the best interests of maintenance of democratic principles.

5. Appointment of Public Information Officers.-(1) Every public authority shall for the purposes of this Act, appoint one or more officers as Public Information Officers.
   (2) Every Public Information Officer shall deal with requests for information and shall render reasonable assistance to any person seeking such information.
   (3) The Public Information Officer may seek the assistance of any other officer as he considers necessary for the proper discharge of his duties.
   (4) Any officer whose assistance has been sought under sub-section *(3)*, shall render all assistance to the Public Information Officer seeking his assistance.
6. Request for obtaining Information. A person desirous of obtaining information shall make a request in writing or through electronic means, to the concerned Public Information Officer specifying the particulars of the information sought by him:

   Provided that where such request cannot be made in writing, the Public Information Officer shall render all reasonable assistance to the person making the request orally to reduce it in writing.
7. Disposal of requests. (1) On receipt of a request under section 6, the Public Information Officer shall, as expeditiously as possible, and in any case within thirty days of the receipt of the request, either provide the information requested on payment of such fee as may be prescribed or reject the request for any of the reasons specified in sections 8 and 9:

   Provided that where it is decided to provide the information on payment of any further fee representing the cost of providing the information, he shall send an intimation to the person making the request, giving the details of the fees determined by him, requesting him to deposit the fees and the period intervening between the despatch of the said intimation and payment of fees shall be excluded for the purpose of calculating the period of thirty days referred to above.

   (2) Before taking any decision under section (*1*), the Public

Information Officer shall take into consideration the representation made by a third party under section 11.

(3) Where a request is rejected under sub-section (*2*), the Public Information Officer shall communicate to the person making request,—

(i) the reasons for such rejection;

(ii) the period within which an appeal against such rejections may be preferred;

(iii) the particulars of the appellate authority.

(4) Information shall ordinarily be provided in the form in which it is sought unless it would disproportionately divert the resources of the public authority or would be detrimental to the safety or preservation of the record in question.

8. Exemption from disclosure of information. (1) Notwithstanding anything hereinbefore contained, the following information not being information relating to any matter referred to in sub-section *(2),* shall be exempted from disclosure, namely:—

(a) information, the disclosure of which would prejudicially affect the sovereignty and integrity of India, security of the State, strategic scientific or economic interest of India or conduct of international relations;

(b) information, the disclosure of which would prejudicially affect public safety and order, detection and investigation of an offence or which may lead to an incitement to commit an offence or prejudicially affect fair trial or adjudication of a pending case;

(c) information, the disclosure of which would prejudicially affect the conduct of Centre-State relations, including information exchanged in confidence between the Central and State Governments or any of their authorities or agencies;

(d) Cabinet papers including records of deliberations of the Council of Ministers, Secretaries and other officers;

(e) minutes or records of advice including legal advice, opinions or recommendations made by any officer of a public authority during the decision making process prior to the executive decision or policy formulation;

(f) trade or commercial secrets protected by law or information, the disclosure of which would prejudicially affect the legitimate economic and commercial interests or the competitive position of a public authority; or would cause unfair gain or loss to any person; and

(g) information, the disclosure of which may result in the breach of privileges of Parliament or the Legislature of a State, or contravention of a lawful order of a court.

(2) Any information relating to any occurrence, event or matter which has taken place occurred or happened twenty-five years before the date on which any request is made under section 6 shall be provided to any person making a request under that section:

Provided that where any question arises as to the date from which the said period of twenty-five years has to be computed, the decision of the Central Government shall be final.

9. Grounds for refusal to access in certain cases.-Without prejudice to the provisions of section 8, a Public Information Officer may reject a request for information also where such request—

(a) is too general in nature or is of such a nature that, having regard to the volume of information required to be retrieved or processed would involve disproportionate diversion of the resources of a public authority or would adversely interfere with the functioning of such authority:

Provided that where such request is rejected on the ground that the request is too general, it would be the duty of the Public Information Officer to render help as far as possible to the person making request to reframe his request in such a manner as may facilitate compliance with it;

(b) relates to information that is required by law, rules, regulations or orders to be published at a particular time and such information is likely to be so published within thirty days of the receipt of such request; or

(c) relates to information that is contained in published material available to public;

(d) relates to information which would cause unwarranted invasion of the privacy of any person.

10. Severability. If a request for access to information is rejected on the ground that it is in relation to information which is exempted from

disclosure, then notwithstanding anything contained in this Act, access may be given to that part of the record which does not obtain any information that is exempted from disclosure under this Act and which can reasonably be severed from any part that contains exempted information.

11. Third party information. Where a public authority intends to disclose information on a request made by a party which relates to, or has been supplied by a third party and has been treated as confidential by that third party, the Public Information Officer shall by notice to such third party invite representation against the proposed disclosure, if any, within fifty days from the date of receipt of such notice:

    Provided that except in the case of trade or commercial secrets protected by law, disclosure may be allowed if the public interest in disclosure outweighs in importance any possible harm or injury to the interests of such third party.

12. Appeals. (1) Any person aggrieved by a decision of the Public Information Officer may, within thirty days of receipt of such decision, prefer an appeal to such authority as may be prescribed:

    Provided that such authority may entertain the appeal after the expiry of the said period of thirty days if it is satisfied that the appellant was prevented by sufficient cause from filing the appeal in time.

    (2) A second appeal against the decision under sub-section (*1*) shall lie within thirty days of such decision, to the Central Government or the State Government or the competent authority, as the case may be:

        Provided that the Central Government or the State Government or the competent authority, as the case may be, may entertain the appeal after the expiry of the said period of thirty days if it is satisfied that the appellant was prevented by sufficient cause from filing the appeal in time.

    (3) The appeals referred to in sub-sections (*1*) and (*2*) shall be disposed of within thirty days of the receipt of such appeals or within such extended period, as the case may be, for reasons to be recorded in writing.

    (4) If the decision of the Public Information Officer against which the appeal is preferred under sub-section (*1*) or (*2*) also relates

to information of third party, the appellate authority shall give a reasonable opportunity of being heard to that third party.

## CHAPTER III
## MISCELLANEOUS

13. Protection of action taken in good faith. No. suit, prosecution or other legal proceeding shall lie against any person for anything which is in good faith done or intended to be done under this Act or any rule made thereunder.
14. Act to have overriding effect. The Provisions of Official Secrets Act, 1923 (19 of 1923), and every other Act in force shall cease to be operative to the extent to which they are inconsistent with the provisions of this Act.
15. Bar of jurisdiction of courts. No court shall entertain any suit, application or other proceeding in respect of any order made under this Act and no such order shall be called in question otherwise than by way of an appeal under this Act.
16. Act not to apply to certain organizations. (1) Nothing contained in this Act,—
    (a) shall apply to the intelligence and security organisations, specified in the Schedule being organisations established by the Central or a State Government or any information furnished by such organisations to the respective Governments;
    (b) shall until Part B of the Schedule is amended under sub-section (*2*), apply to the intelligence and security organisations by whatever name called discharging their functions as such under the State Governments.
    (2) The Central Government may, by notification in the Official Gazette, amend the Schedule by including therein any other intelligence or security organisation established by the Central or a State Government or omitting therefrom any organisation already specified therein and on the publication of such notification, such organisation shall be deemed to be included in or, as the case may be, omitted from the Schedule.
    (3) Every notification issued under sub-section (*2*), shall be laid before each House of Parliament.
17. Power to make rules by Central Government. (1) The Central

Government may, by notification in the Official Gazette, make rules to carry out the provisions of this Act.

(2) In particular, and without prejudice to the generality of the foregoing power, such rules may provide for all or any of the following matters, namely:—

(a) intervals at which matters referred to in sub-clauses (*i*) to (*vi*) of clause (*b*) of section 4 shall be published;

(b) the fee payable under sub-section (*1*) of section 7;

(c) the authority before whom an appeal may be preferred under sub-section (*1*) of section 12;

(d) any other matter which is required to be, or may be, prescribed.

18. Power to make rules by State Government.-(*1*) The State Government may, by notification in the Official Gazette, make rules to carry out the provisions of this Act.

(2) In particular, and without prejudice to the generality of the foregoing power, such rules may provide for all or any of the following matters, namely:—

(a) the fee payable under sub-section (*1*) of section 7;

(b) the authority before whom an appeal may be preferred under sub-section (*1*) of section 12;

(c) any other matter which is required to be, or may be, prescribed:

Provided that initially the rules shall be made by the Central Government by notification in the Official Gazette.

19. Rule making power by competent authority. (1) The competent authority may, by notification in the Official Gazette, make rules to carry out the provisions of this Act.

(2) In particular, and without prejudice to the generality of the foregoing power, such rules may provide for all or any of the following matters, namely:—

(a) the fee payable under sub-section (*1*) of section 7;

(b) the authority before whom an appeal may be preferred under sub-section (*1*) of section 12;

(c) any other matter which is required to be, or may be, prescribed.

20. Laying of rules. (1) Every rule made by the Central Government under this Act shall be laid, as soon as may be after it is made, before each House of Parliament, while it is in session, for a total period of thirty days which may be comprised in one session or

in two or more successive sessions, and if, before the expiry of the session immediately following the session or the successive sessions aforesaid, both Houses agree in making any modification in the rule or both Houses agree that the rule should not be made, the rule shall thereafter have effect only in such modified form or be of no effect, as the case may be; so, however, that any such modification or annulment shall be without prejudice to the validity of anything previously done under that rule.

(2) Every rule made under this Act by a State Government shall be laid, as soon as may be after it is notified, before the State Legislature.

21. Power to remove difficulties. (1) If any difficulty arises in giving effect to the provisions of this Act, the Central Government may, by order published in the Official Gazette, make such provisions not inconsistent with the provisions of this Act as appear to it to be necessary or expedient for removal of the difficulty:

Provided that no such order shall be made after the expiry of a period of two years from the date of the commencement of this Act.

(2) Evey order made under this section shall, as soon as may be after it is made, be laid before the Houses of Parliament.

## THE SCHEDULE

**(*See* section 16)**

## PART A

### Intelligence and security organisations established by the Central Government

1. Intelligence Bureau.
2. Research and Analysis Wing of the Cabinet Secretariat.
3. Directorate of Revenue Intelligence.
4. Central Economic Intelligence Bureau.
5. Directorate of Enforcement.
6. Narcotics Control Bureau.

# Credits

We have tried to put together the names of our fellow travellers in the struggle and campaign for the RTI act. It is probably a credit to the movement that it was beyond impossible to keep count of every individual who contributed to the journey. We apologize to those whose names we have missed, but do hope that they will find themselves somewhere as chronicler or participant in the stories and recollections shared in these pages.

- A.B. Bardhan
- A.K. Shiva Kumar
- Abha Sharma
- Achin Vinayak
- Ajay Mehta
- Ajit Bhattacharjea
- Akashvani
- Amar Singh
- Amitabh Chaudhary
- Amitabh Mukhopadhyaya
- Anant Krishan, *Indian Express*
- Anil Bordia
- Anil Loda
- Anil Sadgopal
- Anjali Bhardwaj
- Anjana
- Anna Hazare
- Anshi
- Anu Rao
- Anurag Vajpeyi
- Arora
- Arun Kumar
- Arundhati Roy
- Arvind Kejriwal
- Asha
- Asha Patel
- Ashok Gehlot

- Ashok Mathur
- Ashok Sain
- Ashok Yadav
- Atta Mohammad
- Ayub
- B.D. Sharma
- Baba Adhav
- Baburam Saini
- Bahadur Singh
- Bajrang Lal
- Balu Ram Saini
- Banna Lal
- Basanta Devi
- Bela Bhatia
- Bhairon Singh Shekhawat
- Bhanwar Gopal (Bhurji)
- Bhanwar Lal Jain
- Bhanwar Meghwanshi
- Bhanwar Singh
- Bhanwar Singh Kushalpura
- Bharat Dogra
- Bharatiya
- Bhikhamchand
- Bhuri Bai
- Bhuri Ya
- Biraj Patnaik
- Bodhu
- Bunker (Sanjit) Roy
- C.G. Somiah
- C.P. Joshi
- Chandra Bhandari
- Charu
- Charul and Vinay
- Chhaggan Singh
- Chimanba
- Chunni Bai
- Chunni Singh
- D.L. Tripathi
- Damodhar Thanvi
- Danvir Singh
- Deepak Gyanchandani
- Deepak Nayyar
- Deva Ba
- Devilal
- Dhowba
- Digvijay Singh
- Dinabandu Chaudhary
- Dinesh Shrimali
- Dinkarlal Mehta
- Dr. Indira Hirvey
- Dr. Kanta Ahuja
- Dr. Manmohan Singh
- Dr. Narainmurty
- Dr. Neelima Dhar
- Dr. P.C. Alexander
- Dr. Patwa
- Dr. Sharada Jain
- Dr. V.S. Vyas
- Durg Singh
- E.A.S. Sarma
- Fatima Begum
- G.R. Khairnar
- Gagdeep Dhankad
- Gajanand
- Galku Ma
- Ganga Singh
- Girija Vyas
- Gopalkrishna Gandhi
- Gopi
- Gopilal Raigar
- Govind Chaturvedi
- Gunjal
- Guptaji
- H.D. Shourie

- H.K. Shastri, PTI
- Haggu
- Hameed
- Hanswarup
- Hanuman Chaudhary
- Hanumantha Rao
- Hari Shankar
- Hari Singh
- Harish Bhadani
- HarishankarBhabra
- Harivansh Bhai
- Harsh Mander
- Heeralal Devpura
- Hemant Kr. Paliwal
- Hemlata Prabhu
- Hukam Singh.
- J.S. Verma
- Jai Prakash Narain
- Jairam Ramesh
- Jait Singh
- Jamna Bai
- Jamunalal Lavati
- Jean Dréze
- Jeevan
- Jeremy Seabrook
- John Singh
- Justice Dinkarlal Mehta
- Justice P.B. Sawant
- Justice Rajinder Sachar
- Justice V.S. Dave
- K.B. Saxena
- K.C. Choudhary
- K.K. Mathew
- K.R. Venugopal
- K.S. Srivastava
- K.S. Subramanian
- Kakiji
- Kalpana Sharma
- Kalu
- Kaluram
- Kamayani Swami
- Kamla Bai
- Kamla Dagdi
- Kanku Devi
- Kavita Srivastava
- Keli Bai
- Kesar Singh
- Kesrimal
- Kheema Ram
- Kheemu
- Kishan Das
- Kishan Lal Gujjar
- Kishen Patnaik
- Kishore Saint
- Komal Kothari
- Koom Singh
- Koop Singh
- Koyali Bai
- Krishan Iyer
- Kuldeep Nayar
- Kunjilal Meena
- Kunteshwar Mahadev
- L.C. Gupta
- Lachhuba
- Lad Kumari
- Ladu Singh
- Lakshman Das
- Lakshman Singh
- Lakshmi
- Lakshmi Krishnamurthy
- Lal Singh
- Laluram
- Laxman Nilwa
- Lokpal Sethi, Hindustan

Times
- M.L. Kheenchi
- M.L. Mehta
- M.P. Parameswaran
- Madhav Godbole
- Madhu Kishwar
- Madhusudan Jhala
- Mahesh Bindal
- Mahesh Bora
- Malini Parthsarthi
- Mamta Jaitley
- Mana Bhil
- Mandata Singh
- Mangilal
- Manini Shekhar
- Mark Tully
- Marudhar Mridul
- Medha Patkar
- Meena Menon
- Meethu Singh
- Mohammad Iqbal, *Hindu*
- Mohan ji
- Mohan Lal Sukhadia
- Mot Singh
- Mota ba
- Moti
- Moti Bai
- Moti Singh
- Mukulika Sen
- N.C. Saxena
- Nagodaji
- Nahar Singh
- Nain Singh
- Narayan Bareth
- Narayan Singh
- Narbada Devi
- Narula
- Nathulal
- Naurti
- Naval ji Chauhan
- Neelabh Mishra
- Nelson Fernandez
- Nemi Chand
- Nikhil Chakravarty
- Nikhil Dey
- Nirdesh Kumar Yadav
- Nirmal Wadhwani
- Nirmala Laxman
- Nitya Ramakrishnan
- Noji (Ya)
- O.P. Jain
- O.P. Mathur
- Om Mahawar
- Om Prakash Darzi
- Om Thanvi
- Onkarnath Tripathi
- P.B. Sawant
- P.N. Bhandari
- P.S. Appu
- P.V. Rajagopal
- Pablo Barthalomew
- Pal
- Panini
- Piyush Mehta, Aaj Tak
- Prabhash Joshi
- Prabhu Das
- Pradeep Bhargava
- Pradeep Loda
- Pradeep Prabhu
- Pragya Paliwal
- Prakash Bhandari
- Prakash Chaturvedi
- Prakash Kardalay
- Prakash Kumar

- Prakash Sharma
- Prasanna Mohnti
- Prashant Bhushan
- Prem Krishen Sharma
- Pushpa Bhave
- Pyarchand Khatik
- R.N. Misra
- Rabi Ray
- Radhakant Saxena
- Radhika Kaul Batra
- Raghu Rai
- Raj Kanwar
- Rajan Mahan
- Rajeev Malhotra
- Rajendra Boda
- Rajendra Gunjal
- Rajesh Sinha
- Rajni Bakshi
- Ram Jethmalani
- Ram Lal
- Ram Sagar
- Ram Singh
- Ramanathan
- Ramesh Nandwana
- Ramesh Vyas
- Ramkaran
- Ramkumar Mishra
- Ramlal Gujjar
- Ramnivas
- Ramprasad Kumawat
- Ranjeet
- Ravindra Shah
- Rekha
- Renuka Pamecha
- Rodrigues
- Rohit Kumar
- Rohit Parihar, *India Today*
- Romila Thapar
- Roop Kanwar
- Roop Singh
- Rukma Ma
- S. Guhan
- S. Regunathan
- S. Srinivasan (Vasu)
- S.R. Sankaran
- Saba Naqvi
- Sam
- Samsud Joh
- Sandeep Pandey
- Sandeep Shrivastav, *Indian Express*
- Sanjeev Kumar
- Sanjoy Ghosh
- Santosh
- Santosh Mathew
- Sarpanch Ramlal
- Satish Sharma, UNI
- Savanchand Chandel
- Sawai Singh
- Sawar Lal Chandel
- Seema Chishti
- Seeta Bai
- Shankar
- Shankar Lal
- Shankar Singh
- Sharada Jain
- Sheila Dixit
- Shekhar Singh
- Shikha Trivedi
- Shiv Singh Nihal
- Shivaji Rao
- Shobha
- Shreeprakash ji
- Shri Prakash Sharma

- Shubhu Patva
- Siddharth Jain
- Siddhiraj Dhadha
- Sitaram Yechury
- Soli Sorabjee
- Sowmya Kidambi
- Sri Ram Lal
- Sriniwas
- Subhramanya Bharathi
- Suchi Pande
- Sudha Pillai
- Sujaba
- Sukumar Muralidharan
- Suman Sahai
- Sumir Hinduja
- Sumit Chaturvedi
- Sumitra
- Sumitra Chopra
- Sunita Devi
- Sunny Sebastian
- Surendra Mohan
- Surendranath Dubey
- Suresh Pachauri
- Suresh Pareek
- Sushil Kumari Pradhan
- Sushila Bora
- Sushmita Banerjee
- Swami Agnivesh
- T.K. Singh
- Tara Singh Sidhu
- Teelu
- Tej Singhji
- Than Singh
- Tribhuvan
- Trilok Singh
- Tripurari Sharma
- Triveni
- Tulsa Singh
- Tulsi Das
- Uma Shankar
- Upendra Baxi
- Usha Rai
- V.K. Arora
- V.P. Singh
- V.S. Vyas
- Vaimal Chouhan
- Vandana Shiva
- Ved Vyas
- Venkatesh Nayak
- Vijay Nagaraj
- Vijay Shankar Vyas
- Vijendra Vidrohi
- Vijaydan Detha
- Vikas
- Vikram Vyas
- Vimal Chauhan
- Vinod Arora
- Vinod Mehta
- Vipul Mudgal
- Wajahat Habibullah
- Wakar Bhai (CPI-M)
- Yashwant Sinha
- Yeduvendra Mathur

# Index